AA BOOK

NEW ARCHITECTURE, NEW CENTURY: THE AA SCHOOL 2010

LIFE IN WC1

'Design is concerned with the conscious distortion of time, distance and size. Anything less is just the status quo.' – Cedric Price

The academic year captured by this 2010 edition of the AA Book is one of historic proportions for the Architectural Association, and I mean this in the most literal – indeed, the least hyperbolic and the most *architectural* sense imaginable. Last September, for the first time in the school's modern history, the AA welcomed its largest class of new and returning students to a unified central campus in Bedford Square. Since the AA originally settled into Bloomsbury in the early years of the last century, it has not undertaken an architectural project at the scale of the one currently underway.

In 2010 the AA at Bedford Square is nearly twice the floor area it was as recently as 2005, and is correspondingly more generous, public and inviting than ever.

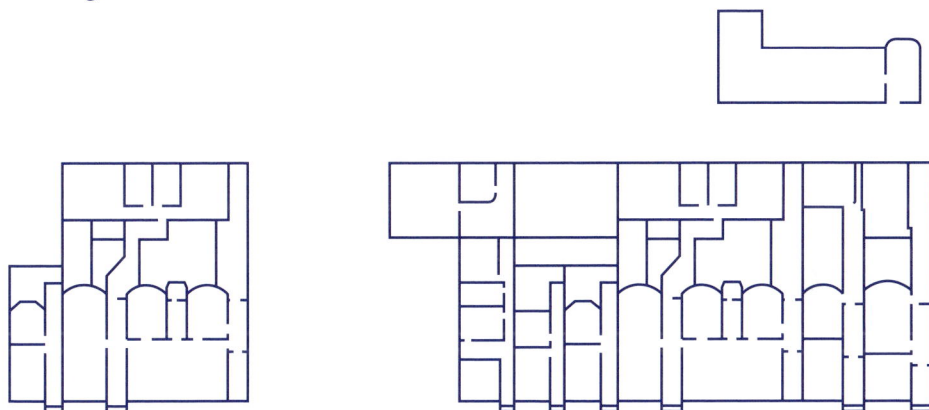

AA campus floorplan in 2005 (left) and today (right)

As the world's leading experimental school, the AA is also daring enough to experiment with its own form, organisation, even daily life. With students and staff travelling hundreds of thousands of kilometres to convene in London each autumn, the AA's dramatic transformation of its own architecture has set the stage for yet bigger changes to come.

I write these words from an office overlooking one of London's last intact Georgian squares. The quiet, classical facades of the AA and its neighbouring buildings provide an understated, unexpected, even ironic *front cover* behind which the world's most avant-garde school of architecture lies. Think of the straightforward typography on the front of this book as an equivalent kind of design statement – a timeless, rectilinear wrap for an interior where bright colours and rousing images leap out from the page page. Nestled beyond the AA's front door, visitors encounter room after room of small, highly focused groups of shared-believers pursuing architecture not as it is already known, but in future forms that have yet to fully appear.

For decades the AA has been committed to architecture's present, aware of its past, and above all committed to its future. From our renewed historic home in London's West End – the heart of the twenty-first century's preeminent global capital – we continue the hard work of building a truly great school of architecture for this new century.

The AA terrace overlooking Ching's Yard

BETWEEN BEDFORD SQUARE & THE WORLD

'The best time to plant a tree was 20 years ago. The second-best time is now.' – Chinese proverb

If we look beyond the traditional borders of Bedford Square, we see that some of the biggest changes and most positive signs of the AA's growth lie well beyond it.

Early this year the AA received consent from the planning authorities in West Dorset for an outline masterplan to develop, through the work of students and staff over the next several years, a new sustainable campus at Hooke Park, the AA's working woodland. The school's new Design & Make programme will launch in September 2010 with a small, highly specialised MArch degree dedicated to the study of architecture through the design and construction of experimental prototype buildings made from timber and other local materials at Hooke Park, an area of outstanding national beauty in the West Country. Through the generosity of Norah Garlick and her family, who share lasting ties with the region and the architectural culture and history of Dorset, the AA was honoured by the Horace and Ellen Hannah Wakeford Bequest. Given in the name of Norah's parents, the legacy will fund the first few years of projects at Hooke Park, as the school seeks other opportunities to support a site-based programme unique in architecture today. Hooke Park seeks to return contemporary design culture to its roots of learning by making, in a world facing unprecedented challenges that demand new and alternative design-build solutions. All of us will strive to live up to the faith in architecture's future that this gift, the largest single private donation ever made to the AA, signifies. To Norah and her family, we are forever grateful.

Installations and the workshop at Hooke Park. Inter 2 pavilion fabricated at Hooke Park and installed in Bedford Square.

To step even further out and away from Bedford Square, more surprising transformations are taking place that connect the AA to the world like never before. In 2008 we established a year-round AA Visiting School, which this year administered nearly 20 different courses in a dozen countries, attracting a thousand or more participants – an experiment in the fundamental ways not only of teaching but also of learning within a globalised architectural culture and practice.

Ranging from sporting infrastructures in Chile to computational cultures with our partners CrystalCG in Beijing, to design workshops in Madrid, Bangalore, San Francisco, São Paulo, Singapore and beyond, the AA Visiting School is a major step in the continuing evolution of architectural education. A long-awaited outcome of the staggering demographics of our school in London (where 90 per cent of our students come from overseas), the AA Visiting School reverses the flow of intellectual life by sending our teachers out from Bedford Square to work alongside local experts and visionaries on projects that demand in-depth investigation. The AA is laying a foundation for the challenges and opportunities that our deeply interconnected world presents.

Shanghai Visiting School 2008

CURATING A WORLD OF LIFE LEARNING

'Books are divided into two classes, books of the hour and the books of all time.' – John Ruskin

In the 1850s the AA extended an invitation to John Ruskin, whose epigram above captures the spirit of the association he visited soon after its formation. Ruskin's spirit survives to this day, in no small part through his former student Walter Crane, who redesigned the AA crest near the end of the nineteenth century to include the motto 'Design with Beauty, Build in Truth'. The words are not only emblematic of Ruskin's belief in a higher calling for architecture, but also signify the importance of beauty in a world with which architects and artists must engage and, if need be, resist everyday assumptions. What was prescient at the brink of modernisation is relevant to us again today, as the world and architecture propel themselves forward at full speed across distances, cultures and individual expectations.

Over the next few months the AA will launch an AA Life Learning initiative that will cultivate our historic commitment to lifelong architectural enquiry. The Architectural Association was established in the mid-nine-teenth century as a 'learned society' committed to the public benefit and defined by public debate on the built world; the objective of operating a full-time school of architecture took more than half a century to realise. (By the time this launched in 1901, Robert Kerr, a youthful AA founder in 1847, was in his 70s.) It is remarkable to ponder the history of the AA in light of developments from the nineteenth century, before the full professionalisa-tion of architecture, to the twentieth-century's educational industry directed at a growing field with insatiable demand for vocational practitioners.

John Ruskin (left) and AA emblem designed by Walter Crane, c 1850s (right)

Architectural culture's global professionalisation – for better or worse – is now complete. So too is the outright industrialisation of architectural education. And yet learning takes on a new role in today's information era, when *knowledge* is ever more valuable. In the coming years the AA Life Learning project will generate a small universe of part-time professional, cultural and educational courses available to AA Members as well as creative and committed individuals of all kinds.

In every way possible the AA seeks to reinvent itself, and not only in the architectural world. If the first 150 years of our history were defined by the 'Architectural', then the century ahead suggests that it will be through the concept of 'Association', that we redefine ourselves, as we seek to associate with architects, creative individuals, audiences and organisations to make our school, and our world, truly better.

Brett Steele
Director, Architectural Association School of Architecture

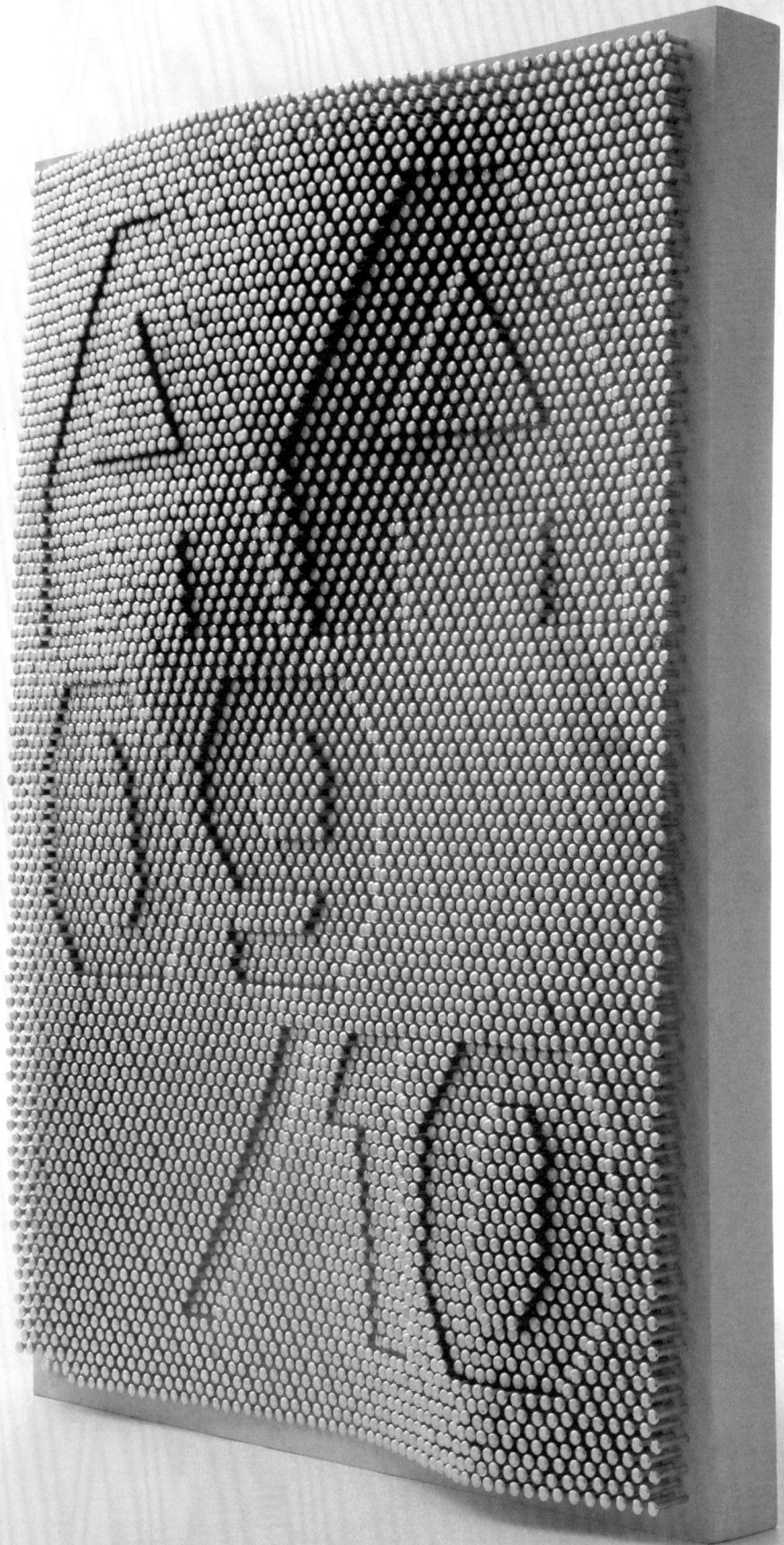

Jeroen van Ameijde, annual AA Projects Review sign,
CNC grid as a nail-pushing machine, 2010. Photo Sue Barr

Architectural Association
School of Architecture

AA

Autoprogettazione Revisted: Easy-to-Assemble Furniture by Enzo Mari and Invited Guests is a group exhibition that traces the influence of Italian designer Enzo Mari's 1970's project for self-made furniture. Using the AA Gallery as a project space, ten artists and designers were commissioned to respond to Mari's instruction-based furniture plans with their own set of instructions.

In a text accompanying the instructions, Mari writes that 'anyone, apart from factories and traders, can use the designs to make them by themselves'. Seen originally by Mari as a means for the self-fabrication of quality design objects, Autoprogettazione continues today as an expression of collaborative design thinking made topical by a recent proliferation of digital technologies.

As part of the exhibition, AA First Year Studio Master Valentin Bontjes van Beek will lead a workshop allowing AA students – Korey Kromm, Alma Wang and Stefan Laxness – to respond to the Autoprogettazione manual, and through the modification of Mari's instructions, generate work that experiments with the scale and material of the furniture.

AUTO-PROGETTAZIONE REVISITED

The Director of the AA School of Architecture Brett Steele invites you to a private view on Friday 2 October 2009 6.30–8.30pm

Inauguration lecture by Enzo Mari 6.30pm AA Lecture Hall Exhibition opening 7.30pm AA Gallery

AA Gallery
3 to 27 October
Monday to Friday 10am–7pm
Saturday 10am–3pm

23 October 2009
6.30pm
AA Lecture Hall
A roundtable discussion with Philliyda Barlow, Clemence Seilles and Travis Broussard, Martino Gamper, Graham Hudson and Joe Pipal

Architectural Association
36 Bedford Square
London WC1B 3ES
Information 020 7887 4145
aaschool.ac.uk

Contributors:
Phyllida Barlow
Broussard/Seilles
Martino Gamper
Ryan Gander
Graham Hudson
Keung Caputo
Lucas Maassen
Joe Pipal

Printed at Bedford Press, London / bedfordpress.org

'**Strikes. Disappea**
Shuttered post offi
Irritatingly long qu
suspicious smells i
survivors. There a
of reasons for the
indulge in the pop
pastime of grumbl
the Royal Mail this

As a design critic, Alice Rawsthorn covers the frontiers of contemporary design, from graphics to publishing and architecture. In this illustrated

Alice Rawsthorn is the d of the *International He* and a columnist for the *Magazine*. She is a boar

Cedric Price revisiting the aviary

Queen with Lord Snowdon at the opening ceremony for the new aviary; Cedric Price and Frank Newby are in the background, 1965. Overleaf: The aviary in 1965

Bernard Tschumi, Fireworks 1974, Architectural Association

With thanks to: Centro Studi e Archivio della Comunicazione, Università degli Studi di Parma; Canadian Centre for Architecture; Fonds Régional

PROJECTS

FOUNDATION COURSE

The Foundation offers a year-long introduction to art- and design-based education. It allows students to develop their conceptual ideas, individually and collectively, in a wide range of media from drawing and painting to filmmaking, pattern-cutting, sculpting and installation. This experimentation opens pathways to a variety of creative disciplines from fine art to architecture.

'All great deeds and all great thoughts have a ridiculous beginning. Great works are often born on a street corner or in a restaurant's revolving door.' – Albert Camus

Do It Yourself Scale, site, scenario and identity. The Foundation cohort featured as both makers and players of the year.

Becoming Fiction The relation of the body to the imagined self and the exchange between atmosphere, character and audience: these self-portraits were exhibited in the Back Members' Room in January.

On Location Consulting films shot in London, we surveyed locations and analysed viewpoints, making drawings and models registering the import of these scenes, their camera angles and architectural surveys.

Prop Master We made a paper replica of a flea market item before casting the original and creating copies in various materials – gradually transforming its identifiable use.

Trip To Paris Cafes. Moments. Scenes. Buildings. Environments. People.

Body Survey We recorded the body at 1:1, examined how it is jointed and how its movement can be exaggerated or restricted.

It's A Wrap All the ways to augment, restrain or subvert the body's movement through garment construction – the most intimate interface between a figure and the immediate surroundings.

Mind Your Head and Mind Your Step The body in relation to millinery and notional furniture/installation.

Take Five One-minute films documenting work made to date – a reflection and projection.

Over to You We wrote our own brief and dictated our final chapters.

UNIT MASTER
Saskia Lewis

TUTORS
Matthew Butcher
Takako Hasegawa
William Martyr

STUDENTS
Vasilis Argyropoulos
Naz Atalay
Camille Corthouts
Albane Duvillier
Soso Joseph Eliava
Despoina Kafetzopoulou
Zaid Kashef Alghata
Vicky Lai
Susan Li
Andra Miruna Mazilu
Cheng Feng Men

Sabrina Morreale
Reem Nasir
Frederique Paraskevas
Heon Woo Park
Steven Price
Mahsa Ramezan Poor
Dania Shams
Justin Hin Yeung Tsang
Fan Zhang
Qin Zhao

Thanks to our consultants/critics:
Leith Adjina
Sue Barr
Mark Campbell
Charlie and Georgie
Corrie Wright
Toby Glanville
Ioana Ili

Bettina John
George Massoud
Flora McLean
Joel Newman
Cher Potter
Antonia Quirke
Damian Rogan
Brett Steele
Trys Smith
Charles Tashima

1

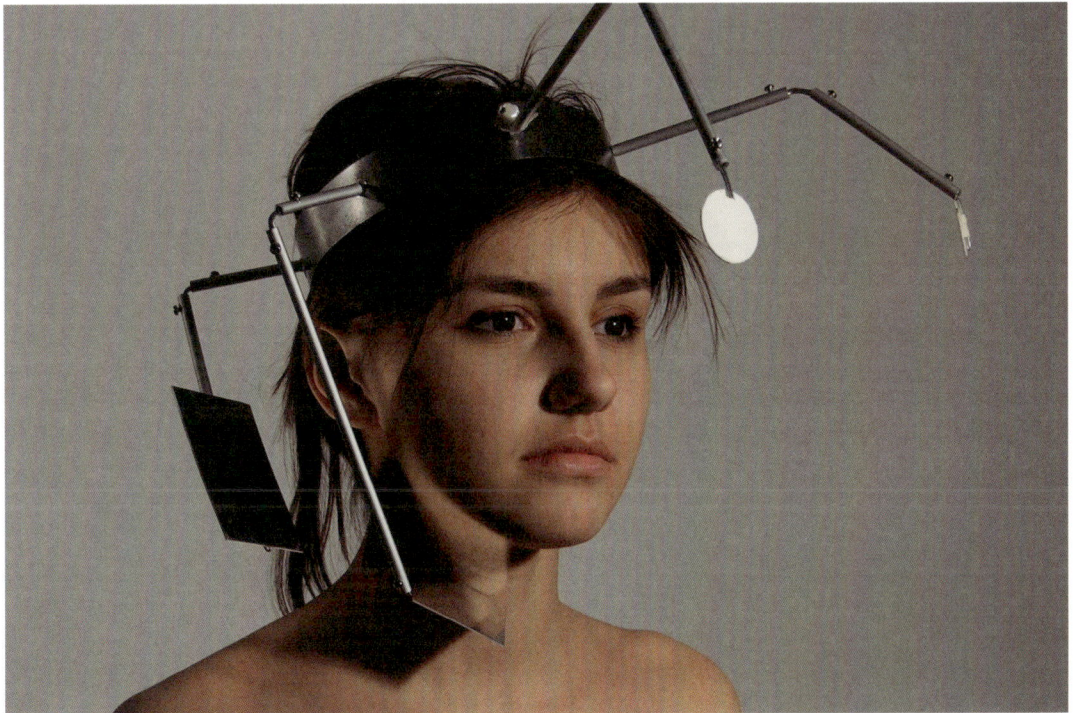

2

3

1. Despoina Kafetzopoulou, When Space Meets Fashion,
a proposal for a body to share the same garment as a wall
2. Andra Miruna Mazilu, headpiece constructed to
examine parts of the body that normally remain hidden
from view

3. Vicky Lai, Mahsa Ramezan Poor and Qin Zhao, the
choreographed moves of the cameraman after seeing
'The Ipcress File'

4

5

6

7

8

9

Borough of Westminster (09/10/09) (0.07) "Thank you for calling Westminster city council, your call may be recorded in order to improve our service"(0.19) "Good afternoon Betty speaking how can I help?"(0.22) "Hi.. ehm.. I'd like to know who I should speak to in regards to balloon releasing"(0.27) "About what sorry?"(0.29) "Balloon releasing"(0.31) "Barroo…"(0.33) "Balloon releasing"(0.35) "Right… Ok hold on"(0.36)(Music plays)(1.44) "Our apologies for the delay, we will do our best to … to keep you waiting"(2…) … I am speaking now … (0.25) "…member of the team will be with you sho… … shortly"(2.50) (Phone rings…)… "…I'd like to know who … very well… could you re… (3.17) "Which releasing?"(3.19) … some balloons… in Covent Garden?(4.26) "… …"(4.29) "Ehm… wait.. I'll just check it…(4.36) "…I've put you on hold please…(4.10) "ah..ok we … … …borough of Camden and … …would it be then"(4.28) "…Let's just check to see if we cover that yr… … you do it"(4.35) "Sure yeah … … … … contact… that would be Westminster …(4.59) "…purpose school project and we'd like to …(4.58)(Phone … … … …maybe you and an email then you w… …(5.31) "Have you … … email (address …(5.33) "Yup I'm ready…..uhm…"(5.40) "It's…. spesh…special…E"(5.43) "Special…E"(5.53) "@ Westminster"(5.56) "@ Westminster"(5.58) "dot..gov"(6.00) "dot…gov"(6.02) "yeah.. dot.. uk"(6.04) "dot….UK"(6.05) "ehm……."(6.07) "And…ehm…. I'd like to know if there's any consequences for doing the balloon release"(6.13) "if theres any sorry?"(6.15) "Consequences… of doing it"(6.19) "Sorry I…i… really cannot hear you"(6.21) (HANGS UP)

4. Qin Zhao, atmospheric painting from a paper model following examination of a scene from 'The Ipcress File'. 5. Justin Hin Yeung Tsang, restraining gestures during conversation – a drawing showing some of the component parts of the proposed garment. 6. Mahsa Ramezan Poor, safely packaged before posting home – packaging designed to protect an individual and allow the inhabitant to have a letterbox view out on the world.

7. Albane Duvillier, distorted vision through movement. 8. Frederique Paraskevas, paper model of a single bicycle wheel. 9. Vasilis Argyropoulos, Zaid Kashef Alghata and Steven Price, transcripts of conversations while trying to arrange a balloon release in Covent Garden laid over one another to create a textual summary of the fictional event.

10

11

12

10. Sabrina Morreale, hats for kissing and whispering
Two hats made out of felt with extensions, one to accept a
hand to aid whispering and the other with finger holds for
a firm grip during kissing.

11. Soso Joseph Eliava, a locked padlock remade at a
scale of 1:1. From left to right: initial paper model, final
paper model. Casts in wax, timber, pewter.

12. Heon Woo Park, An Intimate Environment for Two
for the exchange of secrets and private moments

13

14

15

13. Naz Atalay, Instant City of Lights – a mocked-up London skyline compiled from an extensive series of spinning objects carrying lights and photographed with long exposure

14. Dania Shams, a five-day print in foam board taken from Chesham Street, London
15. Cheng Feng Men, a map fusing and juxtaposing a series of locations used in the filming of 'The Passenger'

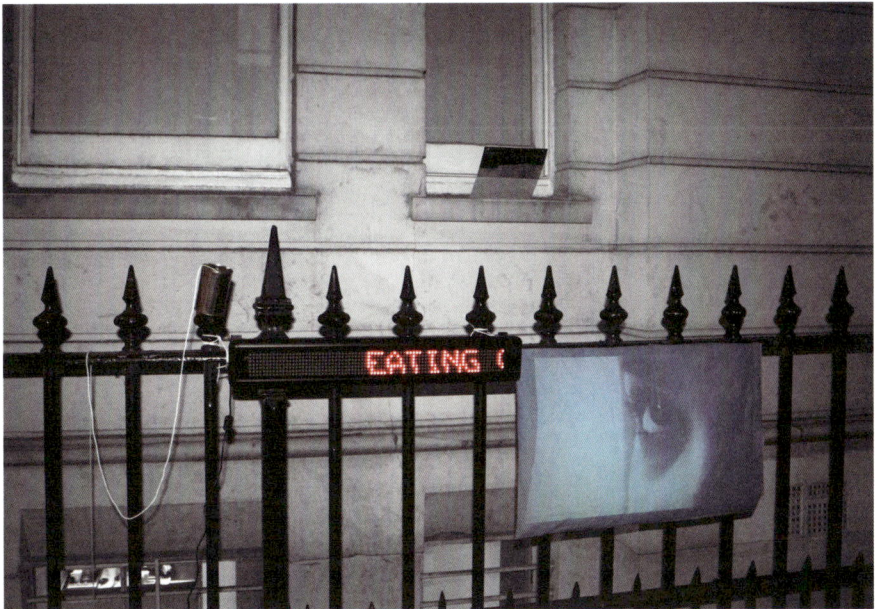

16

16. Reem Nasir, looking out into the street from
the confines of a lower basement floor studio flat

FIRST YEAR STUDIO

The First Year Studio at the AA is an open-ended experiment, a sometimes messy synergy of opposites, a place where problems don't exist – only opportunities. First Year tutors think of design as a mode of behaviour rather than a body of information and consider the diverse teaching methods and ideas discussed to be an accurate reflection of contemporary architectural practice: a twitching territory of instabilities. Students learn to live dangerously and develop their own architectural ideas in the studio, which is organised around a series of projects building in complexity throughout the year.

Projects

Residues of a Meal_Building_Beauty: a construction based on the notion of food production in a city.

Making-Scaling-Re-Scaling 1:10, 1:100, 1:1000: discovering the possibilities of scale using an object palette of domestic implements.

Creepy Crawlies – between man-made and natural objects: drawings that accurately describe the properties of lawnmower parts, a rare beetle.

AA Speed Stop: exploring spatial experience through a short film; footage and montage as a space for imagination.

A New Area of Ultra-Light-Industrial Beauty: an introduction to more orthodox notions of site and architectural typologies.

Design Rethink – 6 Tutors, 6 Briefs: working across distinct agendas to develop a detail of each trans-plant proposal.

Studio Visits, Workshops and Talks

Outside of the studio, visits were made to small-scale UK manufacturers including the Albion Saddlery in Walsall, the Bentley car factory in Crewe and the Brompton bicycle factory in West London. Studio-based workshops introduced everything from orthogonal drawing to CAD to digital design for laser-cutting to rendering to photography.

UNIT STAFF
Valentin Bontjes van Beek, David Greene, Samantha Hardingham, Tobias Klein, Martina Schäfer, Robert Stuart-Smith

STUDENTS
Anouk Ahlborn, Carl Anderson, Francesca Hue-Woon Au, Akhil Mahendra Bakhda, Meliti Bampili Thymara, Andrew Bardzik, William Boscawen, Michelle Choi, Su Yi Choi, Lingxiu Chong, Hunter Devine, Dimitar Dobrev, Philip Doumler, Olle Eriksson, Fatemeh Ghasemi, Nara Ha, MonThi Han, Thomas Holan, Insoo Hwang, Bella Susan Janssens, Rachel Khalil, Wiktor Kidziak, Tae Hyuk Kim, Hanjun Kim, Angelina Kochkinova, Fragkiskos Ioannis Konstantatos, Theodore Koustas, Yu Hin Kwok, Young-Sang Lee, Henry Jinn-Cherng Liu, Donika Llakmani, Sergej Maier, Bruno H. Malusa, Alexey Marfin, Patricia Mato Mora, Linnea Natalie Moore, Lucy Mary Moroney, Sonia Moss, Anna Muzychak, Anand Naikhavare, Shi Qi Ng, Dariga Nurmanbetova, Ekaterina Obedkova, Maria Olmos Zunica, Alexandra Paritzky, Fortune Penniman, Maria Elena Popovici, Vidhya Pushpanathan, Sophie Jane Ramsbotham, Marie-Louise Raue, Kira Sciberras, Sofia Sfyri, Andreani Maria Stephanou, Eleni Maria Tzavellou Gavala, Louise Amy Underhill, Phung Hieu Minh Van, Han Zhang Wang, Mary Wang, Guan Xiong Wong, Lara Yegenoglu, Yifat Zailer, Min Zhang, Yu Zheng

GUESTS
Jozef Amado, Sue Barr, Dana Behman, Phil Cooper, Rose Davey, Christina Doumpioti, William Firebrace, Annika Grafweg, Korey Kromm, Dominic McCausland, Mark Miowdownik, Jan Nauta, Joel Newman, Peter Salter, Toby Shew, Eva Christina Sommeregger, Brett Steele, John Walter, Ray Winkler, Gary Woodley, Catalina Pollak, Xin Wang, Denis Lacej, Simon Whittle, Jaime de Miguel, Ena Woret, KwunJoo Park, Yheu-Shen Chua, Jeroen van Amejde, Iain Maxwell, Eva Sopeoglon, Calvin Chua, George Douglas Thomson, Lukas Schrank, Larissa Begault, Faraz Anoushehpour, Nancy Ni Bhriain, Alex Haw... not to mention all of our jurors

1. AA First Year Studio 2010
Reviewing the digital workshop, Term One

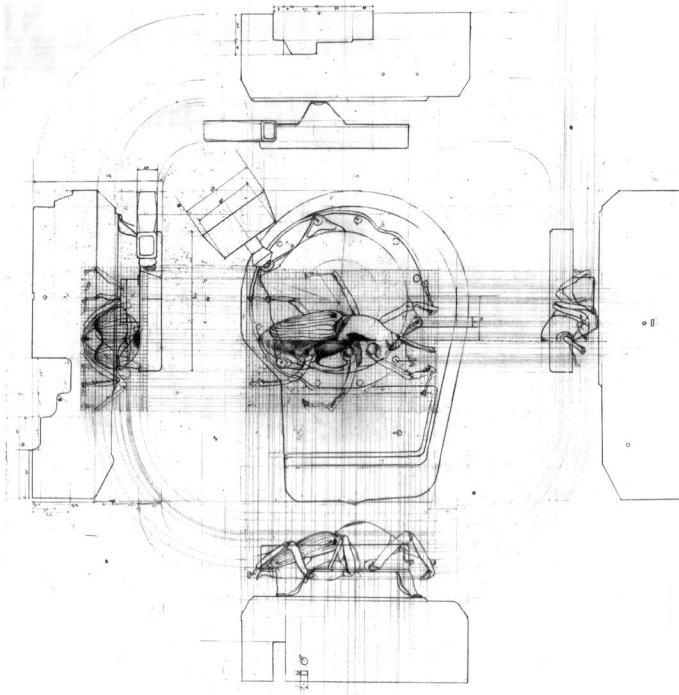

2

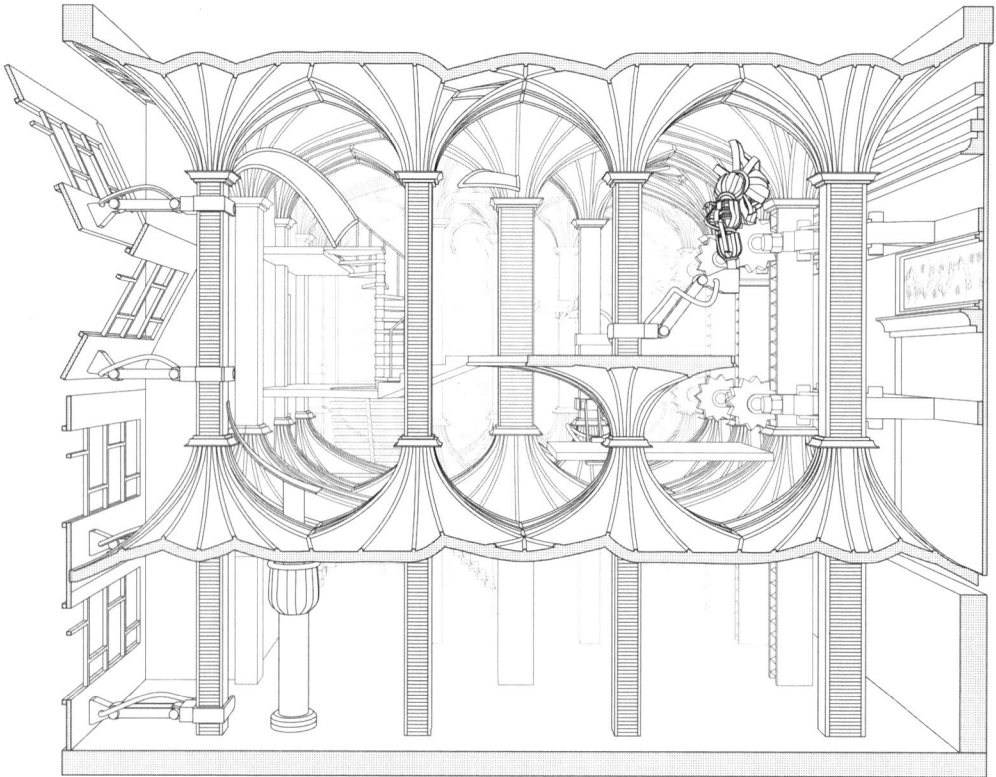

3

2. Nara Ha, drawing between man-made and natural objects

3. Alexey Marfin, Mechanical Baroque: rethinking the locksmith's workshop after a visit to Cologne

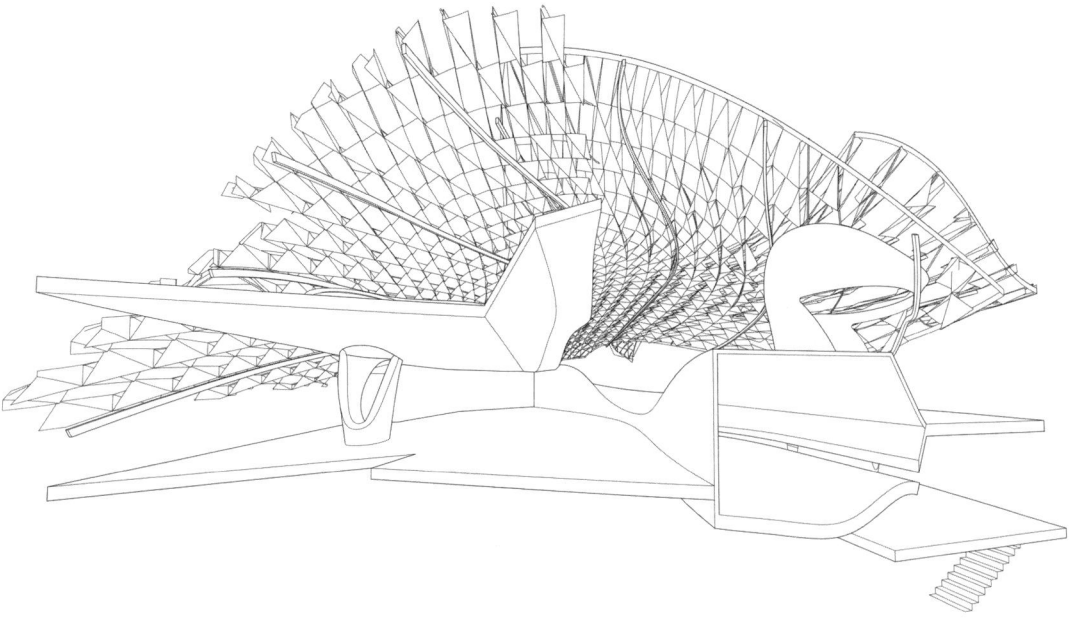

4

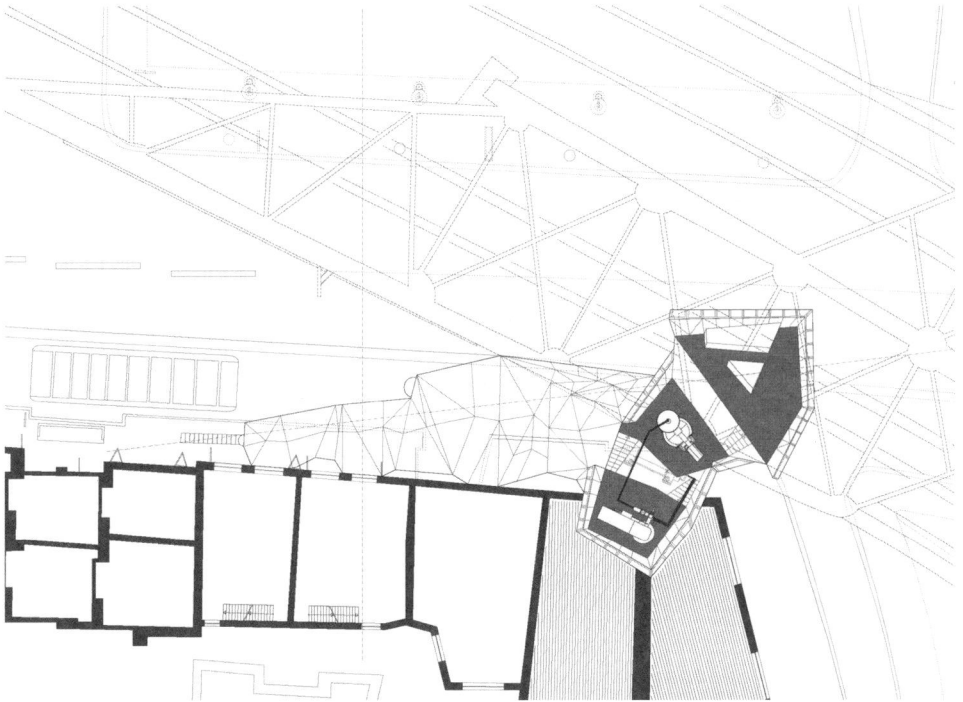

5

4. Yu Hin Kwok, Design Phase Two
Light industrial roof study

5. Marie-Louise Raue, plan for a shoe repair and
chocolate trans-plant. Site: East London Line

23

6

7

8

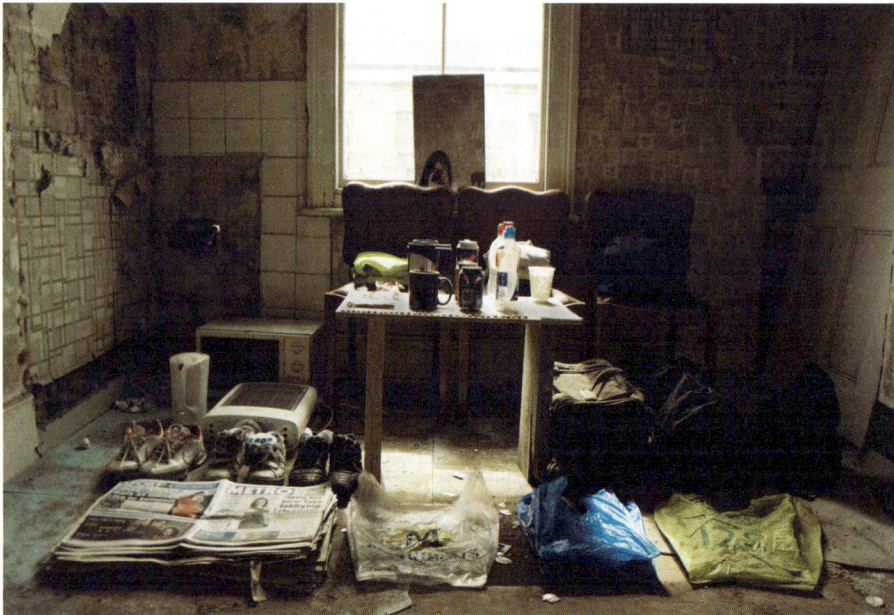

9

6. Louise Underhill, a pink-powder-bomb trans-plant – final model, Scale 1:20

7. Dimitar Dobrev, Design Phase One: a pre-fab unit trans-plant

8. Angelina Kochinova, Sofia Sfyri, Yu Zheng, Form to Scale, Mobius's dog, Scale 1:1000

9. Mary Wang, Design Phase Two: a catalogue of the traces of life found on a construction site

10

11

10. Francesca Hue-Woo Au, Shi Qui Ng,
Thi Han Mon, Scale 1:1000
Cable-tied superstructure for Hong Kong

11. Lucy Moroney, Anand Naiknavare, Ekaterina
Obedkova, Scale 1:100
An imaginary landscape, embedding a city in the distance

12

13

12. Wiktor Kidziak, Design Phase One
A printworks

13 Young-Sang Lee, Design Phase One
A biofuel service stop at Hoxton Station

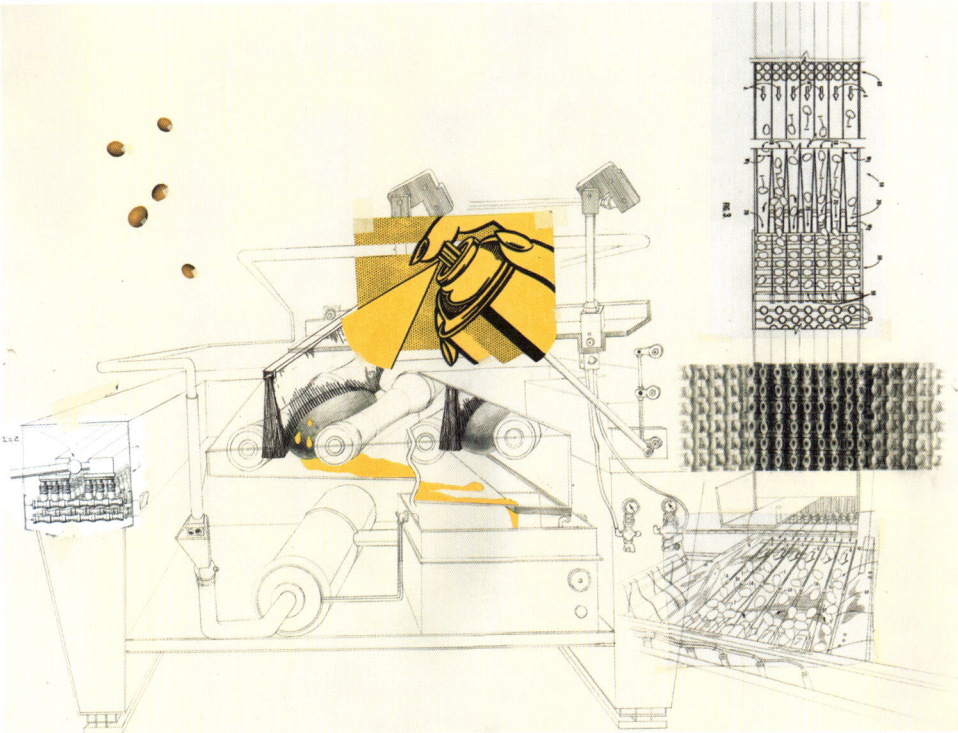

14

15

14. Nara Ha, Design Phase One
Production of vinyl records combined with a chicken
farm. Site: Shoreditch

15. Phung Hieu Minh, Design Phase Two
Manufacturing the sublime: a floodwater
processing plant for East London

INTERMEDIATE 1

'The archaeologists of some future age will study the freeway to understand who we were.' – David Brodsly

The Lost Highway

We started out with the Autobahn. Concrete, schnitzel, ghostdrivers and Krautrock. Ballard, Can and Kraftwerk, segueing into Tom Waits, Johnny Cash, Don DeLillo and even more Johnny Cash as we rode the US Interstate system, driving through California, Nevada and Arizona. LA, Barstow, Vegas, the Grand Canyon, Quartzsite and onto Palm Springs.

With this year's study of the Eisenhower National System of Interstate and Defense Highways (STRAHNET), Inter 1 began a multi-year exploration into the architectural possibilities of land-, sea- and air-based networks. The 'Lost Highway' was an apt place to start. The Interstate ties together every aspect of American life through its tributaries and interchanges, but is also obsolete, dysfunctional and – in parts – just plain broke.

To understand such a complicated system we embarked on a strenuous research project, mapping, drawing infographics, compiling information on highway culture, viewing 70s road movies and road-testing a number of experiments, methodologies and techniques. In the US students counted French Fries, rode in RVs, slept in the desert, ate barbecue and interviewed a cast of miscreants in an attempt to understand the Interstate, an entity that – in DeLillo's memorable words – laid America 'out flat as birdshit on a Buick.'

Students were tasked with designing a 'drive-thru' and studied optimisation, individuation and dysfunctionalism – from 'anti-social' practices at truck stops to the informal domesticity of RVing retirees, strip malls, garages, strip clubs, saloons and highway hypnosis. The programme of drive-thru served as an architectural platform for testing the spatial, temporal, social, economic and political implications of these varied phenomena, and finding ways of occupying the highway's unloved residual spaces.

Inter 1 is dedicated to exploring the potentials of a new type of research-based design studio. Next year – Rotterdam, New Orleans, Memphis and the mighty Mississippi.

UNIT STAFF
Mark Campbell
Deane Simpson

STUDENTS
Costantino Balbo Bertone
 di Sambuy
Shu Susan Chai
Hussam Mansour Dakkak
Madoka Furuhashi
Yeon Sung Lee
Scrap Marshall
Arabella Maza San
 Vicente
Jessica Pappalardo
Ka Hee Park
Kristina Pokrovskaya
Roland Shaw
Camille Steyaert

With thanks to:
Roz Barr
Ricardo de Ostos
Oliver Domeisen
Belinda Flaherty
Francesca Hughes
Tina-Henriette Kristiansen
Jesse LeCavalier
Saskia Lewis
Christopher Pierce
Damian Rogan
Andreas Rumpfhuber
Theo Sarantoglou Lalis
Kirsten Scott
Brett Steele
Jörg Stollman
Dora Sweijd
Charles Tashima
Kirk Wooller
Tom Weaver

Buro Happold
The Center for Land-Use
 Interpretation
The Museum of Jurassic
 Technology
Robert Venturi
Denise Scott-Brown

WALL OF
SHAME
BAN LIST

Name	Fr:	To:
Garrett Thomas	Aug 12/09	8/12/10
Gene Gonzales	Feb 26/09	2/26/10
Sammy Valdez	Jan 19/09	1/19/10
Homer Gonzales Jr	Nov 26/09	1/31/10
Cloyce Vigil	Dec 12/09	1/12/10
Joe Pesata, III	Dec 12/09	1/12/10
Carrie Blackbird	Dec 21/09	1/21/10

1. Costantino Balbo Bertone di Sambuy,
Navajo Nation Saloon

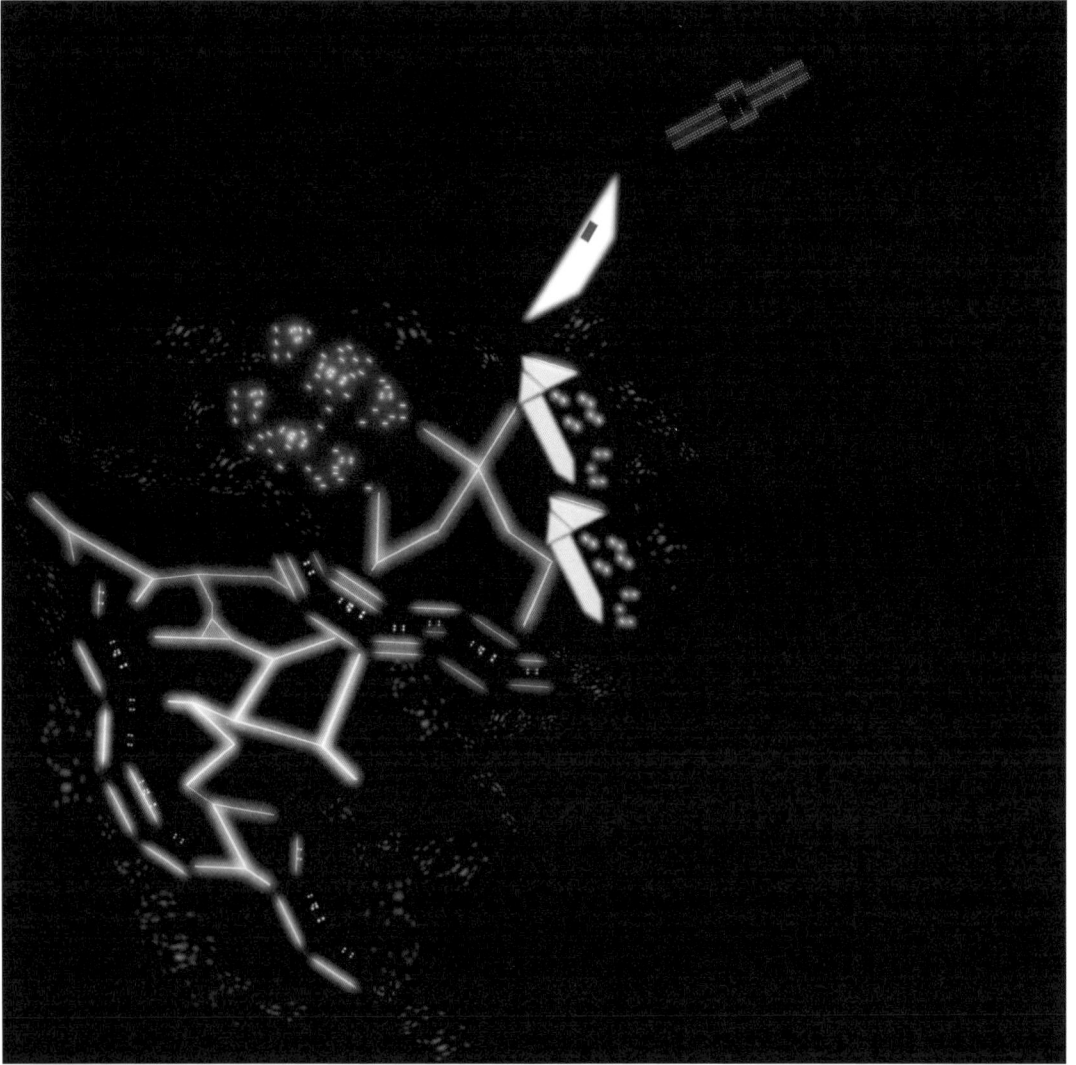

2. Ka Hee Park, RV Park overlooking Las Vegas

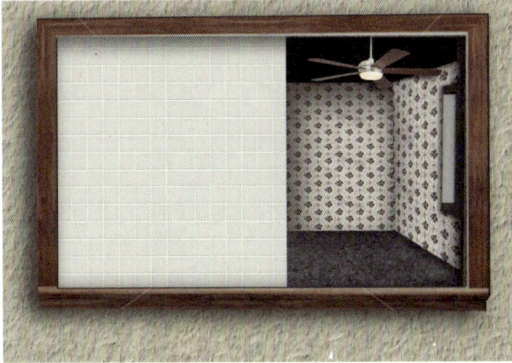

3

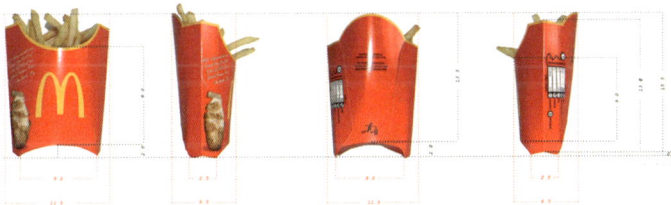

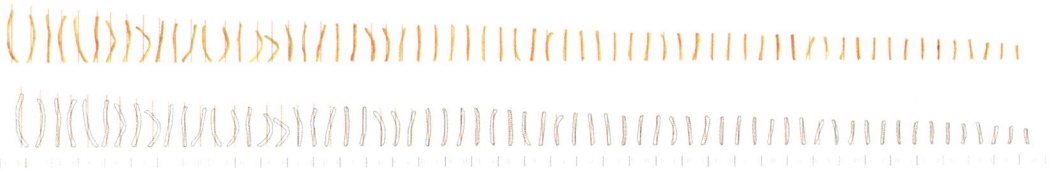

4

3. Kristina Pokrovskaya, Mobile Strip Mall

4. Hussam Mansour Dakkak, McDonald's Drive-Thru

5

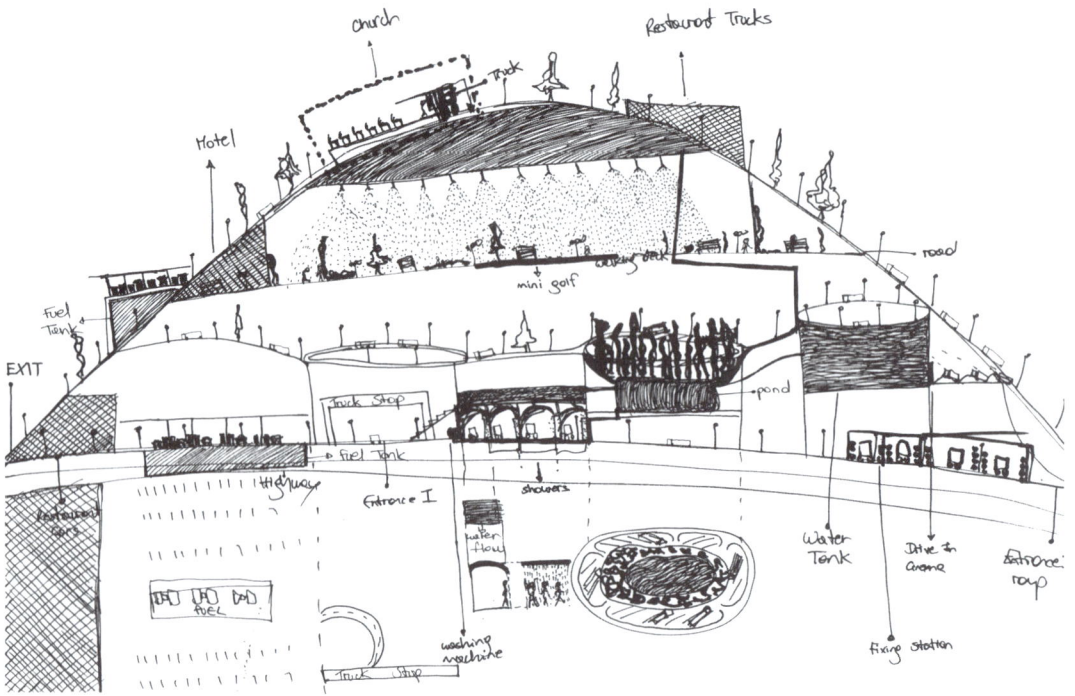

6

5. Arabella Maza San Vicente, Drive-Thru Gas Station   6. Jessica Pappalardo, Californian Truck Stop

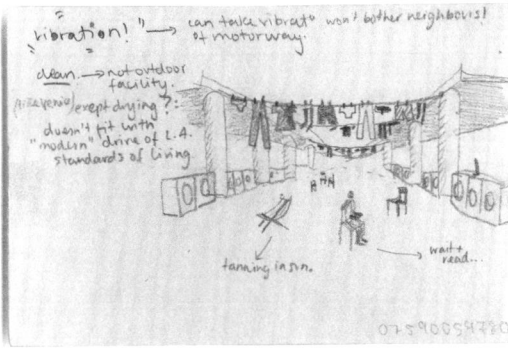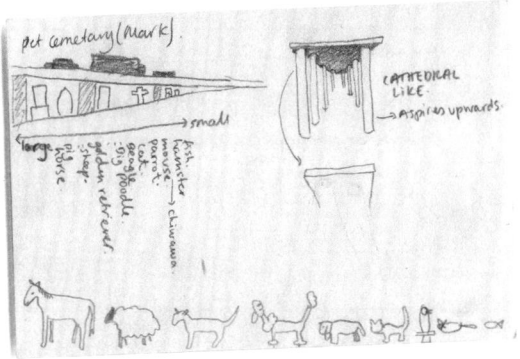

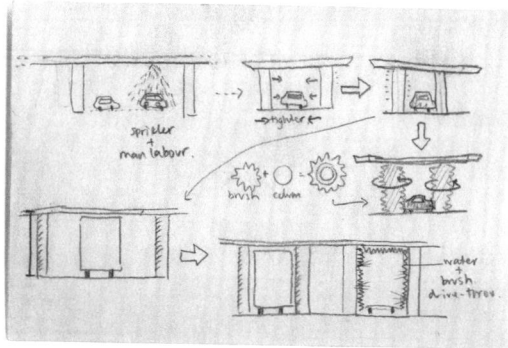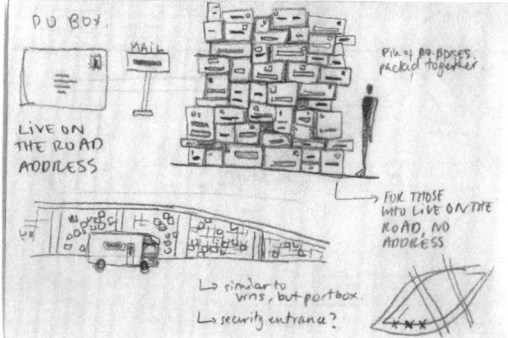

7

8

7. Camille Steyaert, reusing the residual spaces of
Interstate 405

8. Madoka Furuhashi, Venice Boulevard Detour

INTERMEDIATE 2

Hooke Park Caretaker's House

Following four years of the AA Summer Pavilion programme, Inter 2 engaged in a full architectural project: the Caretaker's House for Hooke Park. Taking the opportunity presented by the outline planning permission for the development of the Hooke Park campus, the unit worked through the year to produce, for construction, a fully detailed design for a family house.

The first term consisted of case-studies, site-visits and individual explorations of design concepts for houses leading to competition proposals for the schematic concept. These were developed by pairs of students mentored by architects who had recently received the Manser Medal award for house design. Time spent at Hooke Park exposed students to the subtleties of the site and the lives of the user family. Visits to Frei Otto at his house near Stuttgart and to the Finnforest Merk fabrication facility near Munich introduced the philosophies and technologies underlying the project.

The four competition entries presented a range of responses. David Hellstrom and Elisha Nathoo proposed a free-form three-storey lattice-grid-shell structure; Andrea Kloster and Harpreet Marway's Tree House was based on a spiral of rooms suspended by 'trunks' representing an imagined continuation of the forest; Beom Kwan Kim and William Stanley's Nature Bath proposal placed a single-storey house under an umbrella-like roof that framed views into the woods. The selected scheme, Rebecca Spencer and Harshit Kothari's Breathing House, was arguably the most contextually rich but least developed proposal, provoking strong debate in the competition jury.

In term 2, the unit relocated to Hooke Park and began work as a collective design team. The team worked hard to establish consensus decisions towards a full scheme design. Back in London, the focus turned to detailed design, drawing production, planning application and, with the input of consultants and suppliers, the full definition of the technical systems of the house. Inter 2 has tested the premise of doing architecture (actual construction) in architecture school.

UNIT STAFF
Charles Walker
Martin Self

STUDENTS
David Hellstrom
Beom Kwan Kim
Andrea Kloster
Harshit Kothari
Harpreet Marway
Elisha Nathoo
Rebecca Spencer
William Stanley

MENTOR ARCHITECTS
Sacha Bhavan and
Simon Knox (Knox
Bhavan Architects)
Mike Davies (Rogers Stirk
Harbour + Partners)

Robert Dye (Robert Dye
Associates)
Jamie Fobert (Jamie
Fobert Architects)

**VISITING CRITICS AND
COMPETITION JURORS**
Renato Benedettti, Alison
Brooks, Richard Burton,
Jason Coleman, Simon
Conder, Gordon Cowley,
Mike Davies, Geraldine
Dening, Oliver Domeisen,
Jamie Fobert, William
Moorwood, Ricardo de
Ostos, Alex de Rijke,
Brett Steele

CONSULTANT ENGINEERS
Stephen Jolly
Yannig Robert
Andrew Wylie (Buro
Happold)

Special thanks to:
Frei Otto and Christine
Kanstinger
Finnforest Merk
Chris Sadd and Guy Fabre
(Hooke Park forestry
and sawing)
Richard Burton for his
generous support
Charlie & Georgie
Corry-Wright and family
for their care, support
and patience.

1

2

3

4

1. David Hellstrom & Elisha Nathoo,
Basket Tree House
2. Andrea Kloster & Harpreet Marway
Tree House

3. Harshit Kothari & Rebecca Spencer,
Breathing House
4. Beom Kwan Kim & William Stanley,
Nature Bath

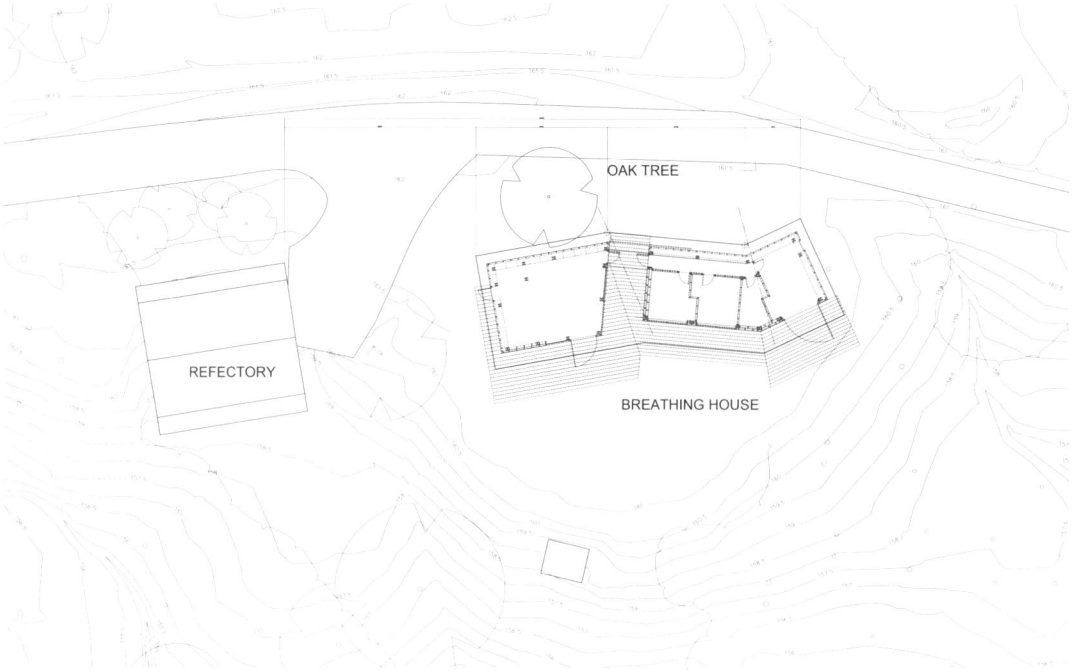

OAK TREE

REFECTORY

BREATHING HOUSE

5

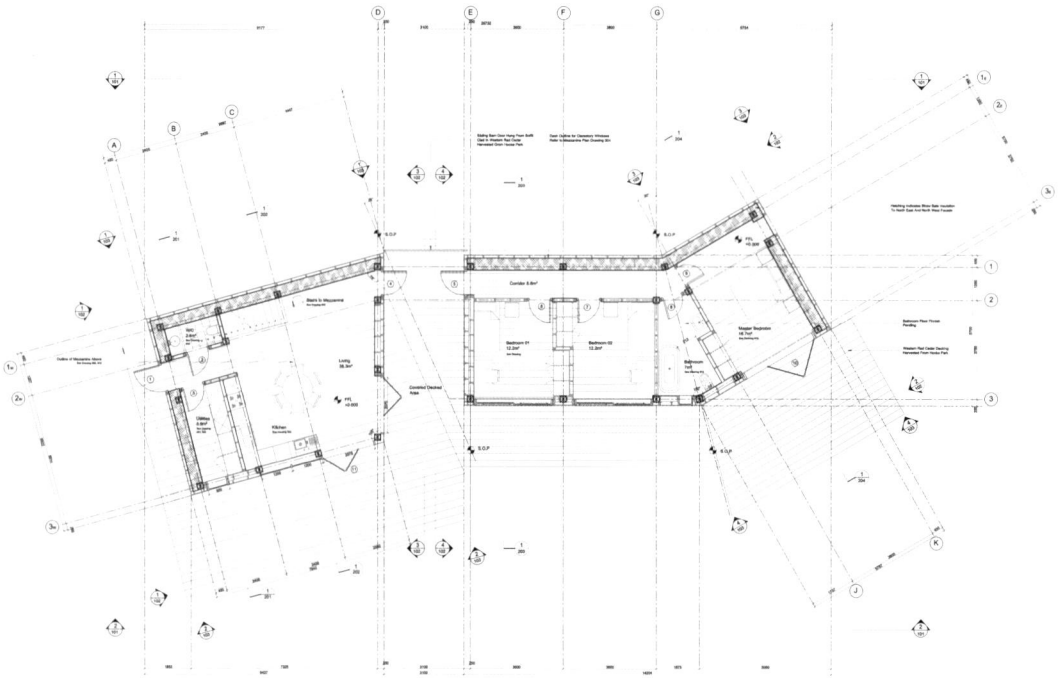

6

5–12. Hooke Park Caretaker's House: Breathing House
general arrangement drawings

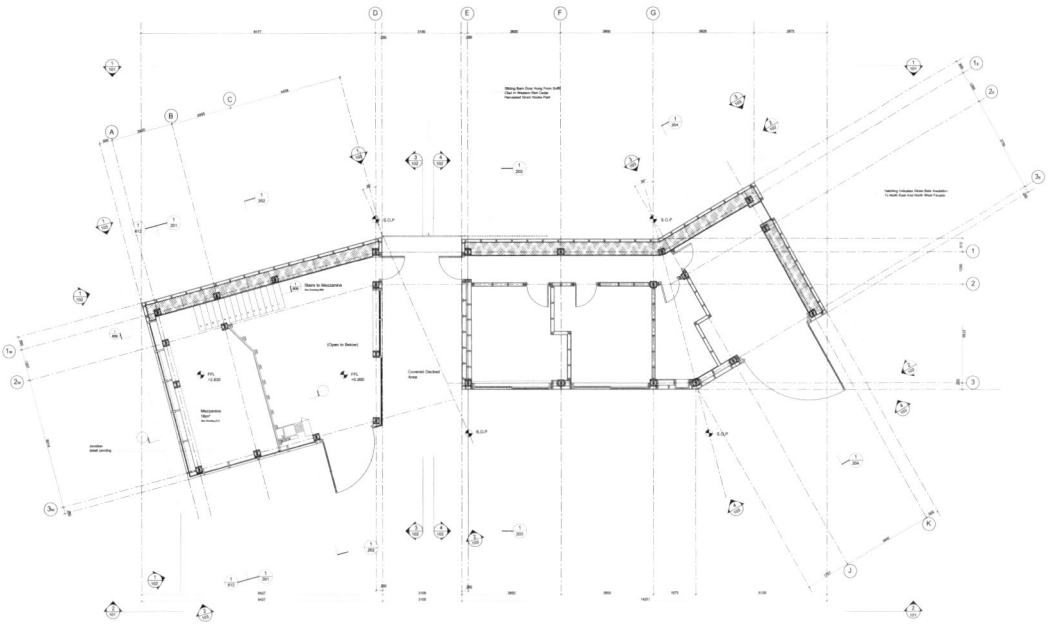

7

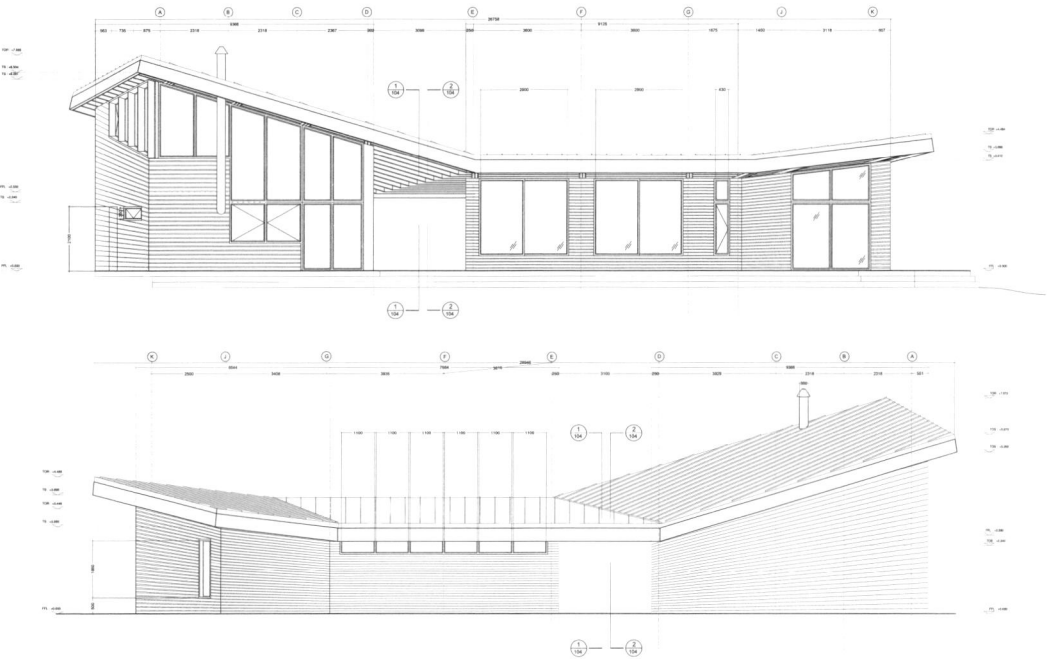

8

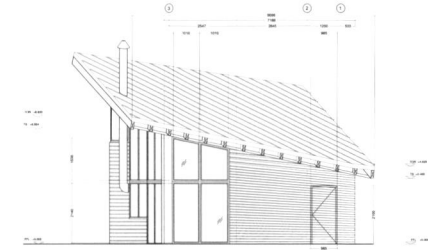

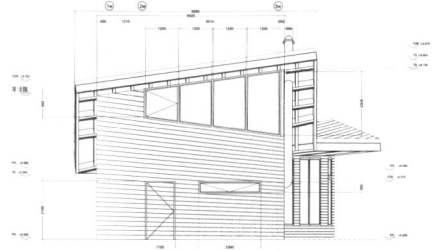

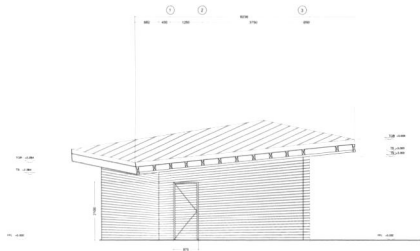

9

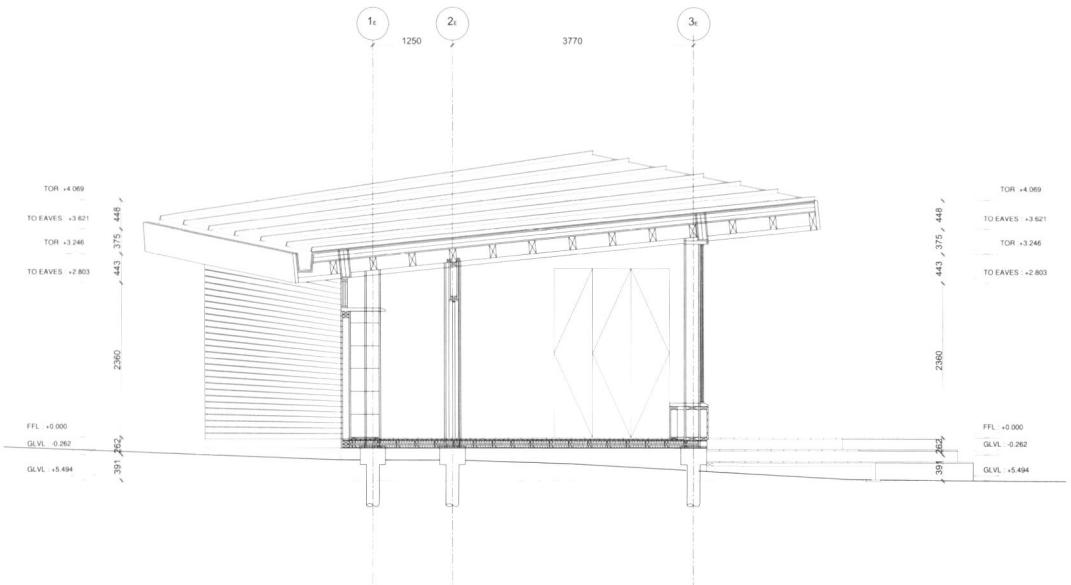

10

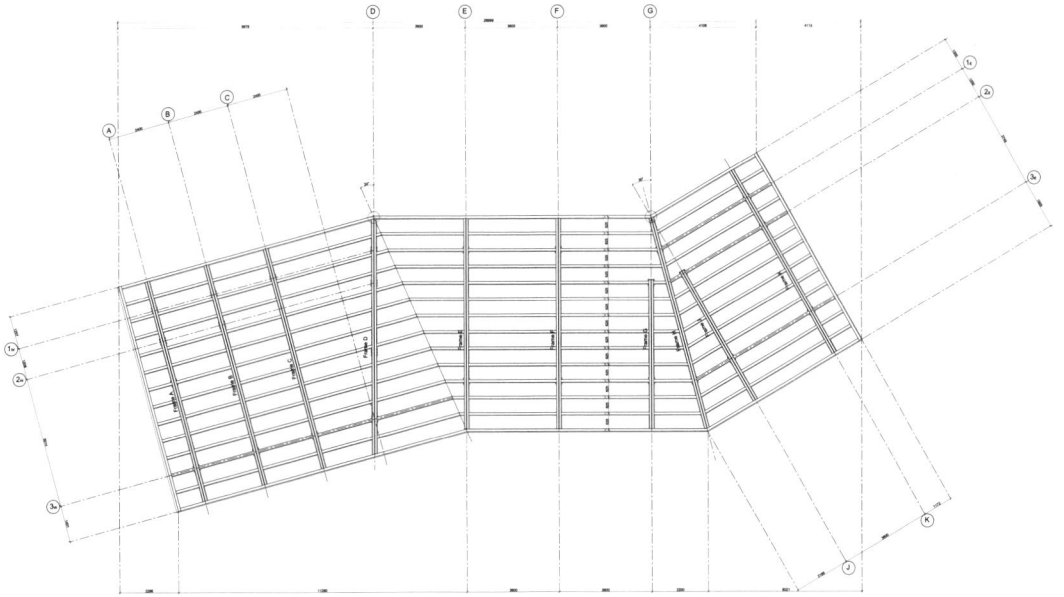

11

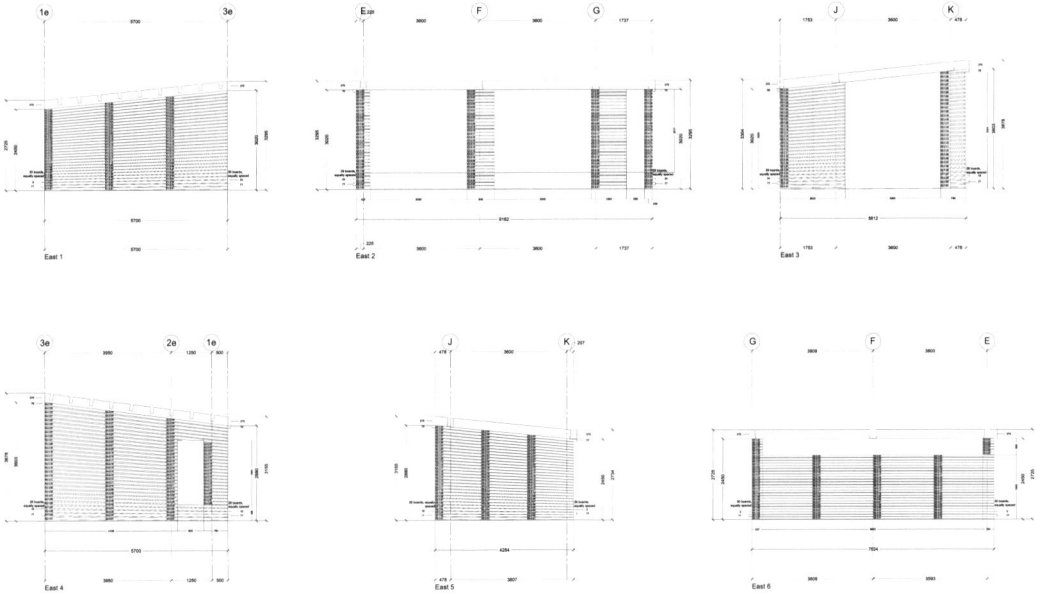

East 1   East 2   East 3

East 4   East 5   East 6

12

39

INTERMEDIATE 3

'Things need not have happened to be true. Tales and dreams are the shadow-truths that will endure when mere facts are dust and ashes, and forgot.' – Neil Gaiman, *The Sandman*

Myths of the Artificial

In an architectural context, Gaiman expands the field in which projects can germinate. Focusing on life's most precious resource, water, Inter 3 leapt outside the strictly scientific approach to infrastructural ecologies and the world of myth for fresh pathways and inspirations. The paramount aim was to consider artificiality as an interface between man and nature, city and resources, culture and environment.

We travelled to north India at the beginning of November. Seeking the sacred traditions of water and its various rituals, the unit experienced the holy city of Varanasi and the River Ganges, as well as ancient step wells, engineered water reservoirs, monkey temples, salt mines, drought zones and vast industrial landscapes where students investigated social and cultural issues – identifying not only problems but also beauty and exuberance.

With the trip as a departure point, students mixed local myths with eccentric devices to construct future narratives. Their final projects crossbreed sacred typologies with effective infrastructure systems to create hybrid traditions and programmatic entrepreneurship. Thirteen students rendered Myths of the Artificial into personal and inspiring architectures. Elegant drawings, exquisite models and delicate tales construct a world of rich and provocative ideas. Charlotte Moe's Purifying Domes and Elina Safarova's Synergetic Threshold: Crematorium along the River Thames eloquently interweave the poetics of scarcity into hopeful landscapes at the human-scale. Song Jie Lim's airborne structure Airavata and Basmah Kaki's meticulously drawn seed bank A Journey in Celebration of Earth, Water and Sun explore deity festivals and propose new narratives. Under the incendiary sun of India and in the toxicity of a sacred river, facts remained secondary. Investigating technological environments inhabited by traditional sensibilities, Inter 3 constructed an ecology of dreams, rituals and machines, a place of celebration and tolerance between past and future.

UNIT STAFF
Nannette Jackowski
Ricardo de Ostos

STUDENTS
Elina Safarova
Maria Brewster
Ingrid Martinsen
Conner Callahan
Mazin Orfali
Ananth Ramaswamy
Charlotte Moe
Ariadna Barthe
Manon Mollard
Song Jie Lim
Yoo Jin Lee
Nikolaos Klimentidis
Basmah Kaki

TECHNICAL ADVISOR
Giles Bruce

Thanks to our
visiting critics:
Abel Maciel, Ben
Masterton-Smith, Paolo
Zaide, Theo Lalis, Natasha
Sandmeier, Monia De
Marchi, Caroline
Rabourdin, Penelope
Haralambidou, Guvenc
Topcuoglu, Stefano
Rabolli Pansera, Goswin
Schwendinger, Bidisha
Sinha, Zubair Surty, Alex
Kaiser, Michael Mitchell,
Jonathan Dawes, Martin
Self, Julian Kruger, Tom
Weaver, Charles Tashima,

Marco Poletto, Joao
Bravo da Costa, Wolfgang
Frese, Marjan Coletti,
Yael Reisner, Christopher
Pierce, Tobias Klein,
Valentin Bontjes Van
Beek, Justin Lau, Kenny
Kinugasa Tsui, Mark
Campbell, Keith Brownlie,
Nuria Lombardero,
Peter Cook

Thanks to our
workshop guests:
Goswin Rothenthal,
Filipa Valente, Alex Kaiser,
Eva Sommeregger

Thanks to Ananth
Ramaswamy and his

family for their generous
help in organising our trip
to India, special thanks to
Narayan Mahadevan in
Delhi and Venkat
Ramanan in Varanasi

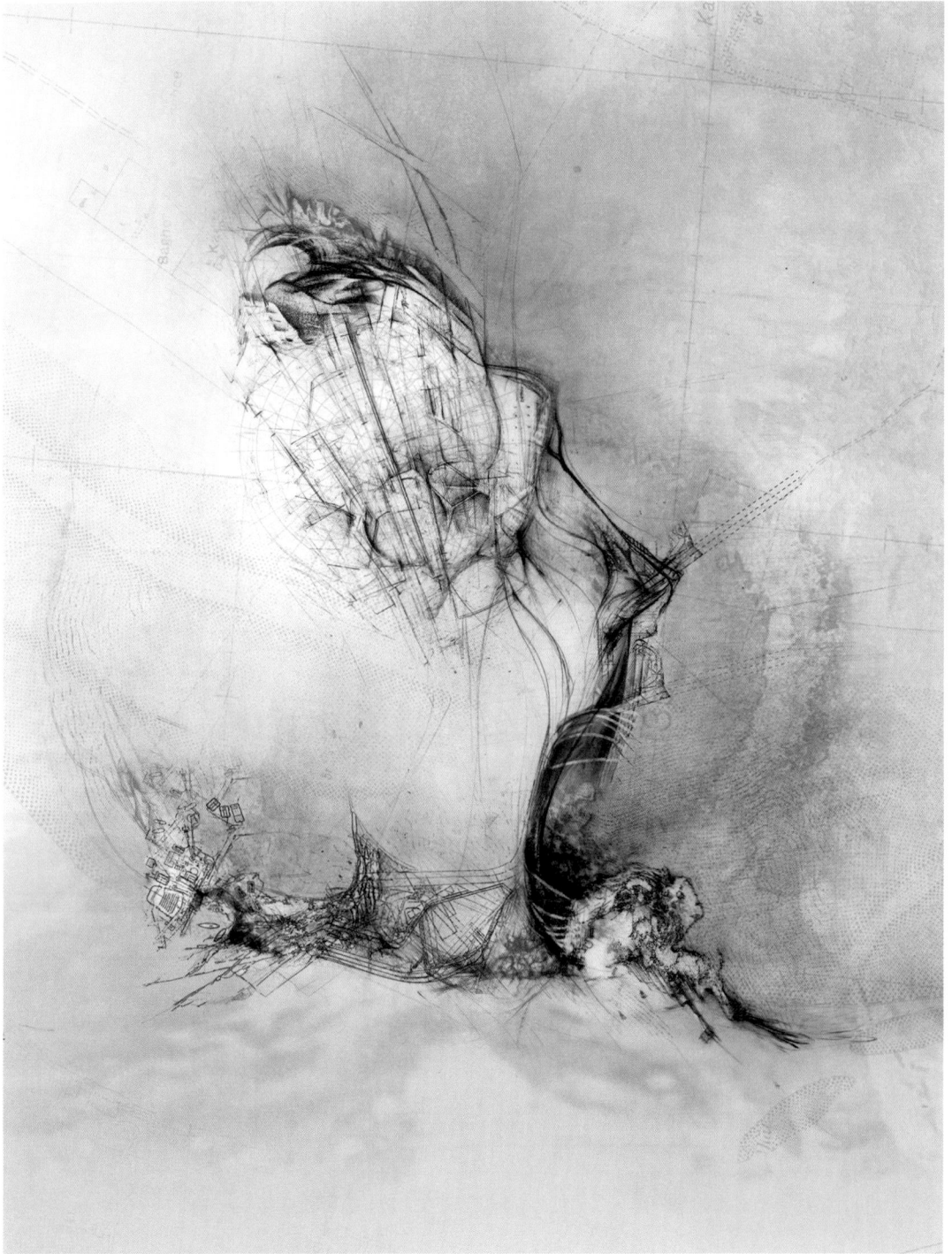

1. Basmah Kaki, A Journey in Celebration
of Earth, Water and Sun
Driven by sun and harvesting rituals the multilayer
seed bank investigates the Pongal festival (beginning
of the harvest), creating a landscape where natural and
artificial spaces coexist in celebrating sustenance and
Surya, the sun god.

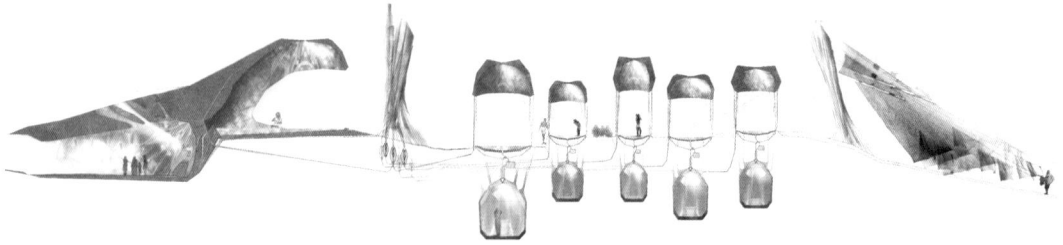

2

3

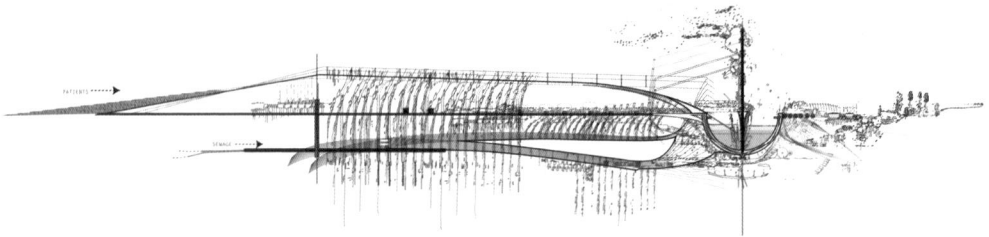

4

2 & 3. Charlotte Moe, Purifying Domes for
Pilgrims to Varanasi
Time is traced by water and read by shadows within the
internal sun clock of the domes. A single drop is released
and controlled within the space according to shadow/light
readings of time. Water is generated from a central tower
that functions as a seasonal clock.

4. Maria Brewster, Healing Gardens: A Hybrid
Ecology of Science and Faith
Inspired by the holistic symbol of the Mandala, the project
focuses on the threshold between the sacred and the
profane. It explores healing and medicinal plants in the
context of the River Ganges, a delicate balance between
water datum and religious needs.

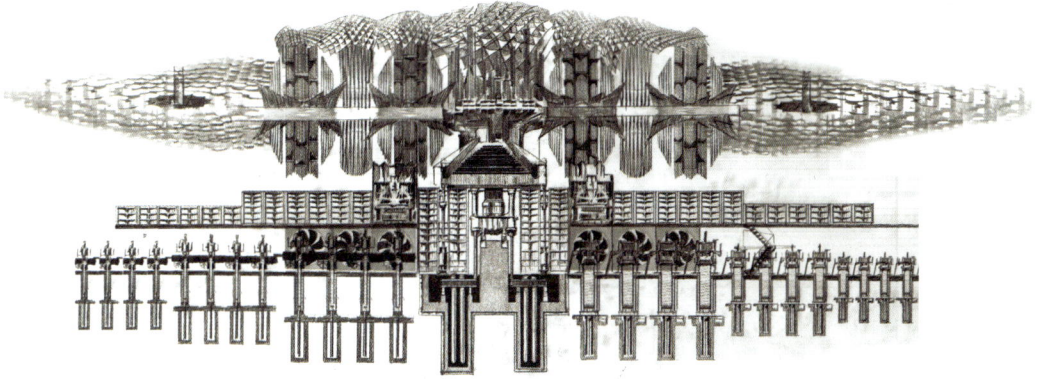

5

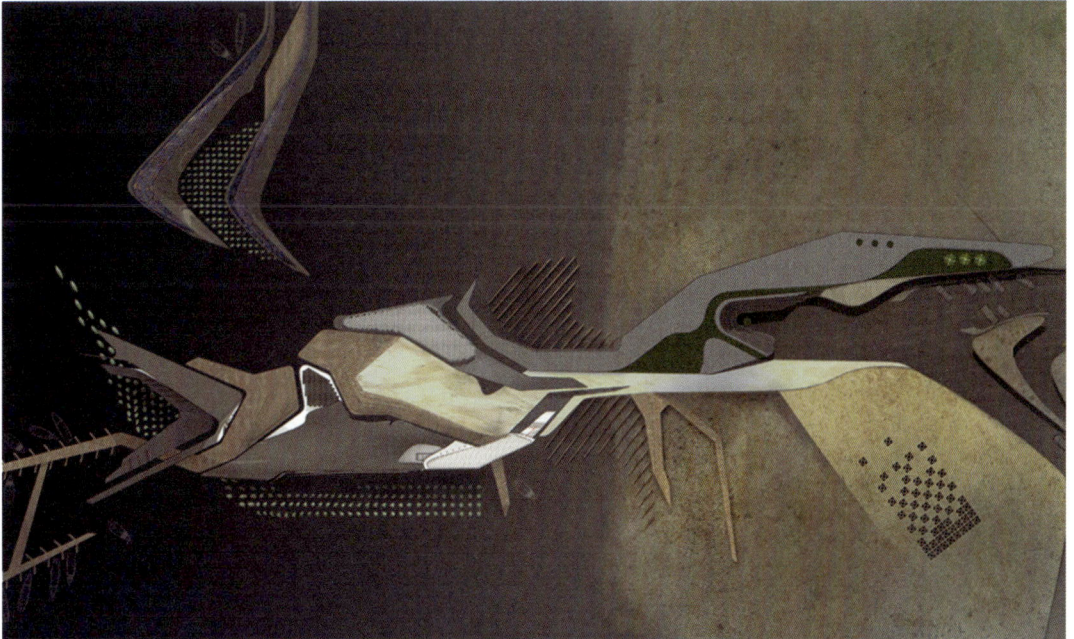

6

5. Ariadna Barthe, Emergent Worlds:
A Hydro-Architecture of Celebration
Explores the process of filtering Ganges water in relation
to people's daily rituals, domestic activities and annual
celebrations.

6. Nikolaos Klimentidis, Aeon Bheema
Observatory and bathing area. A pier-like infrastructure
explores the senses through fluid forms and digital
experimentation.

7

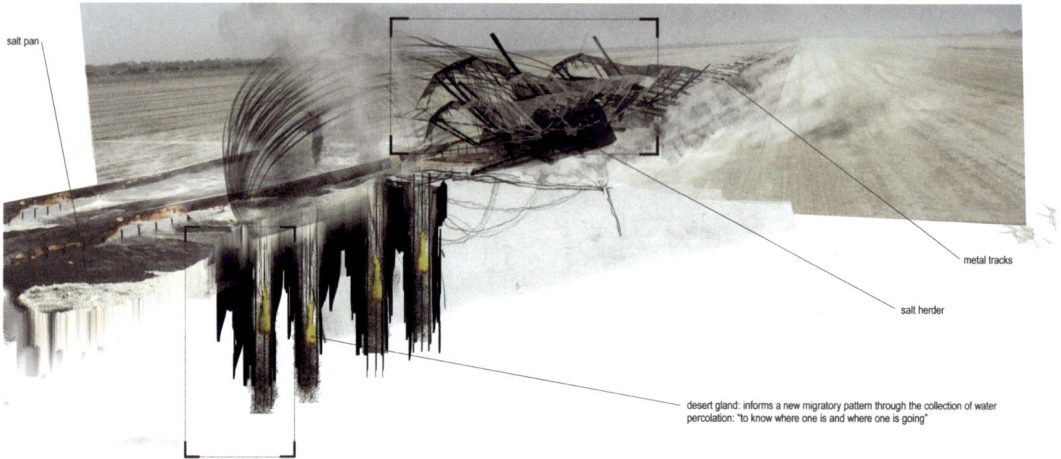

salt pan

metal tracks

salt herder

desert gland: informs a new migratory pattern through the collection of water
percolation: "to know where one is and where one is going"

8

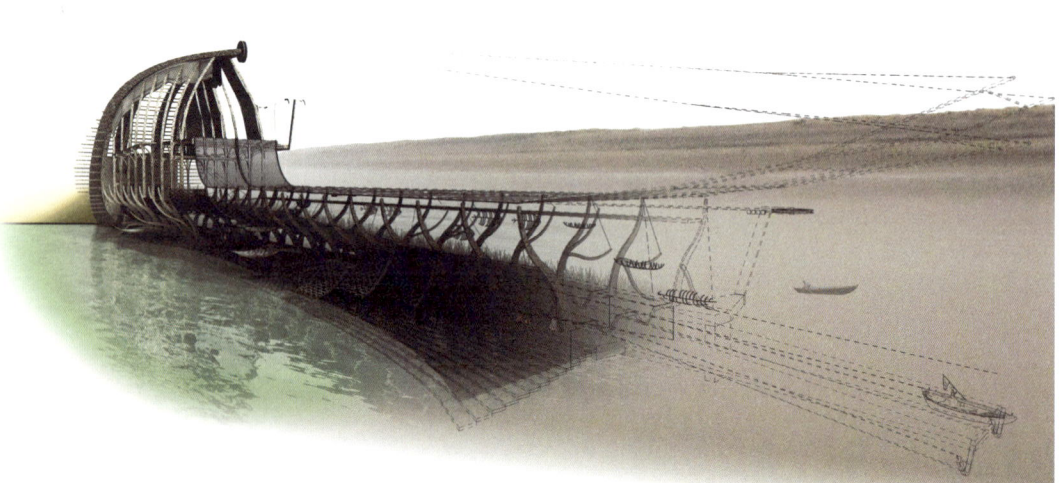

9

7. Song Jie Lim, Airavata. The Bringer of Rain, modern manifestation of the vehicle of Indra, the weather god.
8. Conner Callahan, The White Drought: Experimental Prototypes of Survival. A slow-growth machine explores methods of harvesting hope from the sacred scarcity of the drop of water, as a necessity as well as a techno-social construct.

9. Mazin Orfali, Structural Evolution: Harvesting the Ganga
Harvesting accumulated grunge from boat hulls, the building creates a sense of place for local fishermen and a space where boats can be maintained and new ones produced. Natural algae production purifies the water for those wishing to bathe.

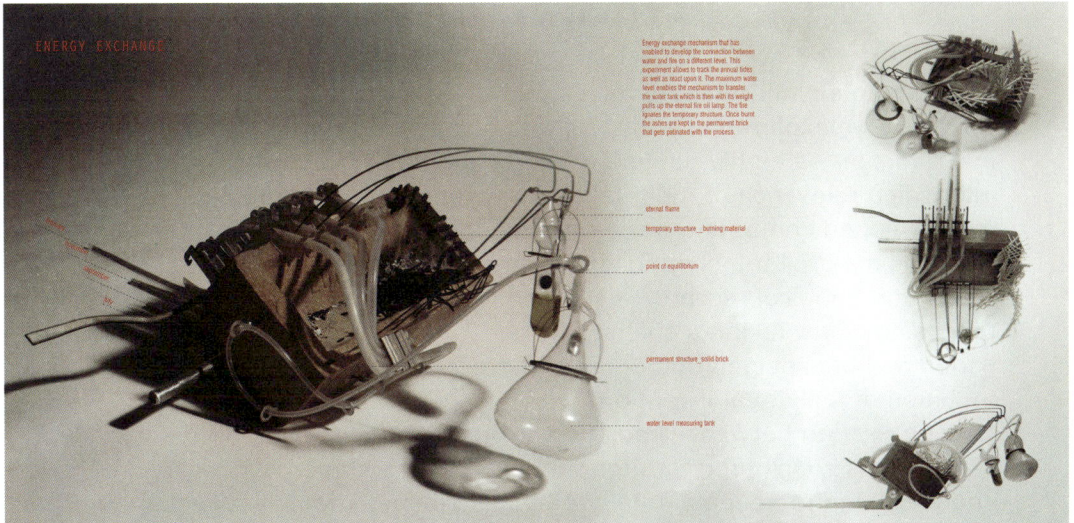

10

ENERGY EXCHANGE

Energy exchange mechanism that has enabled to develop the connection between water and fire on a different level. This experiment allows to track the annual tides as well as react upon it. The maximum water level enables the mechanism to transfer the water tank which is then with its weight puts up the eternal fire oil lamp. The fire ignates the temporary structure. Once burnt the ashes are kept in the permanent brick that gets patinated with the process.

eternal flame

temporary structure _ burning material

point of equilibrium

permanent structure _ solid brick

water level measuring tank

10

11

10. Elina Safarova, Synergetic Threshold: A Crematorium along the River Thames
Between sacredness and contemporary urban life the project explores the River Thames tidal current and London cremation patterns.

11. Yoo Jin Lee, Protocol of a Monsoon Year: An Architectural Interiorisation of a Public Ritual
By addressing the endurance of cremation rituals in Varanasi during the monsoons, the project creates an architecture of spatial sequences of water, smoke and fire.

45

INTERMEDIATE 4

Envelop(e): Inner Beauty

This year we explored quantitative and qualitative density, proposing novel insertions into a highly defined urban condition in Paris. Emphasising the intensified relevance of multi-layered approaches to metropolitan growth, we developed compound design modes for architectural envelopes understood as material transcriptions of contextual negotiations.

Methodological research discussed the extension of a parameter-based process by introducing a spatial and phenomenal approach, observing varied and unexpected outcomes of a prescribed framework and the accumulation of individual inventions.

The relation between predictive design, dynamic input and perceptive reading was considered throughout the year as a staged sequence of analytical and representational media describing various layers of cultural, historical and environmental complexity.

The initial sequencing of urban conditions led to the creation of proposed spatial combinations by hybridising techniques of codified drawing and digital modelling. These three-dimensional diagrams alluded to physical and perceptive qualities of architectural forms and situations. From this logical frame, further sectional study revealed the depth of the Parisian block – its inner beauty in relation to iconic cosmetics.

Students tackled distinguished precedents to expose implicit relationships between forms and modes of living. Starting from overt monumentality we requisitioned past and typical typologies through a simultaneous dialogue between surface, space and experience. Taking into account typological reinventions, we filtered different degrees of materialised envelope designs, regarding them as an interface where culture and history meet both in social arrangement and stylistic expression. The unit also considered environmental responses to architectonic inventions. Designs were abstracted as strategies for urban development in response to the illustrious and deceptive visual continuity of Paris.

Taking the envelope as a magnifying lens, student work explores the contemporary evolution of urban living through the interstitial layer negotiating the public from the private, the ephemeral from the constant, and reinvents this relationship through multi-scale design.

UNIT STAFF
Nathalie Rozencwajg
Michel da Costa
  Gonçalves

STUDENTS
James Kwang-ho Chung
Ni Ding
Ioana-Corina Giurgiu
Dezhi Ho
Charikleia Karamali-Zeri
Seung-Joon Kim
Ja Kyung Kim
Eulalia Moran
Maria Bjerg Nørkjær
Kevin Primat
Wei Ming Eugene Tan
Stefania Triantafyllou
Wai Fung Alex Tsui

Acknowledgements:
Jereon Ameijde
Claude Ballini
Mirco Becker
Lara Belkind
João Bravo da Costa
Giles Bruce
Ines Dantas
Oliver Domeisen
Edgar Gonzalez
Jan-Carlos Kucharek
Nuria Lombardero
Theo Lorenz
Claudia Pasquero
Chris Pierce
Alex Rabe
Natasha Sandmeier
Frances Scott
Therese Severinsen

Marc Simmons
Charles Tashima
Naiara Vegara
Alex Warnock- Smith

1. Maria Nørkjær, Arcade Urban Moment
An urban moment captured in Paris with a focus on
transparency and filtering. The collage expresses the
arcade experience – a transitional space connecting a
sequence from the street into the inner block.

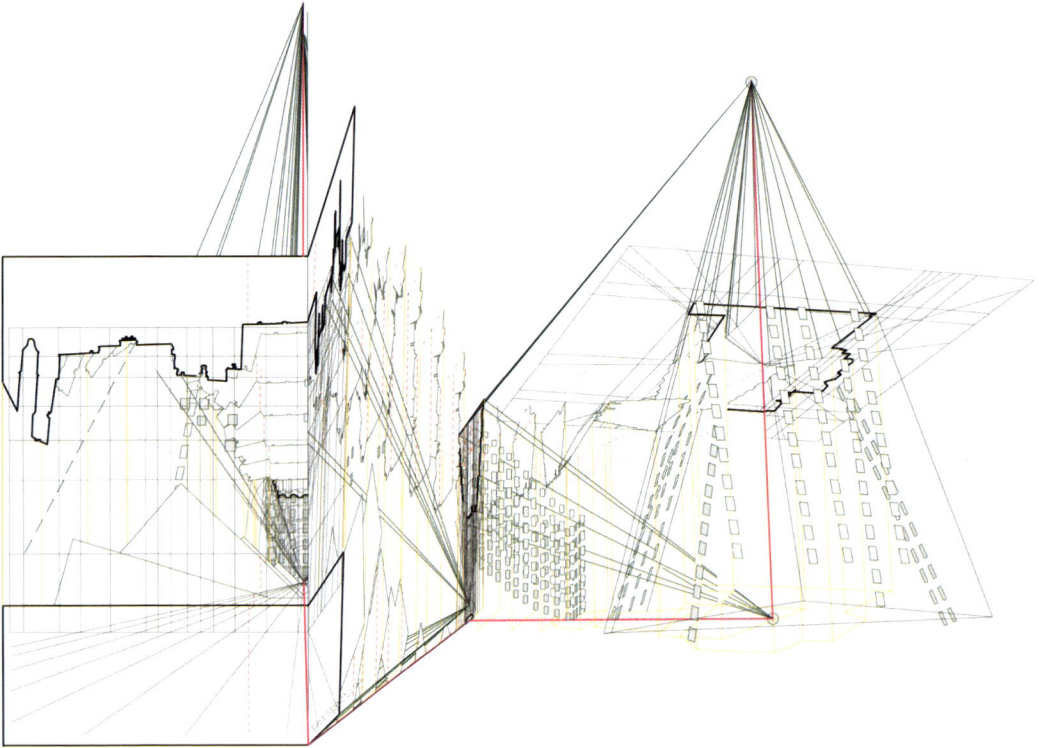

2

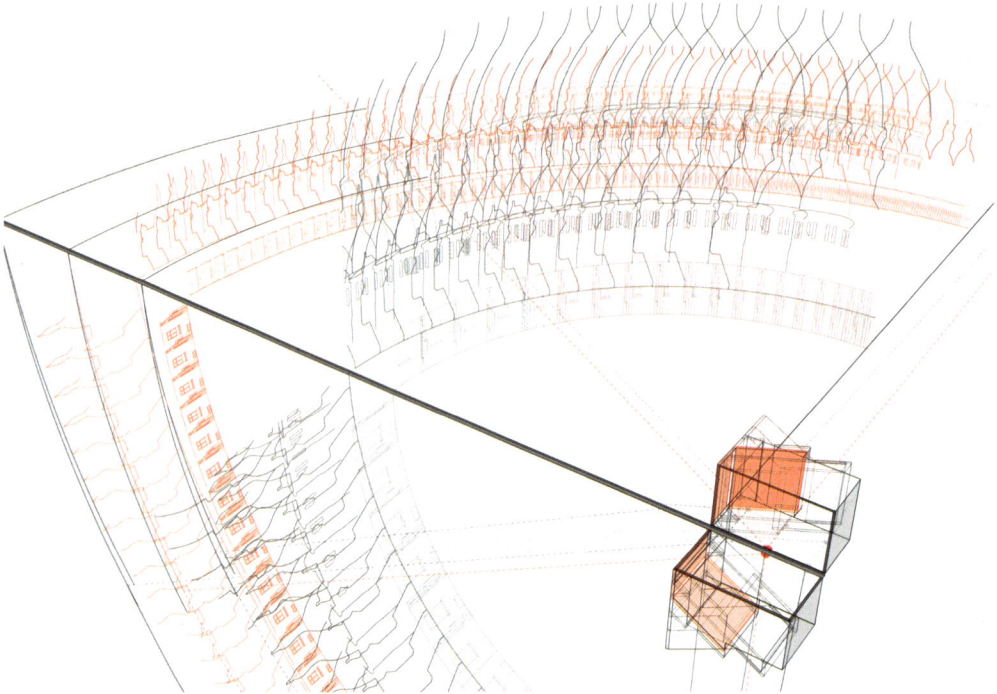

3

2. Charikleia Karamali, Folded Parisian Block
The space folds inwards from the street facade to the
inner block with a transitional space in between. Each is
a step in the process of sequential folding which contains
the inner beauty where the vanishing point of one instant
becomes the point of view for the next.

3. Ja Kyung Kim, Urban Panoramic View of Paris
Banality and specialty of Paris – simultaneous
views from a room with a panoramic view of Paris
are expressed in this collapsed drawing.

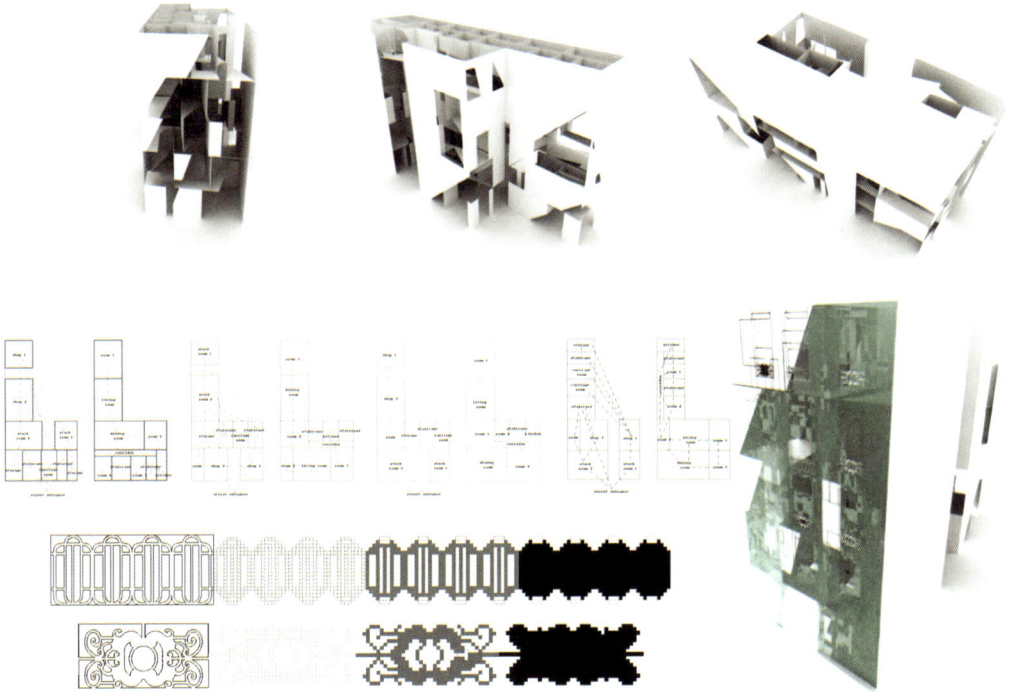

4

5

4. Eulalia Moran, Haussmann 2.0
The Parisian envelope originates in a Haussmannian context. Existing building typologies are reinterpreted at interior and exterior levels resulting in a new spatial distribution that is then carved by the shadows on the site providing additional openings to the traditional fenestration.

5. James Kwang-ho Chung, Folding Parisian Facade
Redefining the formal function of facade elements by folding a Haussmannian facade, respecting stylistic and volumetric aspects of the context.

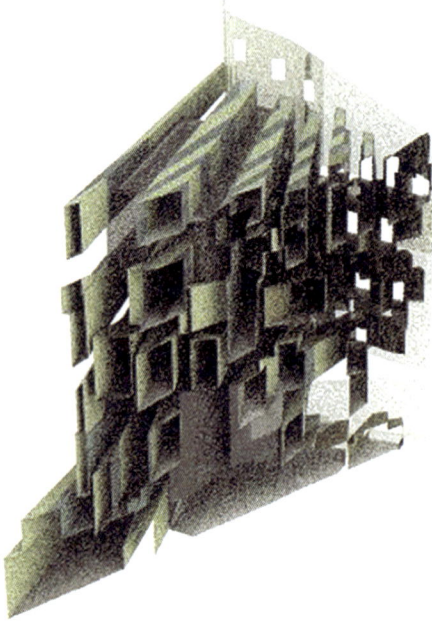

6

7

8

9

6–9. Ni Ding, Visual Arcades
The arcades create an envelope of circulation spaces.
Their intersections at various levels determine the
configuration and variety of internal inhabitable spaces.

50

10. A collection of models produced by students:
3D diagrams, study models and design proposals

INTERMEDIATE 5

Intermediate 5 focuses on performance as the driving force for developing an architectural argument. In a constant dialectic between making, un-making, discerned production and critical assessment, we define tectonic invention and spatial resolution.

Enrique Agudo: Scripting identities and playing roles. Dressing up and tearing down. LA Confidential. The house of an actor. Interstitial spaces.

Hessa Al Bader: I am the original, you are nothing. Monstrosities and Adaptation, Mosque and Sears Warehouse, Olympic Boulevard and Al Aqsa.

Rula Al Sayegh: Second-hand, leather interiors, beneath the valley of the ultra vixen, Monza Cars in Ventura Valley. Copper club, dirty engines.

Oleg Bilenchuck: Weaver of dreams, a silent scream. Griffith observatory and the inverted dome. A pin hole on Mount Lukens.

Stefano Branca: Moonshiner's retreat, stage and saloon. Folkloristic darkness, carcass of the American dream, moonless prairie night, Bonanza.

Joohyun Choo: Territory and text, text and monument, hoodies and uniforms, serve and protect. To punish and enslave, inflate LAPD.

Artemis Doupa: Artemis FULL STOP The Parfum FULL STOP The Los Angeles Theatre. The Diva as typology.

Evangelos Gerogiannis: Nervous meltdown and mechanical breakdown. Accumulation and defect. LA Times, disruptive assembly line. Mechanised distortion.

Kaja Kvande: Intimate and public, the American drama. LA library, invisible boundaries. Edward and Jane. Crucial programme additions.

Nathalie Matathias: Terminal 24, constant time and variable space, constant space and variable time. Universal jet lag, eternal loop.

Wataru Sawada: Imposed monologue. Sea and cemetery, appearing and simulating, Margate pool, oscillating horizon, inverted city.

Graham Smith: The collapse of the projection, the post office and Sigmund's study. An open cinema, a naked performance, Margate plays itself.

Anna Strom: The Phoenix and the river. The sinking shelter. Puente Hill. Energy and Waste. The landfill, a secret garden.

TUTORS
Stefano Rabolli Pansera
Goswin Schwendinger

STUDENTS
Enrique Agudo
Hessa Al Bader
Rula Al Sayegh
Oleg Bilenchuck
Stefano Branca
Joohyun Choo
Artemis Doupa
Evangelos Gerogiannis
Kaja Kvande
Nathalie Matathias
Wataru Sawada
Graham Smith
Anna Strom

Thanks to:
Brett Steele, Charles Tashima, Miraj Ahmed, Nuria Alvarez Lombardero, Dagobert Bergmans, Javier Castañón, Jonathan Dawes, Monia De Marchi, Ricardo de Ostos, Wolfgang Frese, Francisco Gonzalez de Canales, Brian Hatton, Olaf Kneer, Matthew Murphy, Claudia Pasquero, Marco Poletto, Theo Sarantoglou Lalis, Dora Sweijd, Christoph Zeller, Kei Ito, Karl Crick, Kari Rittenbach, Wayne Daly, Wolfgang Frese

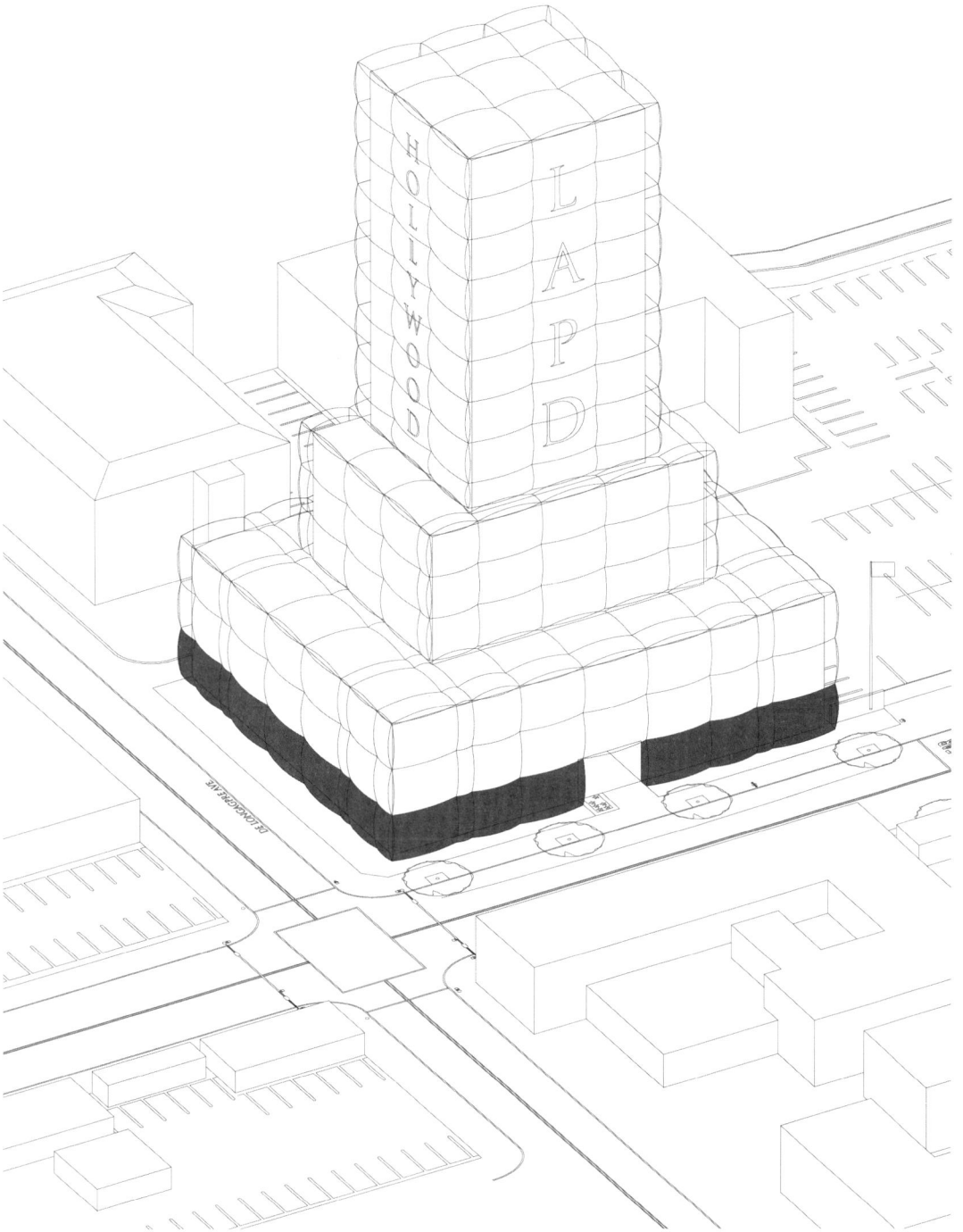

1. Joohyun Choo, territory and authority

2

3

2. Kaja Kvande, the intimate and the public   3. Rula Al Sayegh, the copper club

4

5

4. Artemis Dupa, Full Stop   5. Hessa Al Bader, monstrosities and adaptation

6

7

6. Wataru Sawada, sinking horizon and fire alarm   7. Nathalie Matathias, Teminal 24, universal jet lag

8

9

8. Evangelos Gerogiannis LA Times,
accumulation and defect

9. Oleg Bilenchuck, Silent scream, Inversion 3

INTERMEDIATE 6

Camouflage

Camouflage patterns in the animal kingdom are the outcome of genetics, natural selection and the physical conditions of habitat – creatures mutate to 'become' their surroundings. We are interested in this process of becoming in architecture, one that questions the space we perceive (through illusion) and also our perception of those within it.

A Catalogue of Effects

Our investigation began by developing a critical understanding both of pattern-making and its associated effects. Presented with a range of naturally occurring camouflage patterns, each unit member explored pattern as a device for spatial and material approaches. Iterations evolved using a wide range of camouflage techniques from dazzle to coincident disruptive patterning, counter-shading and mimicry. Developed initially as two-dimensional patterns that featured false perspective, distortion or movement, these were later transformed into an array of small-scale surface and volumetric fabrications with each model evaluated according to spatial and tectonic potential. The studies culminated in an exhibition, A Catalogue of Effects, launched in the AA Back Members' Room. Bringing together individual research as a unit-wide taxonomy of camouflage devices, this speculative material was then used to distort and question the scale of the room and to provide a setting for the work to be displayed.

Responding to Habitat

With Soho as the backdrop, the unit examined the diversity of uses and users as a context into which new building skins, morphologies and spatial organisations were nestled. Each final project has sought to position itself carefully within its setting, with patterns modulating in response to local conditions or movement. Some agendas focused on adjacencies as a way to orientate programmes – using mimicry to create illusions of the familiar. Some enlisted common material systems such as brickwork, transformed with polychromatic patterning and distorted bonding. Others favoured an anamorphic approach, dissolving the distinction between existing surfaces and the building itself.

UNIT STAFF
Jonathan Dawes
Dagobert Bergmans
Fumiko Kato

STUDENTS
Kanachai Bencharongkul
Houssam Flayhan
Jin Uk Lee
Urszula Saniawa
Royce Yue Chai Tsang
Antoine Vaxelaire
Manijeh Verghese
Ruohong Wu
Mohamad Zamri Bin Arip
Chan Zhan

TECHNICAL CONSULTANT
Scobie Alvis

WORKSHOPS
Ricky Rui Li
Suyeon Song

VISITING CRITICS
Douglas Ardhern
Hardy Blechman
Ricardo de Ostos
Cristina Díaz Moreno
Shin Egashira
Efrén García Grinda
Edgar Gonzalez
Nuria Lombardero
Marianne Mueller
Stefano Rabolli Pansera

Dominic Papa
Martin Self
Stephen Sinclair
Brett Steele
Charles Tashima
Tom Weaver

Special thanks to:
Toyo Ito & Associates
Kumiko Inui
Tokyo Geidai University
AA Exhibitions
Department

1. Antoine Vaxelaire, pattern study with false perspective
and shading to explore ambiguous overlapping surfaces

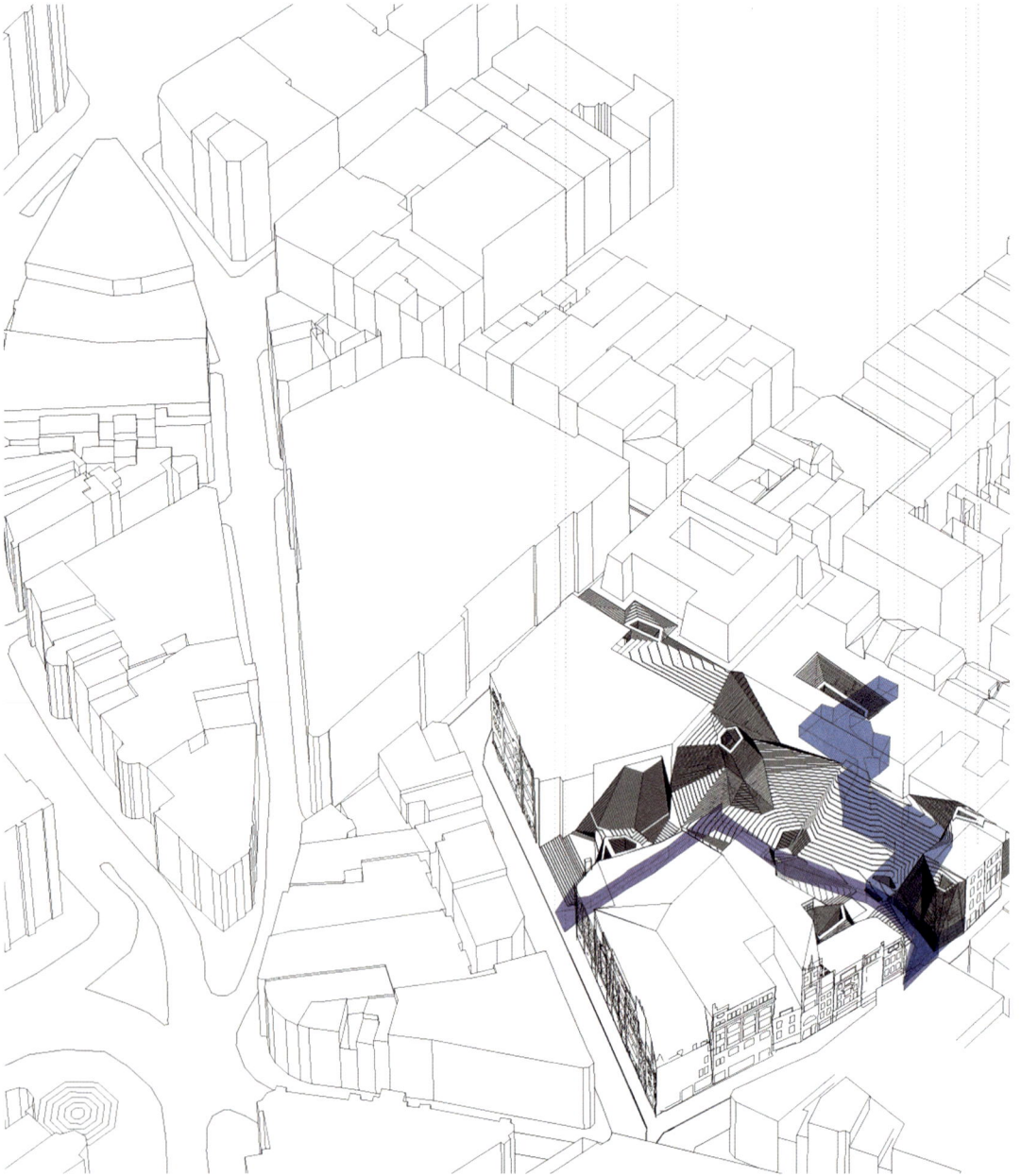

3. Antoine Vaxelaire, adaptive surfaces: the project
interlaces spatial and material relationships, reacting to
local adjacencies and merging the distinction between
background and foreground.

4

5

4. Jin Uk Lee, anamorphic facade of hidden hotel: this projected facade creates an anamorphic illusion by flattening the building's mass in perception.

5. Jin Uk Lee, hotel courtyard: the inner skin of the building is articulated by facets and blades, creating false perspective effects.

6

7

6. Royce Yue Chai Tsang, bathhouse street view: a series of structural profiles varies the degree of transparency within the building, creating an obscure interconnection between the public and private space.

7. Royce Yue Chai Tsang, bathhouse interior: a series of spatial partitioning louvres controls the degree of transparency according to the level of intimacy required for each room.

8. Manijeh Verghese, divergent corner: the camouflage
technique of increasing bond distance as bricks approach
a corner, thereby creating an illusion of spatial expansion
and counterdepth.

INTERMEDIATE 7

'The End of the Universe is very popular,' said Zaphod... 'People like to dress up for it... Gives it a sense of occasion.' – Douglas Adams, *The Restaurant at the End of the Universe*

We sit in wait for the end of the world. We have always regaled ourselves with unnerving tales of a day yet to come. Tomorrow is a dark place and our culture is full of tales of a natural world out of control. Whether it be nuclear apocalypse, viral epidemic, tumbling asteroids or eco-catastrophe our anxieties about our future demise chronicle the flaws and frailties of the everyday.

We have recruited a vagabond troupe of doomsday cultists to join us in this world after the crash; to dance in the shadow of catastrophe and question our fears and misgivings about the future. We have breathed life into the characters and actions of our UNKNOWN FIELDS DIVISION and we have armed ourselves with the props and paraphernalia to survive in the new world.

Together we have voyaged to the edge of the world, 'the last wilderness' of the Arctic. We made a pilgrimage to visit the glaciers before they melt and we shed a tear under the electric skies of the aurora. We have not gone quietly into the night but instead in the Arctic we have forged an intentional community and cult compound of activist architectures, eco-terrorist responses and maverick manifestos.

In our department of Intangible Technology Ioanna and Tobias have encoded the ephemera of web 2.0 into data fossils that calcify on our own bones, and are etched into the layers of glacial ice. Our Illegal Biology Unit has cultivated a psychedelic mushroom farm in which to drown our sorrows, and in Climatology Quiddale is squatting a waterfall to protest for water rights while Heojih has designed a weather-sensitive landscape that broadcasts the song of a dying world.

We are visionaries and reporters, part documentarian and part science fiction soothsayer, critically engaging with the conditions of today through speculation about the coming of tomorrow. Standing at the brink we contemplate an end that is laden with fears and inconsistencies yet at the same time proves to be ripe with unknown escapes and wondrous possibilities.

UNIT MASTERS
Liam Young
Kate Davies

STUDENTS
Tommaso Davi
Jihyun Heo
Kin Pong Ho
Ioana Iliesiu
Tobias Jewson
Seung-Youb Lee
Saif Lassas
Georges Massoud
Borja Miguiro
Nora Nilsen
Quiddale O'Sullivan
Antonis Papamichael
Jack Self
Harri Williams-Jones

VISITING CRITICS
Viktor Antonov, Jon Arden, Tuur van Balen, Johan Berglund, Valentin Bontjes van Beek, Matthew Butcher, Javier Castañon, Revital Cohen, Wolfgang Frese, Adam Furman, Samantha Hardingham, Ben Hammersly, Rosy Head, Simon Herron, Will Hunter, Anab Jain, Matt Jones, Peter Kelly, Christian Kerrigan, Tobias Klein, Joerg Majer, Stuart Munro, Shaun Murray, Tim Norman, James O'leary, Sascha Pohflepp, Matt Shaw, Bob Sheil, Charles Tashima, Guvenc Topcuoglu, Emmanuel Vercruysse

Thanks to
The graphic design crew of Houman Momtazian and Ghazaal Vojdani, Third Plane 3d scanning, Dan Stacey for arranging our Arctic odyssey, the Iceland Meteorological Office, the Iceland Soil Conservation Service and the strange folk of Sudiyeri fishing village in northern Iceland for nursing the seasick on our 12h rite of passage.

1. Ioana Iliesiu, The Ruins Of Twitter
In the north of Iceland a new glacier is forming from
the steams of twitter chatter etched into its surface.
The once invisible datascape becomes a new geology
and the splash of meltwater into the Arctic Ocean is
the last audible cry of web 2.0.

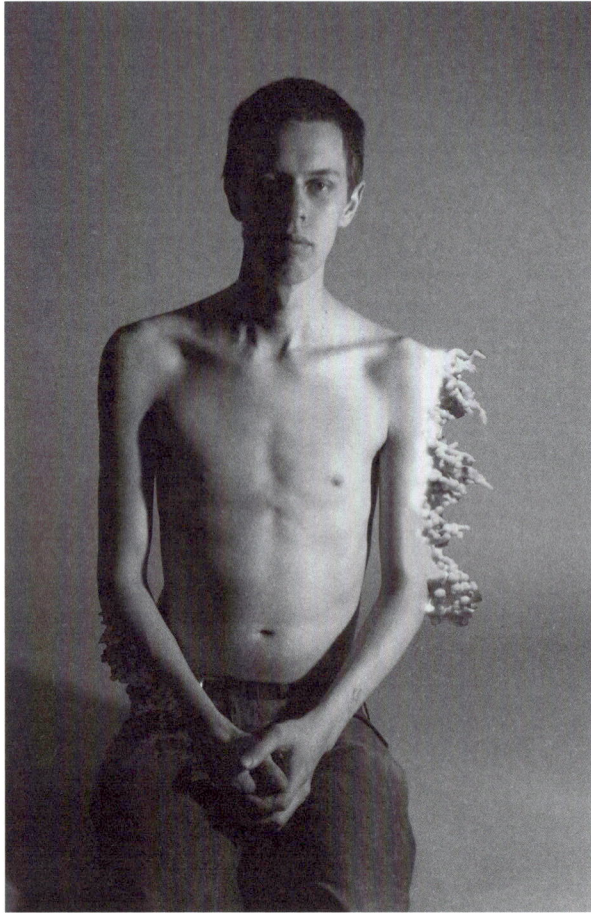

2

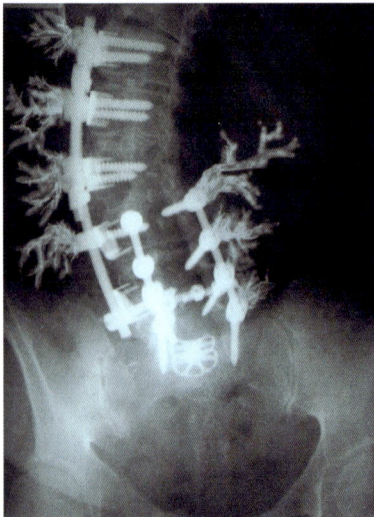

3   4

2–4. Tobias Jewson and Ioana Iliesiu, Data Fossils
With advances in bio-computing, data is now stored as
calcifications under our skin. Illegal immigrants hack their
bones to forge identities; prostitutes blackmail their
clients after they feel their secrets and digital obesity
plagues our teenagers.

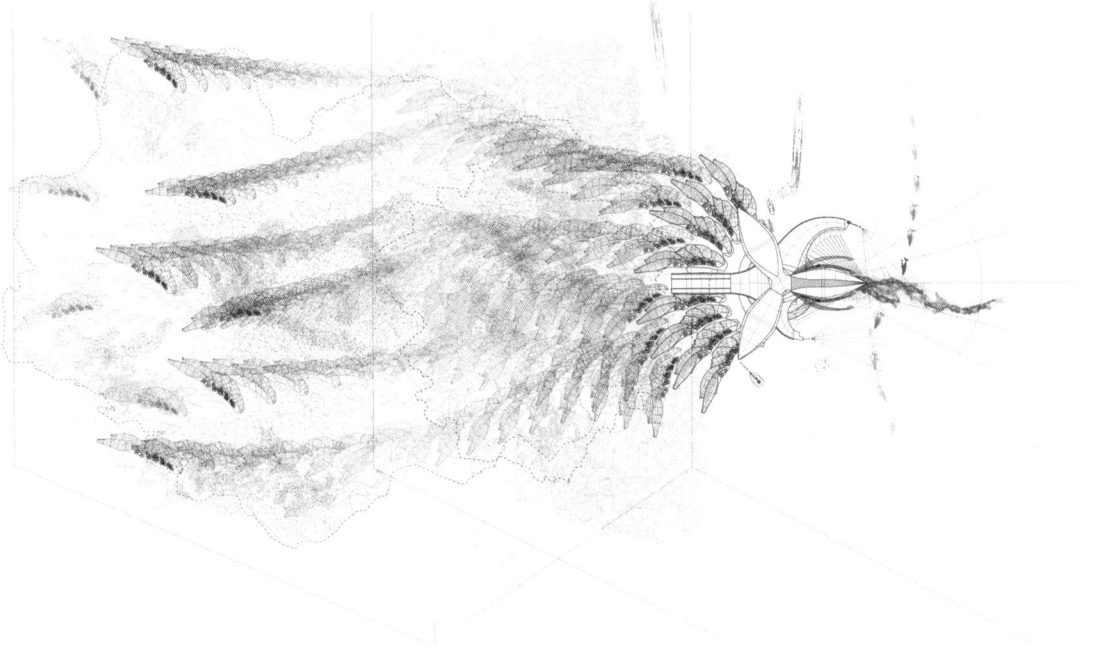

5

6

5. Seung-Youb Lee, Prosthetic from an Ocean Ecosystem
Floating amongst the ice of the Arctic is a strange zoo that
is artificially supporting an ecosystem for the world's last
remaining whale colony.

6. Harri Williams-Jones, Aerospace Agriculture
In the augmented farmlands of rural Iceland a crop of
woven space shuttle nose cones is being prepared for
export. Amongst the flocks of sheep strange bio
technologies have given rise to a new aerospace industry.

7

8

7. Jihyun Heo, *Neurotic Landscapes*
From a remote Icelandic valley, at the precipice of global warming, an array of weather-sensing acoustic instruments is broadcasting across the world a requiem for a changing climate.

8. Quiddale O'Sullivan, *Peak Water Protest Camp*
Rallying against the corporate ownership of water a group of activists deploy a flock of sails and nets to form a protest camp in the mist of a world heritage waterfall.

9

10

9 & 10. Jack Self, Scatterbrain: A Cautionary Tale
The vast intangibile landscapes of the internet have been
consolidated in the physical form of the computational
forests of Scatterbrain Iceland. Across the informatic
seasons the last great machine blinks and flickers silently
in the wilderness.

INTERMEDIATE 8

Politics of Skin Grafting

During the last few years the crisis of capitalist development has redefined our understanding of cities in terms of international policy making, political constituencies and individual and collective political expression in the urban realm. Inter 8 has experimented with new scenarios for political readjustment at a global scale, departing from its most basic manifestation in the city. Students have constructed innovative political arguments by experimenting with relationships between everyday material activities – waiting for a bus, dancing, chatting in the street, wheeling and dealing in the city square – and a particular material organisation. In these common everyday practices, students have found the materials with which to reconstruct the political experience in the city. Exercised in public and constituting a physical expression, these practices acquire political value – Hannah Arendt described the political as action in public – and define new models for the interaction between the individual and the collective in the public arena.

The year began with small workshops in which students became conscious of the political implications of certain architectural elements routinely used in the school. In particular, the door of the Student Forum and the wall of the Director's office were redesigned according to new political arguments. Following these first experiments, students jumped to the urban scale and focused on a design for a very specific public space: the Plaza de la Revolución in Havana, Cuba. Alien to the global market but highly politically charged, the Plaza became a laboratory in which students could speculate about different futures for political expression within the city.

UNIT STAFF
Francisco González
  de Canales
Nuria Alvarez Lombardero

STUDENTS
Uliana Apatina
Merve Anil
Gary Dupont
Max Hacke
Karl Karam
Yong Zaek Kwon
Stavros Papavassiliou
Costa Rivetti
Lyza Rudyk
Maud Sanciaume
Kayvan Sarvi
Atta Yousefi
Olivia Wright

Acknowledgements:
Pier Vittorio Aureli
Jeroen van Ameijde
Miraj Ahmed
Lucy Bullivant
Margarita Camara
Victor Compan
Michel da Costa
Gonçalves
Mario Coyula
Jose Perez de Lama
Mehran Gharleghi
Francisco Gomez
Edgar Gonzalez
Evan Greenberg
Maximilian Gwiazda
Marina Lathouri
Ludovico Lombardi
Alberto Moletto
Rafael Moneo

Jheny Nieto
Ricardo de Ostos
Claudia Pasquero
Marco Poletto
Stefano Rabolli Pansera
Jose Perez de Lama
Tomaz Pipan
Eduardo Rico
Mauricio Puente
Jorge Rodriguez
Nathalie Rozencwajg
Alberto Sabater Alloza
Amin Sadeghy
Cristian Sanchez
Goswin Schwendinger
Douglas Spencer
Brett Steele
Dora Sweijd
Charles Tashima
Melissa Woolford

Manja van de Worp
GEP ETSA Madrid
Antonio Juarez
Paula Montoya
Izaskun Chinchilla
Jose Luis Vallejo

1. Stavros Papavassiliou, a space of confrontation,
friction and free dialogue in the Plaza de la Revolucion

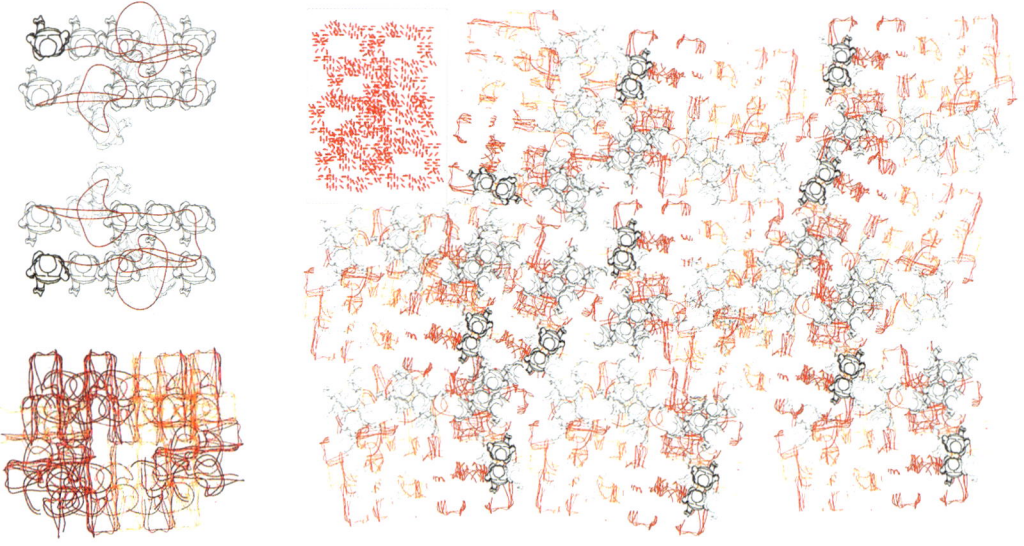

2

3

2. Lyza Rudyk, sharing in the public space: Studies of
two different Cuban dances – Cha-cha, with roots in
African culture, and Reggaeton, a modern dance popular
with younger people

3. Maud Sanciaume, a study on the demonumentalisation of
the Plaza de la Revolución through material fragmentation

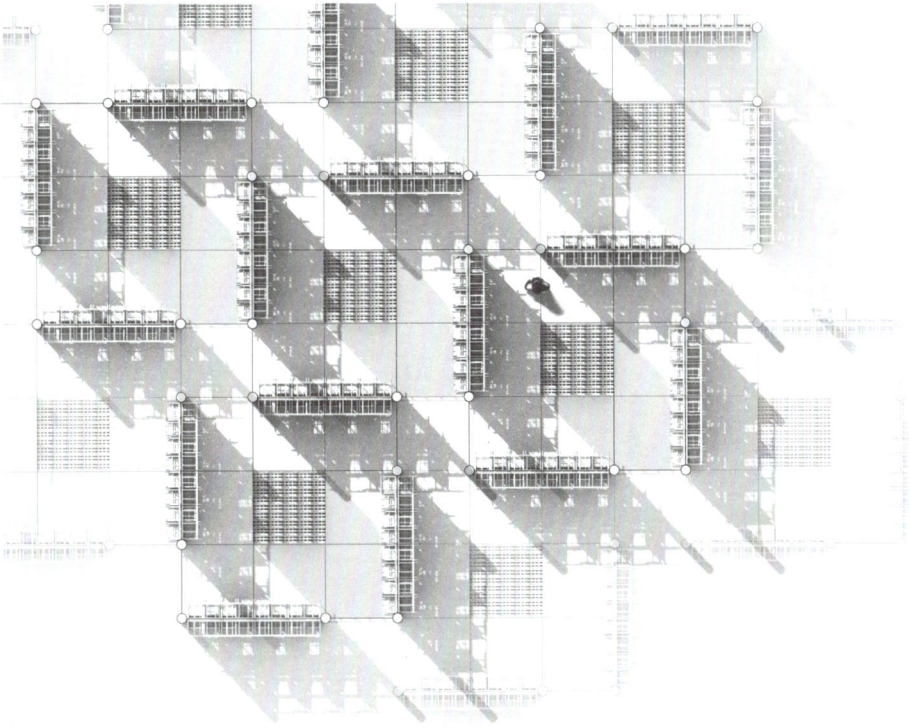

4

5

4. Stavros Papavassiliou, a formal layout of changing spaces for informal political debates and confrontation between Habaneros

5. Gary Dupont, filter system for new bus hubs in Havana: a formal structure supports cavernous, porous and translucent material layers which generate different configurations for gathering spaces.

73

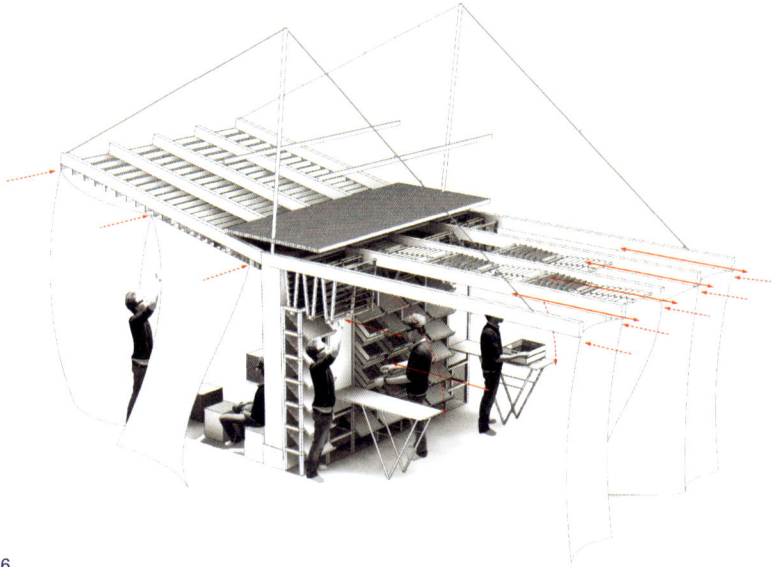

6

7

8

6. Max Hacke, correspondence apparatus: land property
dividers for an urban agriculture intervention in the
Plaza de la Revolución used by Cubans as market spaces
7. Merve Anil, political interference: counterpoint between
projected formal structures and individual informal
appropriations within a new programmatically intensified
area of the Plaza

8. Gary Dupont, spaces of political exchange:
bus hubs in the Plaza responding to a new
decentralised transportation system for Havana

9

10

11

12

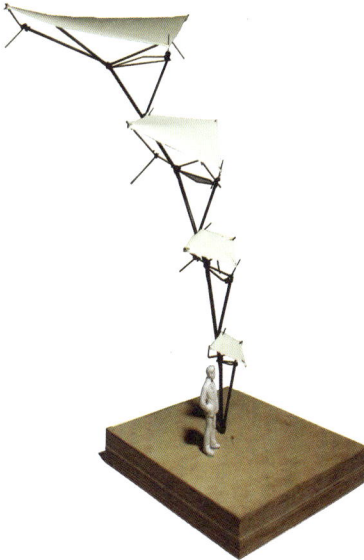

13

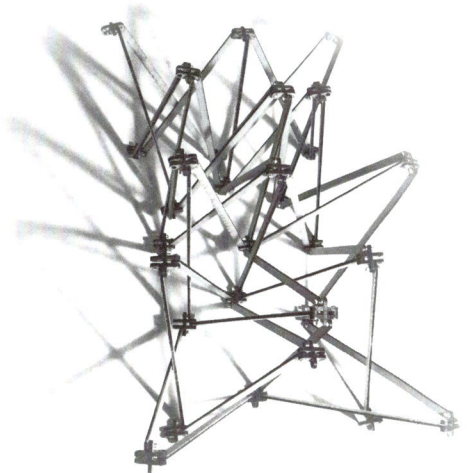

14

9–14. Maud Sanciaume, Atta Yousefi, Merve Anil, Gary Dupont, Max Hacke, Uliana Apatina: these different material experimentations explore low-tech fabrication systems based on local materials configured to articulate political expression in the Plaza de la Revolución.

INTERMEDIATE 9

Inter 9 is crazy about 3D drawing and printing (geeky, we know) but we are also mad for Penélope Cruz, Javier Bardem and FC Barcelona (Christ, who isn't?). Just as Lionel Messi carved up those multi-millionaire, lead-footed Real Madrid galacticos this year, we've sliced up the Camp Nou to invent projects erasing the distinction between city and stadium. We have not redressed Norman Foster's gauche Vegas-style sequined skirt tautology – the 'New Camp Nou'. That his office henchmen wouldn't share their drawings sums up his approach entirely, which is no kind of reply to a club of this quality. We critiqued the stadium typology by taking on the club's Les Corts 'campus' and its connection to the city – its citizens also happen to be the owners and they're currently held at bay, even on game day, by a circumferential 6m-high steel fence surrounded by abandoned training grounds. It's a context we've reinvented.

As ever, our approach wasn't as direct as you might imagine. Starting with hydrographic charts and pilots' maps and then fusing them with other non-architectural drawings we produced a 'composite' drawing and an 'interference drawing' which, when combined, invents a 3D 'drawing/ object' print that is the basis for the scheme. It's a method that lets Max Ernst meet Enric Miralles. In January we were warmly welcomed by the club, who on top of some plum tickets for FC Barcelona v Malaga and our own exhibition at the stadium, also gave us the heads-up on a masterplan competition which formed the basis of work for the next four months. We designed in fragments, which carried the weight of the whole project, and fabricated parts of them under the expertise of Toni Cumella at his enviable atelier in Granollers. We also reinvested our energy in the immaculate portfolio, against a tide of loose-leaf A3s and plasma screen shots.

It's simple: we design through drawing ('beautiful but worrying' – Carlos Villanueva Brandt) and in the process hopefully avoid killing the hallowed grass – which is all Foster's stadia seem to do anyway.

UNIT STAFF
Christopher Matthews
Christopher Pierce

STUDENTS
Frederik Bo Bojesen
Hans-Christian Buhl
Daniel Christiansen
Rebecca Crabtree
Clara Gradinariu
Selim Halulu
Lyn Hayek
Kato Hisashi
Aine O'Dwyer
Ryan Phanphensophon
Emmanuelle Siedes
Gustav Toftgård
Golshid Varasteh Kia
Yuma Yamamoto

Acknowledgments:
London
Thomas Weaver
John Outram
Roz Barr
Nigel Hetherington
Mike Weinstock
Brett Steele
Will Stevens
Jeroen van Ameijde
Fred Scott
Tobias Klein
Samantha Hardingham
Charles Tashima
Ian O'Brien
Nathaniel Kolbe
Max Kahlen
Franklin Lee
Asa Bruno
Noam Andrews

Goswin Schwendinger
Cristina Moreno
Jon Goodbun
Naiara Vegara
Jonathan Wiles
Ricardo de Ostos
Carlos Villanueva Brandt
Sue Barr

Barcelona
Benedetta Tagliabue
Oriol Clos
Aurea Gallén
Toni Cumella
Teresa Ventura
Jaume González-Milà
  Rubio
Angelo Candalepas
Ramon Roger
Iñaki Diez Aguirre

Sponsors:
Ceramic Cumella
FC Barcelona

Photos by Sue Barr
and Inter 9 students

1. Emmanuelle Siedes, Golshid Varasteh Kia
and Selim Halulu, 3D prints

2. Gustav Toftgård, Deep Surface
Frederik Bo Bojesen, Interfered Duality

3. Hans-Christian Buhl & Yuma Yamamoto, Blurring Effect

4. Rebecca Crabtree, Cell Propagation

ecoMachines v3.0: World Dubai Marine Life Incubators

Can architecture claim new roles in this period of economic and ecological turmoil? Can architects contribute new spatial and material practices for the re-functionalisation of the urban landscape?

The World, an artificial marine landscape built off the coast of Dubai City, is the perfect ground to engage with these questions. With its sheer size, embedded fragility, unimaginative design and its massive impact on the surroundings, the $12 billion uncompleted lagoon reveals all the contradictions of the system that fuels major development in Dubai and around the world.

Inter 10's architectural speculation takes the form of 13 visionary projects, the World Dubai Marine Life Incubators, presented here in the form of a *manifesto for systemic architecture*.

Co-envelopes from hi-tech building skins to living membranes of bio-cement that accrete according to user, wind and water pressures (YWK). *Co-pleasures* from passive tourist amusement parks to reactive, self-sustaining coral gardening machines (LM). *Co-boundaries* from fixed barrier to fluctuating field of wave energy harvesters (NM). *Co-farming* from total dependence on imported food to floating fish farm (WH). *Co-n-solid-ate* from underwater desert of loose sand to robotic coral reef garden (WS). *Co-fertilisation* from top-down planning to bottom-up colonisation, coral fertilisation for a diving park (MP). *Co-hubs* from nodal interchanges to catalysts of marine and social life (WY). *Co-public* from spectacular to invisible landmark, a landscape of components for social connectivity and cultural diversity (AB). *Co-nursing* from engineering environmental remediation to coral nursing as a regenerative playground (CA). *Co-structures* from unlimited extraction of natural resources to slow cultivation of luxury through bio-marble components (ZF). *Co-operation* from segregated realms to intense behavioural spaces of social and economic trading (MDLLL). *Co-growth* from artificial foundations and construction systems to mangrove infrastructures for growing inhabitable landscapes (IMF). *Co-healing* from psycho-pharmaceutical abuse to dolphin therapy (ME).

UNIT STAFF
Claudia Pasquero
Marco Poletto

STUDENTS
Yu Won Kang
Leila Meroue
Noam Hazan
Wei Hou
Wesley Soo
Michalis Patsalosavis
Wenlan Yuan
Alessandro Bava
Caterina Albertucci
Zachary Fluker
Maria Dolores Lola
   Lozano Lara
Iker Mugarra Flores
Masaki Echizenya

Research partners:
Maria Arcero, Artist,
   London
Dr Abeer Shaheen
   AlJanahi, Academic
   British University
   in Dubai
Brendan Jack, Nakheel
   property developers,
   Dubai

Special thanks to all the
colleagues, supporters
and guests who have
contributed to stimulating
juries and debates

1

2

1 & 2. Masaki Echizenya, DolphinATOL: an architectural
mechanism for the production of artificial coral atols and
their evolution into natural aquaria for dolphin therapy

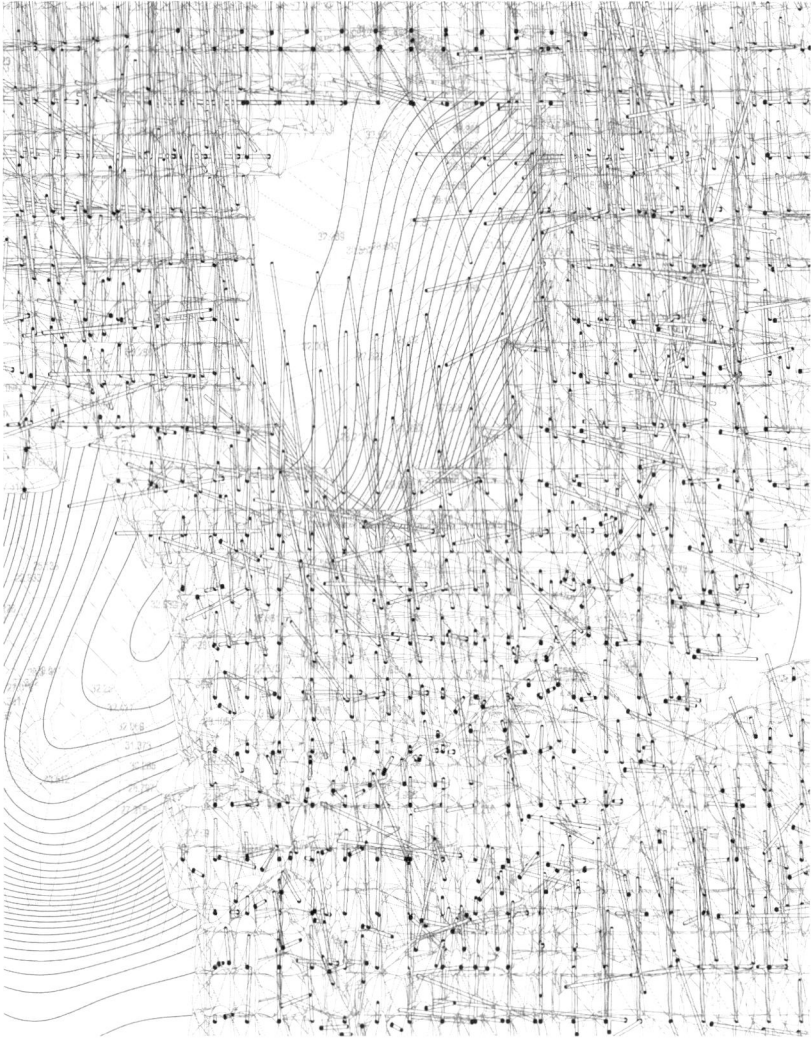

3

4

3 & 4. Alessandro Bava, Moral Garden: the introduction of
an artificial aggregate system transforms the sandy
bumps of the Dubai World islands into an accreted HQ for
the pharmaceutical industry and a related new form of
Arabic public space.

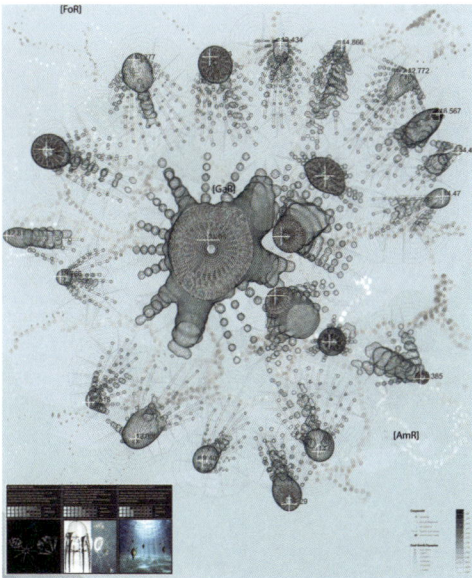

5

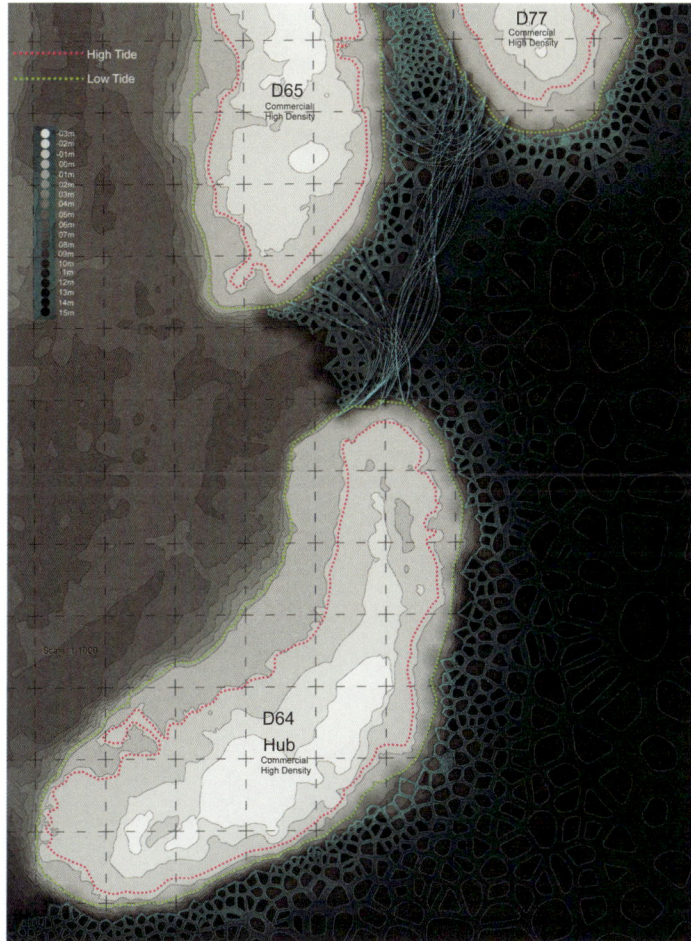

6

5. Caterina Albertucci, CoraLAB: from the engineering of environmental remediation systems to coral nursing as a regenerative playground for tourists, scientists and swarm robots

6. Iker Mugarra Flores, Co-Growth: plan of the mangrove plantation strategy for the formation of natural beaches and living architectural platfoms

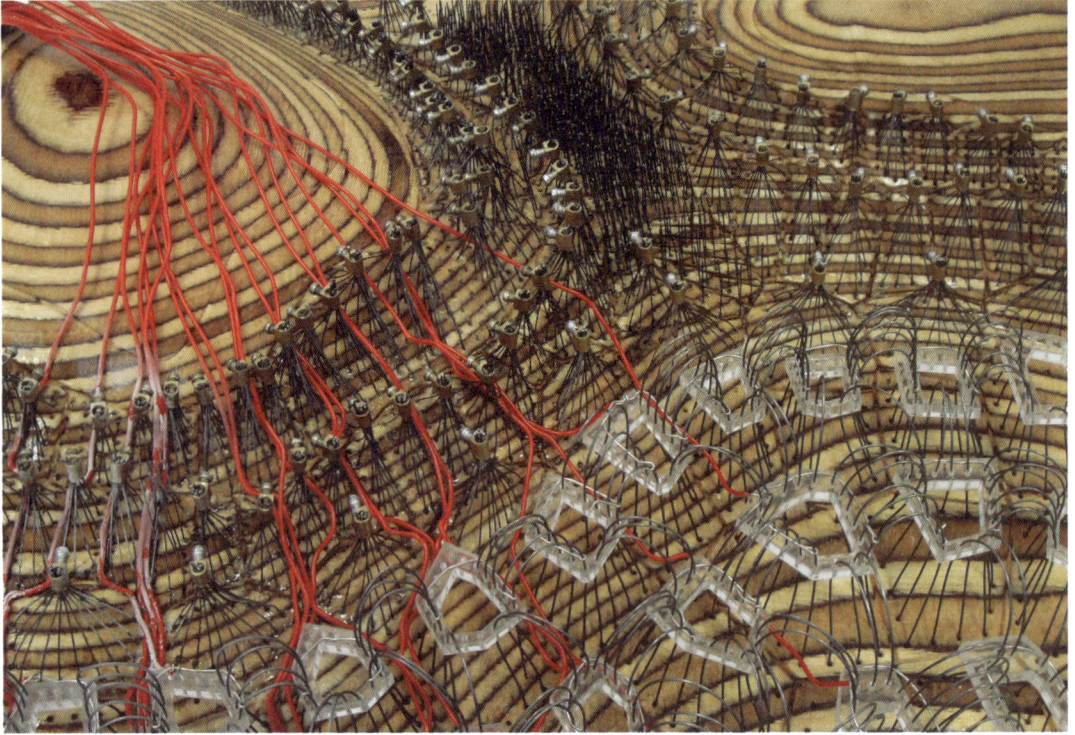

7

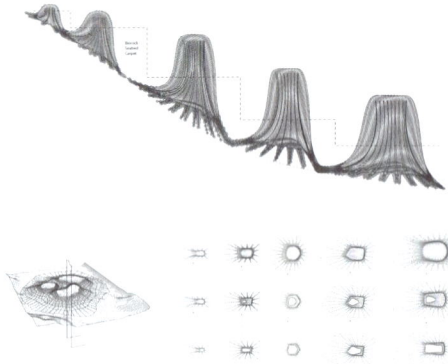

8

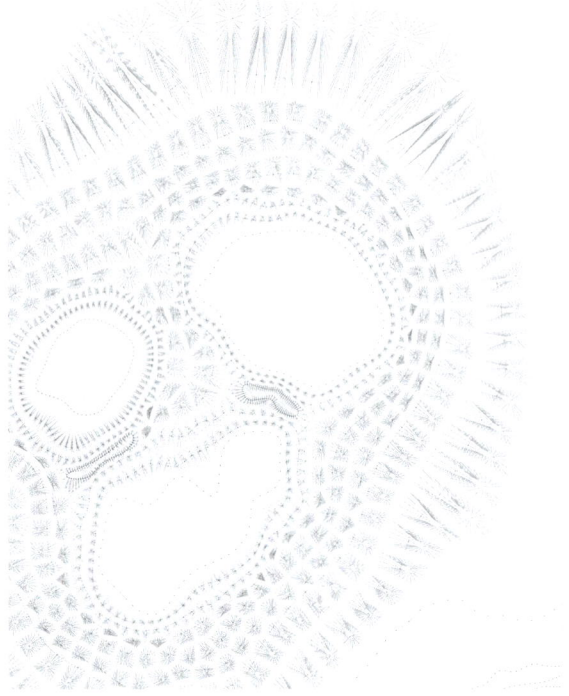

9

7–9. Zachary Fluker, Bio-quarry island: a biorock gardening infrastructure transforms the island into a marine garden to grow custom-designed bioStones – detail of the gardening apparatus and the low-voltage current network for electrodeposition of minerals.

10

11

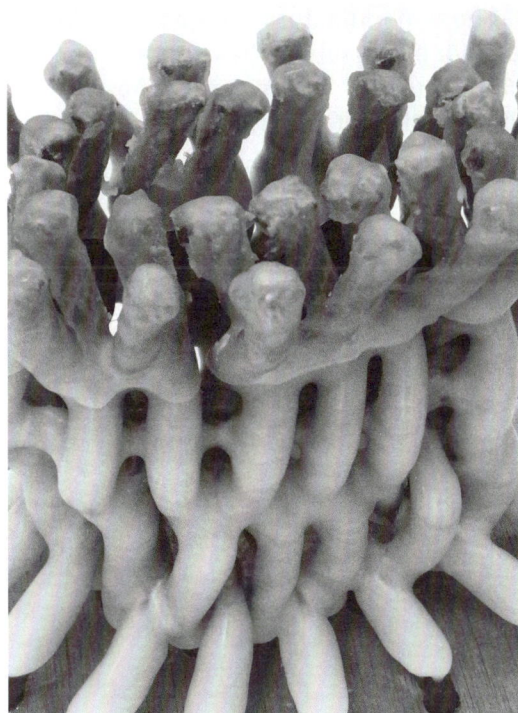

12

13

10–13. Details, clockwise from top: study of artificial aggregate structural system; prototype of co-envelope system of semisubterranean desert dwellings; prototype of accreted BIO-MARBLE; prototype of robot agent for bio-cemented reef formations

INTERMEDIATE 11

Latent Territories

Inter 11 pursues a critical investigation of issues related to urbanism through the study of undefined and residual spaces surrounding transportation networks such as airports, harbours, train and highway interchanges. Originally planned for the periphery, these large inaccessible territories have gradually been surrounded by inhabited areas. This year the unit has been more specifically focused on the inaccessible archipelago of traffic islands adjacent to highway interchanges. We reclaimed these latent territories as new territory for design with a particular outlook on subjects such as subcultures, urban erasure, social fragmentation, cinematic perception and climate.

We began the year with a series of intuitive design workshops exploring both generic and specific spatial attributes related to the interchange. As a group we concurrently produced a resource book compiling documentation from each student's particular perspective and field of interest. The outcome formed the basis of a distinctive vocabulary and a conceptual framework that would later feed into individual proposals at the scale of the interchange.

As part of the unit's interest in transfer of technologies, we organised a series of visits to fabricators from the aerospace, automotive and naval industries. The unit is interested in a synergy between the critical engagement and playfulness of the 60s and 70s architectural avant-gardes and today's enthusiasm for computation and new manufacturing processes. We concluded our investigation with speculative proposals addressing a variety of historical, climatic, socio-political and cultural issues, sometimes polemically, sometimes simply driven by a desire for progress.

UNIT STAFF
Theo Sarantoglou Lalis
Dora Sweijd

STUDENTS
Elora Brahmachari
Yheu-Shen Chua
Tom Hatzor
Ilina Kroushovski
Ashkan Sadeghi
  Lavasaninia
Stefan Einar Laxness
Perrine Planche
Luke Shixin Tan
Elizaveta Tatarintseva
Konstantinos Zaverdinos
Shaoxiong Zhang

TEACHING ASSISTANTS
Yousef Al-Mehdari
Kasper Ax

VISITING CRITICS
Keehyun Ahn
Mark Campbell
Jonathan Dawes
Alan Dempsey
Ricardo de Ostos
Yannick Denayer
David Erkan
Ronan Friel
Alvin Huang
Robert Ivanov
Martin Jameson
Holger Kehne
Tobias Klein
Nuria Lombardero
Yan Pan

Claudia Pasquero
Christopher Pierce
Stefano Rabolli Pansera
Goswin Schwendinger
Brett Steele
Charles Tashima
Jeffrey Turko
Eduardo McIntosh
Mike Mitchell
Thomas Weaver
Chris Ziegler
Li Zhen

Special thanks:
Rob Edkins (2D3D)
John Baker (Baker's
  Patterns)
Allard Bokma
  (Centraalstaal)

1

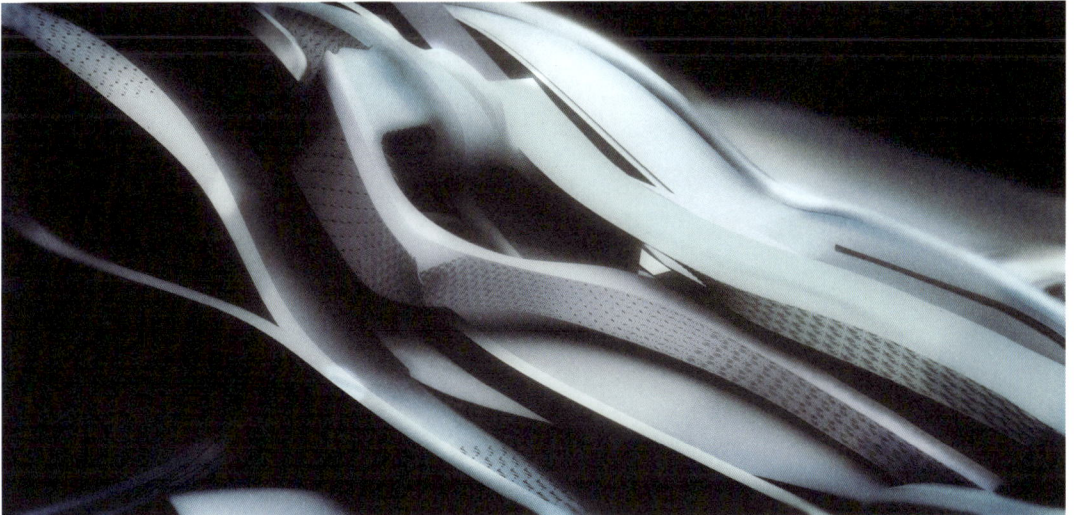

2

1 & 2. Luke Tan, Osprey, Beijing
Commensal infrastructure city for transient cultures:
inhabitable spaces are conceived as mobile
units orbiting around Beijing's ring road network.

3

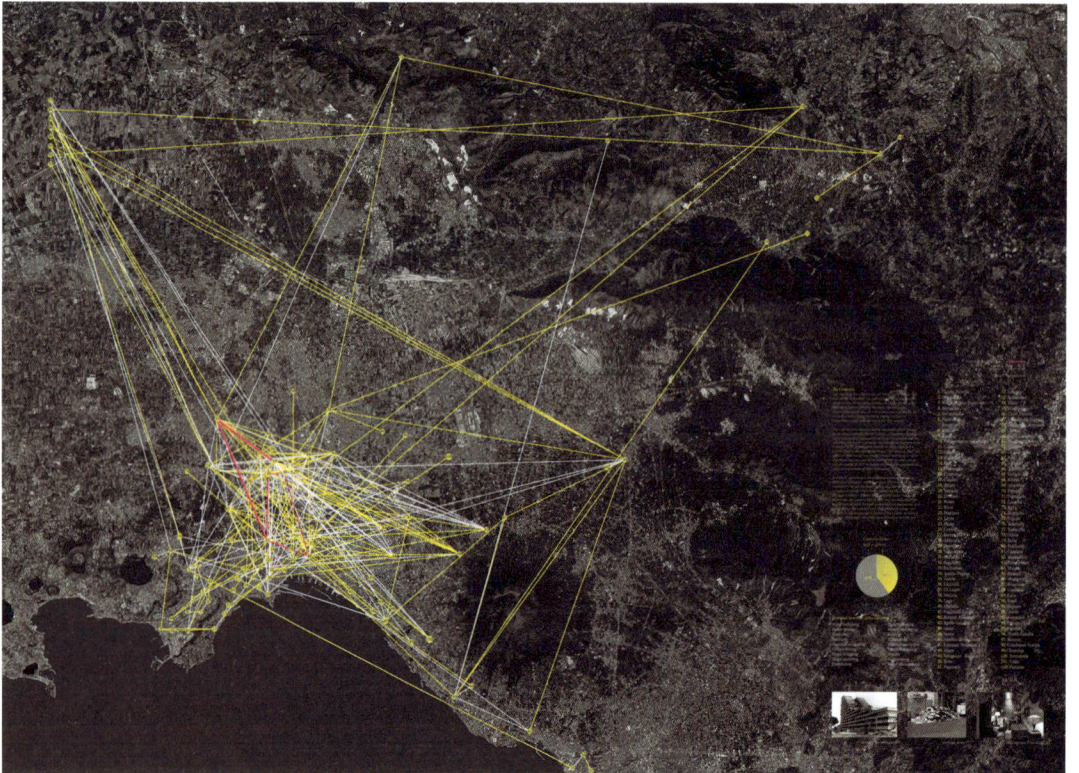

4

3 & 4. Perrine Planche, Italic, Naples
Carceral monument for the Camorra

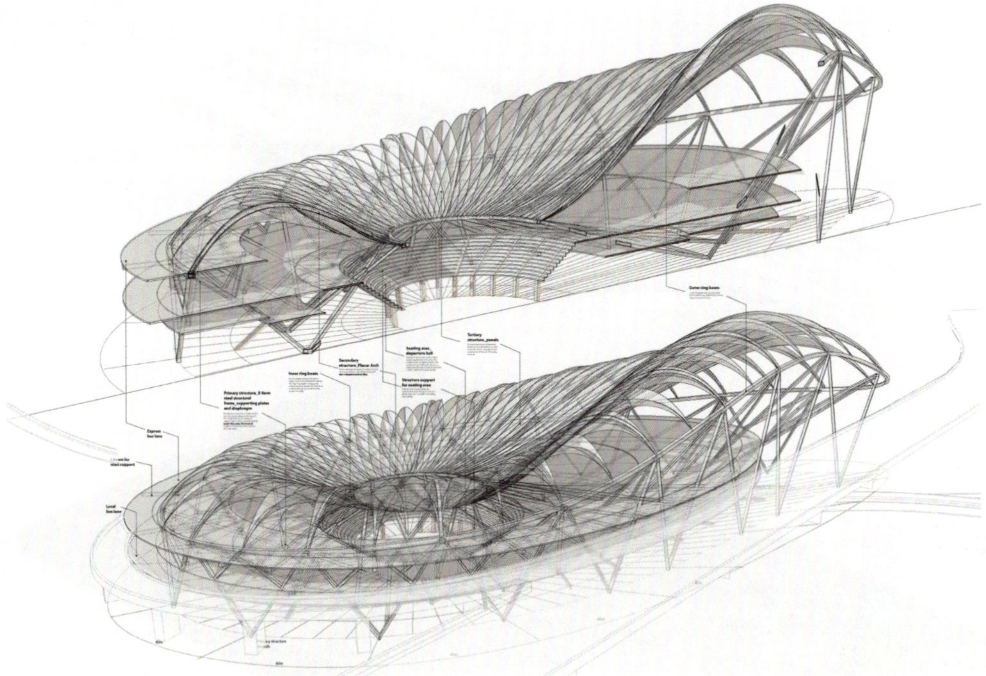

5

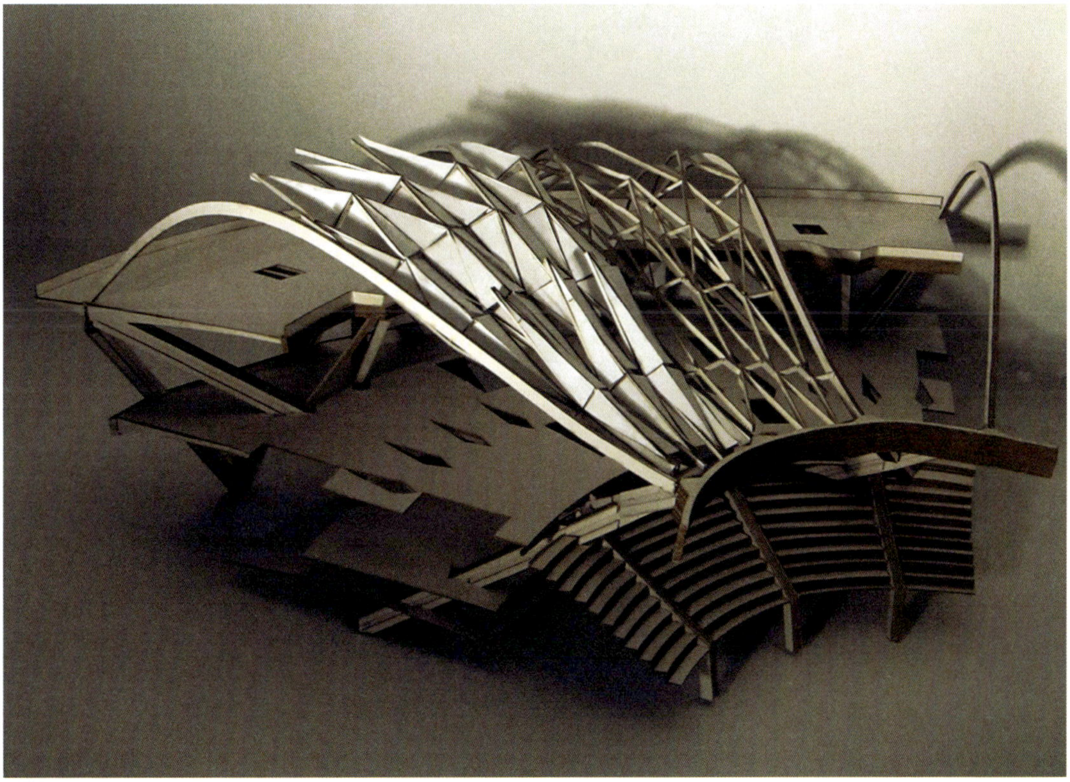

6

5 & 6. Yheu-Shen Chua, Cinematic Exchange,
Kuala Lumpur
Environment-responsive transport hub

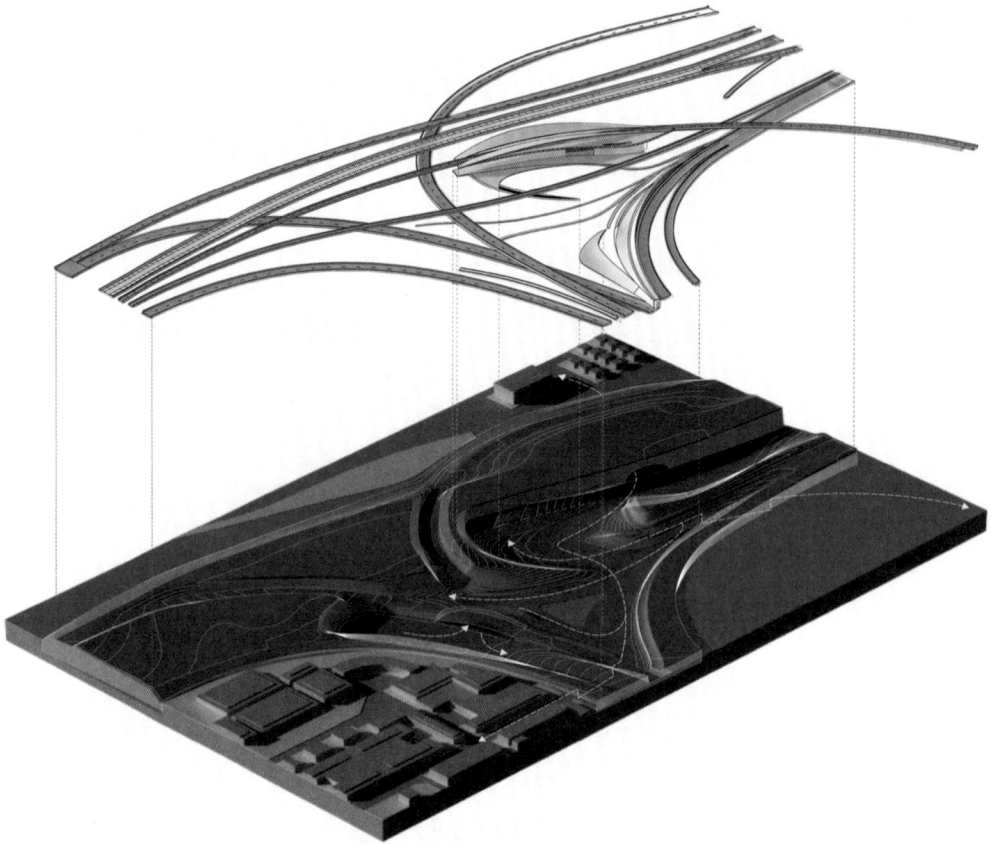

7

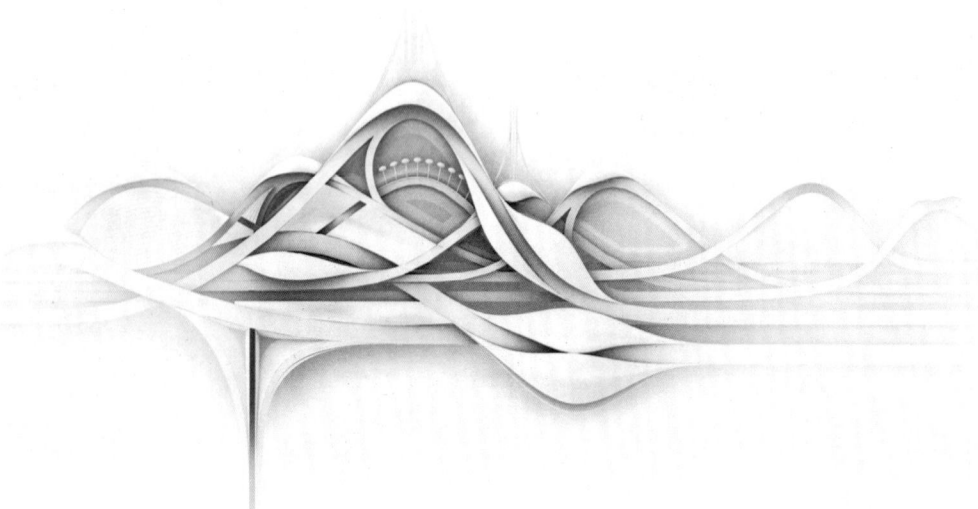

8

7. Konstantinos Zaverdinos, homo ludens landscape
proposal, Amsterdam
The importance of the play element in culture and society

8. Ashkan Sadeghi Lavasaninia, adaptable infrastructure,
Iran. Proposal for a phased symbiosis between
infrastructure and geological formations

9

10

11

9. Ilina Kroushovski, transitional urbanism, Antwerp
The project discusses the overlap between the medieval
defence system of historical cities and twentieth-century
infrastructure deployment.

10. Stefan Einar Laxness, a need for speed, Los Angeles
Parasitic subculture urbanism
11. Elizaveta Tatarintseva, cinematic landscape, Germany
A drive-through visual experience

INTERMEDIATE 12

According to pollsters, the UK 2010 general election was swung by the votes of Motorway Man and Motorway Woman. These offspring of Soccer Mom and Mondeo Man, we are told, live near a motorway junction and drive to work at an office near another motorway junction. Young, healthy and childless, they have little contact with place, community or any of those other things urbanism usually expects.

Our question this year was how this lonely, boring, decoupled, place-less landscape might be a testing ground for our deepest-held architectural truths. Might these apparently negative characteristics contain more positive possibilities?

For example, does the idea of community exist at a place like Beaconsfield Service Station? Perhaps in the large numbers of Eastern European lorry drivers engaged in global logistics or the businessmen plugging their printers into power sockets at Starbucks or the schoolkids hanging out there after class.

The unit examined the relationship between the town of Beaconsfield and the service station. Through fieldwork and close reading as well as speculative proposals, scenarios were developed in which programmes and iconographies forged new connections between apparently disparate conditions.

Design experiments developed a toolkit for exploring architecture as a cultural and communicative act. Genre-bending exercises remade canonical architecture drawings in multiple ways: John Hejduk as Persian inlay, Walking City as Piranesian etching, Chernikov as Pop Art and so on. Explorations of the ways in which architectural languages communicate complex cultural issues were made with large-scale models.

The projects find possibilities to understand a contemporary landscape through an architectural lens. They form new kinds of vernaculars for a networked world whose forces erode traditional conceptions of place. Here, architecture examines its role as a cultural device and a social proposition in an attempt to understand the narrative of Motorway Man and Woman.

UNIT STAFF
Sam Jacob
Tomas Klassnik

Thanks to Finn Williams

STUDENTS
Jen Andersson
Teeba Arain
Win Assakul
Byron Blakeley
Doyeon Cho
Brian Fung
Saki Ichikawa
Summer Islam
Kitae Kang
Vasundhara Sellamuthu
Natalia Sherchenkova
Kasym Ulykbanov
Jacob Wiklander

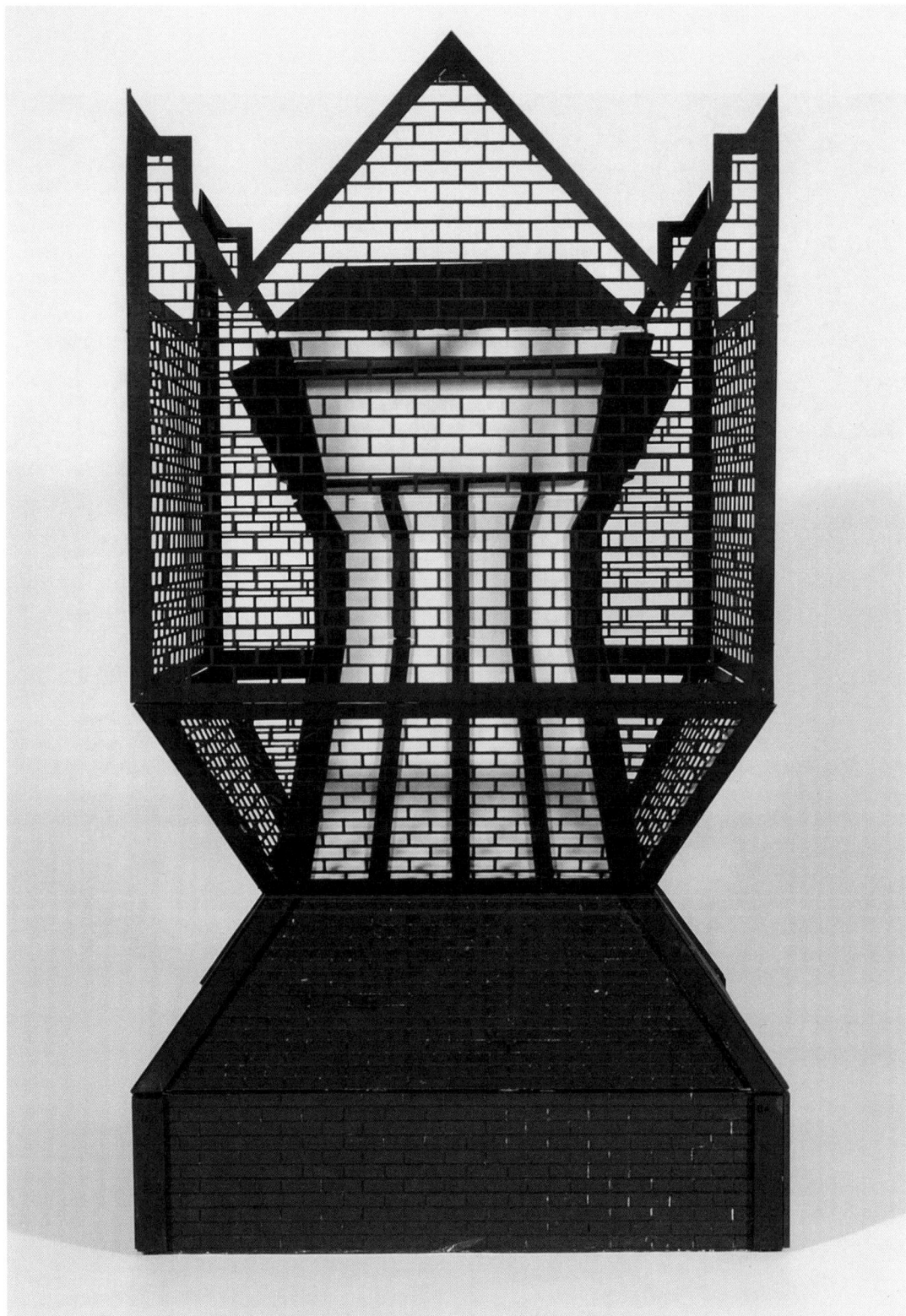

1. Kasym Ulykbanov, military watchtower for a model
village combining the design langages of 1930s suburbia
and 1980s militarised Northern Ireland

2

2. Summer Islam, extension to Town Hall at Bekonscot
Model Village, using the site of a model village to explore
narrative architectural qualities

3

4

3. Summer Islam, The Wall House as Persian miniature, reinscribing John Hejduk as ethnic artform

4. Saki Ichikawa, Golden Clouds Retirement Village – a landscape of half-remembered and vanishing vernaculars

5

6

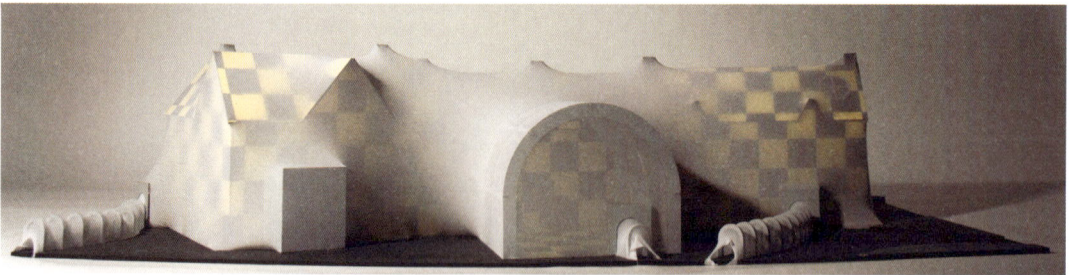

7

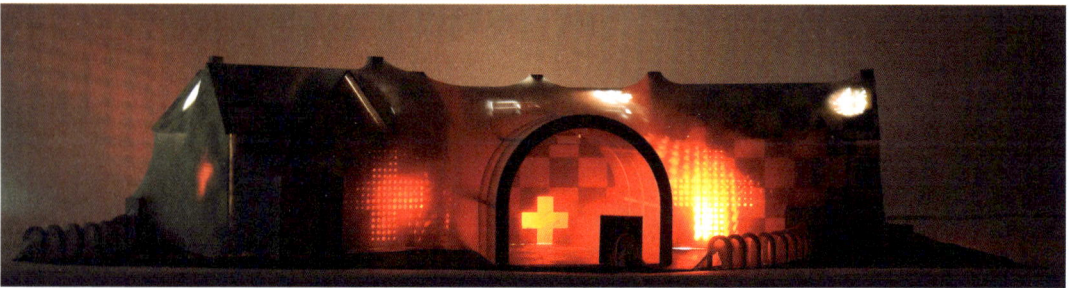

8

5. Natalia Sherchenkova, restaging architectural culture
through the lens of Photoshop. Lebbeus Woods remade
as Breugel
6. Jacob Wiklander, OMA's CCTV as a quilt

7 & 8. Doyeon Cho, quarantine facility for a model village

9

10

9. Doyeon Cho, Piranesian Constructivism   10. Jacob Wiklander, Tesco Town

INTERMEDIATE 13

Visions of Heterotopia

Michel Foucault's lecture, 'Of Other Spaces, Heterotopias' (1967), provided the backdrop for our discussion of how we might contemplate the contemporary city. His famous list of 'other' spaces includes asylums, brothels, cemeteries, carnivals, refuges, theatres and prisons. These create alternative readings of space that are networked, relational, cultural – somewhere between 'real space' and utopia. Foucault posed the question then of whether heterotopias might set up critical juxtapositions within urban and social contexts – against conformity and homogeneity. Today, Inter 13 asks: how do we build in our dense, diverse cities with this perception of space in mind?

Four compromised areas of London were explored in search of the 'other'. King's Cross, Paddington, the City and Southwark became sites of experience and scrutiny. Early observation and investigation provided the raw materials for heterotopic interventions grafted onto various found spaces. Hidden communities, alternative lifestyles and estrangement became the basis for larger propositions in London – to create spaces where 'other' aspects of society can be performed and represented. Projects explored the real and unreal, the ideal and the contingent, in order to 'contest and invert' as well as reflect all other sites of the city.

Urban cultural communities are explored through refuges and retreats, such as Adora's Storytelling Space over a supermarket and Jin's Black Cab Club tucked into a carpark. Death and decay trouble Adelina's vertical Paupers' Necropolis, while Octave offers a transgressive cultural strip on the no man's land of the Thames riverbed. Conrad's subversive food recycling organisation and Shaelina's Urban Reclaimers' Gymnasium accommodate platforms for corporate irritants. Spatial transience and temporality are at the core of Tala's Museum of the Lost and Found over Paddington Station and of Faraz's 'Caravanserai' for the canal community of King's Cross. Eleanor's Working Men's Club and Raha's Theatre challenge the city's financial culture and lifestyle, while Xia's Garden of England, floating above the Bank of England, proposes another mode of production. Ambiguities of illusion and reality explored though Brian's Film School in Somerstown reframe the view of a depressed area.

UNIT STAFF
Miraj Ahmed
Martin Jameson

STUDENTS
Faraz Anoushehpour
Adelina Chan
William (Jin) Chang
Brian (Hwui Zhi) Cheng
Eleanor Dodman
Raha Farazmand
Tala Fustok
Conrad Koslowsky
Shaelina Morley
Octave Perrault
Adora Shahriman
Huida Xia

Special thanks to:
Pierre d'Avoine
Peter Carl
Isabel Carreras Baquer
Kevin Cash
Charlie and Georgie
  Corry Wright
Adam Furman
Marco Ginex
Francisco Gonzalez
Katharina Jacobi
Sam Jacobs
Nuria Lombardero
Theo Lorenz
Rebecca Harral
Teresa Hoskyns
Andrew Houlton
Ricardo de Ostos

Nina Power
Ingrid Schroder
Tanja Siems
Emanuel de Sousa
Brett Steele
Charles Tashima
Patrick Usborn
Tom Weaver
Paul Wintour
Ada Yvars

1

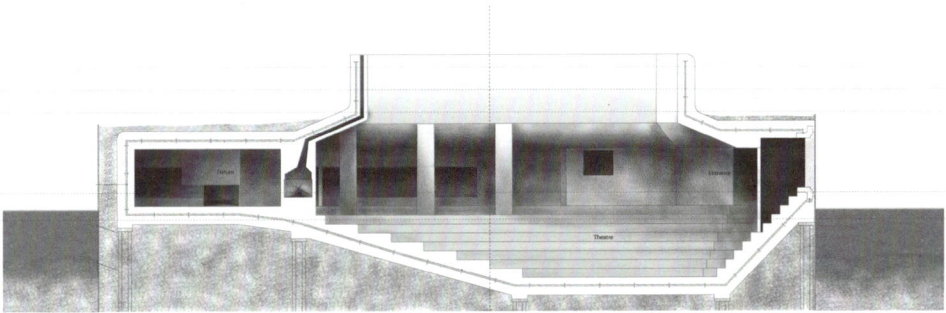

2

1. Octave Perrault
Thames Riverbed Cultural Strip: early
iteration of white cube gallery at high tide

2. Octave Perrault
Thames Riverbed Cultural Strip: a gallery that is
accessible during low tide, with participants becoming
voluntary captives for the hours of high tide

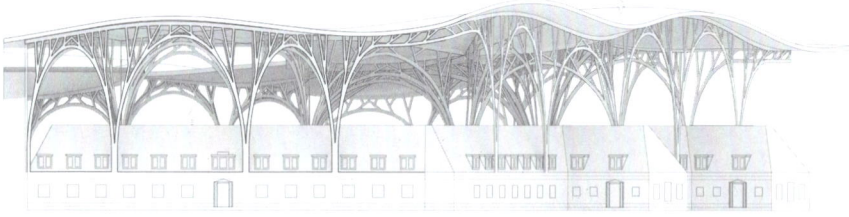

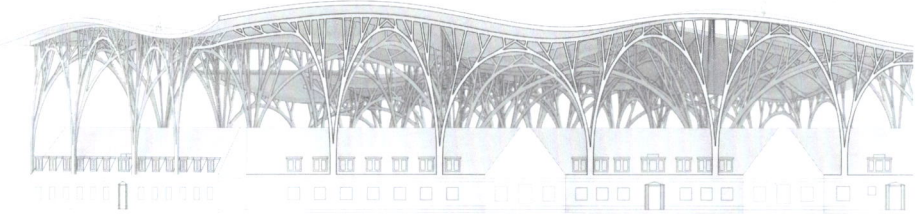

3

4

3. Huida Xia
Garden of England over Bank of England rooftop,
suspended on steel structural system

4. Huida Xia
Garden of England over Bank of England, early collage:
an alternative active layer of horticultural production

5

6

5. Adelina Chan
Interior view of vertical Pauper's Necropolis, Southwark: a monument to the forgotten people of the London streets

6. Faraz Anoushahpour
Short-stay boathouse accommodation for the canal community of the Regent's Canal in King's Cross

7

8

7. Raha Farazmand
A bank and pub are transformed, with the collaboration
between bankers and thespians expressed architecturally
by a theatre bridge

8. Raha Farazmand
Existing materiality of a small square and its adjacencies
in the city morphed into a public performance space

104

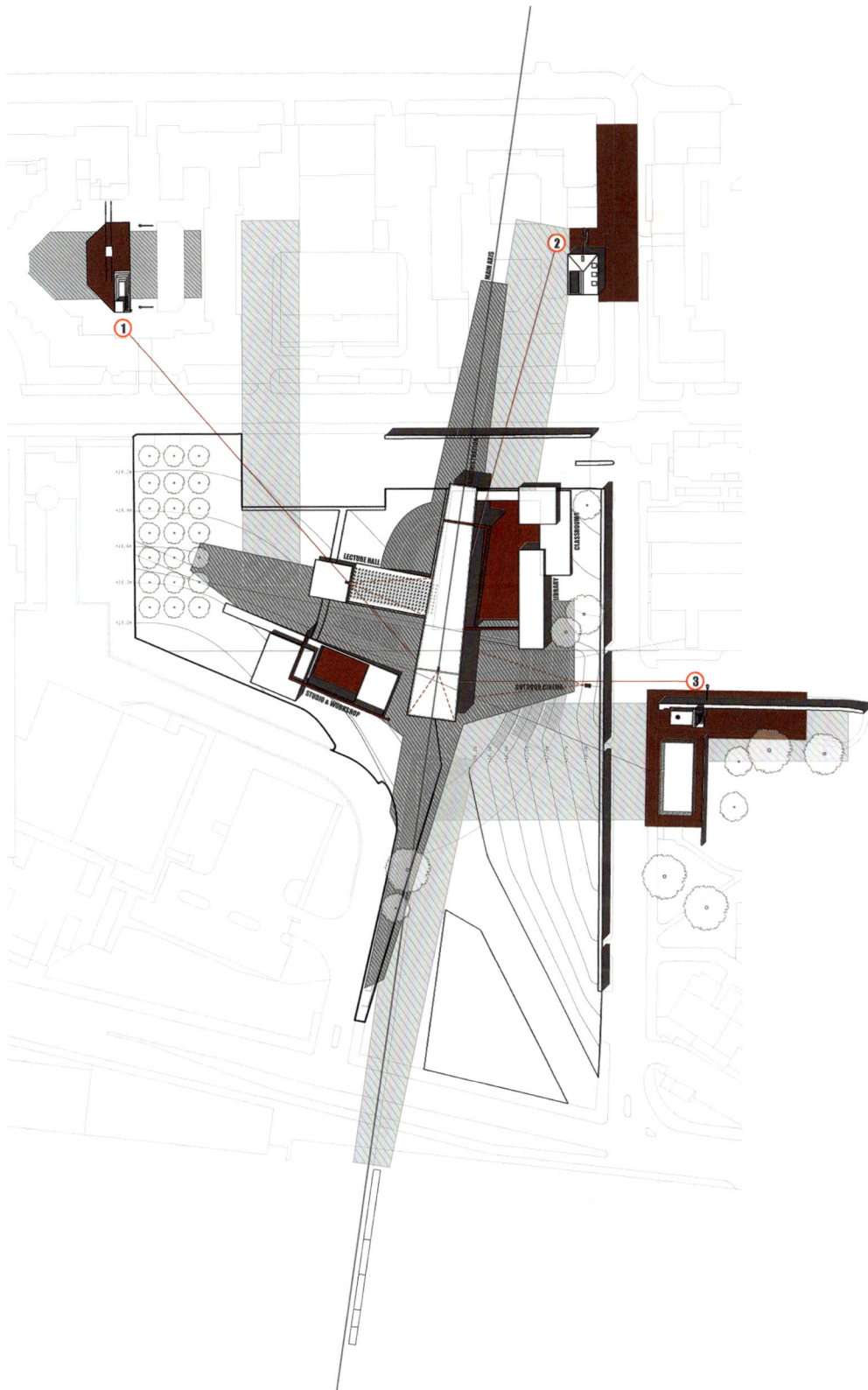

9. Brian Hwui Zhi Cheng
Film School in Somerstown, King's Cross; plan and
context studies. The film school cinematically reframes
and reinvents the local area while providing a space for
multiple perceptions – both real and illusory.

DIPLOMA 1

Mineral Architecture

Unit 1 explored mineral paradigms to challenge spatial and material conventions. Navigating between utopian models and the realities of building, the unit developed architectures of solidity, interiority and groundedness.

The site for the year was Berlin, a city in which the notions of ground and void are particularly acute. Students worked on one of two mirror sites, both models for developing city centres and recurring acts of erasure due to ideology shifts in the city's violent history. Schloßplatz, until recently occupied by the GDR's Palace of the Republic, is probably the most contested site in reunited Germany. Under the new programme of 'Critical Reconstruction', future plans entail the controversial resurrection of the nineteenth-century castle. The Kulturforum, a site initially developed according to a masterplan by Hans Scharoun – and a rare fragment of his vision for a 'Stadtlandschaft' (city landscape) – has been overshadowed by the development of Potsdamer Platz since the fall of the Wall, and has lost a sense of direction.

Students worked with the scripting and modelling of crystalline properties, which provided a reservoir for formal and material systems. Empirical experimentation helped to exploit their habits and capacities to produce physical and sensory effects. Monolithic construction provided a technical focus while mineral matter such as sand, cement, silicates, clays and gypsum delivered a material palette of plastic qualities.

Grounded yet autonomous, the unit sought to radicalise ideas of context and address public space: from Nas' super-museum, a heavily sunken body sitting precariously in Berlin's water-saturated ground, to Akis's strategy of building with Berlin sand to establish a dynamic relationship between the city's public spaces and its rising and falling water levels. Thomas's project for new ground treatment takes after Scharoun's obsession with Berlin's condition as a glacial valley and further explores the technology of landcasting. Alan's contextual erosion and formal echoes synthesise a site of differing ideologies. Takamasa's strategy for material and mnemonic inclusions reacts against the political, historical and cultural erasure all too present in Berlin.

UNIT STAFF
Olaf Kneer
Marianne Mueller

COMPUTATIONAL SUPPORT
Toni Kotnik

STUDENTS
Nas Afshar
Anna Andrich
(Alan) Ho Chiang
(Sunny) Zhuobin He
(Sean) Si Heon Hong
Sara Jaafar
Takamasa Kikuchi
Miscia Leibovich
Akis Patthis
Tomas Pohnetal
Katarina Scoufaridou
Carine Stanton

GUEST CRITICS
Anne Save de Beaurecueil
Alain Chiaradia
Jonathan Dawes
Oliver Domeisen
Shin Egashira
Max Kahlen
Toni Kotnik
CJ Lim
Taneli Mansikkamaki
Monia De Marchi
Fabian Neuhaus
Stefano Rabolli Pansera
Ann-Sofi Rönnskog
Charles Tashima
Jeff Turko
Tom Weaver
Ines Weizmann

Special thanks to:
Thomas Arnold, Elke Knöss and Justus Pysall in Berlin; Hans-Jürgen Commerell at Aedes Network Campus Berlin; Dr Gordon Cressey and Peter Tandy, Natural History Museum; Michael Driver, The Brick Development Association

1. Tomas Pohnetal, Cultural Groundscape
New cultural and material groundscape for
the Kulturforum

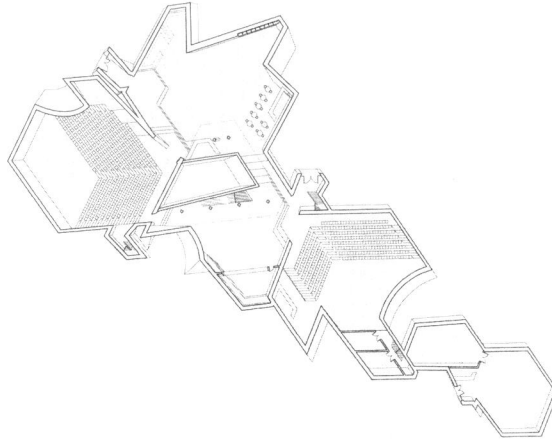

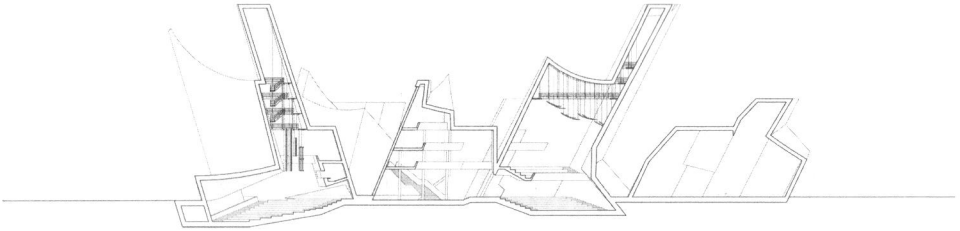

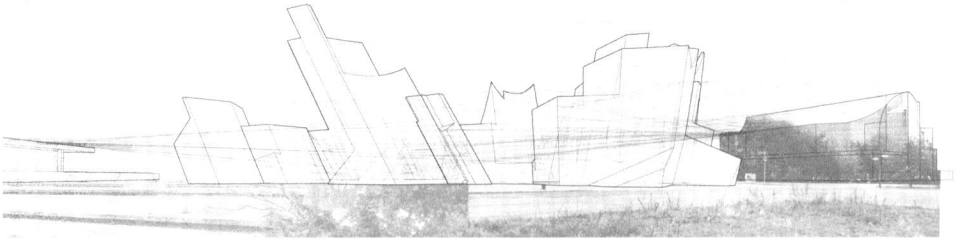

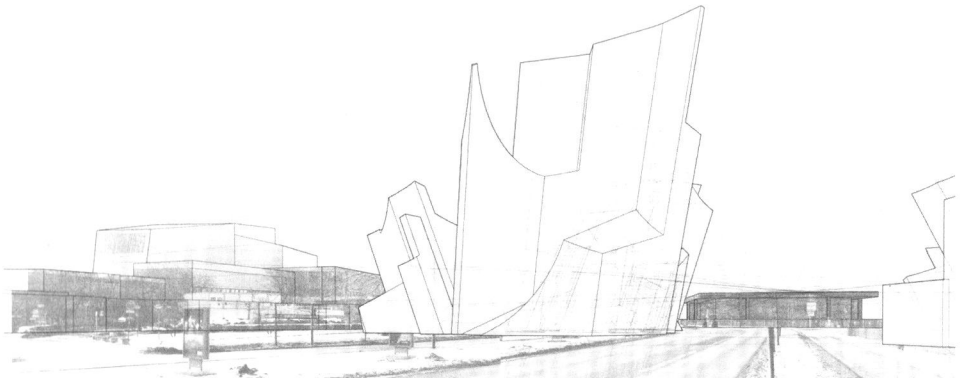

2. (Alan) Ho Chiang, Contextual Erosion
Proposal for a new public theatre, situated amongst the
stylistically opposed buildings of Hans Scharoun and
Mies van der Rohe

3

4

3. Takamasa Kikuchi, Building on the Past
Crystal Architecture is understood as the literal and
metaphoric inclusion of history, reacting against
political, historical and cultural erasure.

4. Katarina Scoufaridou, Stadtkrone
Proposal for a cultural building in the centre of Berlin

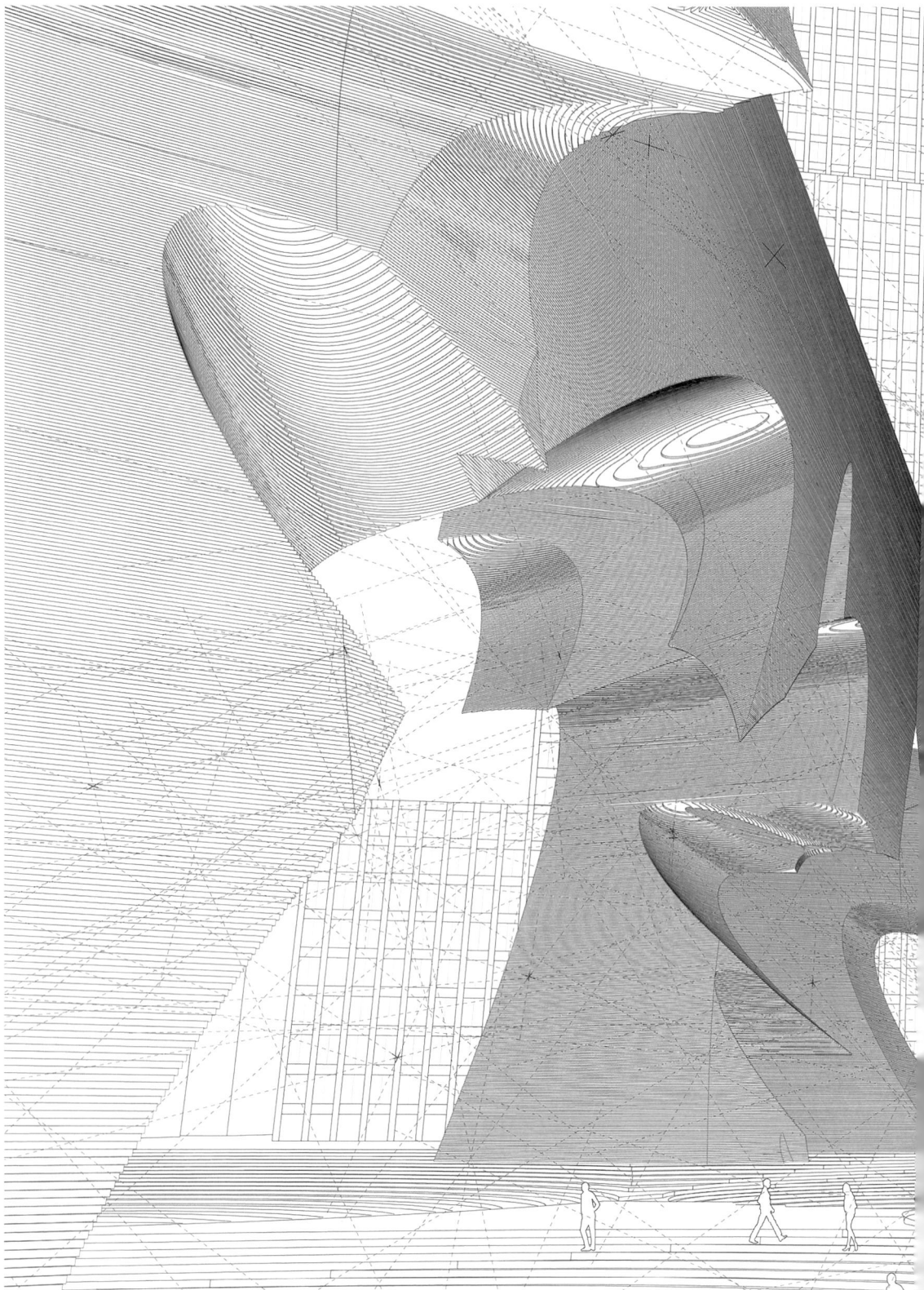

5. Sara Jaafar, De-monumentalising Kolhoff
A radical reworking of Hans Kolhoff's 1994 proposal
for Alexanderplatz

DIPLOMA 2

Choreographing Micro-Revolutions

Diploma Unit 2 set out to invent a new social and aesthetic agenda for ecological architecture, calibrating environmentally responsive geometries to choreograph both climatic and cultural flows within precarious urban conditions. The unit worked on alternative urban organisational structures to mediate between private interests and government bodies, as a way of transforming decaying urban forms that are disconnected from current local cultures and environments. Informed by Félix Guattari's and Suely Rolnik's Molecular Revolution in Brazil, the unit investigated how micro-political movements could escape the 'standardisation of desire' imposed by capitalist and autocratic governments, so as to define 'completely original forms of expression'. The unit collaborated with micro-organisations, networking between the public and private sectors to create multiple-scaled micro-infrastructures that mediate between formal and informal socio-economic, environmental and cultural forces.

Students chose their own sites for intervention, working with existing specific micro-agencies. In Brazil, a former boxing champion attracts homeless people to train in his impromptu boxing academy under the highway viaducts in São Paulo; a former prostitute-turned-community-leader creates a football club for impoverished Gliçério neighbourhood children; evangelist missionaries move into and set up a crèche in the Moinho Fluminese favela, and a self-organised association of Paraisópolis favela inhabitants battle for literacy and citizen rights. In Egypt, a newly formed marine archaeology group looks to further study and exhibit the sunken remains of a former Alexandria; in Sofia, Roma youth seek cultural relevance in a prejudiced Bulgarian society; and in Iceland, environmentalists establish a new presence in the aftermath of the corruption-fuelled national bankruptcy. Extending the ambitions of these micro-agencies, students proposed their own programmatic, formal and aesthetic 'protest' against obsolete regimes, proposing new social programmes to empower local inhabitants. For this, the unit worked on a choreography of aesthetic, programmatic and environmental negotiations to produce controlled emergent spatial effects for a performative architecture that mediates structural, climatic and circulatory flows to reclaim and transform stagnant economies and contexts.

UNIT STAFF
Anne Save de Beaurecueil
Franklin Lee

STUDENTS
5th Year
Ragnhildur Kristjansdottir
Arya Safavi, Tamim
Snegm, William Yam,
Adel Zakout

4th Year
Vicky Chen, Kim Diego
Azevedo, Tolga Hazan,
Yoo Jin Kim, Tae Young
Lee, Stephanie Peer
Edward Pierce, Yvonne
Weng

Special Thanks to:
Local Consultants
Lawrence Friesen, Adam
Davis, John Noel, Philip
Rode, Joana Gonçalves,
Shajay Bhooshan, Matej
Hosek, Vyonyx (Christian
Flores-Nunez, Vladin
Petrov, Nikolay Salutsk),
Kengo Skorick, Arthur
Mamou-Mani, Emiliano
Cevallos

Agencies/Site Consultants
Brazil: Gilson Rodrigues,
Nilson Garrido, Alisson
Faria and Ana Beatriz,
Douglas Nascimento, Ciro

Biderman, Igor Guatelli,
and Zezão

Egypt: Dina S. Taha and
Emad Khalil

Bulgaria: Ivan Minchev,
Stolipinovo National
Railway Infrastructure
Company and Peter Dikov

Jurors
Yota Adilenidou, Noam
Andrews, Valentin Bontjes
van Beek, Alison Brooks,
Lucy Bullivant, Mark
Campbell, Alain Chiradia,
Molly Claypool, Alan

Dempsey, Ricardo de
Ostos, Cristina
Díaz Moreno, Efrén
García Grinda, Marco
Guaneri, Alex Haw,
Francesca Hughes, Max
Kahlen, Jonas
Lundberg, Marianne
Mueller, Kris Mun, John
Palmesino, Eva
Spogelou, Rob Stuart
Smith, Charles Tashima,
Jeff Turko, Jeroen van
Ameijde, Chiafang
Wu, Andrew Yau, and
Chris Yoo

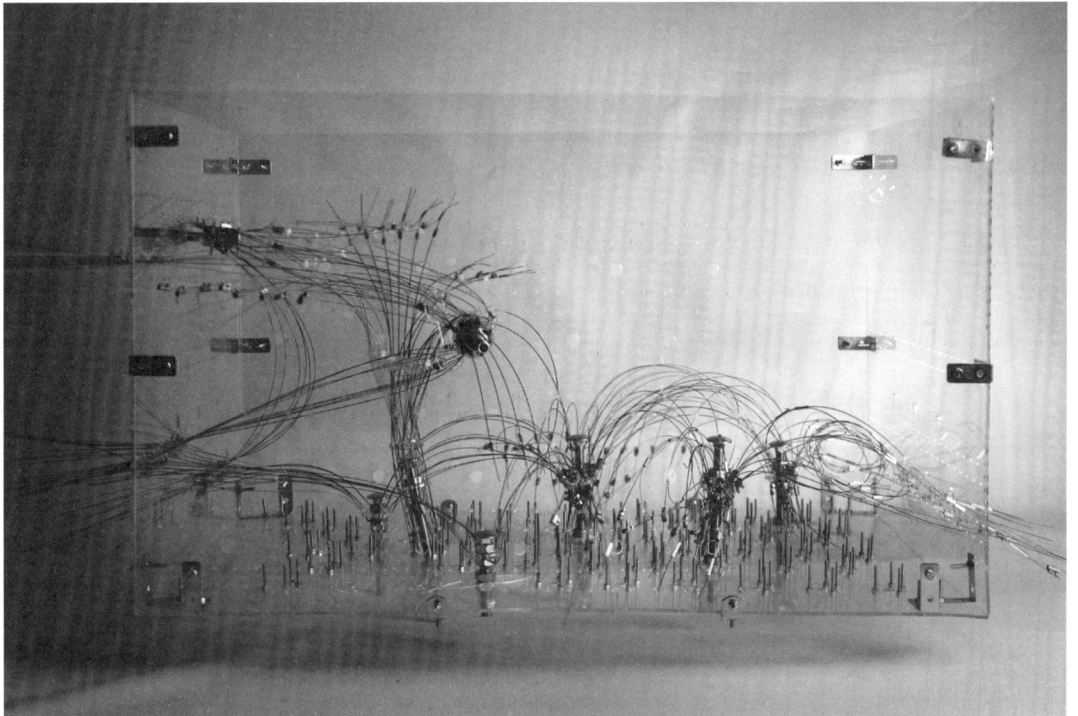

1. Arya Safavi, former prostitute Tia Eva's Gliçério Community Sports – football pitch+vocational school – military barracks occupation. Site: São Paulo

2. Arya Safavi, Gliçério military barracks occupation – cable mesh structure assembled by soldiers and football-players. Site: São Paulo

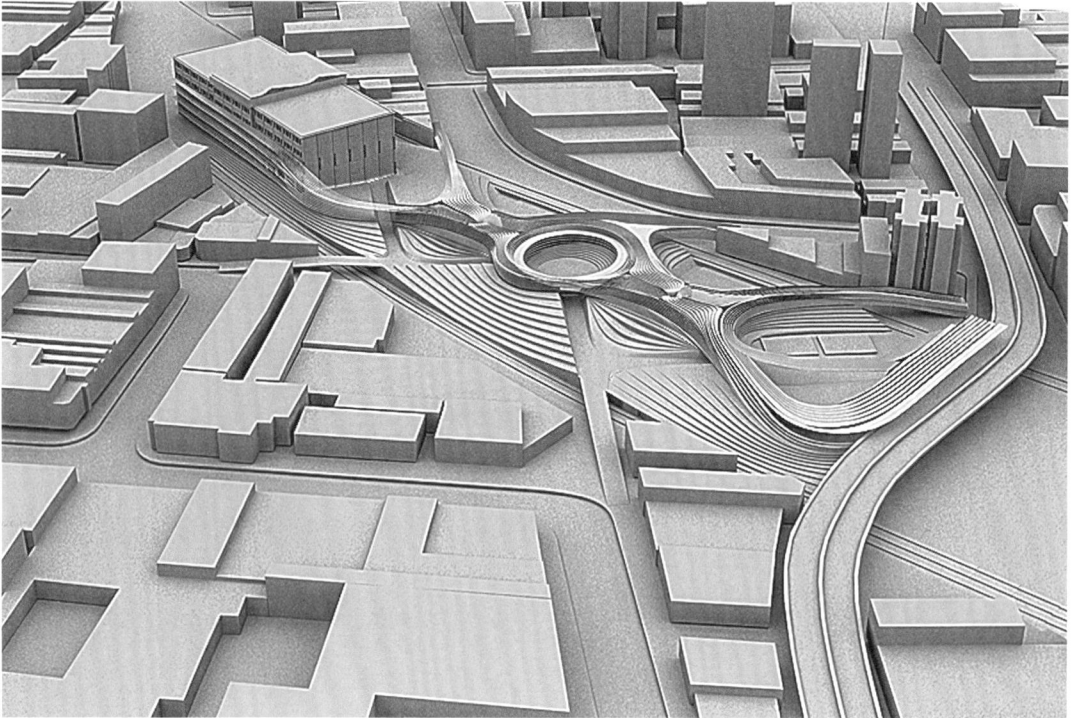

3

4

3. Kim Azevedo, Sitopia hydroponic farming and sports intervention at Moinho Fluminese Mill. Site: São Paulo

4. Tolga Hazan, Nelson Garrido Boxing Academy – new agriculture and sports intervention. Site: São Paulo

5

5. Edward Pierce, re-manufacturing shop-house and
self-build housing intervention at Moinho Fluminese Mill.
Site: São Paulo

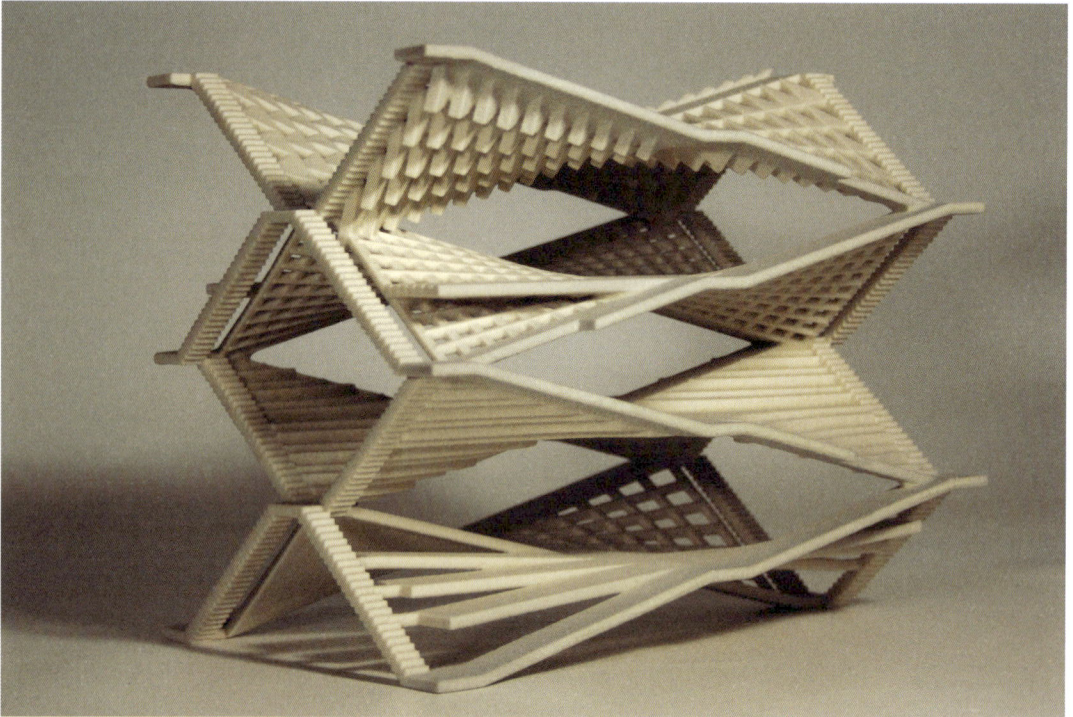

6

7

6. Stephanie Peer: Paraísópolis – community market, classrooms and monorail-station bridge linking favela high street to new Union of Inhabitants Cultural Centre. Site: São Paulo

7. Yvonne Weng: Paraísópolis – community and Honda car sponsored showroom and mechanical vocational school. Site: São Paulo

8

9

8. Adel Zakout, Sofia Central Train Station – Roma Youth Performance Centre. Site: Sofia

9. Ragnhildur Kristjansdottir, community pools, soup-kitchen, aquarium and natural history research centre. Site: Reykjavik

DIPLOMA 3

Meta Urbanism: White City Ecologies
This year Dip 3 Meta Urbanism reassessed the potential of collective, *eco-logical* urban housing and the role of masterplans in the aftershock of the 2008 global economic crisis. Although transformations in communication such as blogging, youtube, facebook, etc. have allowed radically new forms of connectivity, start-ups and vast e-communities, the impact of these communication tools and networks on our urban environment and on the places we live remains to be seen. Felix Guattari's seminal 1989 text *The Three Ecologies* argues, prophetically, that in order to resist the homogenising forces of visual and electronic media, rampant consumerism and the crisis of global climate change, societies need to support individual creativity and social life within a new collective cultural/environmental project. Such an approach would contribute to 'a widespread shift in current value systems' – encouraging our evolution into a more deeply eco-logical society.

Responding to this challenge, Dip 3 has worked from the dwelling *micro* to the urban *macro* scale. Our initial project reconsidered the 'living room' – its evolution, meanings and conventions – to produce conceptual transformations. The emerging concepts of 'living room' fed directly into the 'Concept House' project, a reinvention of the British terraced house as a new 'ecothetical' urban typology. The social and organisational dwelling concepts developed in the terraced house have become the seeds for the final project: experimental high-density urban housing in White City, the derelict site of the obsolete OMA masterplan. Each of these large-scale propositions has claimed part of the White City site; each project could be considered the catalyst or 'lone ranger' in the territory of the anti-masterplan. Reformatted urban dwelling and hybrid programmes express an urbanism of found local potentials, transformed infrastructures, pioneer eco-communities and productive landscapes. Dip 3's idiosyncratic and hyper-active projects propose an alternative density of *social/ecologies* – attuned to the crises of our time.

UNIT STAFF
Alison Brooks
Max Kahlen

STUDENTS
Azri Syazwan Abdul Gani
Suram Choi
Ying-Chih Deng
Yong Bum Kim
Jin Kim
Sergey Kudryashev
Timothy Tin-Che Lee
Inga Maria Wolanczyk
Kai Yang

Thanks to:
David Akera (Akera Engineers), Catherine Burd (Burd Haward Architects), Gary McCluskie (Co-lab Architects), Sarah Hare (Sarah Hare Architects), David Mikhail (Riches Hawley Mikhail), Sarah Featherstone (Featherstone Young), Marcus Lee (Flacq), Levent Kerimol (LDA), Mark Brearley (LDA), Chris Bagot (Softroom), Roger Zogolovitch, Charles Tashima, Marco Guarnieri (KGA), Anne Save de Beaurecueil, Franklin Lee, Carlos Villanueva Brandt, Nate Kolbe (Superfusionlab), Dominic Papa (S333), Marianne Mueller, Javier Castañón

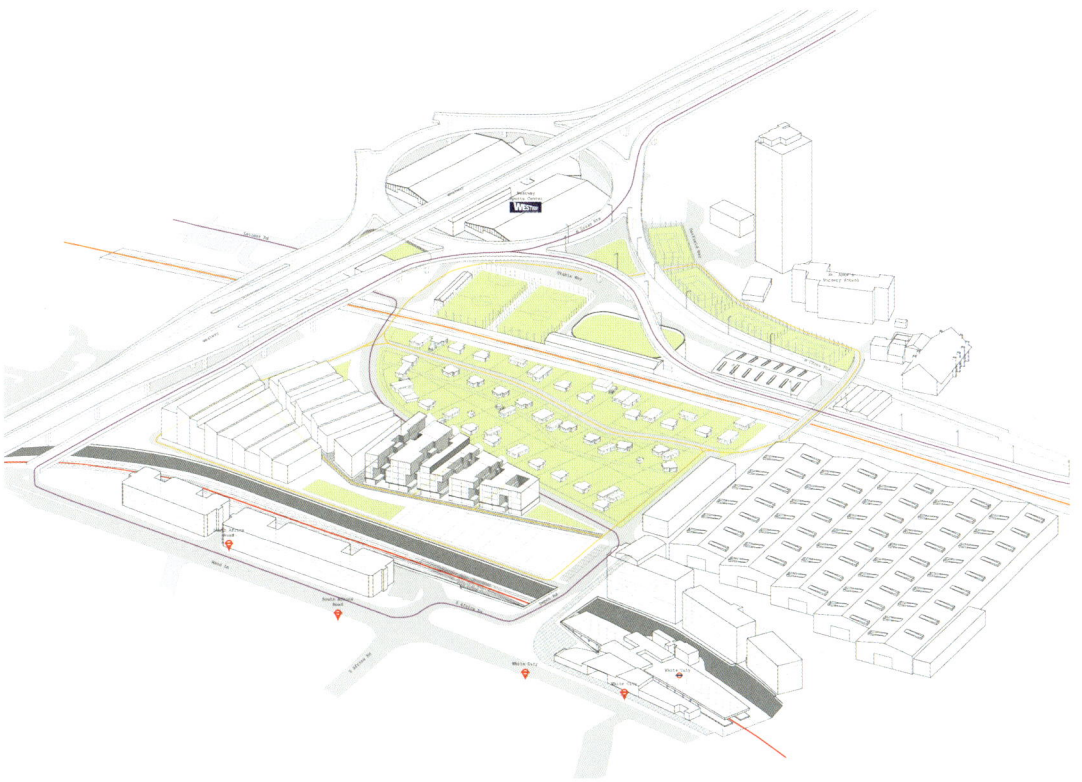

1

2

3

4

1–4. Sergey Kudryashev
The idea of the chimney, found in the typical London
terraced house is re-established as a new social and
environmental strategy for deep high-density housing.

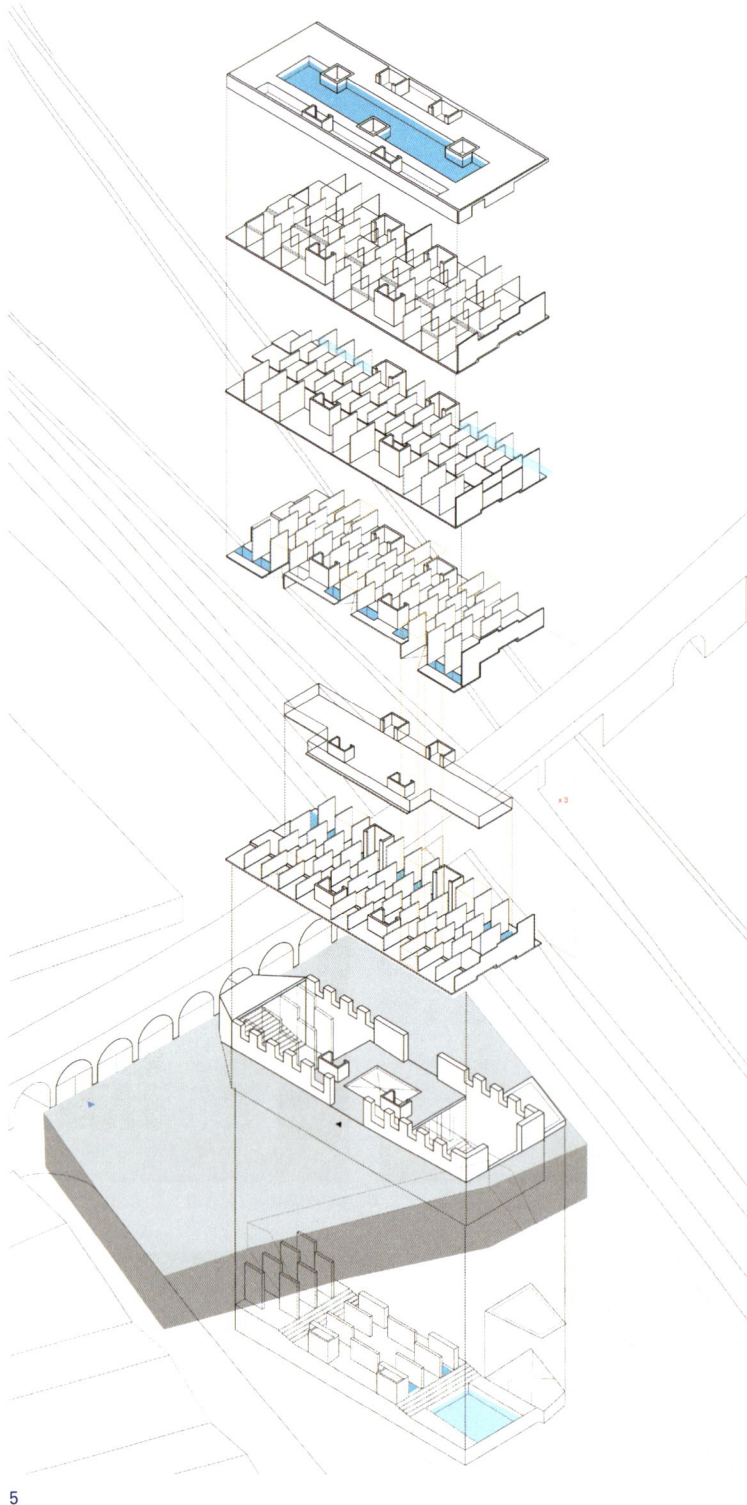

5

5–8. Ying-Chih Deng
Get Naked House redefines the role of the bathroom as an
instrument to reconfigure the dwelling and encourage
new forms of cohabitation: bathing as a spatial organisation of rituals; bathroom as theatrical experience; the
fragile moment of nudity as social tool.

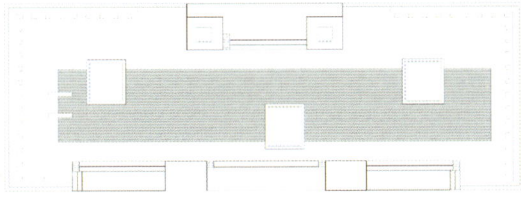

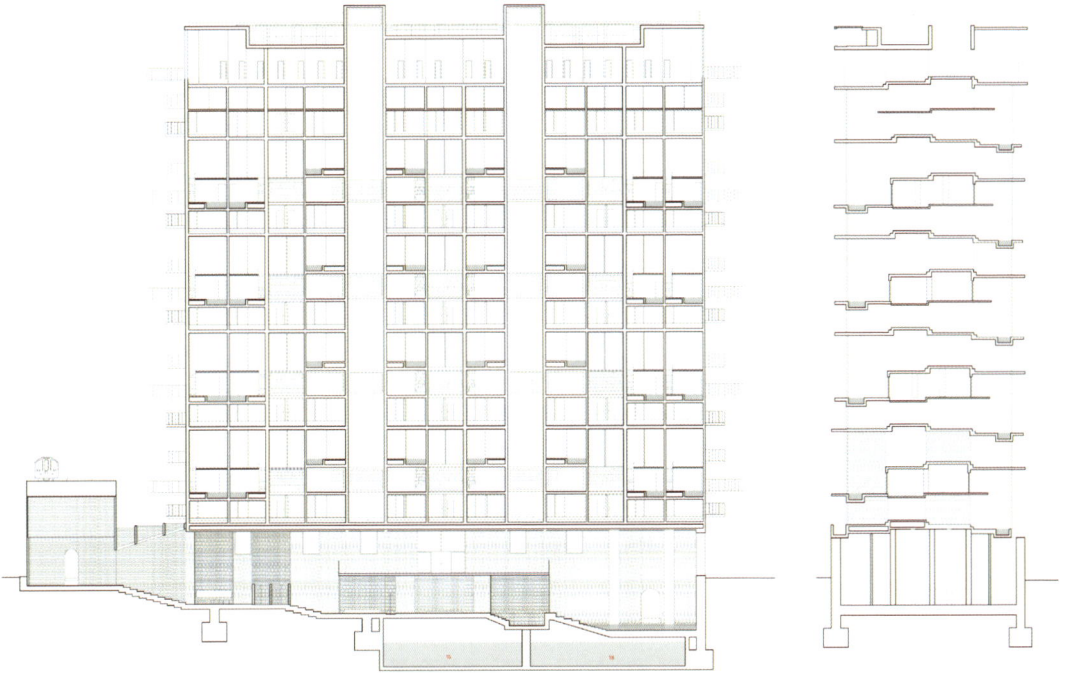

6

7

8

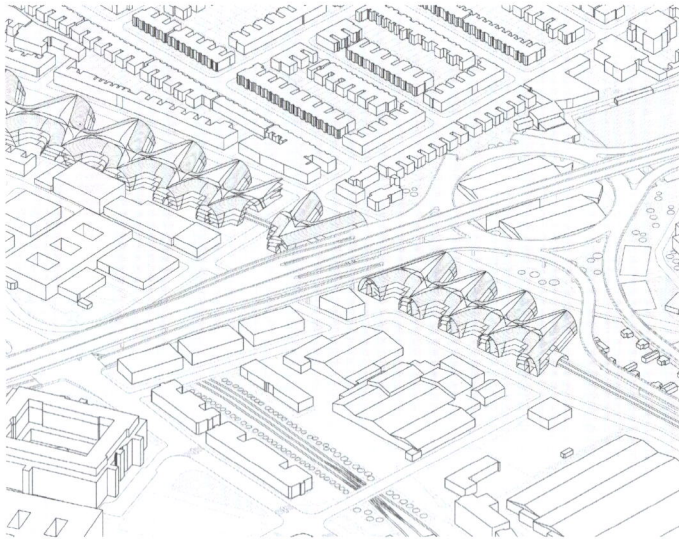

8

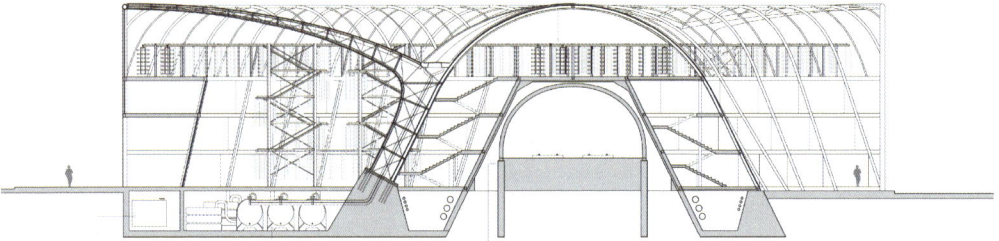

9

10

9–12. Timothy Tin-Che Lee
The Green Mile implements hybrid housing and high-
density food production to reactivate linear infrastructural
voids and reestablish existing urban boundaries as new
socio-economic activators.

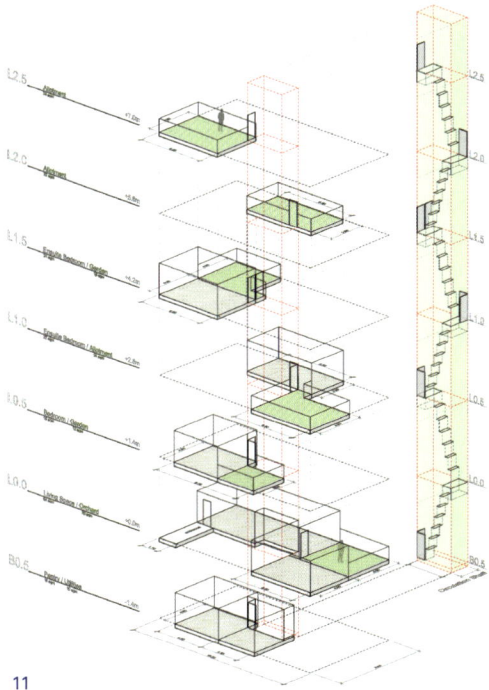

11

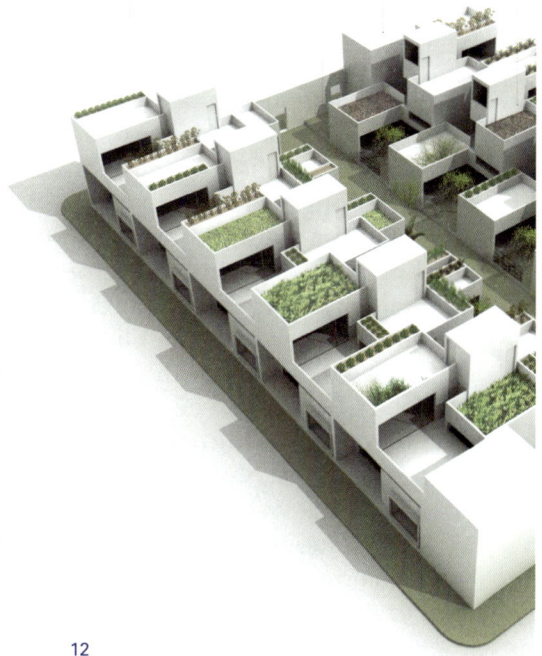

12

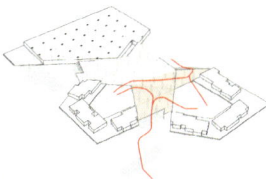

13

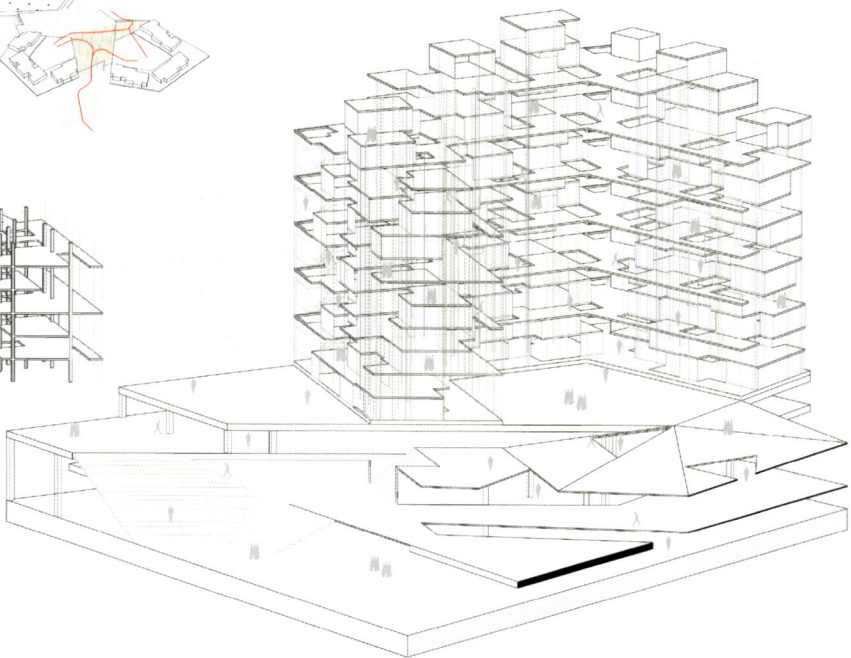

14

13 & 14. Jin Kim
Urban Stage organises a distinct hierarchy of public and
residential programmes through a sequence of foyers and
stages to reactivate the site.

DIPLOMA 4

The Coast of Europe: The Architecture
of Territorial Transformations

Diploma Unit 4's research and design work considers contemporary transformations of the European territories. By looking at the material forms and spatial configurations of the multiple lines of evolution, conjunction, erosion, accretion, intensification and compression of the inhabited space of Europe at a time of profound change, we positioned architecture within the fields of tensions that make up contemporary human environments, to intercept, modify, intensify and shape the materials that constitute Europe today.

Our work starts with the hypothesis that the contemporary spaces of Europe's coasts can be much more than they are. How can we identify the current transformation processes that shape and mould these inhabited spaces? How can we activate architectural intelligence to produce sites beyond what we already know?

The enquiry into how contemporary architecture and urbanism should be positioned amidst the myriad other processes seeking to shape Europe led to the production of new territorial images: on one side we examined new remote-sensing technologies that carve out spaces of operation and sovereignty, and on the other we focused on the agency that such new technologies elicit and entail.

The new models of agency that the research projects investigate show how architecture functions today within an ecology of differentiated spatial practices.

The work presented here is a series of reflections on the multiple objects, situations, actors and spaces, social processes and individual subjectivities currently active in Europe's liminal spaces. How can and should architecture work amongst the complex systems that are shaping Europe? Can architecture draw out unmarked and often overlooked possibilities embedded in these systems and processes?

UNIT STAFF
John Palmesino
Ann-Sofi Rönnskog

STUDENTS
Sanem Alper
Ai Bessho
Yi-Jen Chen
Georgios Eftaxiopoulos
Tom Fox
Oscar Gomes
Agnes Mun Khwan Yit

Thanks to:
Brett Steele
Irit Rogoff
Monia De Marchi
Kirsi Rantama
Antti Nousjoki
Eyal Weizman
Elena Pascolo
Shumon Basar
Barbara Campbell-Lange
Thomas Campbell
Dmitry Vorobyev
Paulo Tavares
Stefano Rabolli Pansera
Charles Tashima
Mark Cousins
Marina Lathouri
Histories and Theories
    MA students

1. Agnes Mun Khwan Yit combined civil protection management and evacuation plans to reshape the metropolitan areas around Vesuvius in Naples.

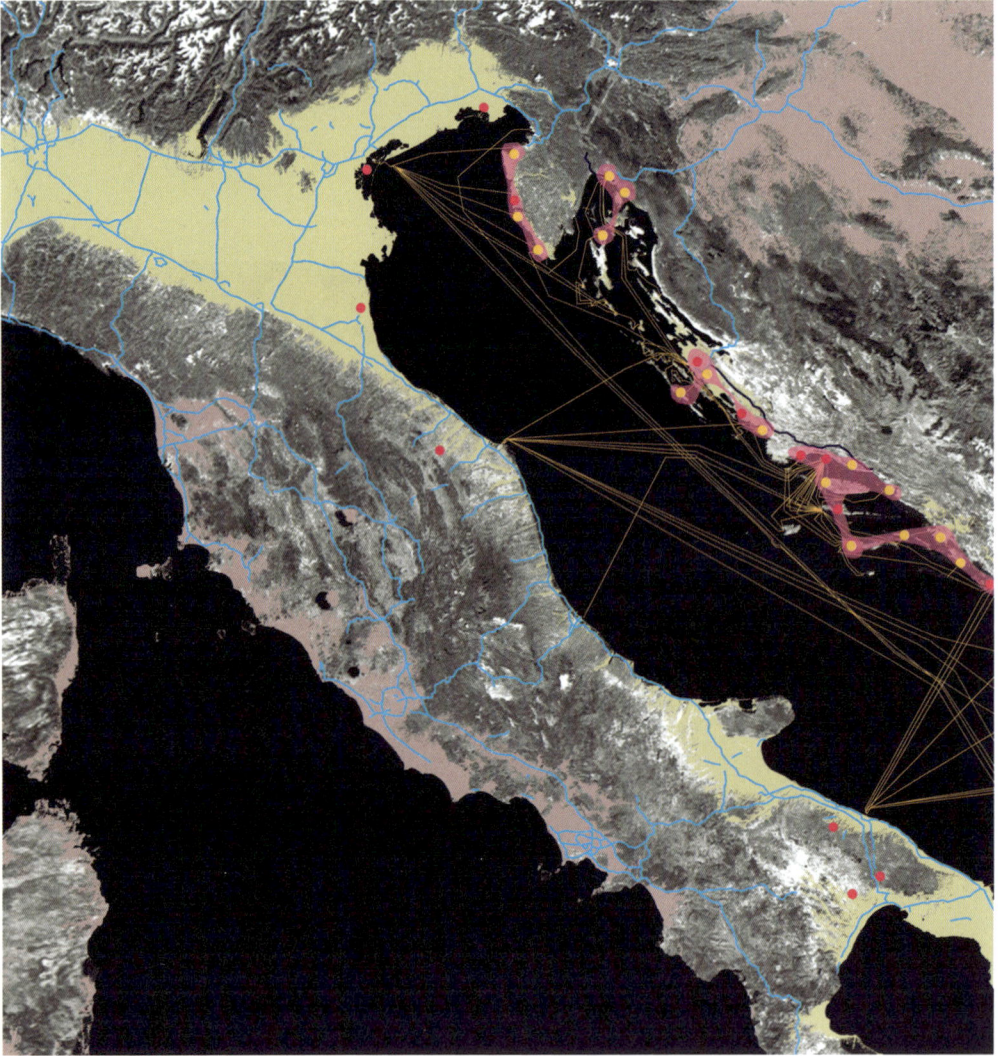

2

3

2 & 3. Ai Bessho focused on UNESCO's management techniques in developing a series of new citadels in the Adriatic.

4

5

4 & 5. Tom Fox explored the impact of the spatial products
of orthodox politics and economic policies on the
transformation of the Atlantic Coast.

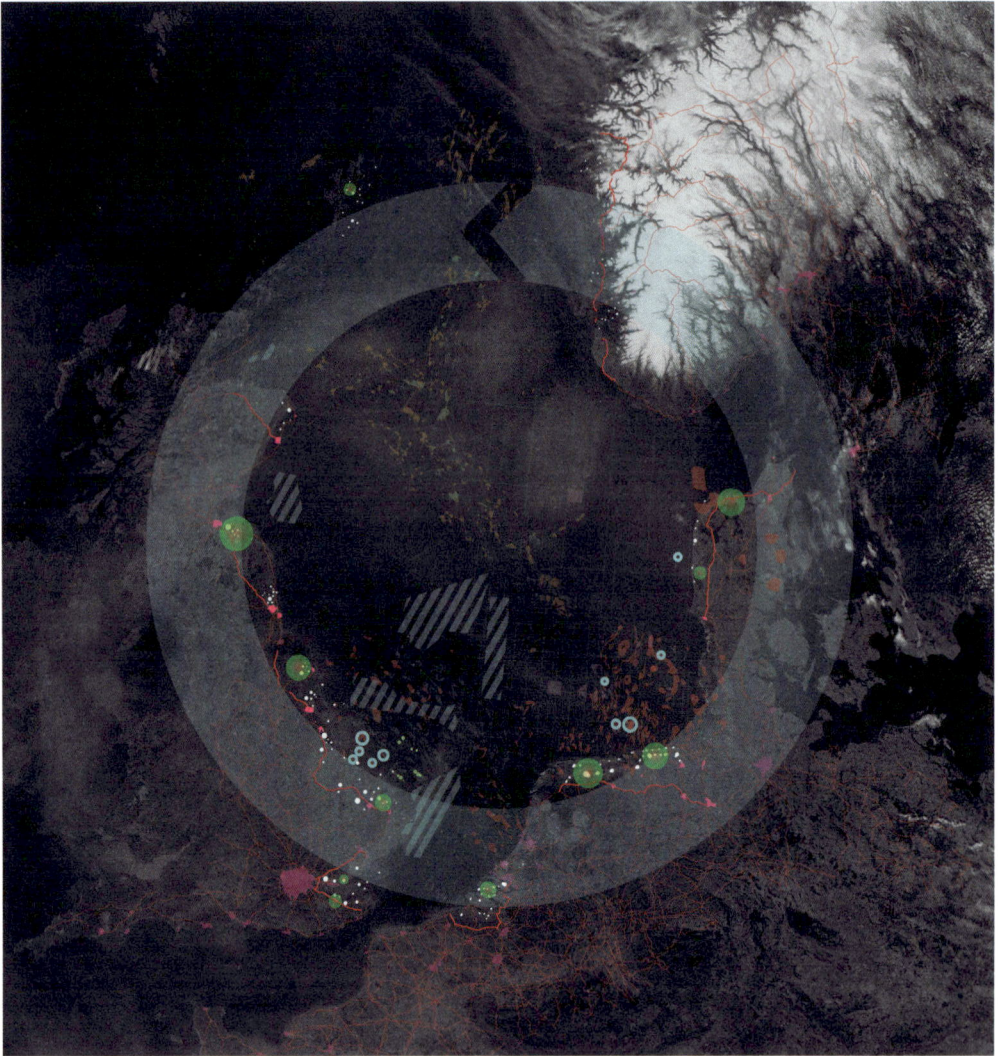

6

7

6 & 7. Yi-Jen Chen's project addresses renewable energy as a potential for innovative metropolitan development in a vast ring-city around the shores of the North Sea.

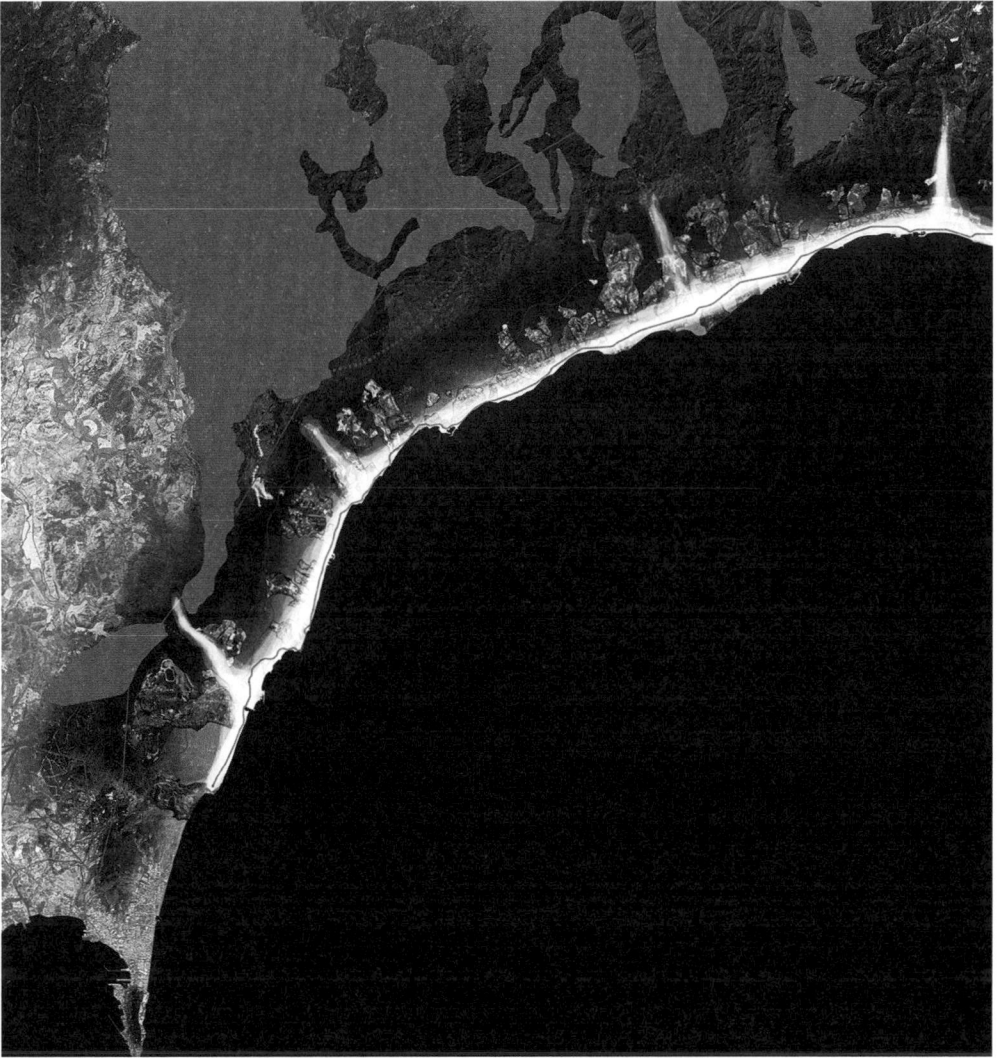

8

9

8 & 9. Georgios Eftaxiopoulos looked at the potential
of solar energy to address the collapsing tourist urban
system in the western Mediterranean.

DIPLOMA 5

Re:Public – Third Natures

Dip 5 focuses on the role of architecture as complex ecologies that act as linking mechanisms between living beings, social groups and technological objects. The unit explores the notion of buildings as *third natures* – deliberate material and intellectual manipulations of our biotope. To encourage a deep rethinking of buildings as public spaces, we focused this year on the conceptual and technical development of a small to medium-scale project that involves linking inert and living materials. Engagement with technology was paired with a new consciousness of the identity of our body – redefining the role of artificiality, perception or carnality within our experience.

The work of the unit is highly contextual, extending the notion of context beyond its conventional limits. The context of the public space is defined not just in relation to its physical surroundings, but in terms or the congregation of people that use it. A congregation, here, is understood beyond the usual meaning of a single social group bound together in worship or by politics. Rather, it implies links with other social groups, natural species, ecosystems and objects, including technological ones. In this way, the congregational public spaces become assemblies, meetings of members of numerous communities of different backgrounds.

UNIT STAFF
Cristina Díaz Moreno
Efrén García Grinda
Tyen Masten

STUDENTS
Francesco Matteo Belfiore
Thomas Wai Tong Chan
Benedetta Gargiulo
Fedor Gridnev
Kyung Tae Jung
Ji In Kim
Eugene (Duck-Jong Lee)
John Ng
Seung Joon Oh
Niklavs Paegle
Pei-Yao Wu

SEMINARS
Vicente Soler
Nerea Calvillo
Santiago Huerta
Teresa Galí
Lluis Viú

GUESTS
Alisa Andrasek
Anne Save de Beaurecueil
Oliver Domeisen
Christina Doumpioti
Shin Egashira
Juan Elvira
Uriel Fogué
Evan Greenberg
Francesca Hugues
Andrés Jaque
Holger Kehne
Franklin Lee

Nuria Lombardero
Monia de Marchi
Miguel Paredes
Claudia Pasquero
Marco Poletto
Natasha Sandmeier
Brett Steele
Charles Tashima
Jeffrey Turko
Carlos Villanueva Brandt
Andrew Watts
Andrew Yau

Thanks to:
Mike Weinstock
Charles Tashima
Ricardo de Ostos
Nannette Jackowski

1 & 2. Pei-Yao Wu, A Fun Building: Pop subculture in Tokyo. A series of follies, each dedicated to a different Japanese urban subculture (Lolita, Otaku, Ganguro), is proposed along a route within Yoyogi Park, Tokyo. The project focuses on contemporary folly for Lolitas, constructed with kaleidoscopic spaces that project the aesthetic exuberance of fashion and lifestyle.

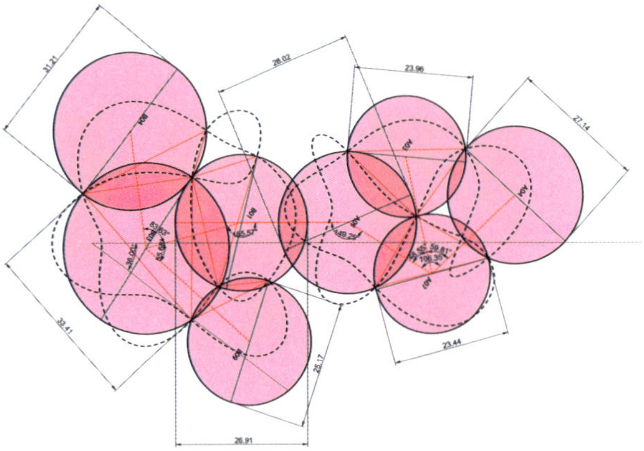

3

5

4

3 & 4. John Ng, Isle of Samba
Dancing sambistas, mobile spectacles and stealthy
bird-watchers. The Isle of Samba's annual carnival infects
with an atmosphere made real even for a single day.

5. Eugene (Duck-Jong Lee), Serpentine Flow
The Brazilian martial art of Capoeira describes the blurred
boundary between different social groups and induces
spontaneous social conditions.

6

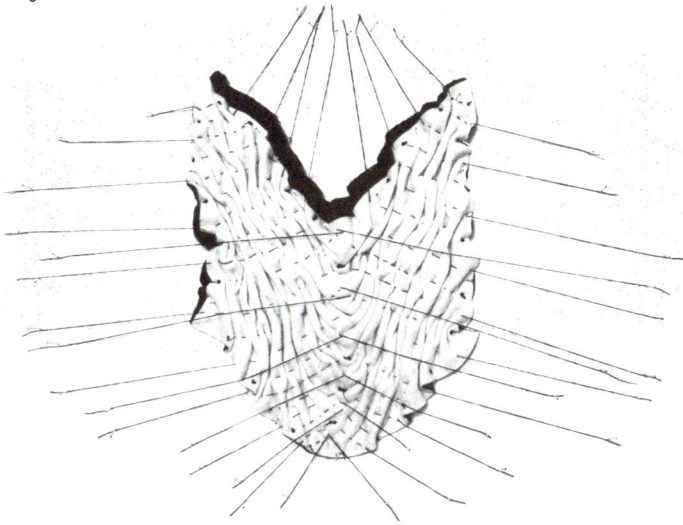

7

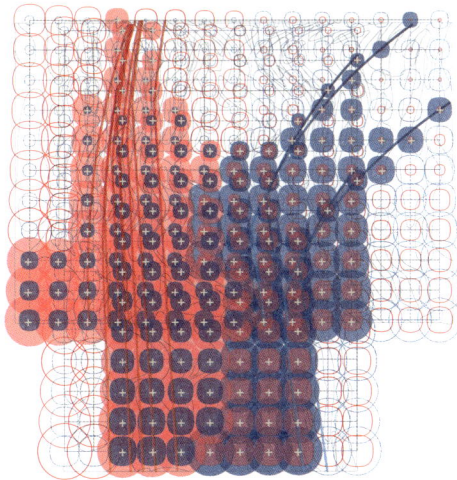

8

9

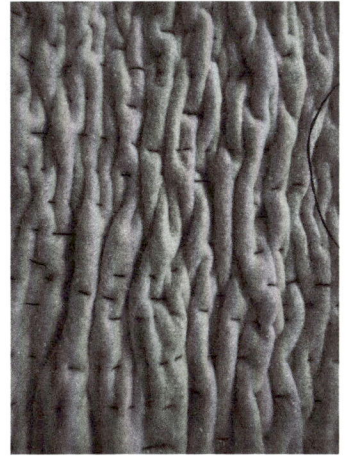

10

11

6–11. Ji In Kim, Eco-Body
The Eco-Body creates a series of mediating devices
between our naked skin and surrounding nature. This
third skin establishes a new relationship between our
body perception, water, ice and a constructed geology.

12

13

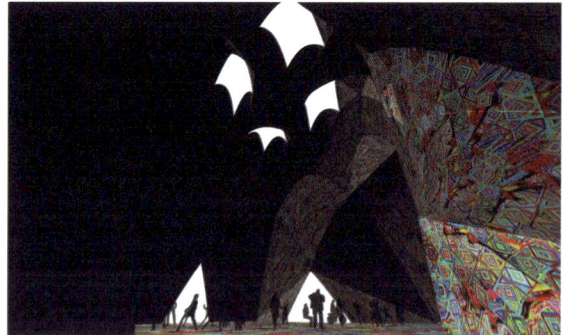

14

15

12–15. Niklavs Paegle, Discotheque
The Discotheque assembles the gentrifying hipster culture alongside the Bangladeshi diaspora in East London. It is juxtaposed with Brick Lane market, the protected view corridor of St Paul's Cathedral and the newly constructed London Overground line. The programmatic reconstruction of the layered domes assimilates local mythology in the same way emerging social groups do.

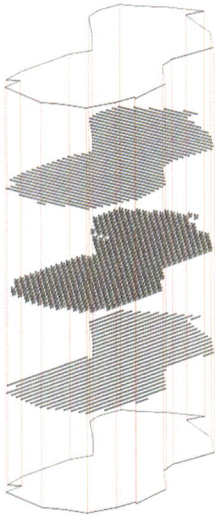

16

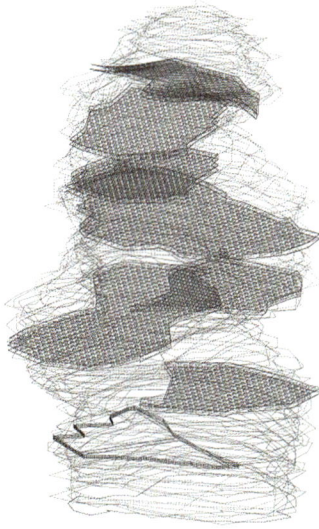

17

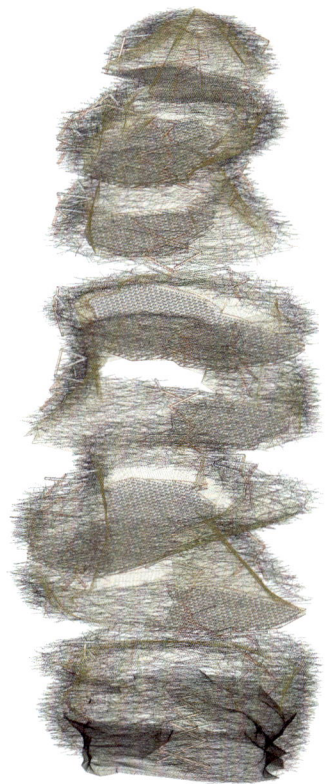

18

19

16–18. Seung Joon Oh, Educational Building of Nature Integrated facilities for an alternative education system and a shanty town community in Seoul. Its tectonic nature offers itself as a pedagogical instrument.

19. Benedetta Gargiulo, The Embassy of Third Natures A multi-climatic territory in London's Nine Elms defines a new reality between existing allotments, winter gardens, farmer's markets and gastronomic societies.

135

DIPLOMA 7

'We must subject technology and science to the economy of the poor and penniless. We must add the aesthetic factor because the cheaper we build the more beauty we should add to respect man.' – Hassan Fathy

Schools are important public buildings; the experience of school is culturally defining and registers dominantly in personal memory and development. Yet school design remains largely indifferent to changes in teaching theory, technology and the broader role of education within communities.

Our projects this year were set in southern Lebanon in the context of Palestinian refugee camps and the divided city of Beirut. Our focus was on school design as a means to shape the many reciprocal relationships within its setting: ecological, hydrological, material resources, climatic as well as cultural and aesthetic. With optimism we rigorously pursued a green agenda, one by nature transdisciplinary and reliant on collaboration and context.

In an area which has always known conflict, the school building is a place to restore community and a safe haven, effectively a 'child-friendly-space'. What proved challenging and informative to us was a lack of readily available data, which forced us to take a forensic approach to our analysis.

By designing for long-term development as well as humanitarian issues, we mean not only dealing with natural disasters and conflict but involving ourselves in systemic issues. We intervene by layering positive impacts on local economic and social well-being.

Two technical ambitions guided the unit's work and research: an investigation into tool-making in a digital age (the inherent obsolescence of high-end fabrication machinery creates an opportunity to adapt low-cost analogue tools) and research methods for accurately predicting the behaviour of natural light (to restore an operational means of calculation for digital modelling).

Participation and communication are essential – this also involves raising awareness. By engaging directly in the field and finding active networks and collaborators including technologists, theorists and NGOs, we encourage projects to outlast the timescale of school terms.

UNIT STAFF
Simon Beames
Kenneth Fraser

STUDENTS
George Woodrow
Imogen Long
Andrew Tam
Yi Ling Wong
Sanaa Shaikh
Helen Evans
Julin Ang
Ting Ting Dong
Andreas Poullaides
Helena Westerlind
James Rai
Aditya Aachi

Thanks to
Kevin Fellingham
Theo Lorenz
Will McLardy
Terry Raggett
Shireen Hamdan
Barnaby Gunning
Michael Evans
Timm Schoenberg
Simon Dickens
Charles Tashima
Iain McDonald
Souraya Ali
Asif Khan
Julia King
Gary Grant
David Bakins
Anies & Itab Al-Hroub

1. Helen Evans

2

3

2. Yi Ling Wong
A therapeutic dance school inserted into war-torn buildings next to the Green Line in Beirut regenerates scarred buildings and heals war-torn minds

3. Sanaa Shaikh
Glass school: varying levels of transparency promote cohesion and allow users a multi-faith education while maintaining independent identity.

4

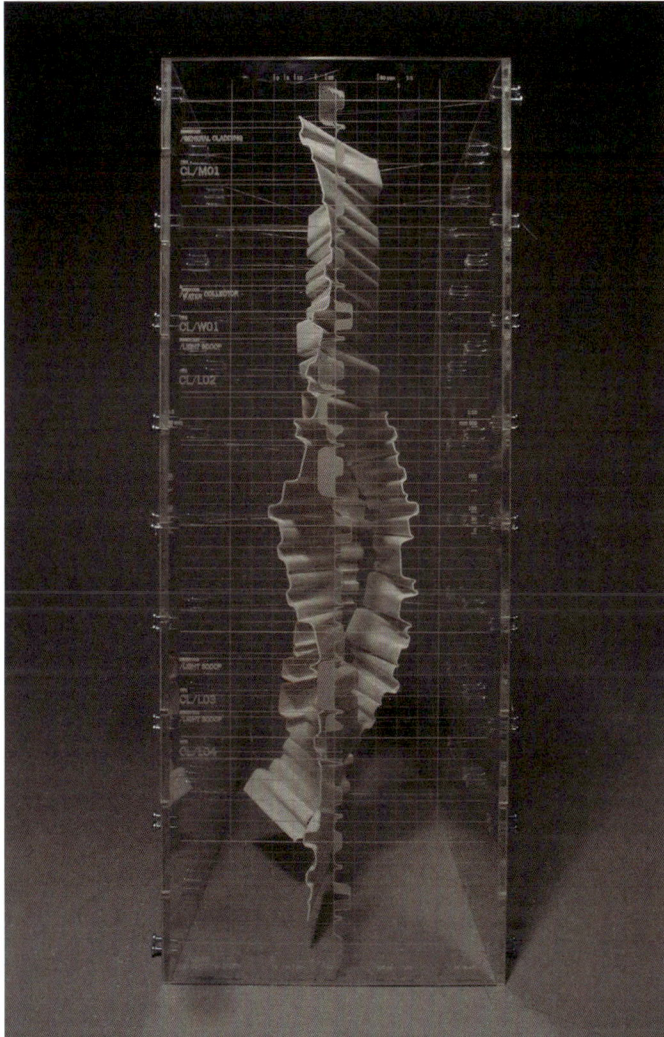

5

4. Imogen Long
en-roll: taking the existing refugee camp as its anchor, the mass-customised stitched fabric system infiltrates, encloses, links and remakes this densely packed, deteriorating urban environment.

5. Andrew Tam
Corrugated self-reinforcing PET panels (from recycled bottles) convert the 10,000m^2 north facade into a dew harvester, providing water for a vertical urban farming institute.

139

6

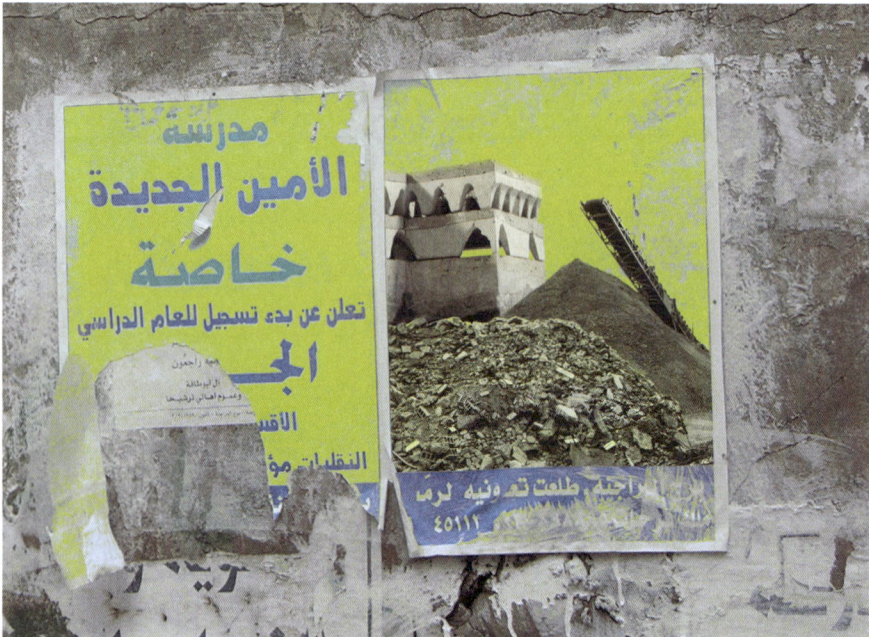

7

6. George Woodrow
The scheme addresses educational and infrastructural
deficiencies of a UNRWA refugee camp in Beirut,
proposing an 'extended' school which acts as an
earthquake safety zone for the entire community.

7. Helena Westerlind
Space as form: the proposal casts a new school in an
abandoned square, making the invisible tangible. Newly
created spaces within the cast present themselves as the
locus of memory as the refugee camp disperses.

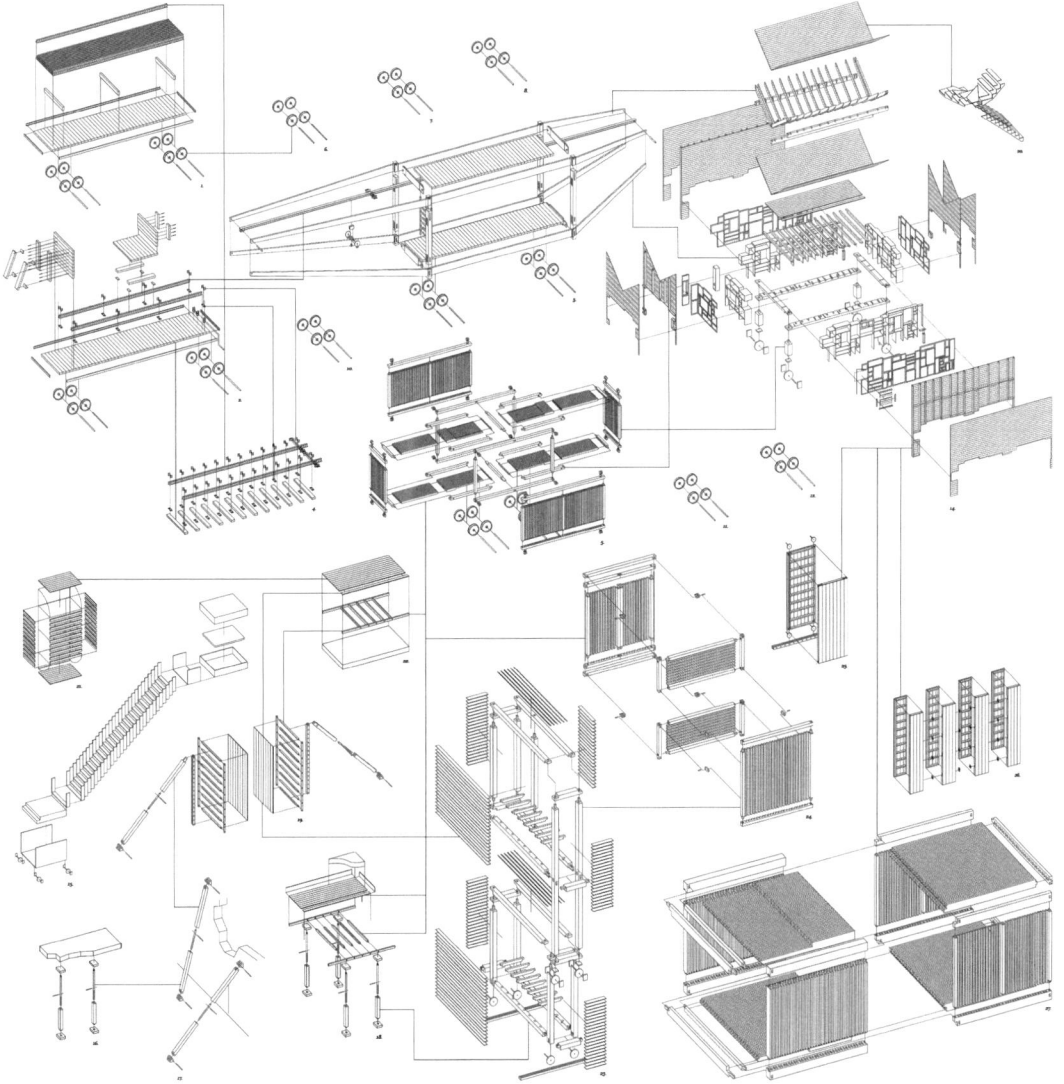

8. James Rai
Through a forensic study of the aftermath of conflict
the proposal generates a series of vehicular machines
to reconstruct and reskill the population.

141

DIPLOMA 8

Evolving from the unit's focus on systems-based design, the emphasis for the year was on the development of open frameworks that are inherently applicable to a range of architectural situations. Student projects explored the potential of establishing design methods that fundamentally question the paradigm of rule-based architecture.

The chosen context for this year was Hashima Island, an abandoned coal-mining facility at the southern end of the Japanese Archipelago. The island was chosen as it served as a prime example of an incomplete and incoherent architectural assemblage of missed opportunities, developed with the support of heavy industry, yet lacking any clear organisational logic. To allow for the development of both a framework and a coincident architectural example, the programmatic brief was left open to interpretation. By the year's end, projects had naturally begun to prioritise one of the following two categories:

The Procedure – some projects focused solely on either architectural attributes or methods, using their identification and elaboration as a means to stipulate the necessary requirements for any subsequent architectural instantiation. As the projects show, these procedurally driven methodologies emphasised organisational tactics, yielding formally specific structures as the basis for architectural propositions of high definition.

The Object – by contrast, object-driven proposals underlined the value of identifying generic classifications that could then be informed by context-sensitive instances, the objects themselves. The objects possess directives their associated attributes as well as methods for the express purpose of architectural strategies. Procedural operations were then implemented piecemeal to articulate object collections that remain relatively neutral in their formal output yet coherent in their phased implementation.

In all the architectural speculations this year, the eventual success of the project depended on finding a congruence between the roles of inevitable probabilistic models of proposed architectural systems and an overriding counterpart, the non-determinism of open frameworks. Such a congruence would then serve as the criterion for each project's logical stability.

UNIT STAFF
Eugene Han
Chris Yoo

STUDENTS
Michal Ciomek
Yung Kyoo Kim
Emmanouil Matsis
So Jung Min
Ji Hyun Lee
Kwan Joo Park
Claretta Pierantozzi
Yvonne Tan
Sakiko Watanabe

INVITED CRITICS
Javier Castañón
Toni Kotnik
Chris Lee
Monia De Marchi
Francesca Hughes
Anne Save de Beaurecueil
Mike Weinstock

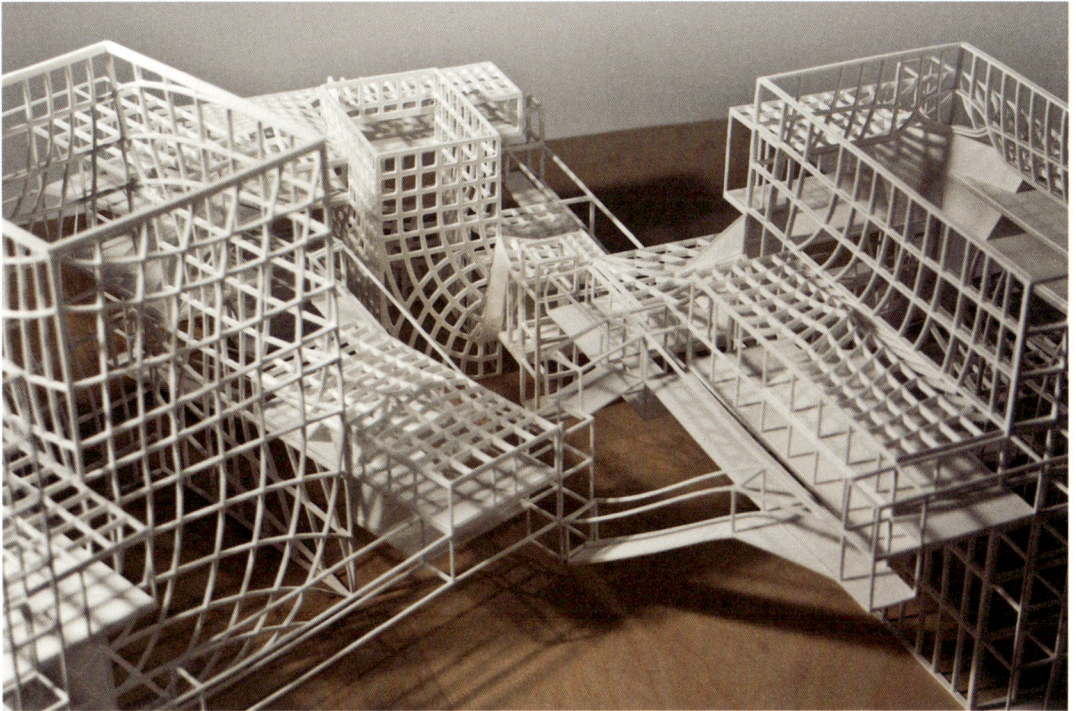

1

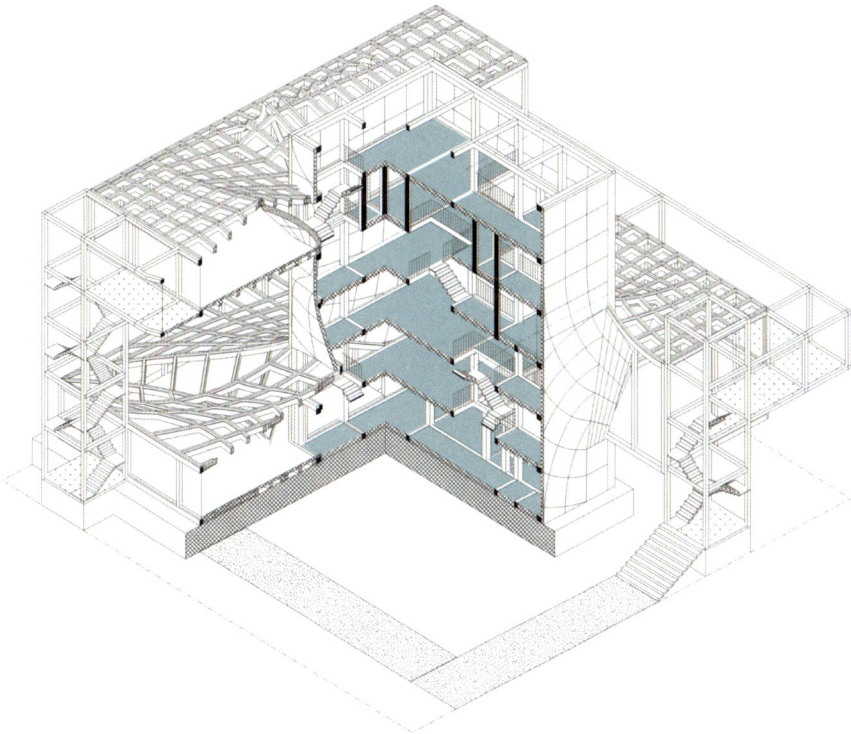

2

1 & 2. Yvonne Su Zen Tan. This proposal for an on-site library complex clearly placed procedural methods within spatial arrangements, whereas organisational strategies were addressed when determining architectural clusters, to produce a prototypical alternative to the mono-programmatic nature of the existing site.

3

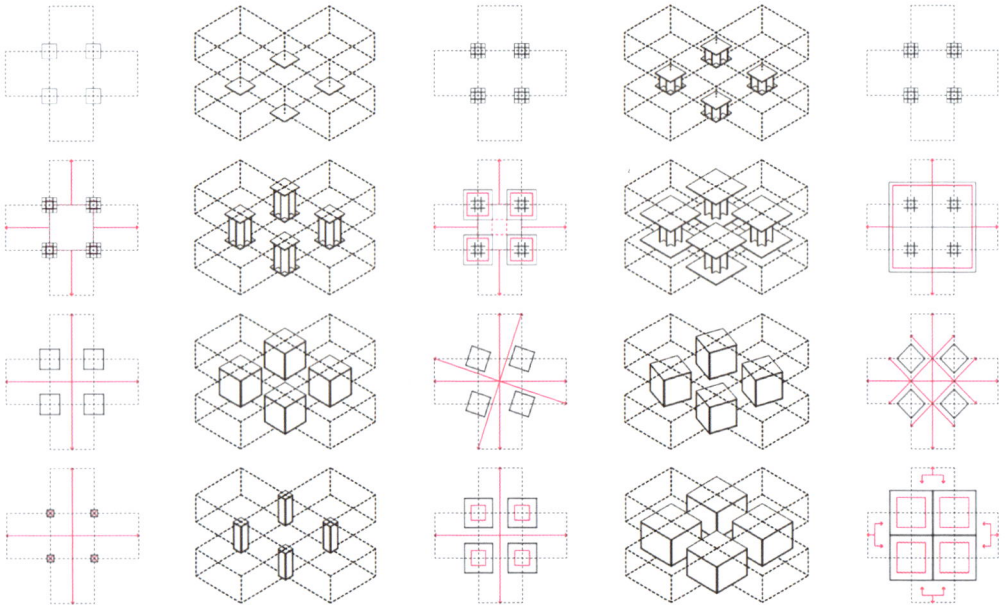

4

3 & 4. Emmanouil Matsis. Agora integrated the contextual architectural distribution inherent in the existing community with sequence-dependent organisations. By exploiting the behaviour of simple formulae to produce unequivocal architectural foci, the proposal aimed to demonstrate an architectural language based on a geometric vocabulary of context-sensitive objects.

5

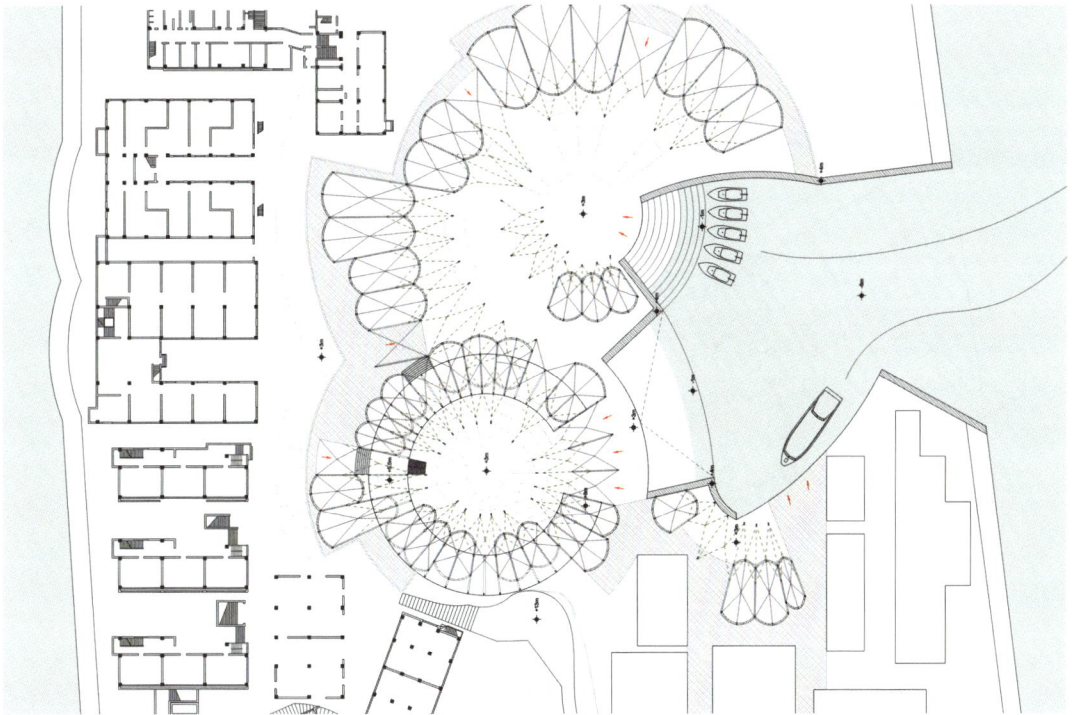

6

5 & 6. So Jung Min. A primarily procedural approach that responds to the lack of existing hierarchical architectures by proposing a micro-harbour. The project was finalised through the definition of seamless compositions of typically incongruent geometries to yield a framework independent of constituent types.

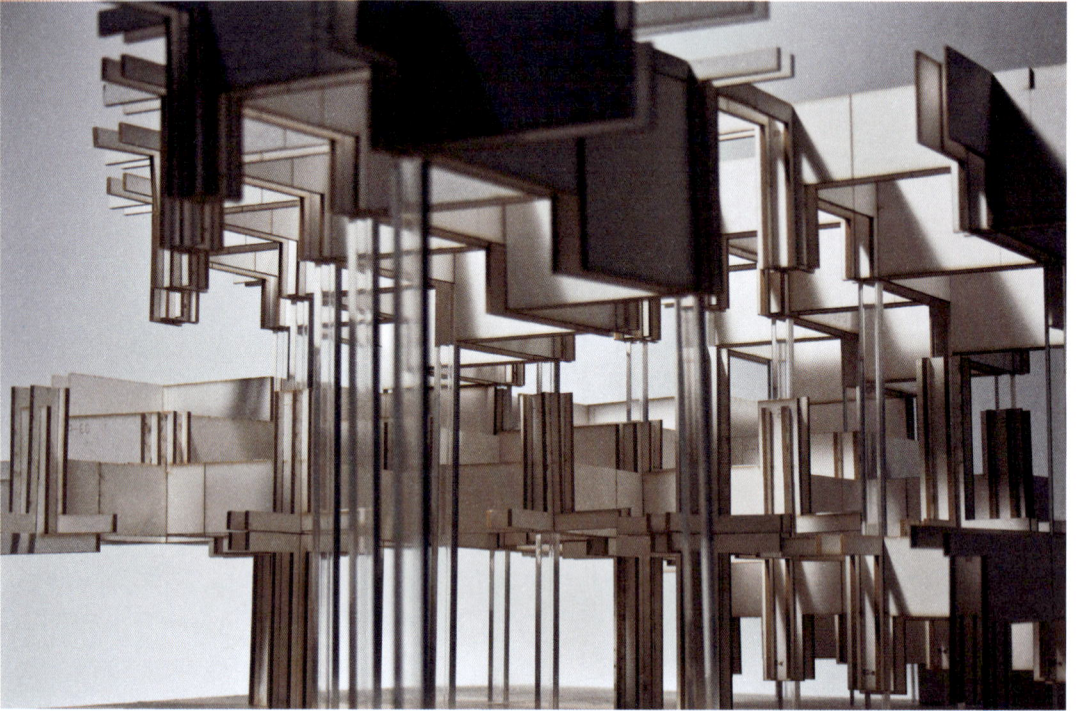

7

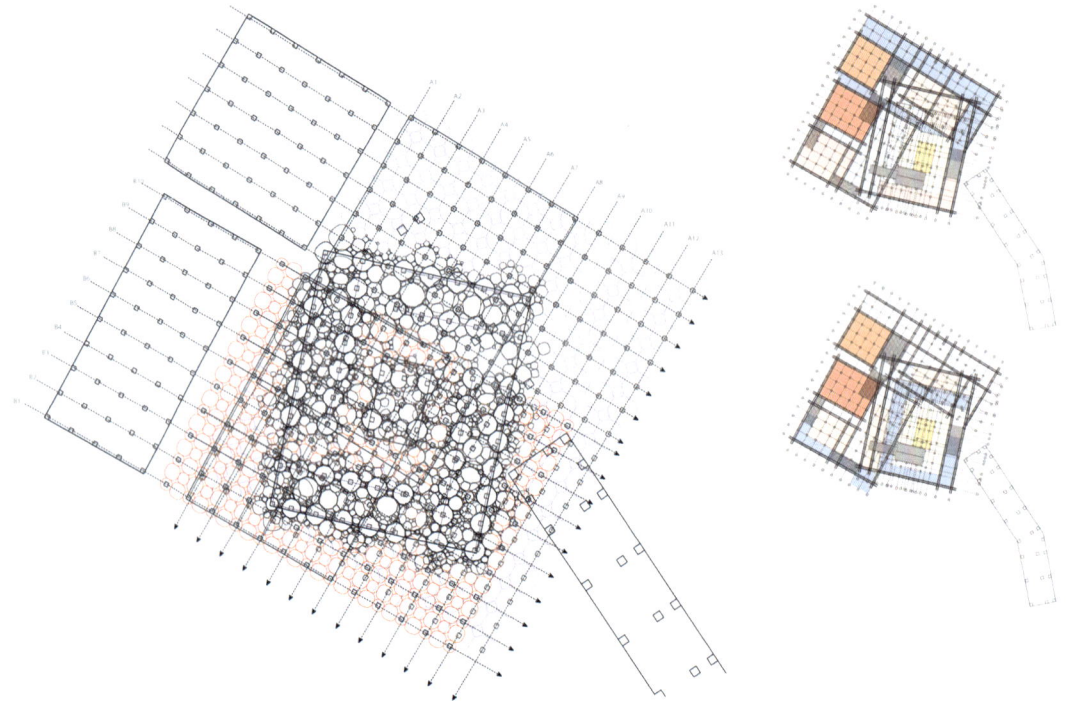

8

7 & 8. Yung Kyoo Kim. An on-site museum that would
demonstrate extended capacity of primitive architectures
through a reductive grammar of procedurally driven
construction types.

9

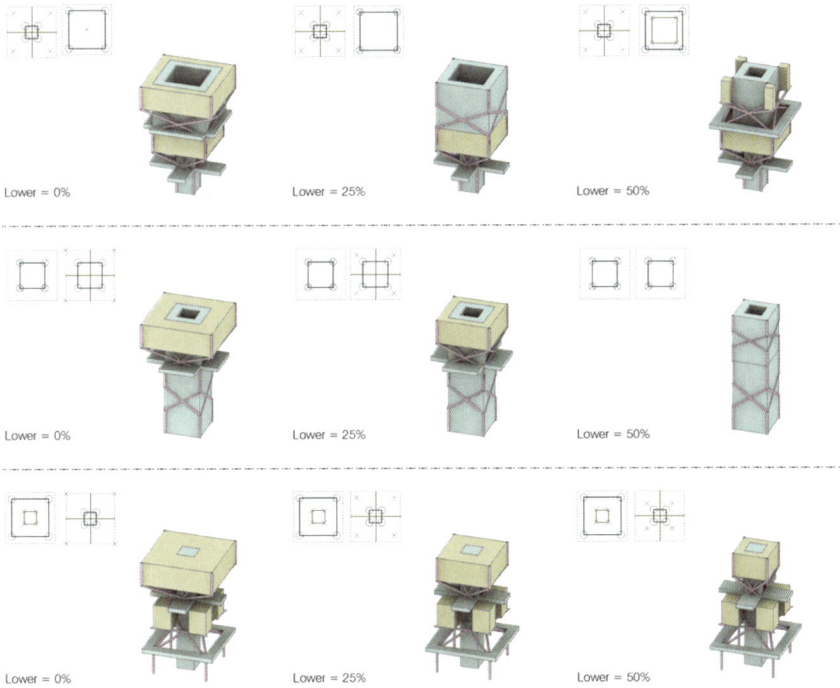

Lower = 0% Lower = 25% Lower = 50%

Lower = 0% Lower = 25% Lower = 50%

Lower = 0% Lower = 25% Lower = 50%

10

9 & 10. Sakiko Watanabe. A two-fold investigation of the propagation of complex field systems resulting in a polymorphic architectural grammar and a proposal for a particle acceleration laboratory on the island.

147

DIPLOMA 9

Iconic Fictions

Fiction set the tone and the agenda for this third year of Diploma Unit 9's foray into Iconic Architecture. Our projects were set in contexts hovering between real and imagined worlds. Some slipped forwards and back in time, sideways to alternate (at times catastrophic or giddy) realities, while others sat in places we know, only built from materials we don't yet have and inhabited in ways our lives don't yet allow. Oddly, the crazier the fiction, the more believable the project.

Flavie developed a split personality and portfolio between architect and archivist as she took on the legacy of the Guggenheim Museum. She presented new ways to design and read an architectural project – tightly woven with faux contextual and institutional material.

Amandine never left her room. Her fiction treats the city as an interior experience extending from the bedroom to the street to the city block. The eliminated exterior provokes a rethinking of architecture that becomes less an issue of what objects to shape than of what to inhabit.

Tijn was incarcerated in a prison of his own making. It evolved from a self-governing quasi-utopic world to one also focused on rehabilitation. The prison occupies one stage in a cycle of crime, punishment, detention and release – repeating itself behaviourally and architecturally.

Zoe imagined a world of water floating above the city grid. The bathhouse distorted our perception – visual, aural and haptic – to effectively recalibrate our understanding of space and material. Water made and dissolved walls whilst pouring from one space to the next.

Lara's smooth sphere (Seraphina) provides a moment of respite for the frenzied city-dwellers who spend time with her. Patrick brings a bit of New York to Los Angeles in the form of public city-space, while Kitty begins archiving books and ends up archiving a city. Shen gives new meaning to the atrium while Aras imagines a world in which private is public. All the while, Mickey tells of imminent destruction whilst creating an architecture of survival and hope.

UNIT STAFF
Natasha Sandmeier
Monia De Marchi

STUDENTS
Aras Burak
Amandine Kastler
Flavie Audi
Kitty O'Grady
Lara Lesmes
Mickey Kloihofer
Patrick Usborne
Shen Fei Lam
Tijn van de Wijdeven
Zoe Chan

1. Diploma 9 sampler in rows starting from top left:
Amandine, Aras, Flavie, Kitty, Mickey, Lara, Tijn,
Shen, Patrick & Zoe

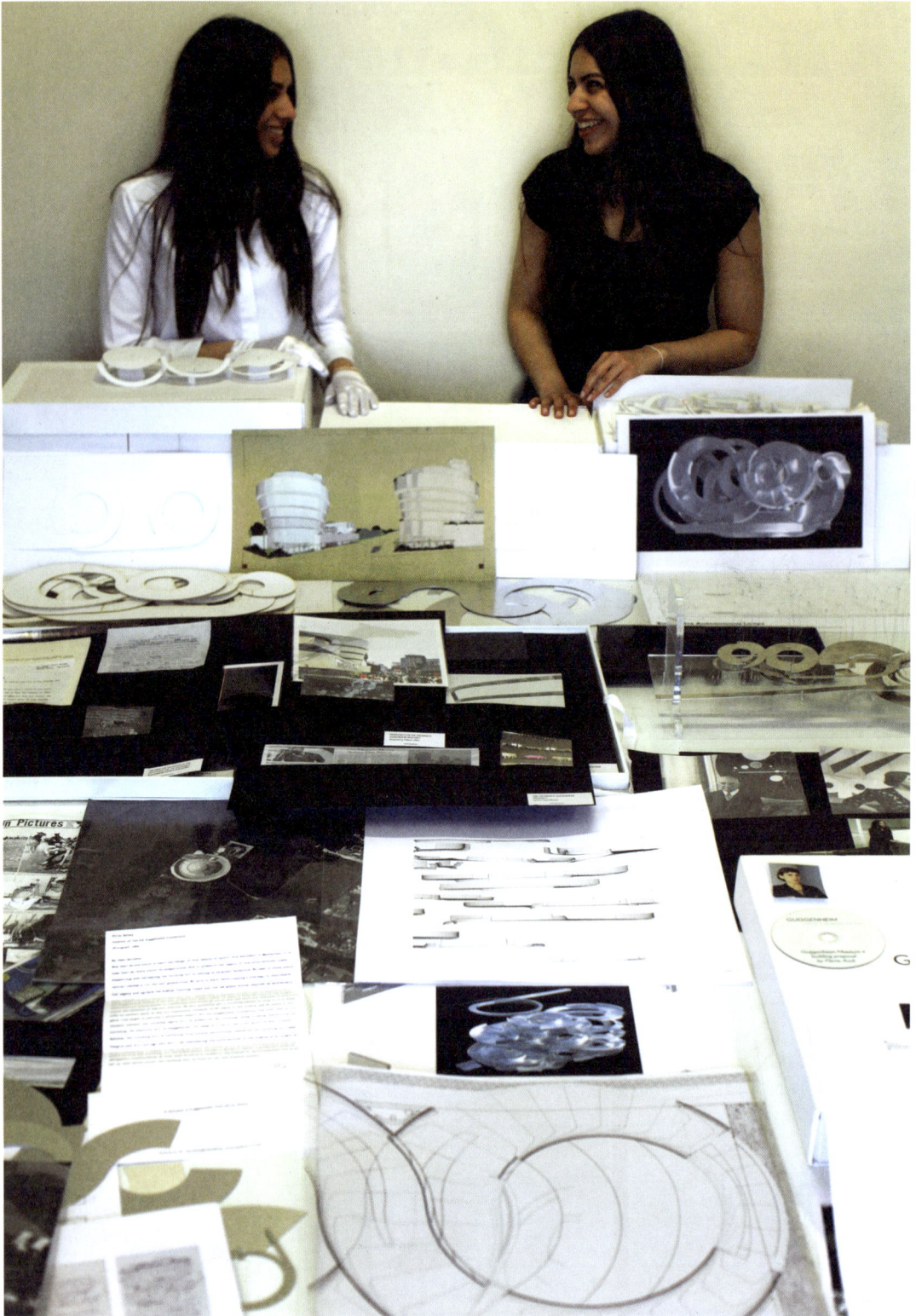

2. Flavie the Archivist (left) and Flavie the Architect (right)
discuss the process of making Guggenheim 4.

3. Amandine sets the stage for her world of interiors.

4. An excerpt of Tijn's prison shows how he used image to explore the varied conditions of incarceration and rehabilitation.

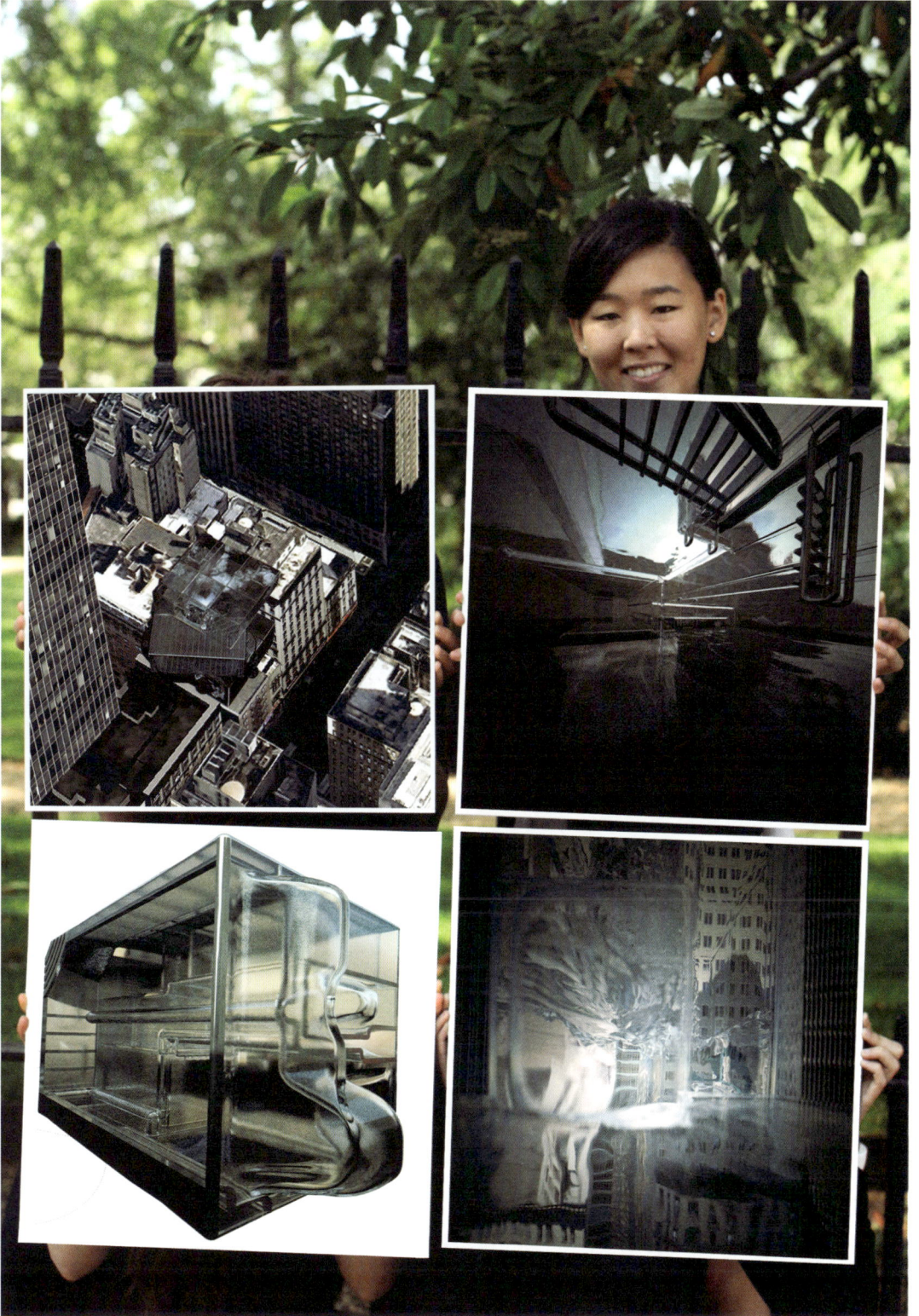

5. Zoe's images of her Melting Space in which
water is as important a material as glass and steel.

DIPLOMA 10

Direct Urbanism: Interactive Rules

In Direct Urbanism: Interactive Rules we have concentrated on urban, spatial and interactive rules and the role that they play in the making of architectural and urban space. We have combined these rules with topical urban conditions in order to further experiment with the relationship between physical and social structures and have then developed methods for designing complex spatial interventions that directly affect the live realm of the city.

As a starting point, we investigated and analysed the strategies and perimeters of three current London projects: the US Embassy in Nine Elms, Battersea Power Station and Chelsea Barracks. In response to these masterplans, we have devised methods of working with the interactive spaces that allow for the overlap of rule-based systems and mediate between the internal and external spaces of the city.

At the architectural scale, we have developed ten suggestions for a composite spatial language of structure, enclosure, components and interactive elements that support the design of an interactive perimeter as a physical structure. At the urban scale, we have expanded this perimeter into a territory of action in order to generate strategic interventions that challenge the city's existing and proposed infrastructure, fabric and rule-based systems.

UNIT MASTER
Carlos Villanueva Brandt

DIRECT ACTION WORKSHOP
Jan Willem Petersen
Domenico Raimondo

TOKYO WORKSHOP
Tom Heneghan
Tamao Hashimoto
Fumi Kashimura

TS WORKSHOP
Alex Warnock-Smith

STUDENTS
Amber Wood
Jan Nauta
Kleopatra Chelmi
Korey Kromm
Larissa Begault
Merlin Eayrs
Mita Solanki
Nick Simcik-Arese
Ronald Wong
Stephanie Edwards

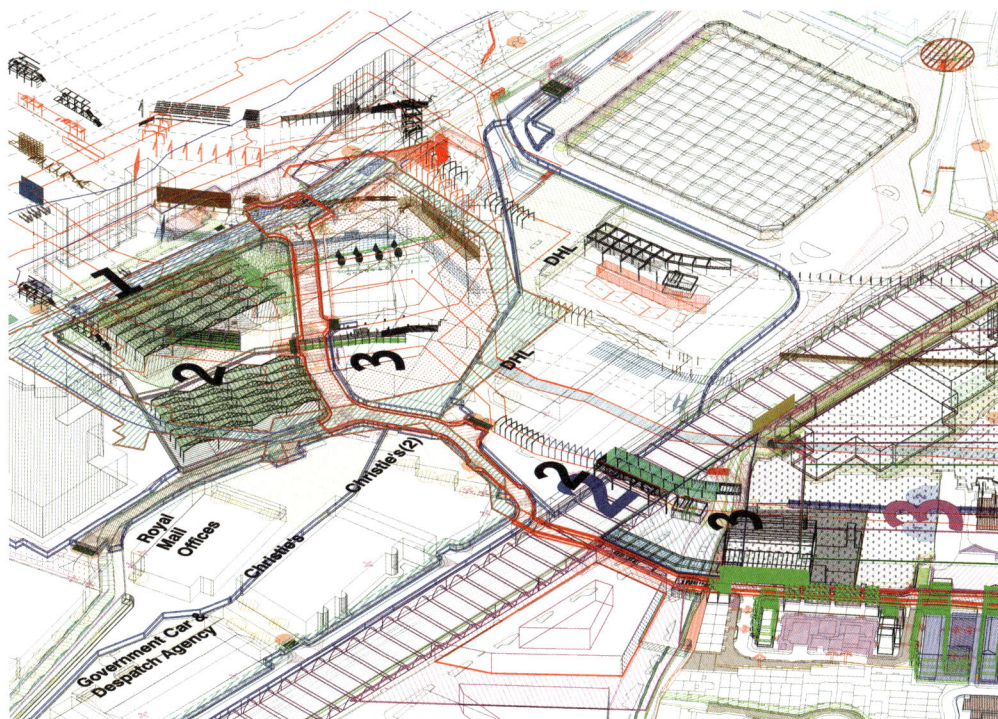

1

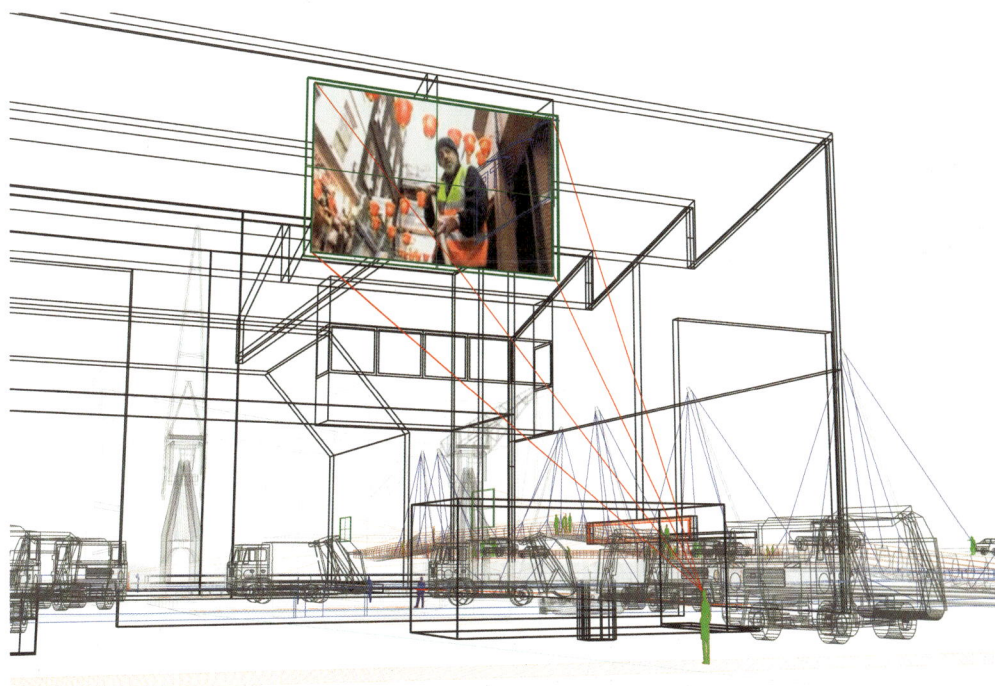

2

1. Korey Kromm, US Embassy, Nine Elms. Best Defence is a Good Offence, two pathways respond to a variety of urban conditions in order to establish the most effective form of security.

2. Jan Nauta, Battersea Power Station. Blurring Boundaries urbanises Viñoly's self-contained development by inserting a new right of way, a new metropolitan service and a system of images.

155

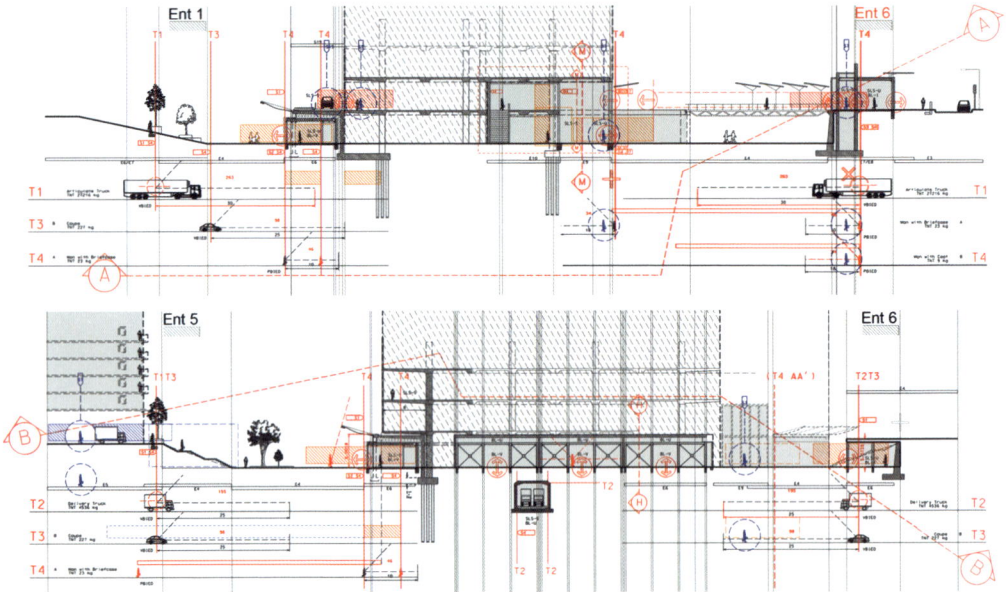

3

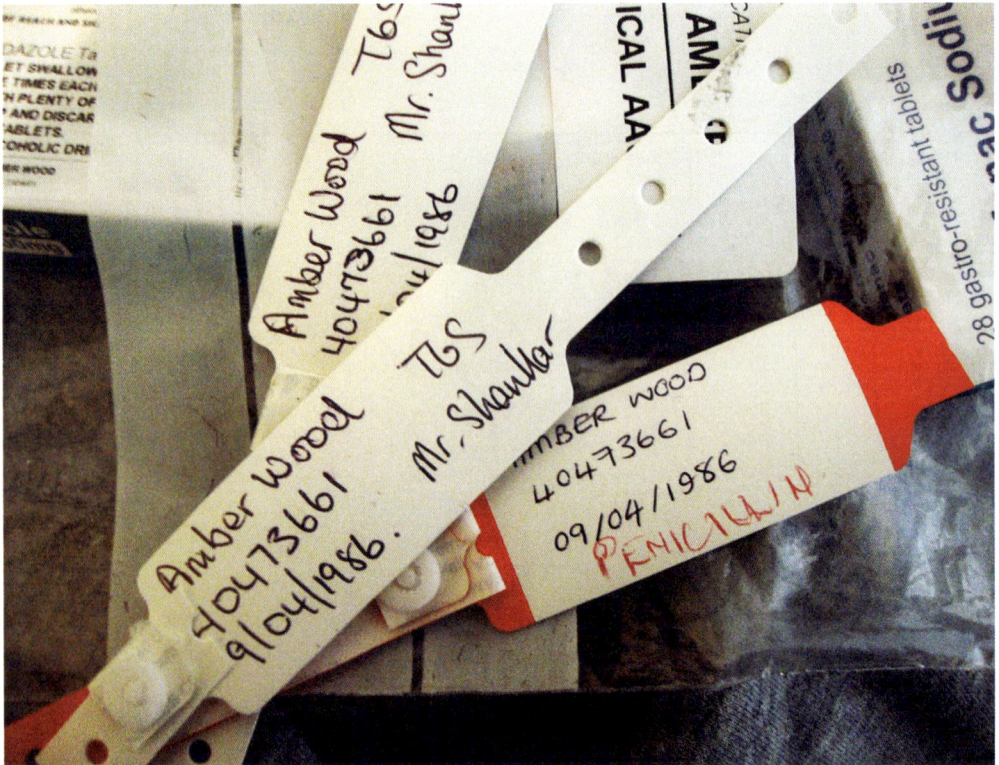

4

3. Ronald Wong, US Embassy, Nine Elms. Inclusion Zone re-appropriates the exclusive security perimeter of the embassy by introducing three stratified perimeters for different embassy user groups.

4. Amber Wood, Chelsea Barracks. Polyclinic, appendicitis: a direct experience of the NHS.

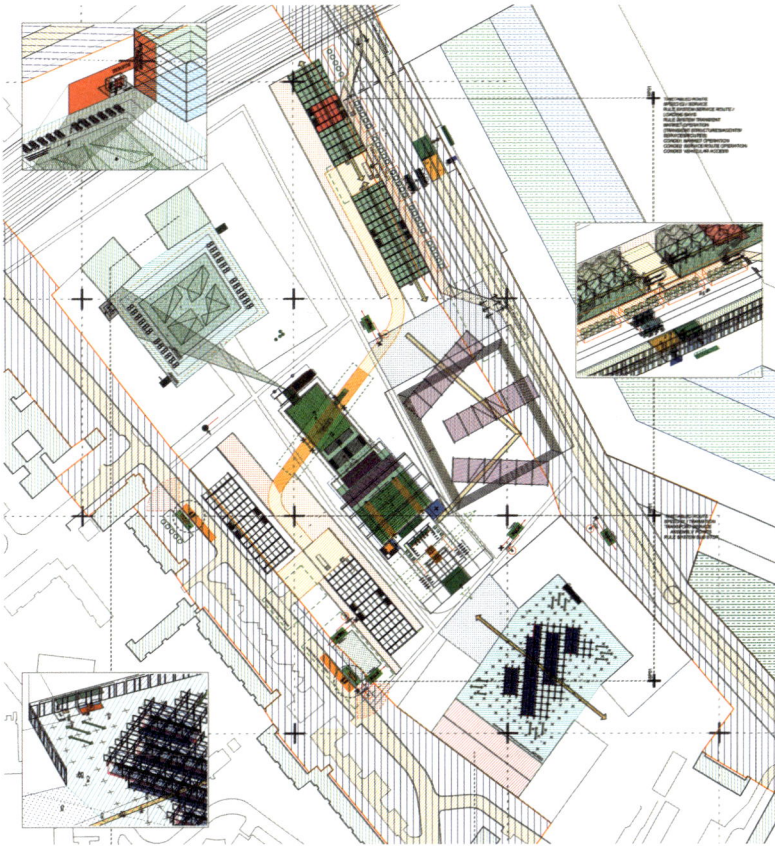

5

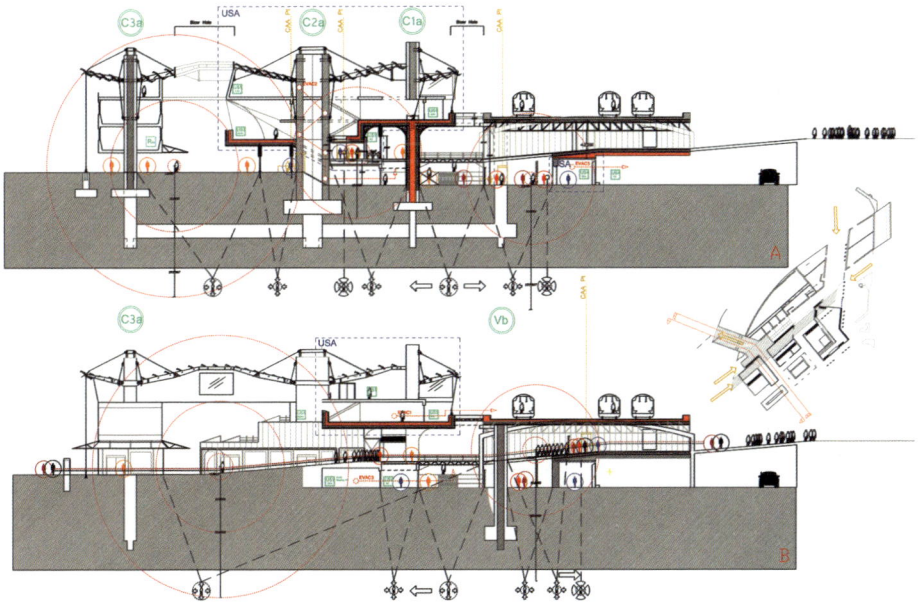

6

5. Kleopatra Chelmi, Nine Elms Opportunity Area. Urban Speeds, two routes and rule systems, slow and fast, demarcate a cultural strip that activates the surrounding context.

6. Nick Simcik-Arese, US Embassy, Nine Elms. Dislocating the Fortress challenges the colocation strategy currently adopted by the US Embassy design policy by proposing an open security framework of public space.

157

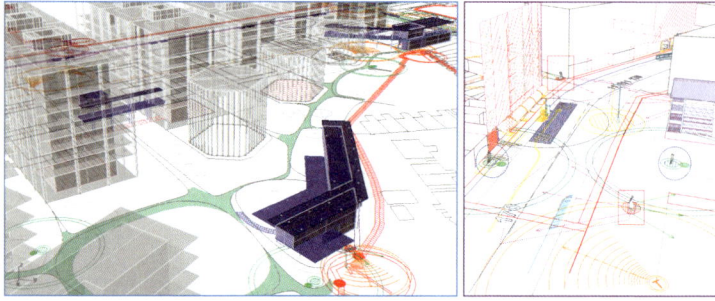

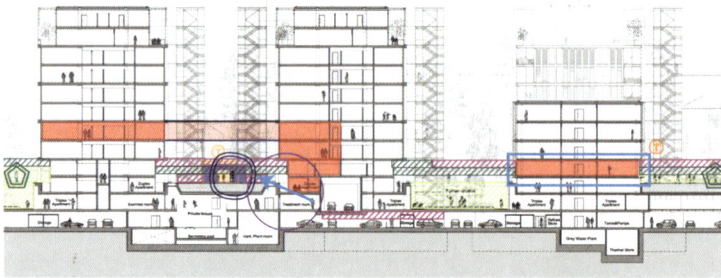

7

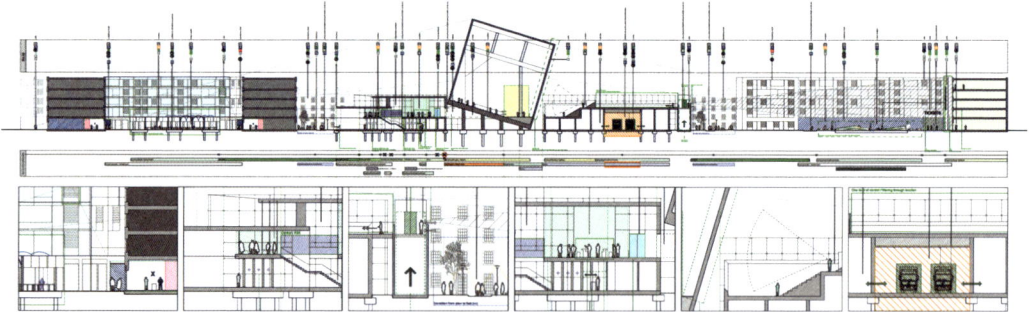

8

9

7. Amber Wood, Chelsea Barracks. Polyclinic adapts
new health care provisions in order to generate new
spatial arrangements, operative systems and institutional
perimeters.

8. Kleopatra Chelmi, Nine Elms Opportunity Area
Urban Speeds
9. Mita Solanki, Nine Elms Opportunity Area, Urban Hub

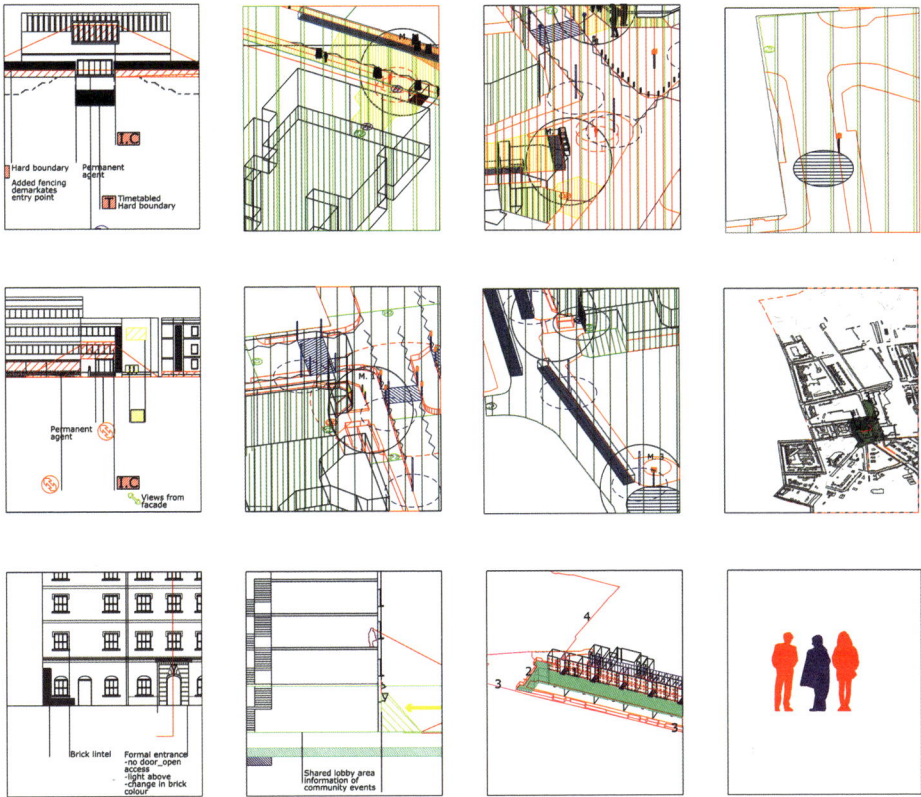

10

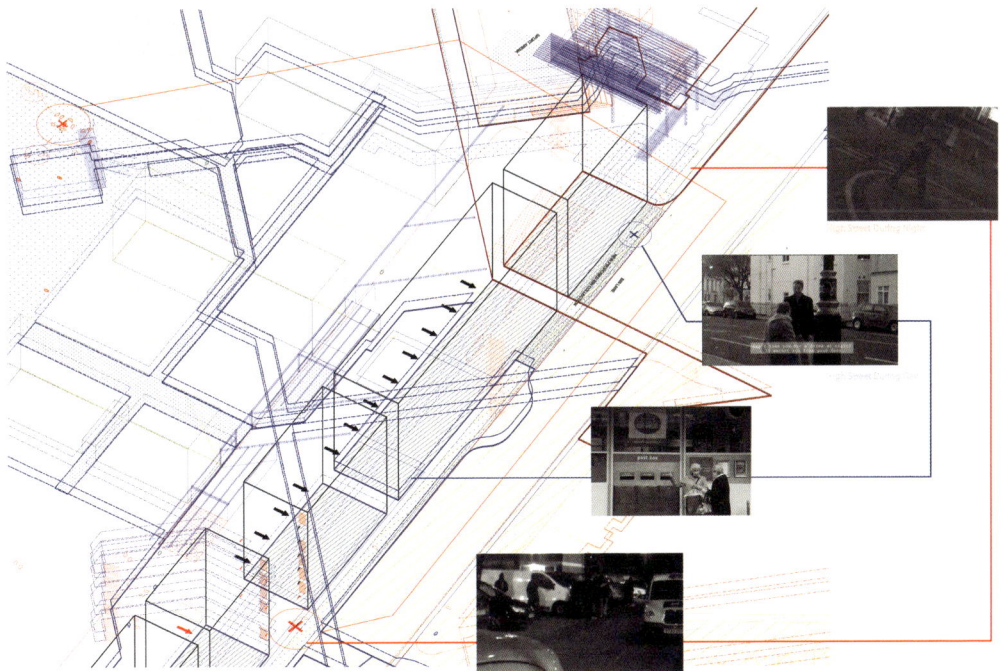

11

10. Larissa Begault, Chelsea Barracks. Reconfigured Institution physically overlaps with the potentially exclusive masterplan and also changes the perceptually rigid boundaries of institutional organisations.

11. Merlin Eayrs, Lupus High Street, Pimlico. High Street speculates on possible ways of designing for two different tribes, epitomised by Hoodies and Grannies, using the same space.

DIPLOMA 11

Micro City Phase 3

What kind of an architecture will our city leave us to design?

Continuing a preoccupation with the post-infrastructural peripheries of London, the unit focused on the area around Whitechapel – a fringe of the city swayed gently by autonomous development, property speculation and the steady decline in industry.

These fluctuations have left the area with a strange accumulation of leftover space, service networks and incomplete urban narratives. By drawing the actuality of this Bataillean 'dust', the unit compiled a matrix of fragments, speculating on their socio-spatial potential whilst reinterpreting the city as a catalogue of beautifully incomplete objects.

By indexing – and then collaging together – the surplus, the historical, the anticipated urban condition, students were able to imagine alternative futures for Whitechapel's major transitions: a super-block extension to the Royal London Hospital and the subterranean tunnelling of Crossrail. Students explored their designs by borrowing from reverse urban engineering, making and remaking the city through drawing, collage and model, the latter used to explore new structural vocabularies and their associated textural details.

Proposals occupy the realm between localised service structures and re-imagined infrastructural typologies, reinvigorating the dge conditions produced by proposed masterplans and explicating intricate cross-utilisations of public facility and service infrastructure, each mindful of the formulation of an inner-city based prototype architecture: the micro city, whereby the exceptions within the city survive to represent a new spatial anthology.

Supplementary investigations this year included: reworking Friedrich Kiesler's Endless House, Brussels fieldwork, two Tokyo workshops on urban erasure and infrastructural possibility, and frequent testing of materials at Hooke Park.

UNIT MASTER
Shin Egashira

STUDENTS
Umberto Ballardi Ricci
Michael James Griffiths
Sarah-Louise Susan Huelin
Kanto Iwamura
Taebeom Kim
Jon Charles Lopez
Nicola Jayne
Amelia Luck
Jussi Taneli
  Mansikkamaki
Nathaniel Mosley
Aimee O'Carroll
Yuko Odaira
Jiehwoo Seung
Erlend Skjeseth
Silvana Taher

SEMINARS AND WORKSHOPS
Shigeru Aoki
Brian Hatton
Hugo Hinsley
Grahame Shane
Yoshiharu Tsukamoto

GUEST CRITICS
Rubens Azevedo
Miraj Ahmed
Larry Barth
Nicolas Boyarsky
Peter Carl
David Greene
Eugene Han
Tom Heneghan
Kisa Kawakami
Olaf Kneer
Makoto Motokura

Hikaru Nissake
Masao Noguchi
Stefano Rabolli Pansera
Natasha Sandmeier
Fred Scott
Theodore Spyropoulos
Brett Steele
Signy Svalastoga
Charles Tashima
Andrew Yeu

1

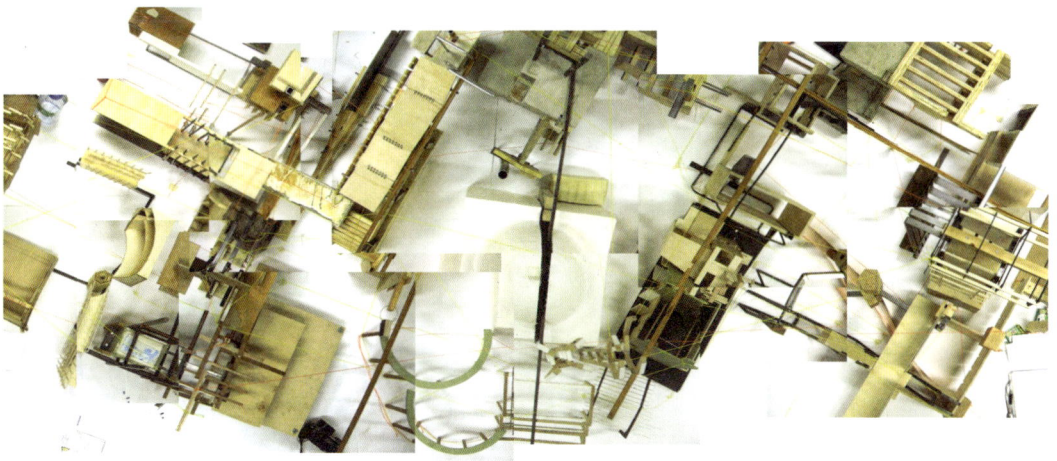

2

1. Whitechapel city samples are de-collaged and rearranged into micro urban components. Families of models at a scale of 1:50 were reproduced in November 2010.

2. Whitechapel reaggregated into a series of urban junctions. Collective working collage, scale 1: 50.

161

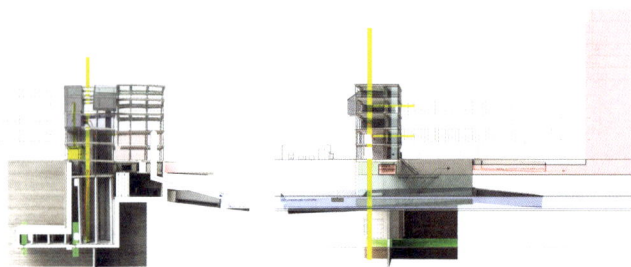

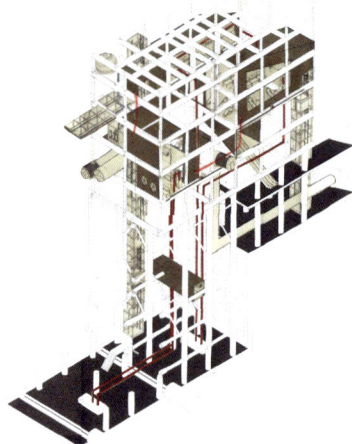

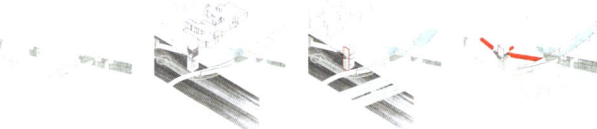

3

4

3. Aimee O'Carroll, Whitechapel Urban Artery
Exposing the historical infrastructure of the mail rail as a 'medi-rail' for London and adaptive reuse of the former East District Post Office building. A new infrastructural hub for the distribution of medical components.

4. Jon Charles Lopez
A groundwater recovery system for Crossrail that supplies a series of underground bathing pools and public spaces, activating and enabling unexpected collisions of time, structure and ritual.

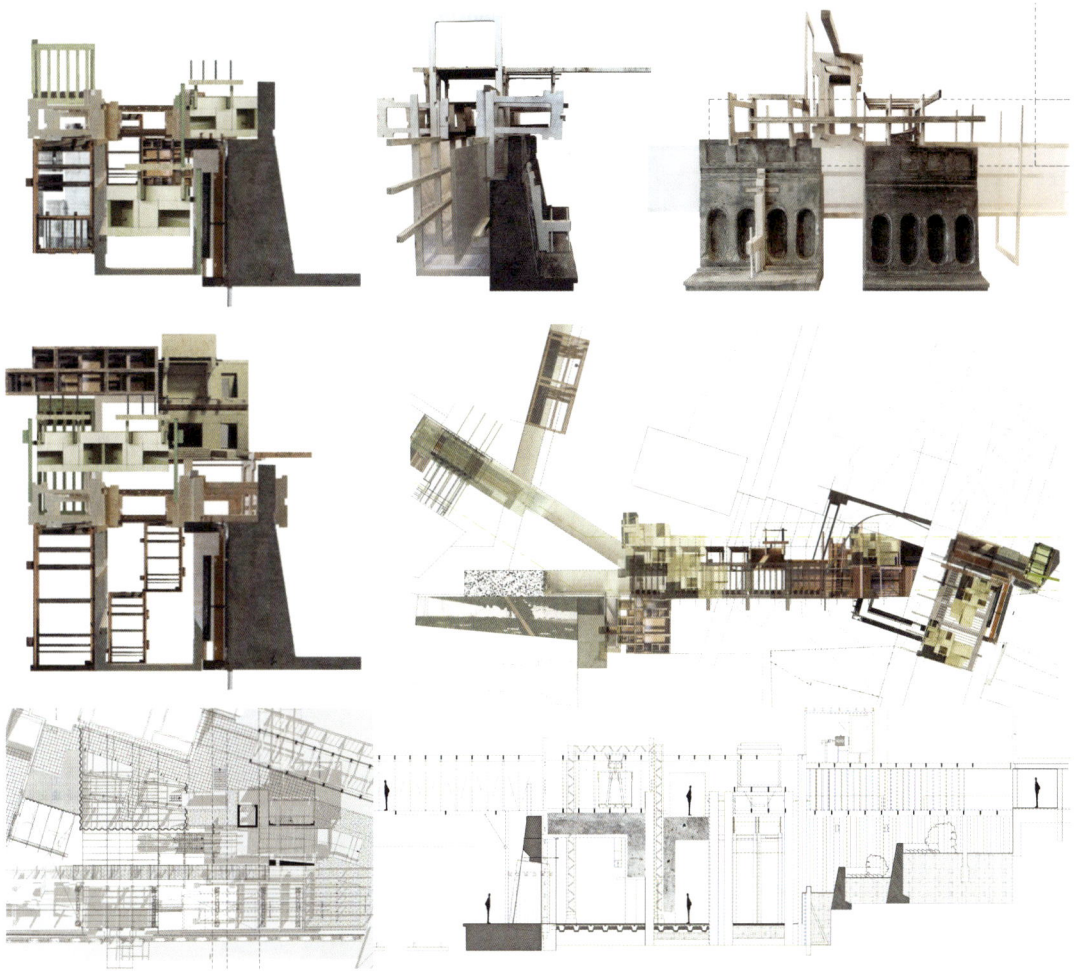

5

6

5. Erlend Skjeseth, Choreographed Construction Site.
Exploring the formation of void spaces at in-between
stages of construction and adaptable structures that will
respond to the changing context, improving public access
to existing local facilities.

6. Kanto Iwamura, Deeper City.
Deeper City proposes to dig deep into the old city of
Whitechapel to create a new Crossrail typology for mixed
flows of ventilation, a train station and public library.

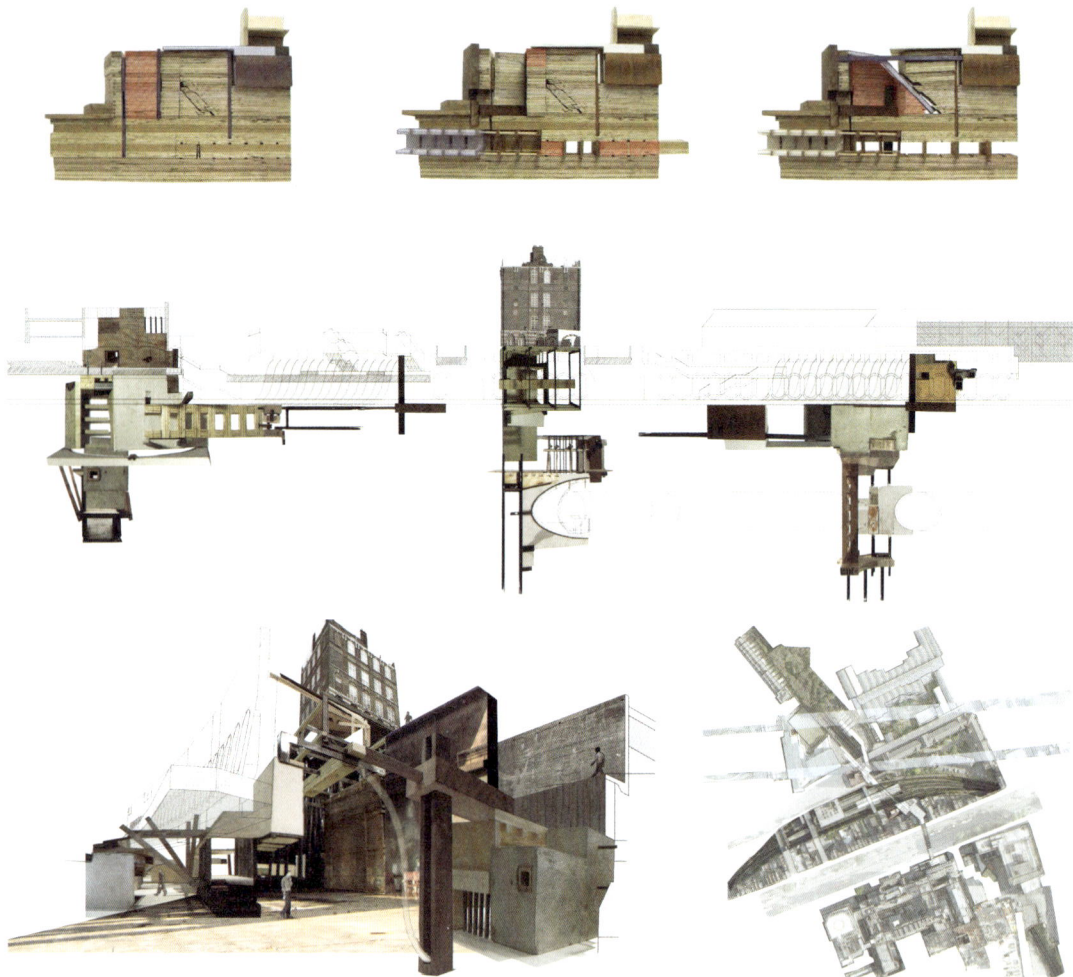

7

8

7. Michael James Griffiths, Urban Jig
The permanence of the city is sustained by an endless
series of deconstructions and recompositions; a blurring
between built and un-built.

8. Taebeom Kim, Reclaimed Void
Demolition as un-urban phenomenon. Speculating
on the preservation of incomplete urban fragments
inside the Royal London Hospital expansion zone.

9

10

9. Jiehwoo Seung, city inside Royal London Hospital
The proposal intervenes in current development phases
and reorganises infrastructural space through a series
of public activities.

10. Taneli Mansikkamaki, Creative Micro City
An architectural response to urban gentrification
processes, focusing on forgotten industrial buildings
and creative micro businesses in London's fringes.

DIPLOMA 12

Nip & Tuck

Diploma 12 pursues an agenda to explore new spatial and social constellations through engagement with infrastructure. This year we developed a network of public bridging systems for the Los Angeles Metropolitan region.

Before the advent of modernism infrastructure was integrated within the experience of cities and buildings. The development of modernist regional planning practices, such as those enacted by Robert Moses in New York, changed all that. According to the modernist paradigm, urban space consists of a series of rationalised and functionally distinct operations. Network transit projects in this tradition built to a regional or national scale tend to sever connections at a local one. Resulting scalar disjunctions and social fragmentations produce 'splintering urbanism', in which the local public realm is ill served by privately funded large-scale projects.

In response to this condition, and in the context of the infrastructural renewal currently underway in the US, we explored alternative infrastructures in Los Angeles. The unit addressed the potential of architecture to mediate between the different scales across which networked infrastructures are mapped, exploring the capacity to accommodate an array of local public interests as well as demands for global forms of connectivity. To this end, the typically linear trajectory and narrow functionality of the bridge typology was reoriented toward a field condition in which multiple programmes are articulated.

The unit travelled to LA to study the complex conditions of infrastructural settings and to visit a range of modernist and contemporary buildings as well as architectural practices working in the region.

Each student selected a condition that runs along, over, under and/or across an existing freeway in terms of structure, topography, geometry, programme and potential. Accordingly, we employed the diagram and the index as methodological tools through which to read and reconfigure these conditions.

Exploiting architecture's capacities to fuse the functional, the projective and the spiritual, Diploma 12 proposes visionary material structures that transpose 'freeway' into a sustainable and inclusive future.

UNIT STAFF
Holger Kehne
Jeffrey Turko

TECHNICAL TUTOR
Federico Rossi

STUDENTS
George Barer
Ville Saarikoski
Fei Wu
Gustav Dusing
Li Gan
Nicos Yiatros
Oliviu Logojan-Ghenciu
Mark Chan
Elena Gaydar
Rosanna Kwok
Tom Lea

Jiatian (Vincent) Gu
Nicholas Ho

Acknowledgments:
Robert Thum
Franklin Lee
Olaf Kneer
Charles Tashima
Brett Steele
Wolf Mangelsdorf
Nate Kolbe
Mehran Gharleghi
Evan Greenberg
Eva Castro
Hitoshi Abe
Marcelo Spina
Georgina Huljich
Tom Wiscombe
Kivi Sotamaa

Dana Cuff
Lorcan O'Herlihy
Duncan Nicholson
Eric Owen Moss
Mark Lee
Sharon Johnston
Andrew Batay-Csorba,
Morphosis
Sci Arc
UCLA School of
Architecture
Efrén García Grinda
Cristina Díaz Moreno
Jonas Lundberg
Andrew Yau
Anne Save de Beaurecueil
Dora Sweijd

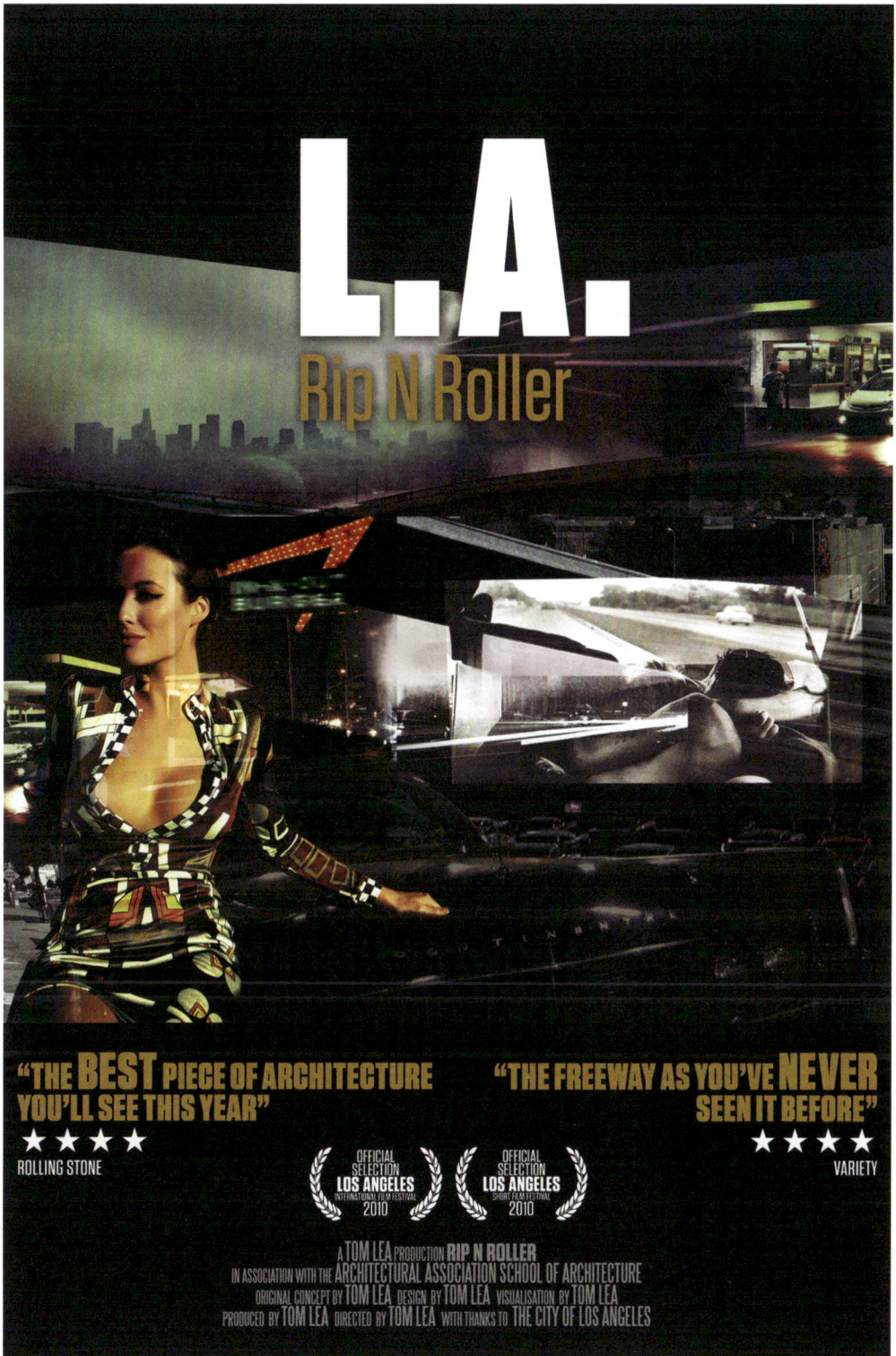

L.A.
Rip N Roller

"THE **BEST** PIECE OF ARCHITECTURE YOU'LL SEE THIS YEAR"
★★★★
ROLLING STONE

"THE FREEWAY AS YOU'VE **NEVER** SEEN IT BEFORE"
★★★★
VARIETY

OFFICIAL SELECTION
LOS ANGELES
INTERNATIONAL FILM FESTIVAL
2010

OFFICIAL SELECTION
LOS ANGELES
SHORT FILM FESTIVAL
2010

A TOM LEA PRODUCTION RIP N ROLLER
IN ASSOCIATION WITH THE ARCHITECTURAL ASSOCIATION SCHOOL OF ARCHITECTURE
ORIGINAL CONCEPT BY TOM LEA DESIGN BY TOM LEA VISUALISATION BY TOM LEA
PRODUCED BY TOM LEA DIRECTED BY TOM LEA WITH THANKS TO THE CITY OF LOS ANGELES

1. Tom Lea, LA Rip N Roller
Shredding and interweaving the Hollywood freeway
101 with Hollywood's walk of fame beneath it creating
multiple filmic sequences and programmatic interstices
that transform a splintering infrastructure into a
glamorous and densified public network.

2

3

2 & 3. Tom Lea, Santa Monica Interlace – a new end to
route 66 that interlaces traffic movement and programme
into an infrastructural civic landscape creating a new
dynamic hierarchy that transforms a service corridor into
an extension of the pier itself.

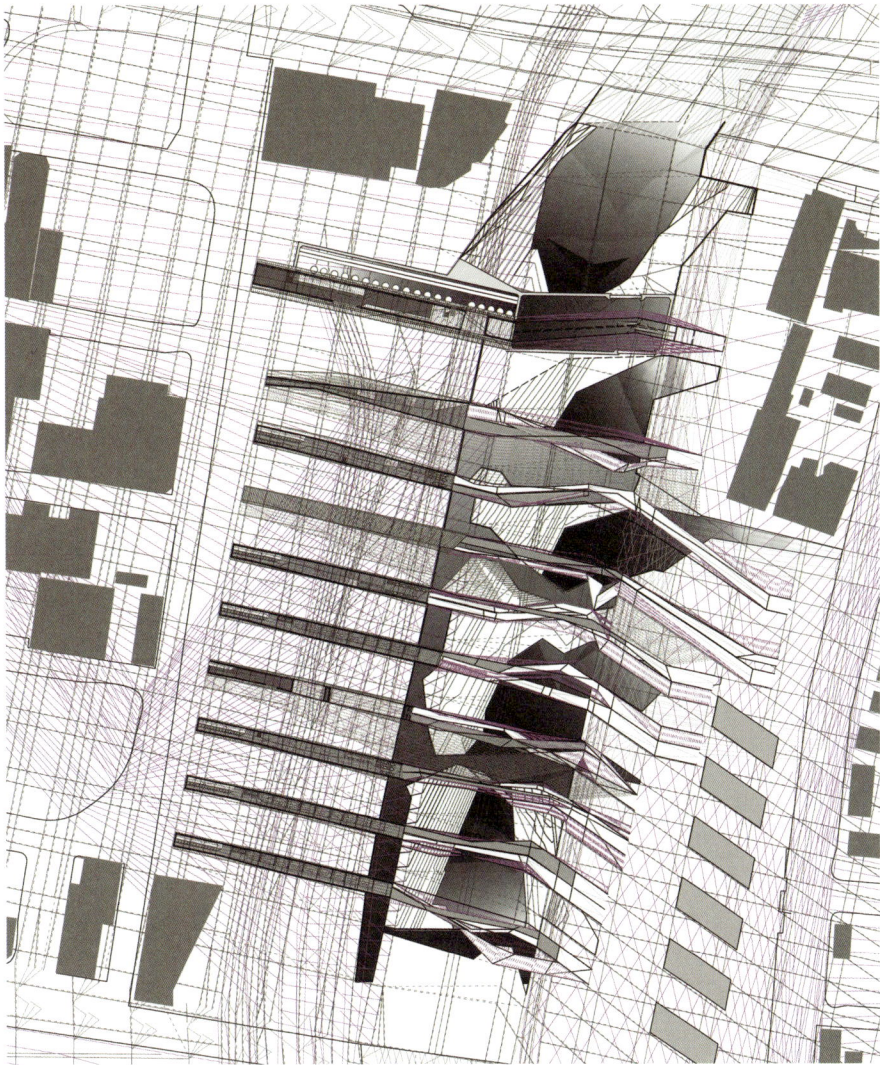

4

5

4. George Barer, Landuse Index
Steps towards the re-use of the archaic LA riverbed as a networking infrastructure. Through manipulation of the given landuse a projection of information is made into the riverbed, resulting in a blurring of territories and clues towards potential connections.

5. George Barer, Waterway Row
The implementation acts as a catalyst for the redevelopment of a centrally located yet underused area. A new urban park is proposed within the riverbed, stitching pedestrian access across the river and incorporating an interwoven public-civic / commercial-private territory manipulation.

169

8

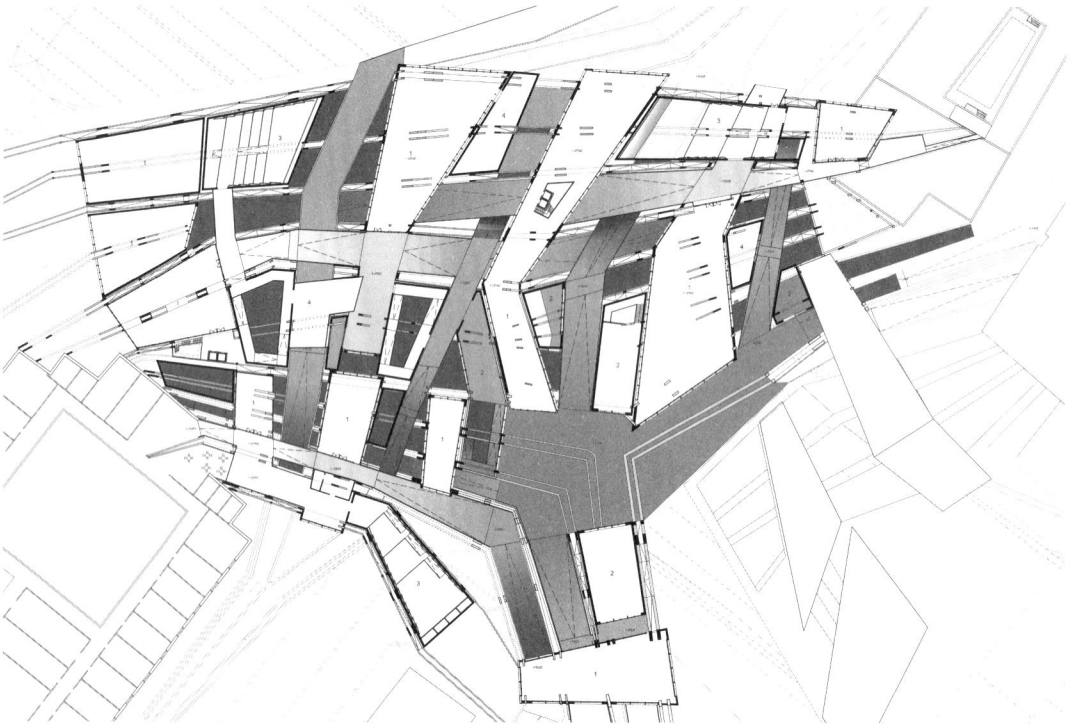

9

8. Elena Gaydar, Depth of Field: enclosures that avoid gestalt. A structural tissue that can help to colonise and integrate the abundant terrain vagues and disjunctions in the inner city fabric of LA.

9. Fei Wu, Superposition of Urban Fabric Embodiment and Index. To question the lifestyle of LA, an innovative public leisure infrastructure is inserted on the boundary of the city centre to re-build the connections between the residents' daily events.

170

6

7

6. Gustav Duesing, Station Stoop
The project seeks to converge transport links into a new urban core that refocuses its two-dimensional suburban neighbourhood. Through the manipulation of existing organisational patterns the project enables vital exchanges between different modes of transportation.

7. Gustav Duesing, Station Stoop
A section-active system enables connections and filters between multi-scale transport networks and local programmes and street life.

DIPLOMA 13

The Reformed Grammar of Ornament

Dip 13's collection of experimental ornament for the twenty-first century takes off from Owen Jones's seminal *The Grammar of Ornament* (1856). Each student developed a catalogue of iconographic, naturalist, geometric and materialist ornament for a new embassy in central London. Their Reformed Grammar of Ornament was developed into architectural details pertaining to structure, circulation, surfaces, joints, openings and services. From these established *loci* of ornamental performance a new ornate architecture emerged. Idiosyncratic ornamental languages were tested against a highly charged site, the complexities of national identity, contemporary political and cultural desires of representation, aesthetic traditions and functional requirements for beauty, meaningful expression and material sophistication.

In Regent's Park, David convoluted the territory into a neo-art-nouveau whiplash for a divided post-colonial Belgium. Chen amalgamated Chinese ornamental with English picturesque landscape traditions to create a mountainous twenty-first-century chinoiserie. Eli's Brazilian embassy redeems the material failure of white wall modernism through indigenous ornamental figuration, whereas Fredrik's manga-architecture confronts the obsessive Japanese manipulations of nature with western metamorphic prototypes such as rustication and arboreal structural metaphors. On Belgrave Square, Aram adopted a neo-orientalist approach in designing a sexually charged veil projecting the Turkish habit of nomadic assimilation. Joy's embassy for Thailand reconfigures the neoclassical site by means of Thai ceramic craft and marries it to the western cultivar of the billboard. Alma's system of ornament oscillates between Egypt's ancient fantasy and Islamic presence as it combines figuration based on the lotus with abstract arabesques, while Kai's Chinese embassy employs Semperian concepts to weave an architectural cloak of visual censorship into the site. At New Zealand House on Pall Mall, Eyal created iterations of Dutch hydrophobia in the form of rippling brick curtain walls. Hyun-Young sliced cracked voids through the building, upon which ornamental motifs project the desires of a split Korean nation. Jaime conquered the building's mid-century purity with lavish Mexican neo-churrigueresque ornament in an exemplary process of constructional occupation. Behold the rise of a new world of ornament!

UNIT MASTERS
Oliver Domeisen
Tristan Simmonds

STUDENTS
Fredrik Valdemar Hellberg
Chen Jin
Eli Lui
Aram Mooradian
David Nightingale
Kai Hian Ong
Eyal Shaviv
Jaime Alberto Sol Robles
Joy Natapa Sriyuksiri
Hyun-Young Sung
Alma Wang

Thanks to
Eleftherios Ambatzis, Noam Andrews, Shumon Basar, Edward Bottoms, Mark Campbell, Javier Castañón, Mark Cousins, Michel da Costa Gonçalves, Monia De Marchi, Eugene Han, Francesca Hughes, Sam Jacob, Sam Jacoby, Alex Kaiser, Tobias Klein, Toni Kotnik, Madam Studio, Graham Modlen, Lars Müller, Marianne Müller, Natalie Rozencwajg, Christopher Pierce, Natasha Sandmeier, Tobi Schneidler, Anne Save de Beaurecueil, Hinda Sklar, Thomas Weaver, Mike Weinstock and Marilyn, Belinda, Victoria, Nadine, Tristan, Nick & Joel at the AA. Special thanks to Abraham Thomas at the V&A and Kent Bloomer at Yale for their insights and advice, *Archithese* magazine for their sponsorship, and to Brett Steele and Charles Tashima for their ongoing support.

1. The Reformed Grammar of Ornament
Ornament Plates by Jaime (I, XIV), Kai (II, VII), Eyal (III),
David (IV, IX), Aram (V, VI, XII, XIII), Chen (VIII, XV), Eli
(X, XVI), Alma (XI).

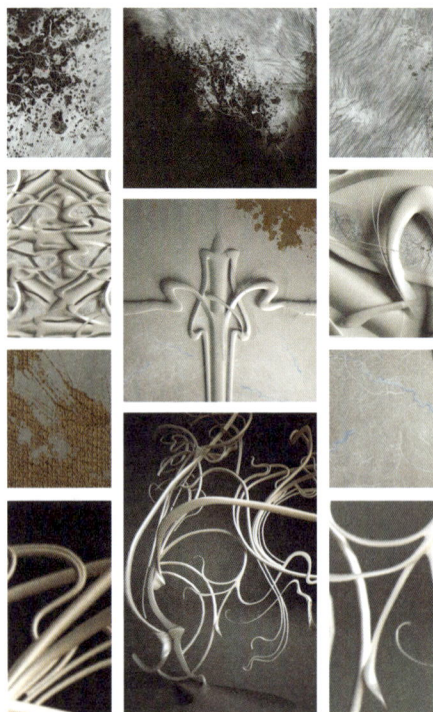

2

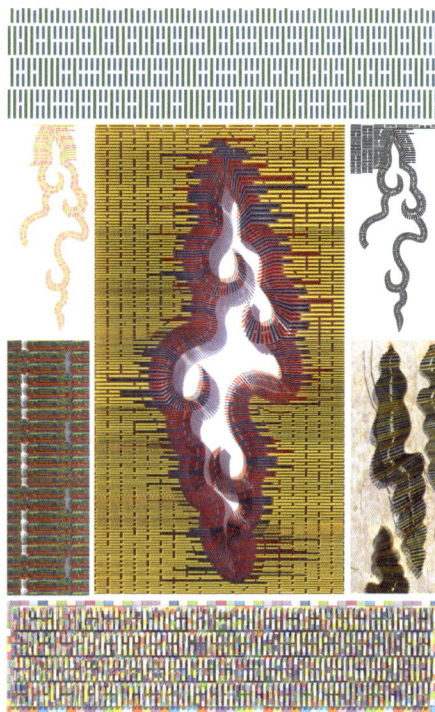

3

4

5

2. David Nightingale, Naturalist Ornament for the Belgian High Consulate in Regent's Park; 3. Hyun-Young Sung, Geometric Ornament for the Korean embassy at New Zealand House, Pall Mall; 4. Fredrik Hellberg, Naturalist Ornament for the Japanese embassy in Regent's Park; 5. Joy Natapa Sriyuksiri, Iconographic Ornament for the Thai embassy on Belgrave Square.

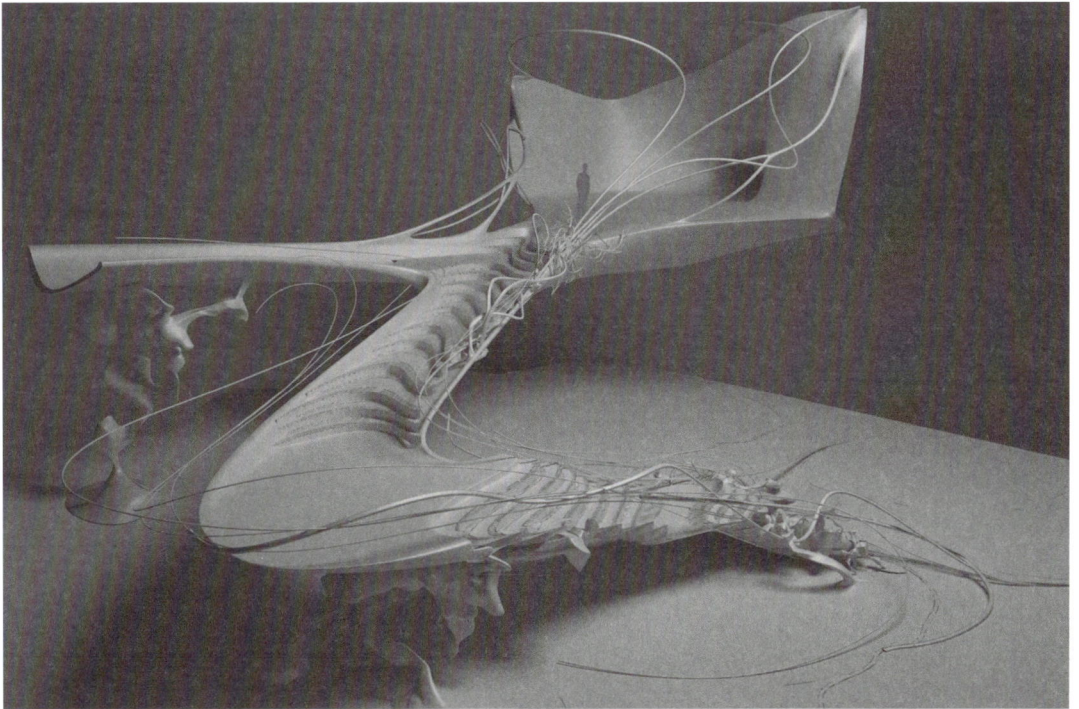

6

7

6. David Nightingale, The Reinvigoration of the Whiplash – grand staircase. An accelerated choreography that structures the movement through the Belgian embassy is drawn from the unifying curvature of art nouveau.

7. Alma Wang, Existing between Dualities – wall detail (drainage). The lithic tectonics of ancient Egypt combine with Islamic copper arabesques to create a rusticated wall fortifying the Egyptian embassy on neo-classical Belgrave Square.

175

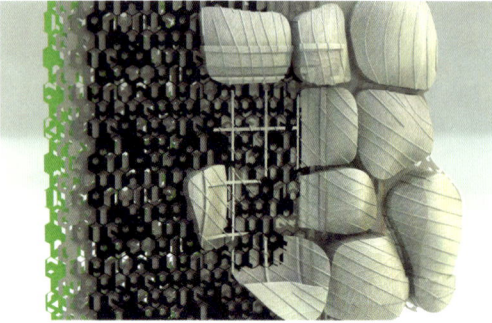

8

9

10

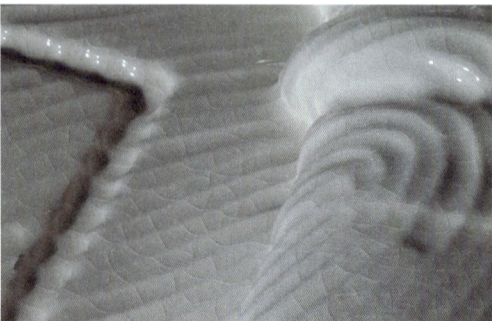

11

12

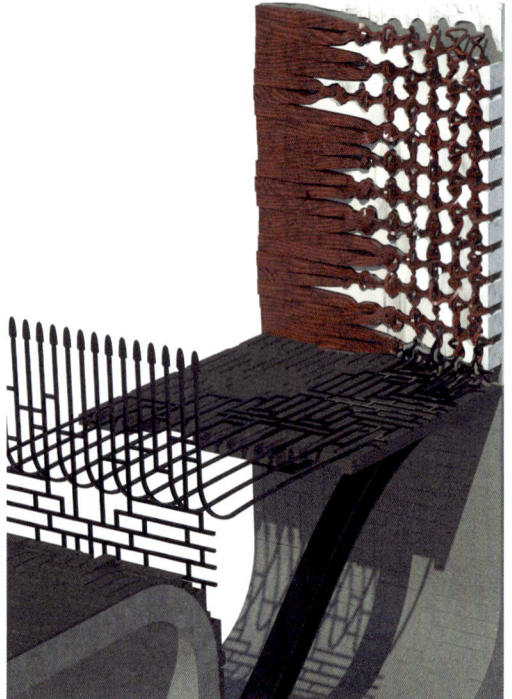

13

8–11. Joy Natapa Sriyuksiri, East meets West: Hybridised Cultures of Economic Demand – manufacture of ceramic facade panels for the Thai embassy, Belgrave Square. The mark of the maker (fingerprint) is left on opposite sides by the Thai craftsman and the CNC mill. 12. Fredrik Hellberg, Naturally Artificial – The Tower of the Folding Stones.

The Japanese embassy's rusticated base dissolves into a kinetic Asanoha pattern that opens with the rising sun. 13. Kai Hian Ong, Keeping Face: Ornament as Textile Mask – entrance detail. Marble, rosewood, cast iron and Portland stone are woven into an impenetrable Semperian veil for the Chinese embassy, Belgrave Square.

14

15

14. Fredrik Hellberg, Naturally Artificial – The Tower of the Folding Stones. Western arboreal structural metaphors are synthesised with origami-*shoji* walls. Manga colours are fed into Owen Jones's polychromatic principles.

15. Jaime Sol Robles, The Neo-Churrigueresque: Ornament as a process of occupation – facade detail. The Mexican embassy infests New Zealand house with the proliferating intricacy of gestural curvature.

DIPLOMA 14

In recent years complex forms, parametric systems of design and diagrams have become the norm in architecture. If these devices promise endless differentiation and adaptability to multiple situations, identities and performances, the results in fact contribute to a monotonous landscape of (value-free) diversity. Against this landscape, Diploma 14 has worked to propose a return to simple forms – not as a retreat into self-referentiality (as in the glossy minimalism of contemporary architecture), but as a polemical way to confront and understand the insurmountability of the city. Instead of naively mimicking urban complexity with architectural complexity, the unit proposes to critically examine urbanity as something that provides architecture with its *raison d'être* while itself remaining irreducible to architectural form.

The design of the Immeuble Cité is intended as an opportunity to put forward innovative and extreme living standards in light of increasingly merging living and working activities.

Issues integral to the design of these buildings are: economy of the means of construction, accessibility, relation between individual and collective spaces, material and structural framework, the dialectic between flexibility and permanence (e.g. no value-free flexibility), the critical relationship between repetition and exception. In addition, the project fundamentally confronts the relationship between poverty and hedonism.

Architecture povera embraces the austerity of form for the sake of affordability. Hedonism concerns the pursuit of pleasure as a fundamental aspect of life. Within our contemporary situation, in which the entirety of existence is dominated by work, hedonism must not be considered as 'consumption' or 'spectacle' (the main modalities of work management today) but is a truly political state of being – one which the philosopher Giorgio Agamben defined as *inoperosità* (a state of unproductivity).

For this reason, the Immeuble Cité must be a contradictory site of extremes in which managerial efficiency and the organisation of collective space coexist with the possibility of escape.

UNIT MASTERS
Pier Vittorio Aureli
Barbara Campbell-Lange
Fenella Collingridge

STUDENTS
4th Year
Kim Bjarke
Calvin Chua
Carlos H. Matos
Anton Medyna
Katrina Anne Muur
Jerome Tsui

5th Year
Cristina Asenjo del Río
Sea Eun Cho
Fabrizio Matillana
Jorgen Tandberg
Simon Whittle
Johnny Gao Yuxian

Thanks to:
Peter Carl
Javier Castañón
Will Hunter
Chris Lee
Mauro Parravicini
Peter Salter
Brett Steele
Charles Tashima
Carlos Villanueva Brandt
Elia Zenghelis

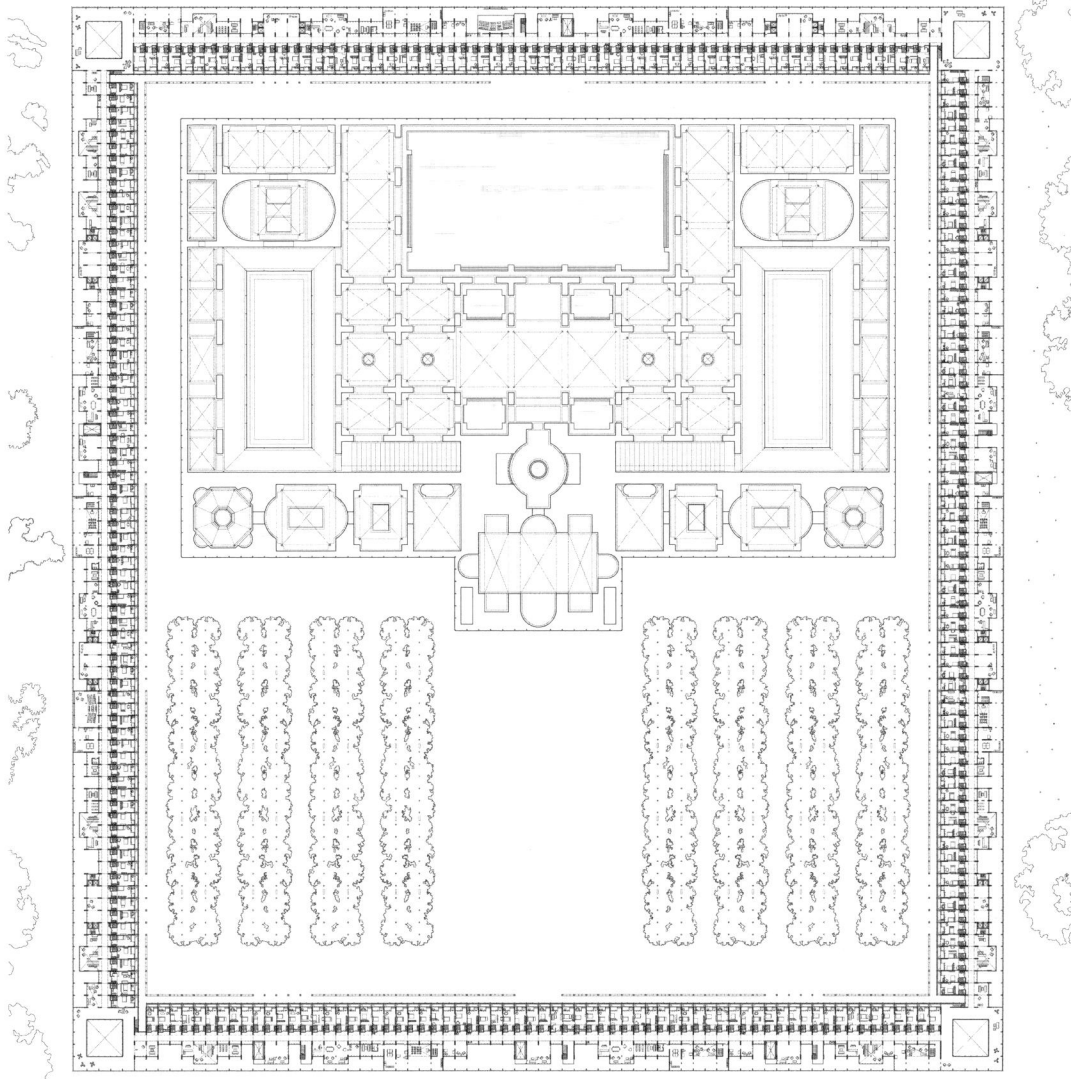

1

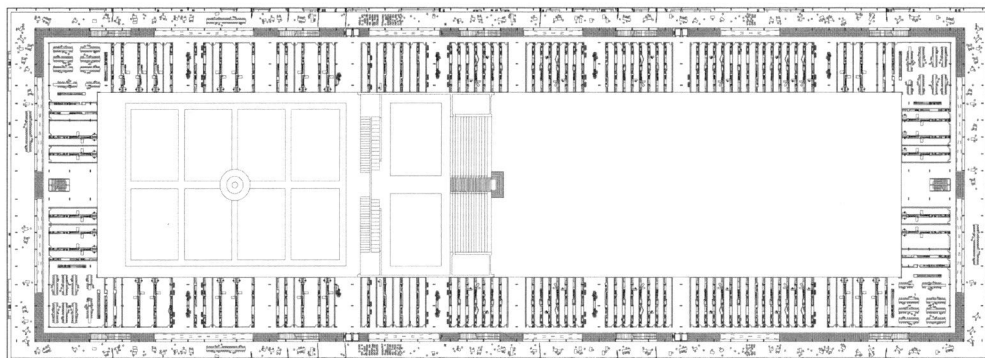

2

1. Cristina Asenjo del Rio
The Immeuble Cité appropriates the form and
programmatic richness of the Roman imperial baths,
addressing the pervasiveness of work and its publicity
through its informality, providing an institution
where communication, in all its forms, prevails as
the source of contemporary productivity.

2. Johnny Gao Yuxian
The project conflates two extreme formal organisations:
the ritualised symmetry of the garden and the relentless
repetition of the frame. The tension between the classicist
courtyard and the modernist living units stages a
spatial paradox where inside is outside, the contained
infinite and the exterior blind.

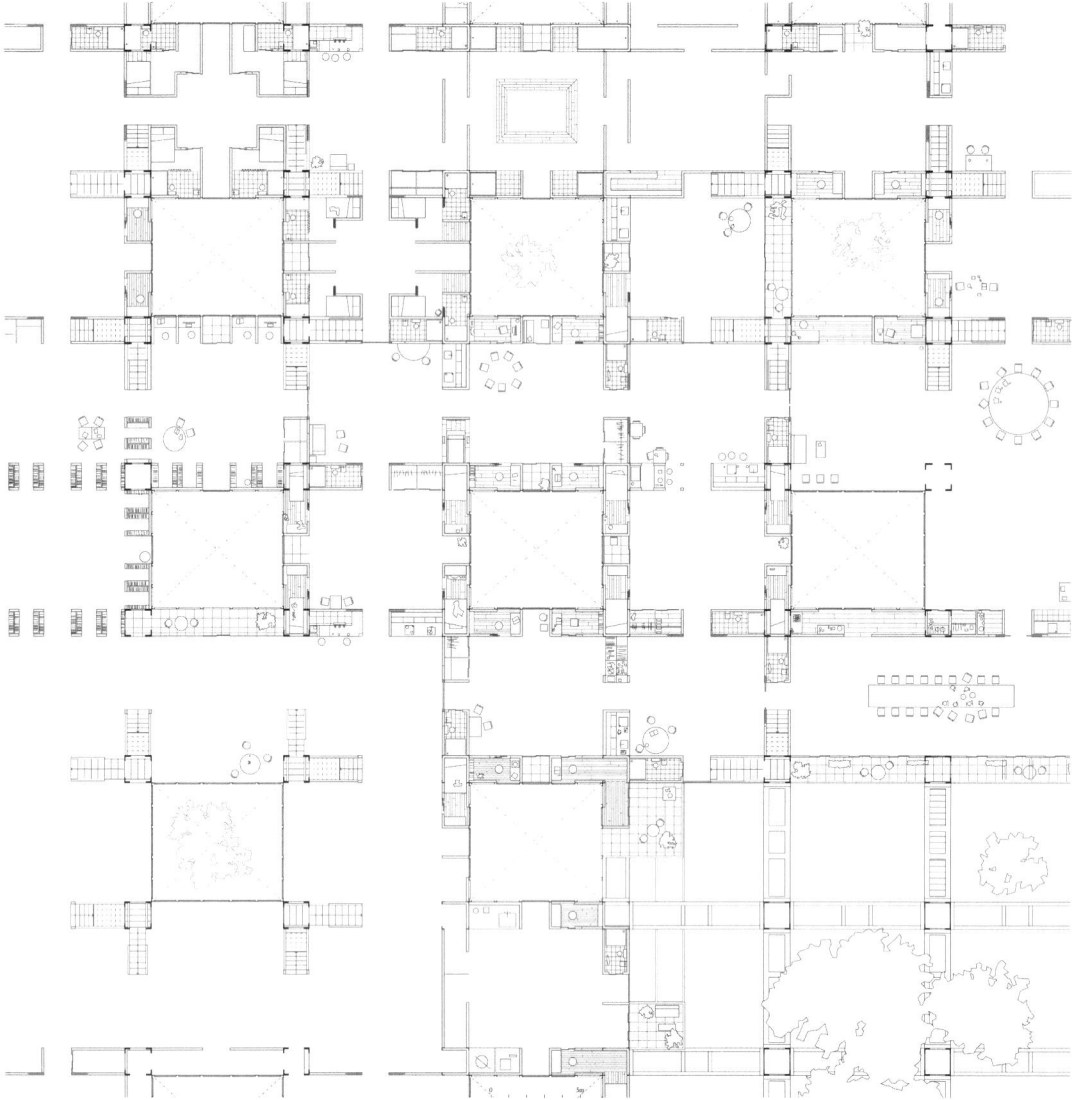

2. Simon Whittle
The project addresses the condition of ubiquitous
production within the intense spectrum of social
relationships. Production today is generated not by
concentration and isolation but by the constant possibility
for relationships. The project takes this condition to the

extreme in order to critically test its spatial consequences.
This involves removing the corridor as the primary
organisational mechanism of the plan and establishing
a matrix of autonomous rooms linked enfilade and
defined by the articulation of the wall.

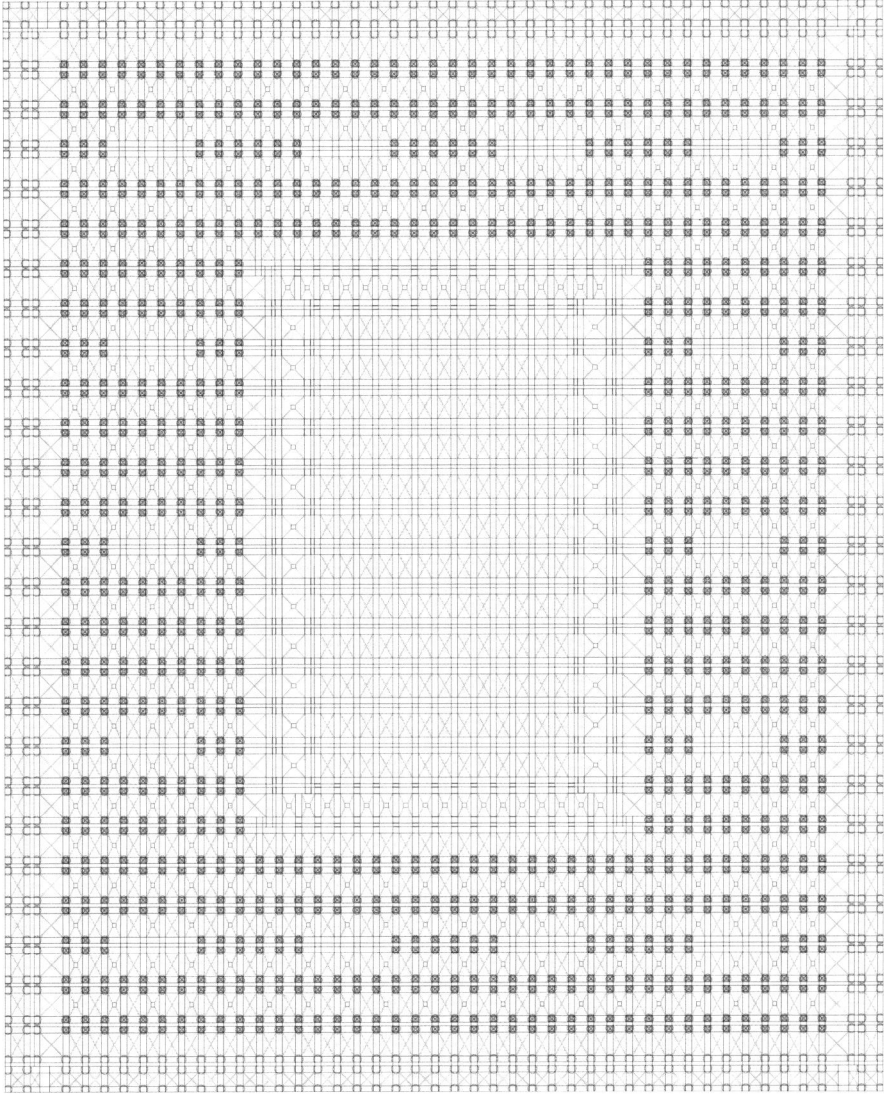

3. Fabrizio Santiago Matillana Sin Joc

Humboldt did not think of the university as a machine for producing professionals or for finetuning scientific knowledge. For him, what was fundamental was the pursuit of truth and the ordering of life around that pursuit. The project represents this condition by merging living and working (studying); the institution is thereby purged of its contemporary internal bureaucratisation by means of a fluid material and circulatory occupancy, the immersion of the individual within the collective.

181

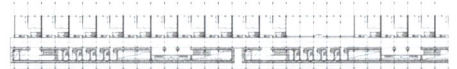

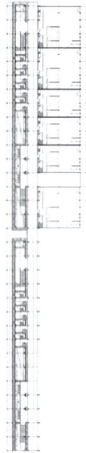

4. Jorgen Tandberg
The proposal's main reference is John Hejduk's North, East, South, West House from 1973; the cynical pragmatism of his project has (paradoxically) as its main goal an almost naive belief in the ability of the generic to cater to different personalities. Where Hejduk separated living areas from circulation areas by means of plain walls, the Immeuble Cité leaves one side of each wall empty, as an extreme form of hedonism.

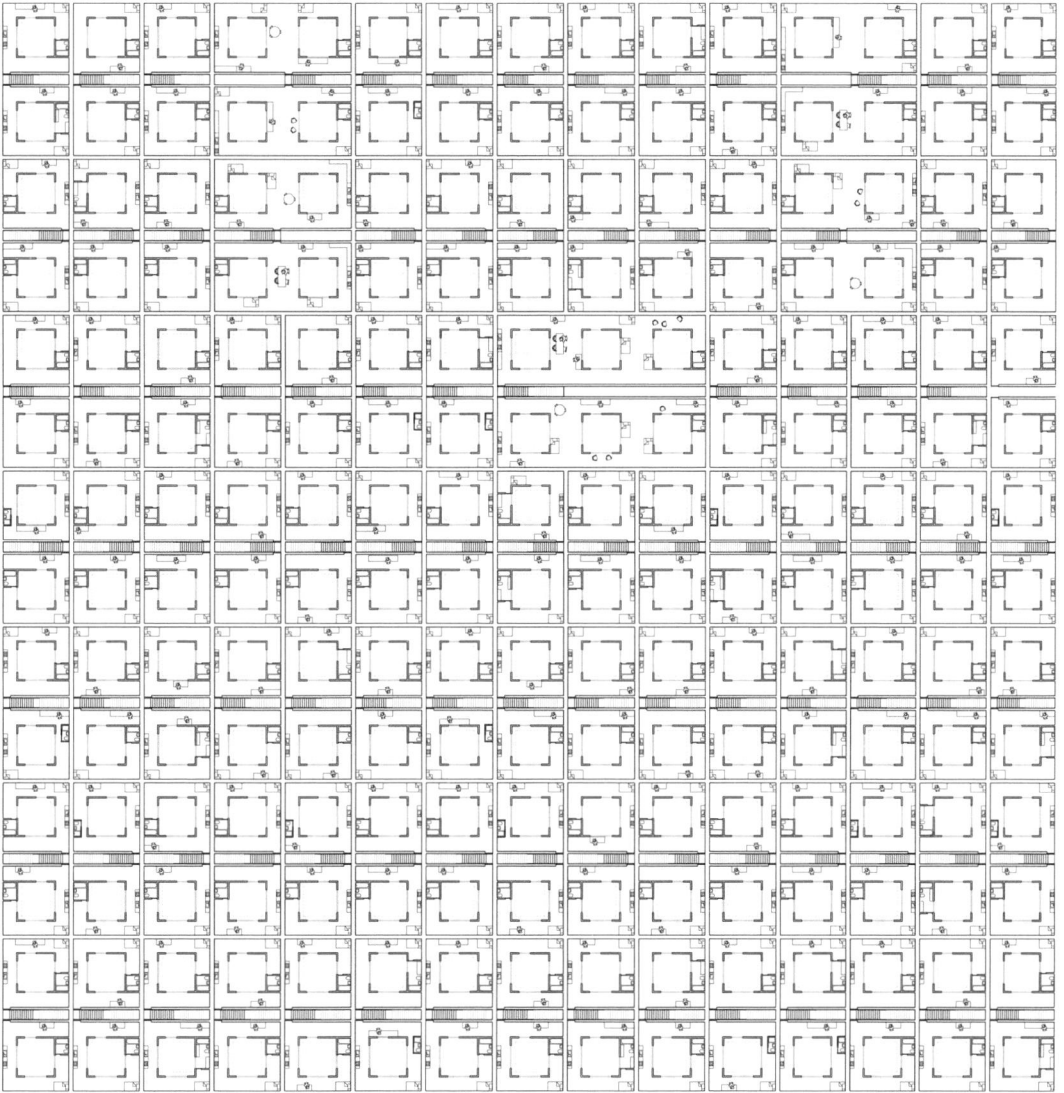

5. Sea Eun Cho

The project is a hypothesis for individual habitation, multiplied to present an extreme condition reliant on an arrangement of rooms without corridors. The aim of organising through the individual is to socially construct a separation where detachment from the ever-present prospect of work is possible and where solitary existence becomes hedonistic. The dichotomy of the project lies within the single unit, formed strictly around the individual and the overwhelming presence of the mass constituted by these single units, thus creating a new collectiveness.

183

DIPLOMA 15

Antique Futures/Future Antiquities II

If the supercontext of Antiquity has always been accessed and reinvented via key supertypes (the ruin, the copy, the collection), then its counter-context, the Future, has always been prescribed via supertypes of technology: data processing, environmental control, transport, telecommunication, representation. After five years of working on extreme cultural contexts, we have found *technology-as-context* to be the most perversely irrational and uncannily fertile of all. As the artifice of the instrumentalist rationale crashes down around our ears, technology (itself fundamentally instrumental) is here ripe for hypercontextual invention: in-built obsolesence, undersirable trait transfer, false autonomy and erroneous calibration are operative strategies for critically reoccupying the space of technology itself.

Nostalgia Outwitted

No less nostalgic than Antiquity, the (ancient) idea of the Future is a minefield of postmodern traps, here outwitted THROUGH ACTIVE INSTRUMENTALISATION OF HISTORICAL RESEARCH. Though selected technologies were studied in their nineteenth-century infancy, their foibles and the precarious futures they promised are still with us today. Thus: the perpetual despair of Theo's Sisyphean landscape is driven by the discovery that early voting machines were designed by gambling engineers – explaining much about recent elections.

Friction in the calculations of early computers is rewritten by Fusako as the friction between calculated and counted, surveyed and surveyor in the ominous melting of the Mer de Glace.

An architecture of suspicion cloaks Jenny's Grand Tour arterial roads for 60kph zootropic kerb crawling. The massive error margin in early telegraph calibration led Sayaka to design an itinerary for getting lost, in more senses than one, in Palermo's quanats. On discovering that Austin's moon towers were effectively sited by the world's first serial killers (only in Texas), Hye Ju has prepared a case for the prosecution for murder of the balconies, dumpsters and traffic lights of Palermo. Identifying the paradoxical similarities between the Ferris Wheel and the panorama machine, and in homage to Byron's Venetian plunge, Angelo proposes a swim through the Grand Canal: a panorama machine for the flâneur aquatic.

UNIT STAFF
Francesca Hughes
Noam Andrews

TECHNICAL SUPPORT
Matthew Wells

STUDENTS
Thomas Cella Burnford
Angelo Sang Hoon Han
Fusako Ishikawa
Sayaka Namba
Eun Joo Park
Hye Ju Park
Theo Wyatt Petrides
Jenny Elisa Schafer

**VISITING CRITICS/
WORKSHOPS**
Lara Belkind, Mark
Campbell, David E. H.
Edgerton, Maria
Federochenko, Adrian
Forty, Eugene Han,
Christine Hawley, Sam
Jacoby, Max Kahlen, Karl
Kjelstrup-Johnson,
Gergely Kovács, Chris
Lee, Monia De Marchi,
Sang Hoon Oh, Anne Save
de Beaurecueil, Charles
Tashima, Franklin Lee,
Carlos Villanueva Brandt,

Alex Warnock-Smith,
Thomas Weaver

Thanks to:
Francesca Arici,
Alessandra Buccheri,
Emmanuelle Cance,
Gabriella Ciancolo, Pierre
Alain Croset, William
Firebrace, Stefano Rabolli
Pansera, Alessandra
Ponte, Maria Chiara Tosi

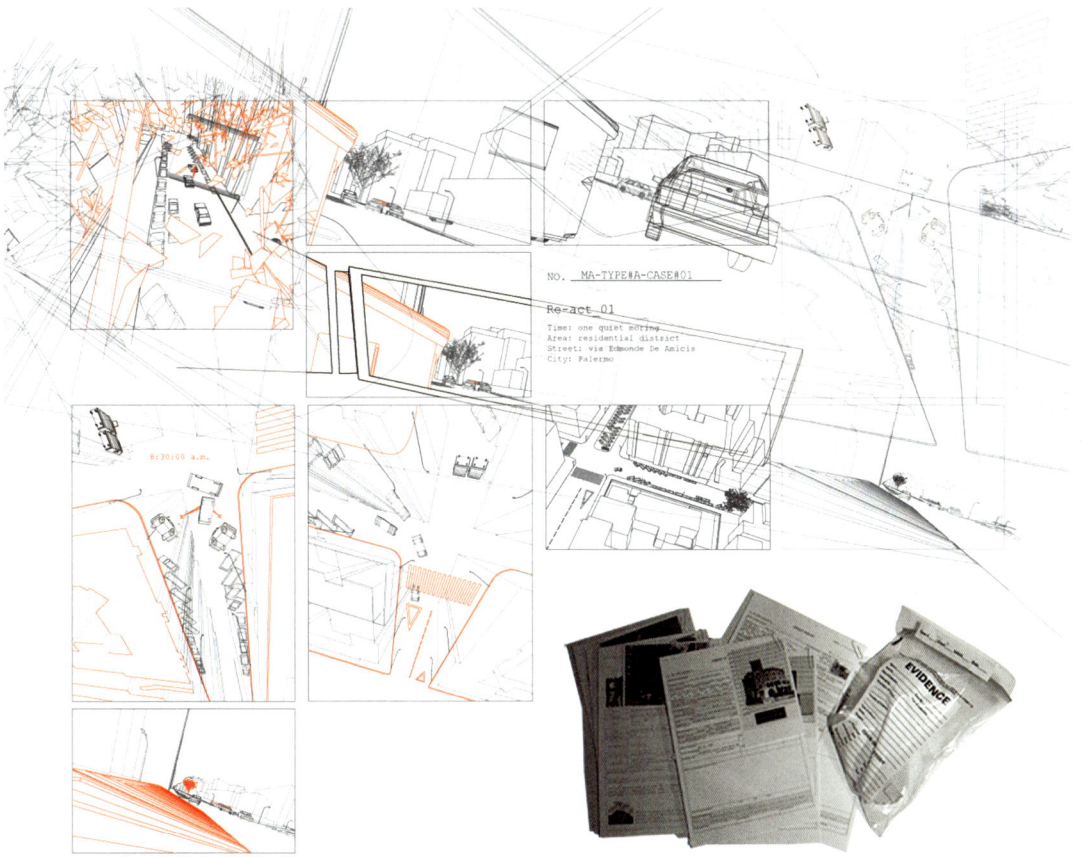

1

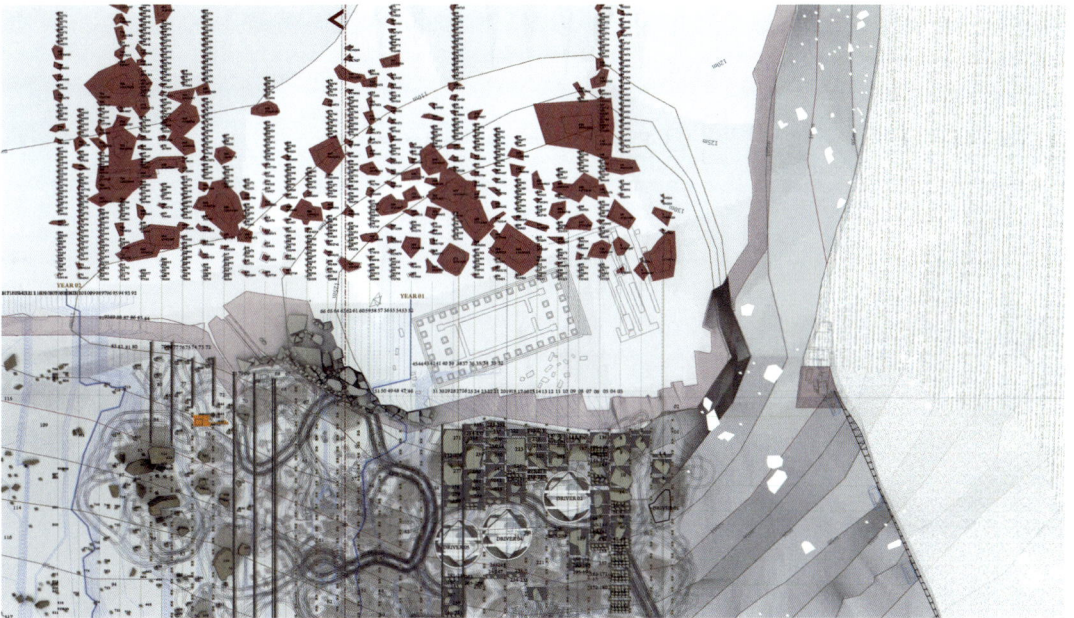

2

1. Hye-Ju Park, People vs. The City of Palermo. Architecture is found to be guilty of enabling high-profile murders leading to its own redevelopment.

2. Theo Wyatt Petrides, The Sisyphean Engine of reconstruction. The endless rebuilding of the ancient city wall at the Valley of the Temples forms an allegory of the democratic ritual of voting.

185

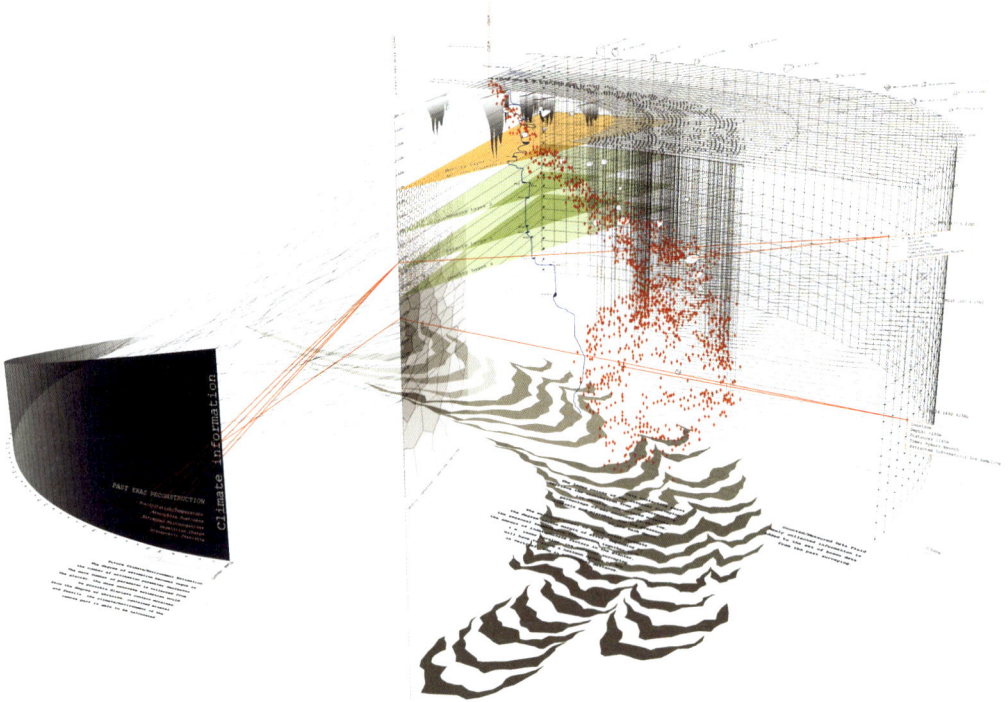

3

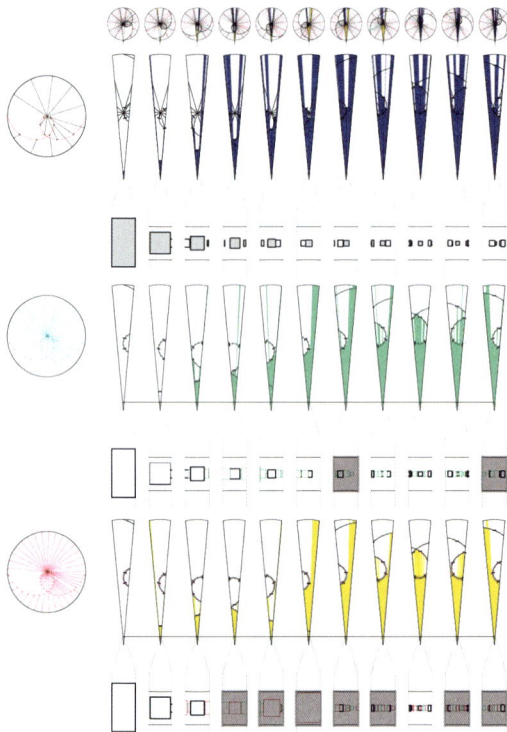

4

3. Fusako Ishikawa, Self-Surveying Glacier
A system of passive surveying installed inside the
Mer de Glace constructs an architecture backwards
from the movements of the glacier.

4. Jenny Elisa Schafer, Line to Loop
A perceptual field of suspicion is constructed through
the occupation of the circular space within the zoetrope.

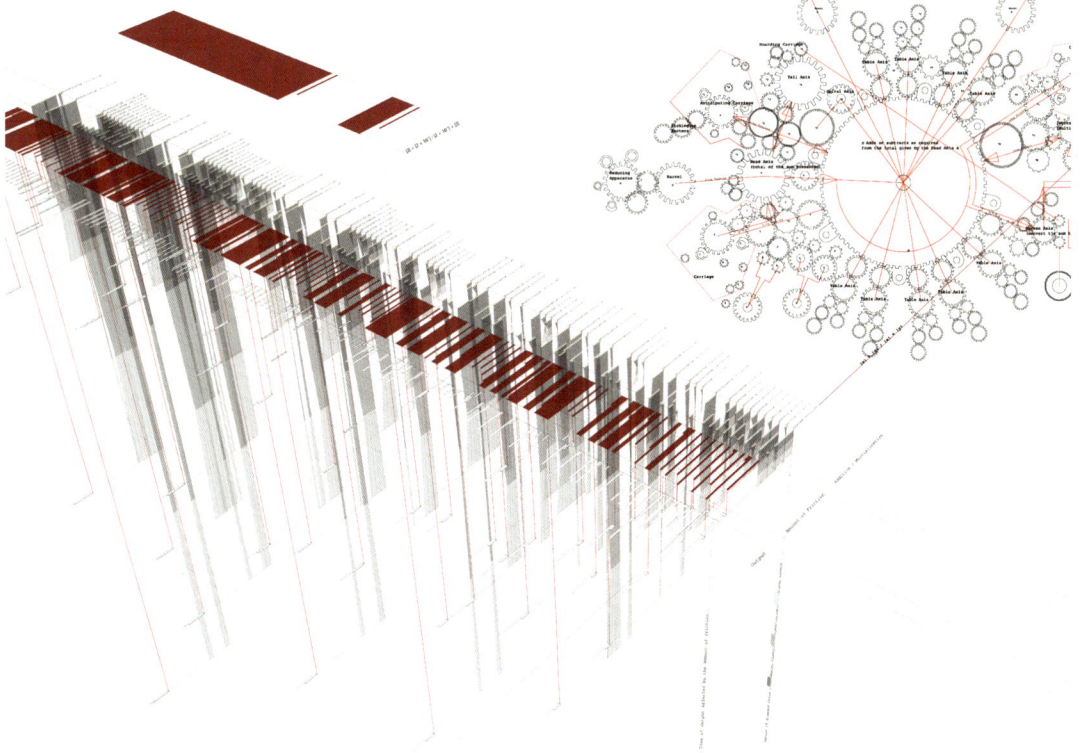

5

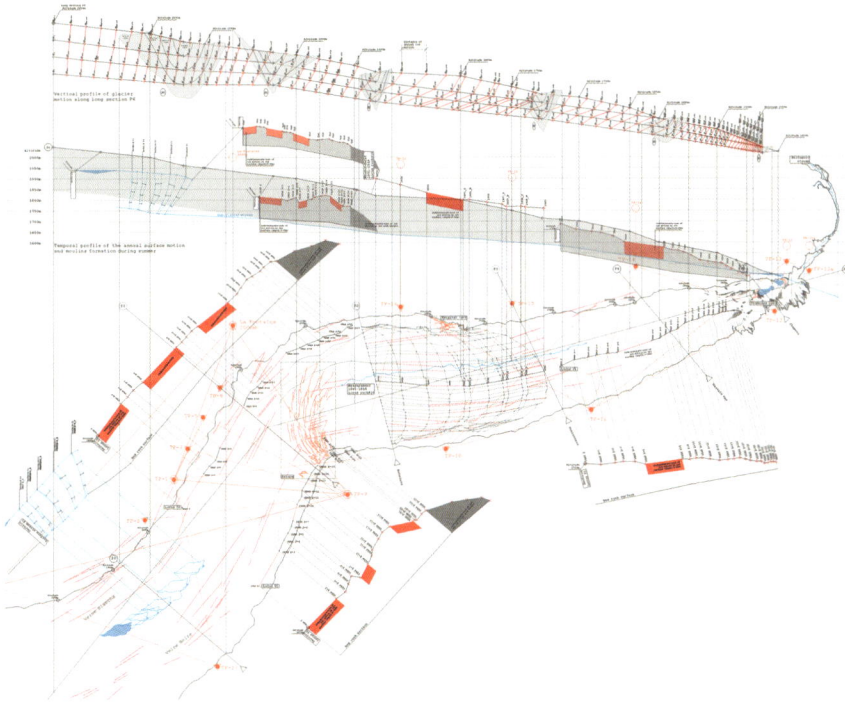

6

5. Fusako Ishikawa, 200 x 2 is not the same as 2 x 200
Calculating is not equal to counting: in anticipation of
Wittgenstein's crisis, Babbage's difference engine
reveals that the amount of energy and time expenditure
of a given calculation relates to the chosen route of the
function through the space of the machine.

6. Fusako Ishikawa, Temporal Glacial Transformations
The behaviour of the Mer de Glace is harnessed to create
a melting architecture of overlapping voids in the ice
using Vallot's nineteenth-century surveying techniques
revamped for the twentieth-century climate crisis.

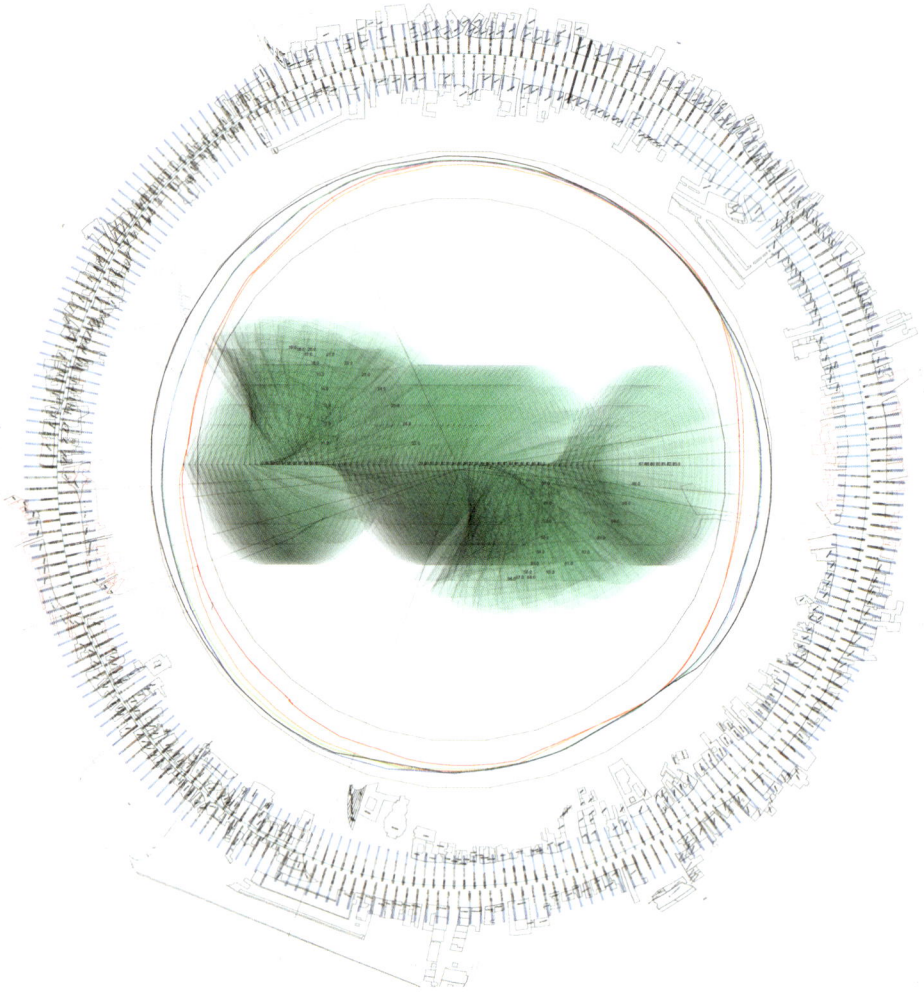

7. Angelo Sang Hoon Han, Lord Byron's Aquatic Venice
Byron's legendary swim down the Grand Canal functions
as a machine of representation and transportation.

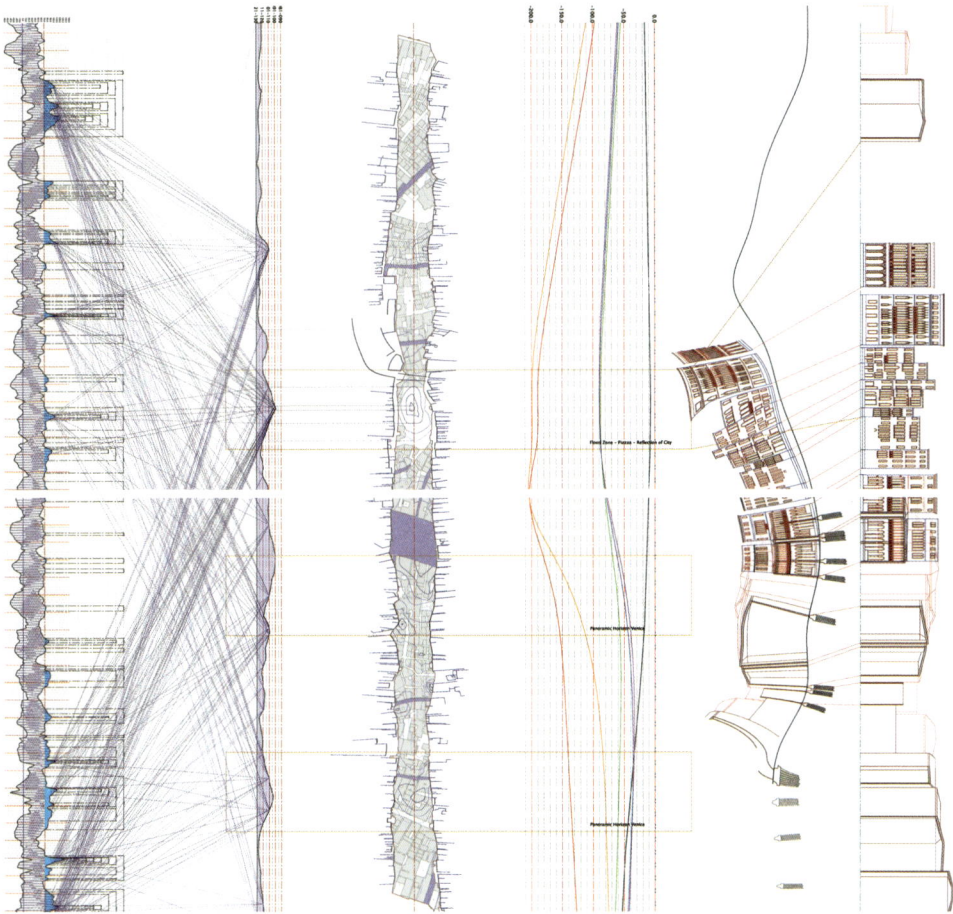

8

9

8. Angelo Sang Hoon Han, Swimming Through
Hypercontextual Venice. The straightening of the
Grand Canal yields historical horizons and a swim
through the earth.

9. Angelo Sang Hoon Han, Machines That Do No Work:
The Ferris Wheel. A technological artefact that does no
work, gets you nowhere, yet endlessly delivers the
horizon.

DIPLOMA 16

Adaptive Ecologies 2: Composite Production

Dip16 have continued their research into environmentally specific yet highly articulated spatial production viewed as an integral part of the overall building ecology. We have been researching recent developments in environmental science, digital design and manufacturing, material science, processes of industrialised building, industrial production economies as well as new organisational models and methods of procurement in close collaboration with multi-disciplinary consultants.

We have continued our quest for a new architectural aesthetic and spatial quality based on the idea of the composite. Our goal is an increasingly articulated and context-specific architectural space arising from an environmentally conscious ecology of industrialised architectural production with an innate capacity for redeployment and adaptation. We see new environmental conditions, building standards and legislation as a springboard for imaginative and innovative environmentally conscious design to emerge.

Dip 16 attempts to nurture environmentally conscious design talent by exploring how one goes about appropriating and developing individual design techniques and directing one's own research. All briefs and sites have been defined by the students.

www.dip16.net

UNIT MASTERS
Andrew Yau
Jonas Lundberg
in collaboration with:
Jonas Runberger &
Tom Tong

STUDENTS
Michael Ahlers, Josiah Barnes, Yee Hong Chong, Adam Holloway, Soo Hyun Jin, Elliott Krause, Chi Sung Lee, In Sub Lee, James McBennett, Emily Thurlow, Sharon Toong, Claudia White, Hyun Suk Yi, Seung Hyun Yuh

TECHNICAL STUDIES CONSULTANCY
Javier Castañón,
John Noel, Wolf Mangelsdorf, Martin Self, Mike Weinstock
STRUCTURAL

CONSULTANCY
Reuben Brambleby AKT

GEOMETRY CONSULTANCY
Kengo Skorick, Arthur Manu-Mani & Ying Wang
Timber consultancy:
Daniel Fagerberg, UFO Stockholm

BEIJING WORKSHOP
Prof. Xu Wei Guo, Dean of Tsing Hua University, Prof. Liu Jian, Tsing Hua University, Peter Davidson of LAB, Mark Harrison of Atkin Beijing, Tsing Hua University and Beijing Central Academy of Fine Art

SUPERSTUDIO
Magnus Larsson,
Andrea Marini, Darren Chan, Levin Lo, Yin Ho, Natalie Chatan, Eda Yetis

HOOKE PARK WORKSHOPS
Charles and Georgie Corry-Wright

Thanks to critics:
Jeremy Kim, Steve Hardy, Tobias Klein, Ulrika Karlsson, Jeff Turko, Stephen Roe, Andrei Martin, Denis Balent, William Chen, Gustav Fagerstrom, Zlatko Haban, Abraham Gordon, Mariam Pousti, Gianni Botsford, Duncan Berntsen, Francesca Hughes, Olaf Kneer, Natasha Sandmeier, Andrei Martin, Iseki

Takehiko, Joao Bravo Da Costa, Katrin Jonas and Nathan Kolbe

Special thanks:
AA and Brett Steele, Charles Tashima, Mike Weinstock, Marilyn Dyer, Belinda Flaherty, Victoria Bahia for making the AA such a special place.

1

2

1 & 2. Prototyping and installation for the WOOD 2010
Exhibition in Virserum Smaland at KLH Scandinavia on
Orsa, Sweden, produced in collaboration with Philip Earley
and Georgina Bister Unit04 LMU and UFO Scandinavia AB

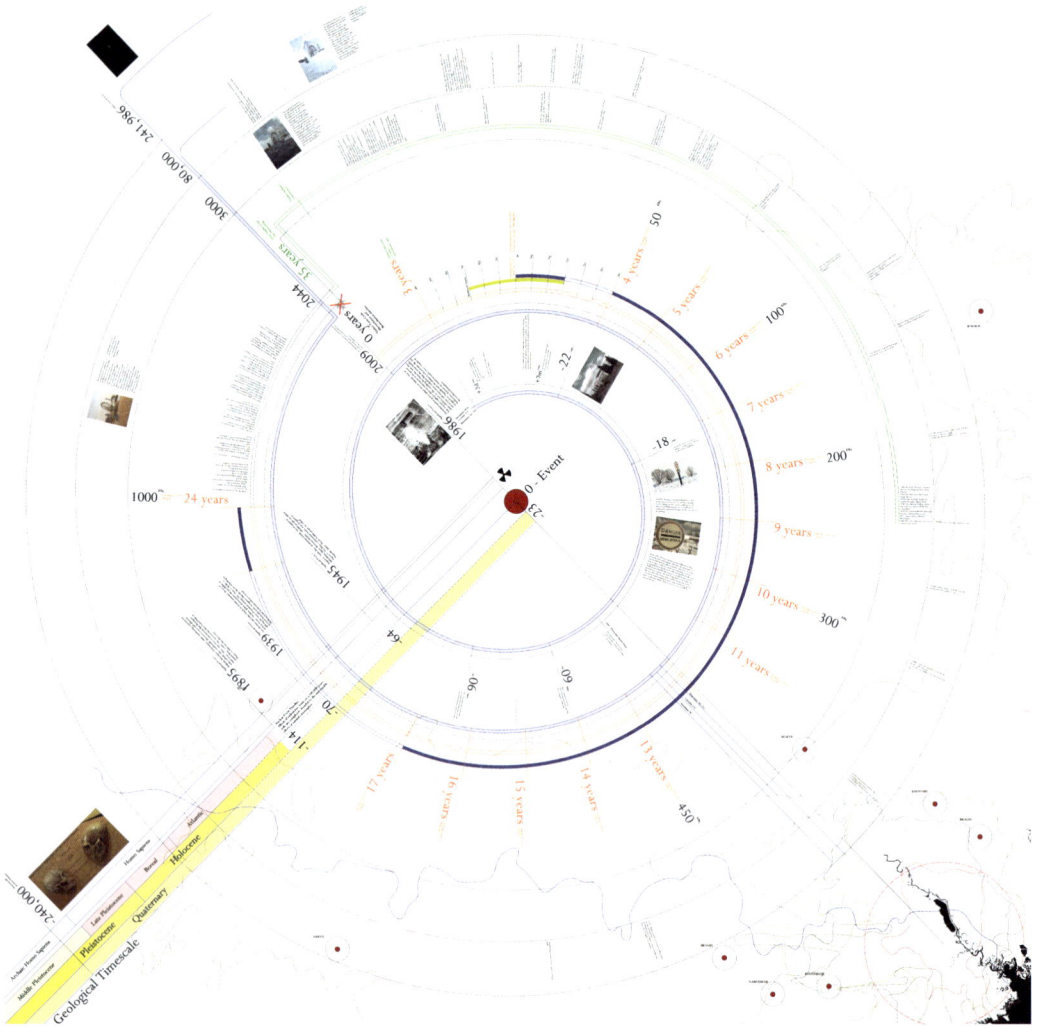

3. Chernobyl's Ghost by Elliott Krause
Chernobyl & Pripyat zones of exclusion and ecosystem

4

5

6

4. Elliott Krause, prototypical cross laminated wood
jointing condition produced at Hooke Park

5 & 6. Elliott Krause, proposed Chernobyl World Heritage
Centre: conceptual views of exterior

193

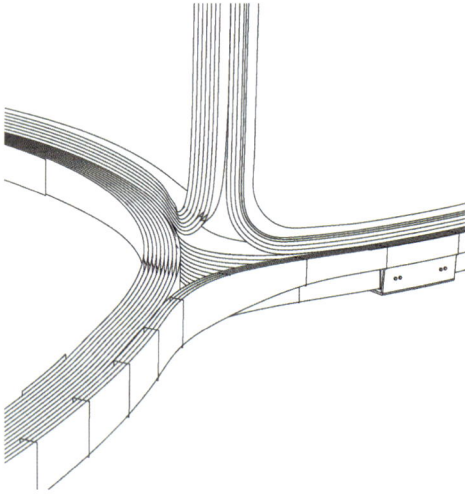

8

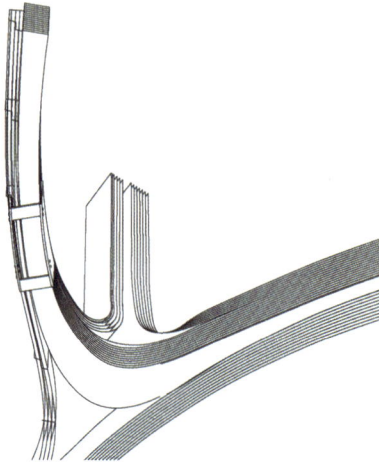

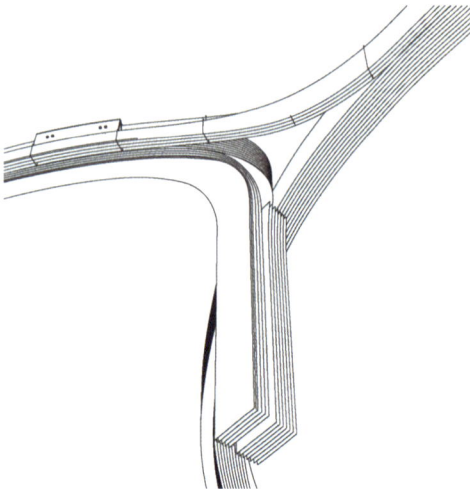

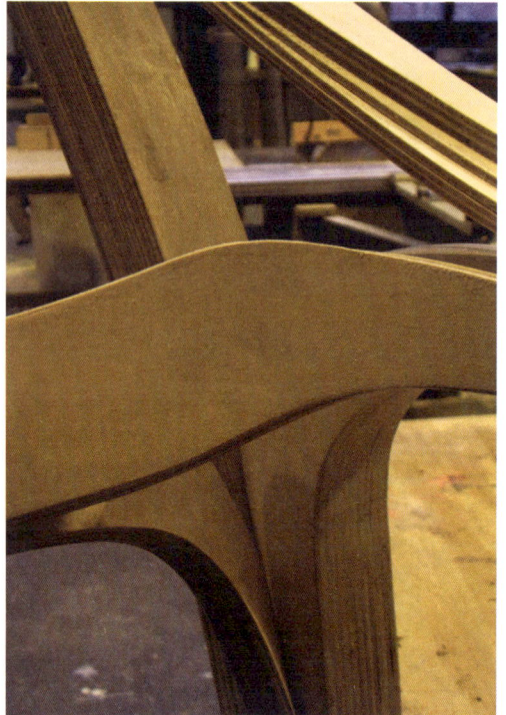

7

9

7–9. Claudia White, curved timber laminations

10

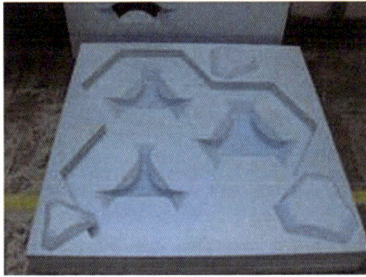

11

12

13

10. Yee Hong Chong, woven bamboo
concrete reinforcement

11–13. Sharon Toong, porous concrete screen CNC-milled
formwork and casting process and final concrete cast

195

DESIGN RESEARCH LAB

The DRL has concluded the first year of a new three-year design research agenda: Proto-Design. Proto-Design investigates digital and analogue forms of computation in the pursuit of systemic design applications that are scenario- and time-based. Considering controls systems as open acts of design experimentation, the DRL examines production processes as active agents in the development of Proto-Design systems. The challenge is to find systems that can articulate urban deployment through poly-scalar correlations. Parametric and generative modelling techniques are coupled with physical computing and analogue experiments to create dynamic feedback processes. New forms of spatial organisation are explored that are not type- or context-dependent. The aim is to detect scenarios that challenge the parameter-identification that directs systems to evolve as ecologies of machines or as material and computational regulating systems, instead moving towards an architecture that is both adaptive and hyper-specific. This performance-driven approach seeks to develop novel design proposals concerned with the everyday. The iterative methodologies of the design studio focus on the investigation of spatial, structural and material organisations, engaging in contemporary discourses on computation and materialisation in the disciplines of architecture and urbanism.

The studio was organised as five parallel research projects exploring the possibilities of Proto-Design, led by Yusuke Obuchi, Theodore Spyropoulos, Patrik Schumacher, Alisa Andrasek and Marta Malé-Alemany. Yusuke Obuchi's studio, Proto Tectonics, investigate material systems and multi-scalar fractal logic for large-span structures. Theodore Spyropoulos' studio, Digital Materialism, explore new forms of prototypical housing through evolutionary innovation and morphological novelty. Patrik Schumacher and Christos Passas's studio, Interiority, develop complex, layered and highly differentiated tectonic systems that start to compete with the best historical examples in terms of richness, coherency and precise organisation. Alisa Andrasek's studio, Wetware, pursue computation through the development of poly-scalar coastal infrastructures within high-pressure flooding zones. The Marta Malé-Alemany studio with Jeroen van Ameijde, Machinic Control, examine architectural design processes incorporating digital fabrication methods that challenge repetitive modes of industrial production.

CO-DIRECTORS
Yusuke Obuchi (Foresites, London)
Theodore Spyropoulos (Minimaforms, London)

FOUNDING DIRECTOR
Patrik Schumacher (Zaha Hadid Architects)

COURSE MASTERS
Marta Malé-Alemany (RE-D, Barcelona, Porto), Alisa Andrasek (Biothing, London)

COURSE TUTORS
Jeroen van Ameijde (Digital Prototyping Lab, AA), Shajay Bhooshan (Zaha Hadid Architects) Christos Passas (Zaha Hadid Architects) Rob Stuart-Smith (Kokkugia, AGU, Arup)

PROGRAMME ASSISTANT
Yota Adilenidou

TECHNICAL TUTORS
Lawrence Friesen (Generative Geometries) Hanif Kara (Adams Kara Taylor Consulting

Engineers)
Riccardo Merello (Arup; Arup Associates)

SOFTWARE TUTORS
Brian Dale
Kristof Crolla
Paul Jeffries
Chikara Inamura

VISITING TUTORS
Mollie Claypool
Ryan Dillon

INVITED CRITICS
Ben van Berkel, Evan Douglis, Tom Wiscombe, Matthias Kohler,

Paul Nakazawa, Mike Weinstock, Dana Cuff, Winka Dubbeldam, François Roche, David Ruy, Peter Testa, Robert Somol, Brett Steele

Sponsors:
Festo
Rieder

STUDENTS PHASE 2

Omrana Ahmed
Shany Barath
Knut Brunier
Mehmet Akif Cinar
Gerry Cruz
Jaime de Miguel
Amrita Deshpande
Ning Duo
Mustafa El Sayed
Gary Freedman
Yuxi Fu
Amro Ghazzawi
Subharthi Guha
Soomeen Hahm
Ling Han
Le Ha Hoang
Chia-Liang Huang
Roland Jarosz
Nahed Jawad
Song Jiawei
Spyridon Kaprinis
Immanuel Koh
Shankara S Kothapuram
Denis Lacej
Akhil Laddha
Elizabeth Leidy
Lin Mei Ling
Ena Lloret Kristensen
Xiaosheng Li
Sudhanshu Mandlik
Kanop Manglapurk
Atul Mhatre
Maryam
  Mirmohammedsadeghi

Juan Camilo Mogollon
Alicia Nahmad
Shaju Nanukuttan
Saahil Parikh
Ardes Perdhana
Catalina Pollak
Natalie Popik
Pebyloka Pratama
Michalis Roidis
Diego Rossel
Sara Saleh
Luis Miguel Samanez
Jose Sanchez
Puja Shah
Stuti Shah
Muhammed Shameel
Osbert So
Ricardo Sosa
Anica Taneja
Maria Tsironi
Manya Uppal
Maria Eugenia Villafane
Denis Vlieghe
Xin Wang
Nick Williams
Paul Wintour
Natalie Wong Chauvet
Jie Yuan
Yichi Zhang
Jiali Zhou

STUDENTS PHASE 1

Ahmed Abouelkheir
Federica Capodarte
Brendon Nikolas Carlin

Fabrizio Cazzulo
Povilas Cepaitis
Georgios Ermis Chalvatzis
Sanhita Chaturvedi
Jian Chen
Jang Eun Cho
Kyle Chou
Esteban Colmenares
Giulia Conti
Maria Eugenia Diaz Diaz
John Michael Dosier
Stella Dourtme
Lluis Enrique Monzo
Claudia Constanze Ernst
Patrick Speakman Farley
Afra Farry
Takbir Fatima
Roberto Garcia Velez
Xin Guo
Tyson Hosmer
Shigang Huang
Seo Yun Jang
Manuel Jimenez Garcia
Alexandros Kallegias
Ji-Ah Lee
Wei Li
Anastasia Lianou
Zhihong Lin
Shan Lou
Kai Sun Luk
Alan McLean
Shuyang Mi
Alejandro Mieses
Miguel Miranda Montes
Said Fahim Mohammadi

Carlos Gabriel
  Morales-Olivares
Konstantinos Mouratidis
Thiago S Mundim
Bryan Oknyansky
Diego Ordonez
Igor Pantic
Riddhi Parakh
Eleni Pattichi
Katharina Penner
Walee Phiriyaphongsak
Carlos Piles Puig
Atta Pornsumalee
Tao Qin
Sean Rasmussen
Michael Rogers
Xiao Long Rui
Poonam Sardesai
Behdad Shahi
Andri Shalou
Luis Miguel Silva
  Da Costa
Daniel Silverman Serra
Ryan Szanyi
Faysal Tabbarah
Sukhumarn Thamwiset
Lorenzo Vianello
Kuo Wang
Junyi Wang
Dan Wang
Greg Richardson Williams
Jiang Yuchao
Junjie Zeng
Yifan Zhang

1. Phase 2 Final Thesis Presentation, January 2010

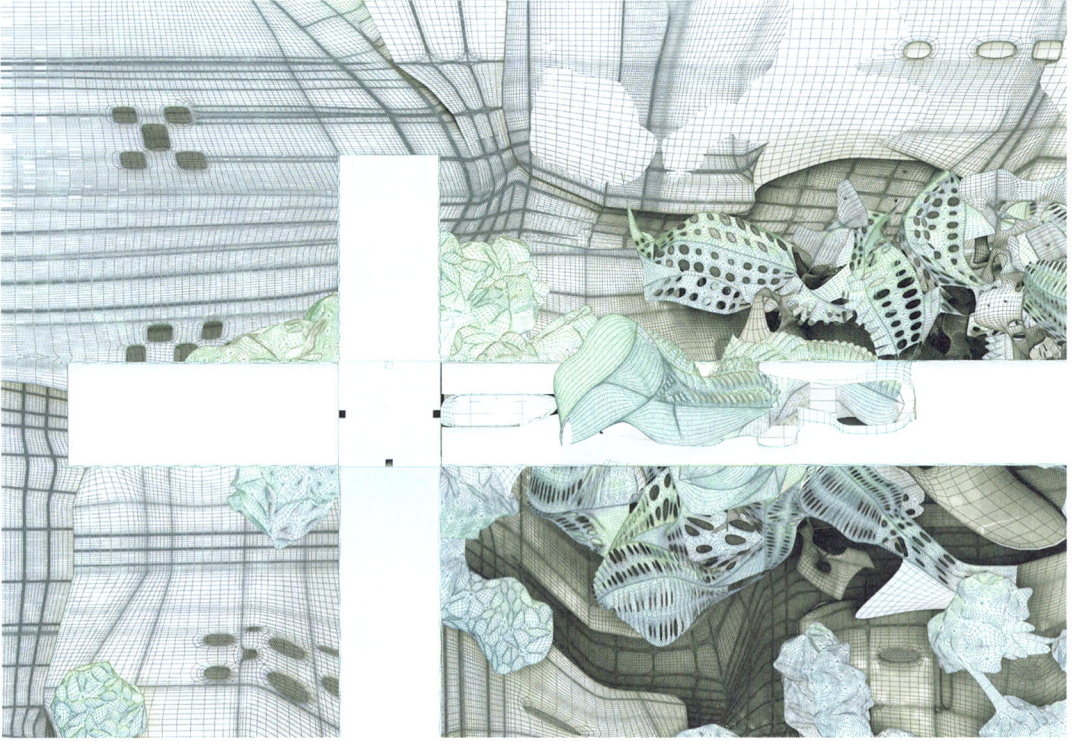

2

3

2 & 3. Anon_SoftCast
Tutor: Theodore Spyropoulos
Team Omrana Ahmed (USA – India), Mustafa El Sayed
(Egypt), Sara Saleh (Italy – KSA), Nick Williams Australia)

4

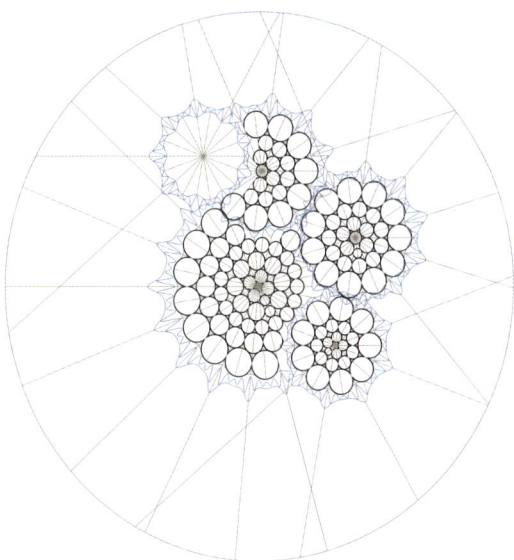
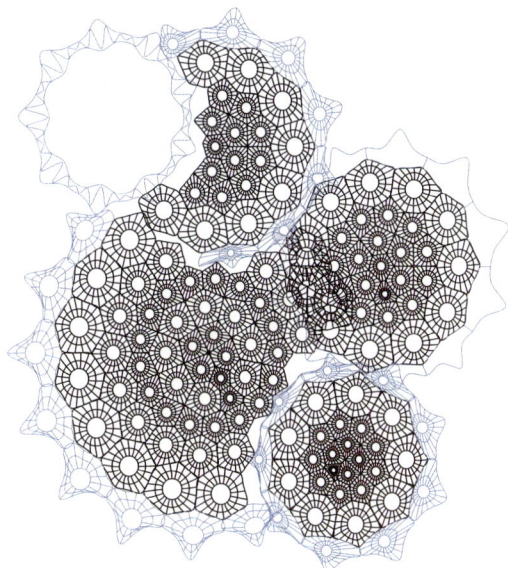

5

4–5. Pasta_Digital Vernacular
Tutors: Marta Malé-Alemany / Jeroen van Ameijde
Team: Song Jiawei (China), Ling Han (China), Lin Mei Ling
(Taiwan), Shankara S. Kothapuram (India)

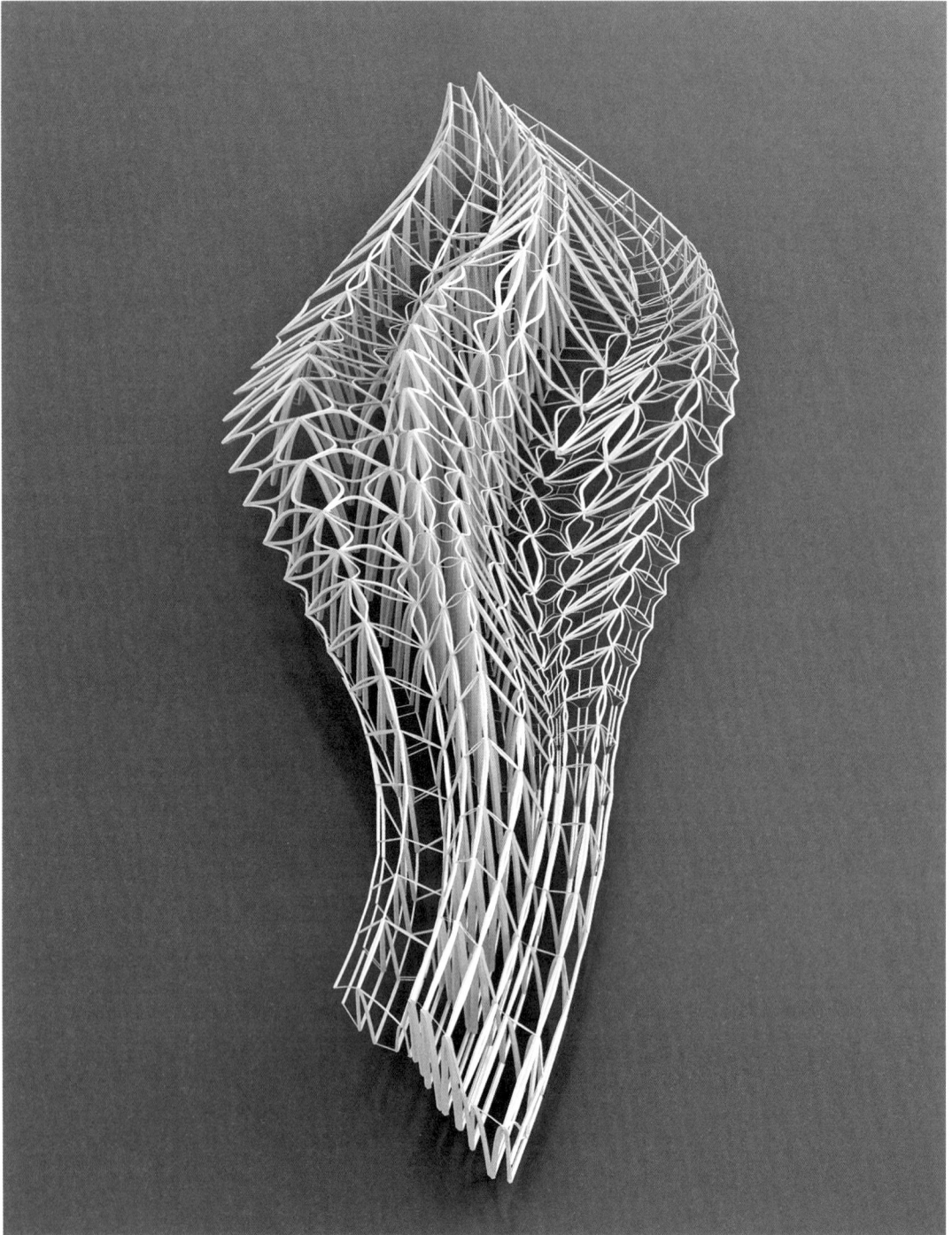

6. 0RN8_Autogenous Reticulations
Tutor: Patrik Schumacher / Christos Passas
Team: Gerry Cruz (Mexico), Spyridon Kaprinis (Greece),
Natalie Porpik (Kazakhstan/USA), Maria Tsironi (Greece)

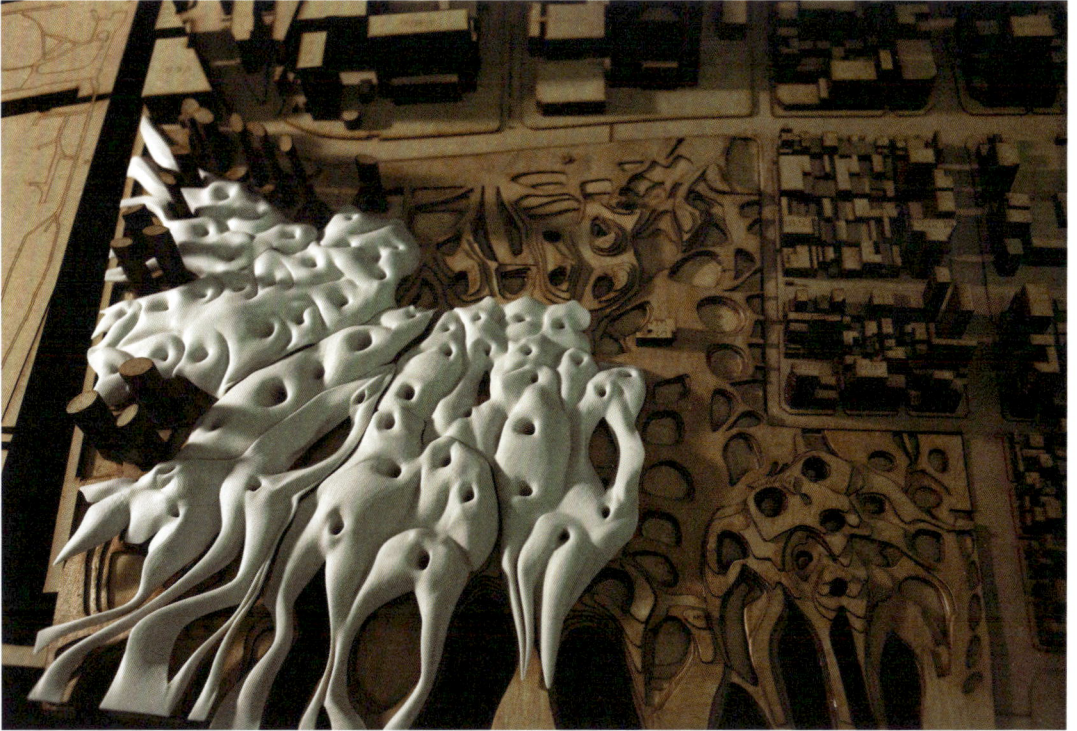

7

8

7 & 8. Synergic
Tutor: Yusuke Obuchi
Team: Ning Duo (China), Roland Jarosz (Poland),
Kanop Manglapurk (Thailand), Michalis Roidis (Greece)

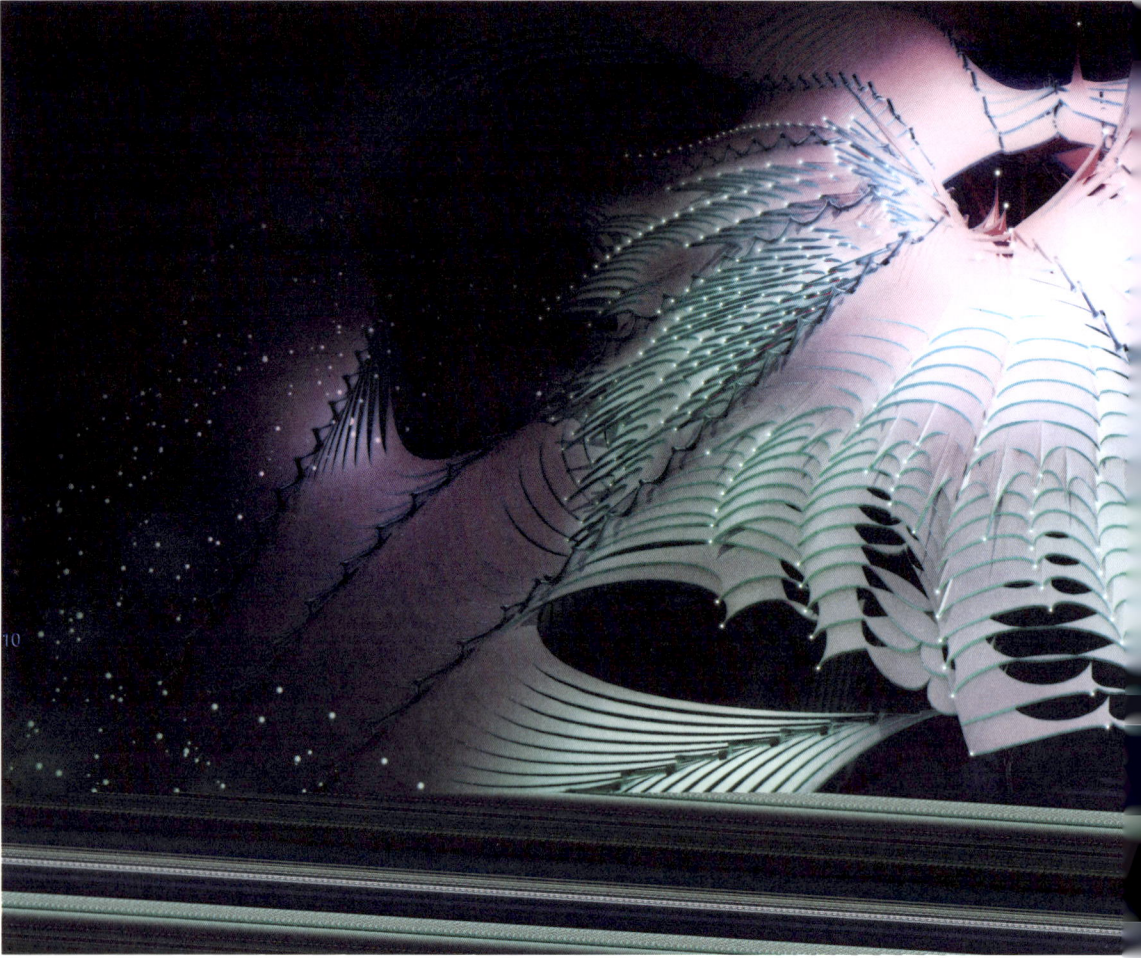

9. Probotics_DataReef
Tutor: Alisa Andrasek
Team: Knut Brunier (Germany), Diego Rossel (Chile),
Jose Sanchez (Chile), Anica Taneja (India)

EMERGENT TECHNOLOGIES

EmTech explores the concepts and convergent interdisciplinary effects of emergence on design and production, and seeks to develop creative inputs to new architectural design processes. Seminars and a core studio familiarise students with EmTech computational processes, their associated conceptual fields and their application to architectural design research. The culminating design thesis derives from this coursework.

The theoretical context of EmTech, encompassing its origins, conceptual structures, instruments and practice is explored in relation to contemporary architectural discourse. The philosophy of emergence forms the logic and processes of evolutionary computation; the application to architectural design focuses on genetic algorithms for structural form-finding and generative design. Emergence is also a central concept of biomimetics, in which biological structures are analysed and understood as self-organised material hierarchies achieved by bottom-up processes – from these structures, properties and performances emerge. Emergent behaviours are also demonstrated by the culture of production at large, a dynamic interaction of diverse forces that follow local rules rather than instructions imposed from above. Larger coherent patterns or 'macro-behaviours' are discernible, arising from material productions that are localised by author, time and geography.

The design research studio enables students to further develop the themes of the course, in three main fields: Active Material Systems with Advanced Fabrication; Natural Ecological Systems Design (currently focused on shorelines and deltas); and Urban Ecological Design (focused on algorithmic design for energetic models of new cities in emergent biomes).

DIRECTORS
Michael Weinstock
George Jeronimidis

STUDIO MASTERS
Christina Doumpioti
Toni Kotnik

STUDIO TUTORS
Evan Greenberg
Konstantinos Karatzas

VISITING STAFF
Achim Menges
Fabian Scheurer
Wolf Mangelsdorf

MASTER CLASSES 08/09
Alan Dempsey
Cristina Díaz Moreno and
Efrén García Grinda
Jalal El-Ali
Hanif Kara
Achim Menges
Fabian Scheurer
Hugh Whitehead

ENGINEERING CONSULTANTS
Buro Happold

EMERGENT TECHNOLOGIES AND DESIGN DEGREES AWARDED 08/09

MSc with Distinction:
Konstantinos Karatzas,
Maria Mingallon:
Fibre Composite Adaptive
Systems

Michel Moukarzel:
Tensegrity for Temporary
Structures

MSc.
Kunkun Chen:
Void-Activated Tubular
Timber Structure

Mohamad Khabazi:
Algorithmic
Morphogenesis

Tamara Lavrovskaya:
Evaporative Cooling
System

Sara Pezeshk: Reinforced
Earth Anticlastic Envelope
Systems

Ioanna Symeonidou:
Surface Nets
Xia Su: Hydrological
Surface System

MArch with Distinction:
Shuai Feng: Branching
Strategies for
Microclimates

Mohammed Makki &
Pavlos Schizas: Urban
Metabolic Growth

MArch
Selim Bayer: Cloaking
Surface Waves for an
Anti-Seismic Urban
Masterplan

Utssav Gupta:
Inhabitable Bridge

Sakthivel Ramaswamy:
Fibre Composite Adaptive
Systems

Jheny Nieto Ropero:
Timber Composite
Surfaces

Revano Satria: Cellular
Solid Morphologies

Kyle L. Schertzing:
Coastal Geodynamics

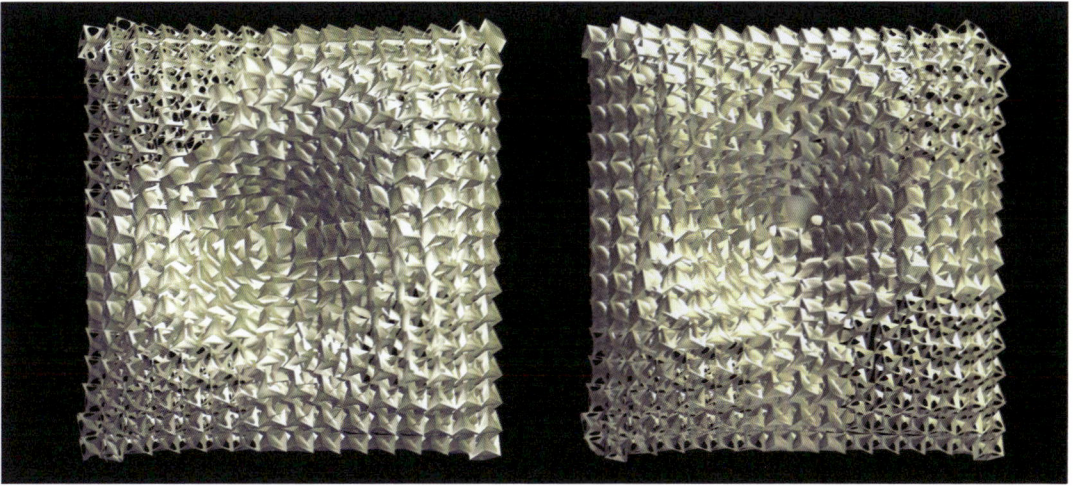

1

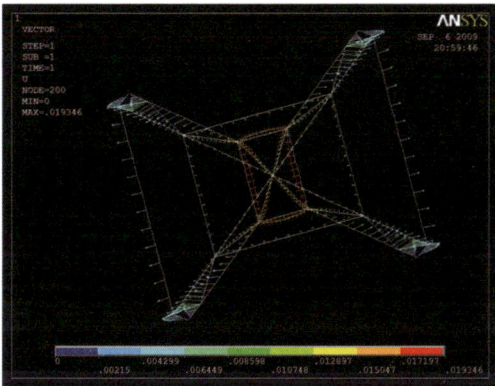
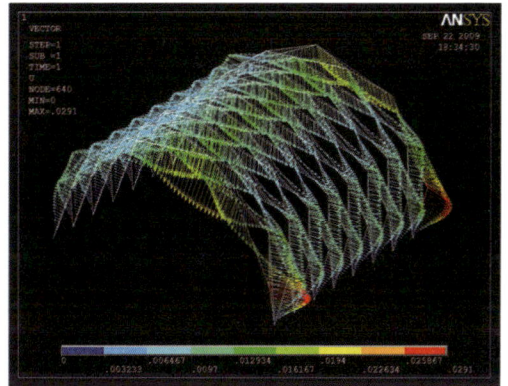
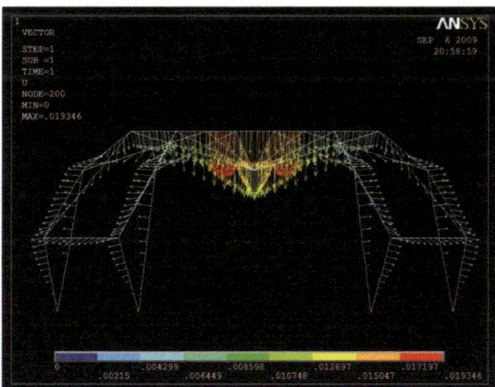
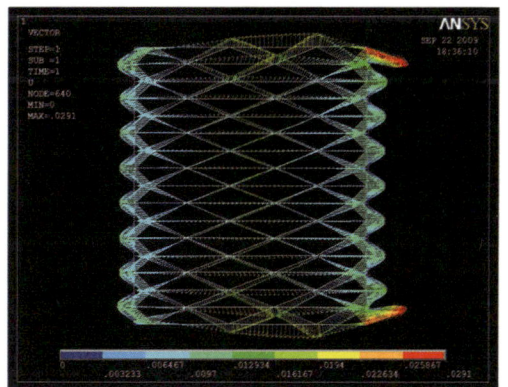

2

1. Fibre Composite Adaptive Systems, Konstantinos Karatzas, Maria Mingallon, Sakthivel Ramaswamy
A composite material system with embedded sensors and actuators of shape memory alloys with high structural capacity, all integrated into a polymer matrix.

2. Tensegrity for Temporary Structures, Michel Moukarzel
A construction system with a high space-to-weight ratio of materials that can be rapidly deployed for disaster relief: bridges establish or restore transportation systems, structures house a field hospital, community and religious spaces, storage and management offices.

3. Urban Metabolic Growth, Mohammad Makki
and Pavlos Schizas
Polycentric urban systems in regions with extreme
climatic conditions are optimised for water, food
and energy flow and grow to an 'equilibrium' state
between resources and population.

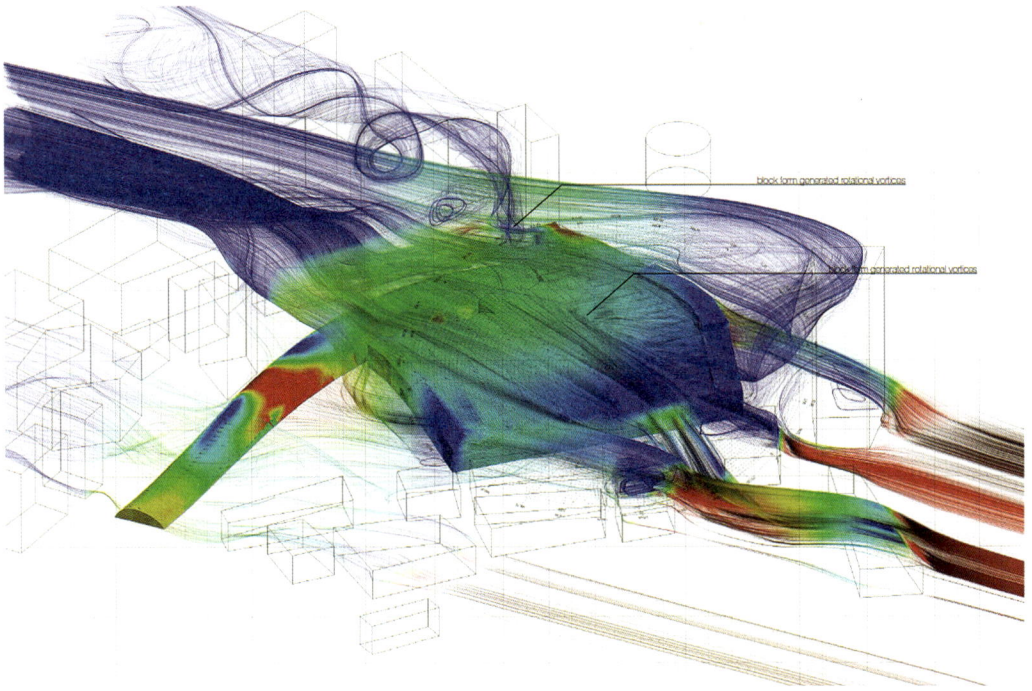

4

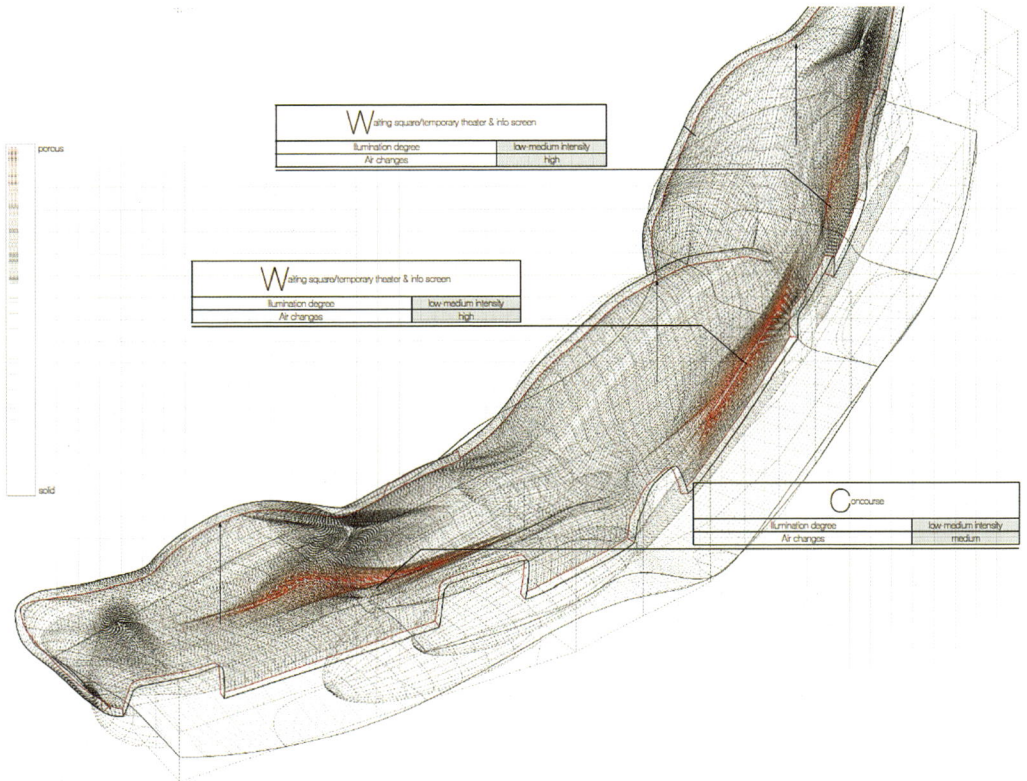

5

4 & 5. Branching Strategies for Microclimates, Shuai Feng
A branching ventilation system within the shell of a new
Waterloo railway concourse, composed of concrete
embedded with fibre optics, responds thermodynamically
to the architectural programme.

6

7

6–8. Wave Canopy, Emtech Staff and Students 2008/09
The canopy has two principal structural systems – wave-like strips of a thin timber composite and upright timber fins that provide local stiffening and connection to the existing steel columns of the upper terrace. A project combining the mathematics of evolutionary development processes and physical experiments in material behaviour. Photo Sue Barr

208

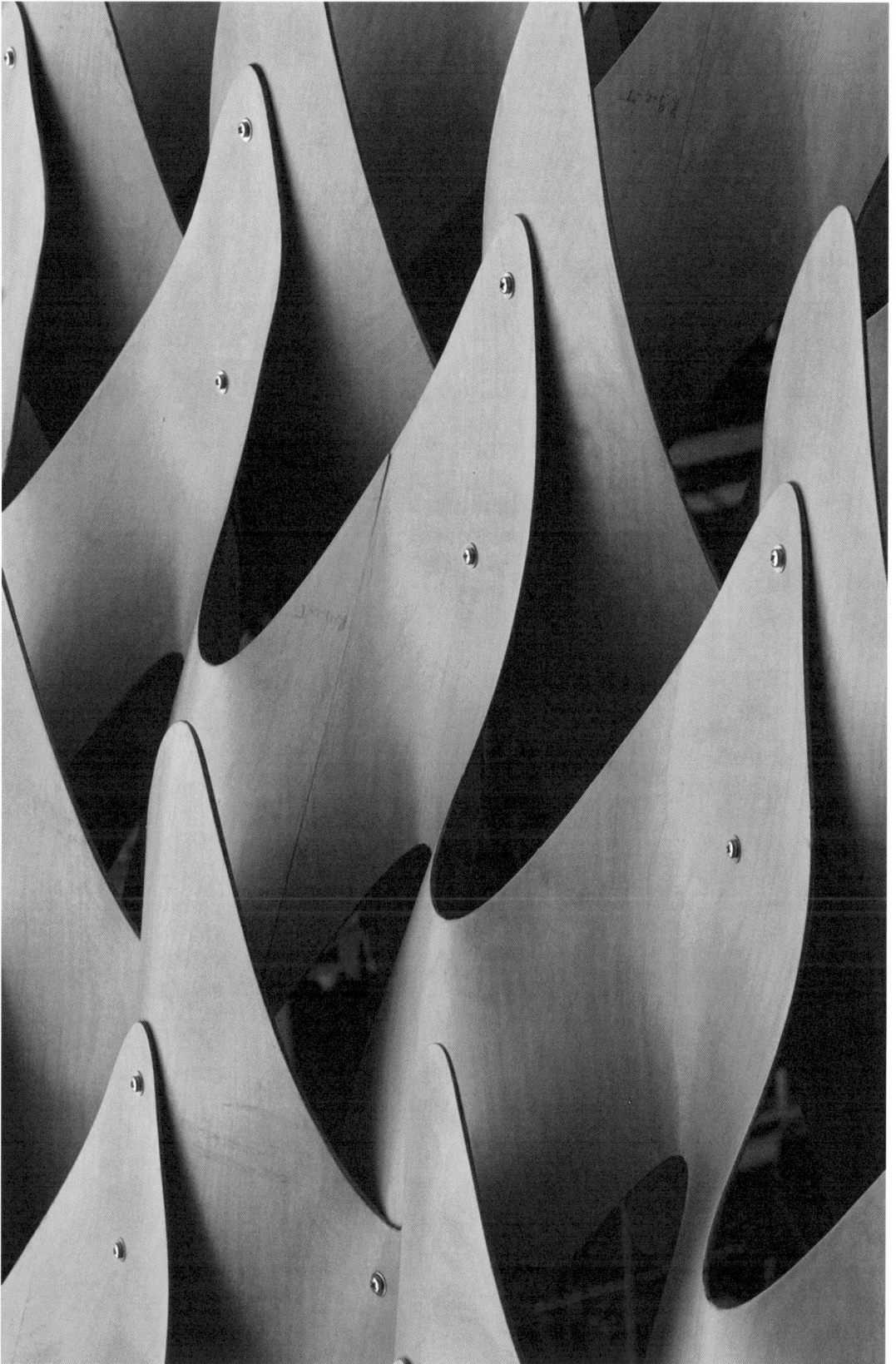

MA HISTORIES & THEORIES

Histories & Theories provides a platform for critical enquiry into the writing of history, theoretical debates and forms of architectural and urban practice. The aim is three fold: to ground contemporary arguments and projects in a wider historical, cultural and political context; to produce knowledge which relates to design and public cultures in architecture, including the AA School; to enquire into new forms of historical, theoretical and architectural research and practice.

A common concern of the different courses is analysing the relation of theoretical debates to particular projects, in order to develop a critical view of the arguments of the design, its mechanisms and effects. Terms are organised around seminar courses, lectures and events, offering students a range of approaches to investigate the contemporary from a historical, theoretical and cross-disciplinary perspective and to expand and reinterpret disciplinary knowledge in a broad cultural arena. The investigation of the modern and modernity through a critical reassessment of modernism, in terms of its narratives and controversies, is our point of departure towards understanding contemporary architecture and debates.

Central to the course is an emphasis on the critical practice of writing. Different forms such as the essay, review, short commentary and interview allow students to engage with diverse forms of enquiry and articulate the various aspects of their study.

This year, the programme drew a wide variety of students from Canada, Hong Kong, India, Italy, USA and the UK. Whereas the majority were trained architects taking a year to either reflect upon the theoretical implications of their design practice or take the first steps in an academic career, three students from graphic design and cultural studies joined the course to acquire an understanding of architectural theory in relation to particular projects.

The theme of the annual Histories & Theories Debates – with visiting critics, historians, writers and architects – focused on the city, politics and spaces and also related to the 'City Cultures' Research Cluster directed by Marina Lathouri. A series of lectures and seminars addressed a number of themes, prompting a lively dialogue between students and visiting lecturers. Also special seminars on writing and contemporary forms of publishing were held with Kirk Wooller and Shumon Basar.

Taking full advantage of AA events, the students have been active in juries and discussions of design work produced in other parts of the school. In particular, a series of workshops and seminars was organised with Diploma Unit 9.

A study trip to Seville and Cordoba was combined with an intensive programme of seminars focused on the MA thesis research.

STAFF
Marina Lathouri
(Programme Director)
Mark Cousins
Francisco Gonzalez
de Canales

VISITING TUTORS
Pedro Ignacio Alonso
Braden Engel

VISITING SPEAKERS
Shumon Basar, AACP,
Printed Matters: An
Informal Discussion on
Writing, Editing and
Publishing

Andrea Cavalletti,
University of Venice,
Biopolitics and the City
John Palmesino, AA
Diploma Unit 4, North

Wendy Pullan, University
of Cambridge, Frontier
Urbanism: Spatial
Discontinuities in
Contested Cities

Emanuel de Sousa,
AA PhD researcher,
Heterotopia: Other Cities

Teresa Stoppani,
University of Greenwich,
Venice after the Modern:
Architectural Devices for
the Contemporary City

Carlos Villanueva Brandt,
AA Diploma Unit 10,
Direct Urbanism

Michael Weinstock,
AA Director Emergent
Technologies Graduate
Programme, Metabolism
and Cultural Evolution

Ines Weizman, London
Metropolitan University,
Double Agency and
Unreasonable
Architectures

Kirk Wooller, AA PhD
candidate, Magazines as
Sites of Architectural
Innovation

STUDENTS
Daniel Ayat, Shumi
Nabaneeta Bose, Man Ha
Chan, Marco Ferrari,
Lori Marie Gibbs,
Roberta Marcaccio,
Deepa Ramaswamy,
Phoebe Stirling,
Troy Conrad Therrien

THESIS RESEARCH
Daniel Ayat, *City and
Farm: The Urban Practices
of Food Production After
Nature and Culture*

Shumi Nabaneeta Bose
*Discourse 2.0 - The Effects
of New Media on Architec-
tural Thought*

Man Ha Chan
*The Emergence of the
Public Sphere: Architec-
ture Writings in China's
Mass Media Since 1949*

Marco Ferrari
*Embassies: A New Paradigm
for Urban Paranoia*

Lori Marie Gibbs
*Constructing Sustainabil-
ity: Interrogating the Role
and Response of the
Architectural Practice on
Issues of Ecological
Building Design*

Roberta Marcaccio
*Fully Air-Conditioned:
Artificiality and Invisibility
in Architecture*

Deepa Ramaswamy
*The Architectural Context
and its Imaginaries*

Phoebe Stirling
Thinking the City as Milieu

Troy Conrad Terrien
*Modernising Architectural
Modernism in the Tropics:
Human Dust and Other
Unimaginables of the
Uncertain*

MA Histories & Theories thesis seminar, Seville,
May 2010. Photo Troy Conrad Therrien

HOUSING & URBANISM

Housing & Urbanism applies architecture to the challenges of contemporary urban strategies. Today's metropolitan regions show tremendous diversity and complexity with significant global shifts in patterns of urban growth and decline. This programme investigates how architectural intelligence helps us understand and respond to shifting urban conditions. Housing is considered both as a critical aspect of urbanism and as a means to reflect upon changing ideas of domesticity, identity and public space.

Student work is divided among design workshops, lectures and seminars, and a final thesis which allows for a focused study within the broader themes of the course. The programme explores the interplay between graphic tools and writing, in order to develop research ideas about the urban condition and skills for intervening through spatial design.

There are three current research themes of H&U work:
1. the role of urbanism in enhancing 'innovation environments' and 'knowledge-based' clusters through their urbanisation;
2. ideas of living space and housing, and issues of mix, density and urban intensification in which architecture is considered in relation to a process of urbanisation;
3. exploring urbanisms appropriate to address urban irregularity and informality and to engage with the interaction of spatial strategies and social policies.

This year's design workshops took place in the Lea Valley in London and in Taiwan in collaboration with the Graduate Institute of Architecture at National Chiao Tung University, complemented by a study visit to Hamburg. The workshops addressed processes of rapid urban development related to knowledge-based economies, as well as the potential for synergies between new and existing urban cultures. H&U reaches beyond the AA through publications, participation in events such as EcoBuild 2009 and exhibitions. H&U staff have contributed to the UN Global Studio in Johannesburg; the INTA International Urban Development Association programme in Taiwan; and are involved in urban projects internationally in the UK, the Netherlands, Italy, Sudan, Spain, Singapore and the USA.

STAFF
Jorge Fiori
Hugo Hinsley
Lawrence Barth
Nicholas Bullock
Kathryn Firth
Dominic Papa
Elena Pascolo
Alex Warnock-Smith

CONTRIBUTORS
Arthur Aw
Chi-Yi Chang
Trevor Flynn
Sascha Haselmayer
Pei-Hsien Hsu
Anderson Inge
Shu-Chang Kung
Charles Lin
Sabrina Puddu

Dirk Schubert
David Tseng
XueXue Institute
Francesco Zuddas

STUDENTS
Ankita Agrawal
Zainab Alireza
Malay Deshmukh
Daniela Djourkova
Vanessa Espaillat
Denny Husin
Chalita Karwattanagul
Bhavana Kumar
Nicola La Noce
Efthalia Lestou
Shan Li
Yanping Liang
Sarah Melsens
Jong In Park

Mariia Pashenko
Dung Phan
Jerome Picard
Bekim Ramku
Bayu Riyadi
Kalliopi Tsiota
Denise Vilela
Lisa Woo

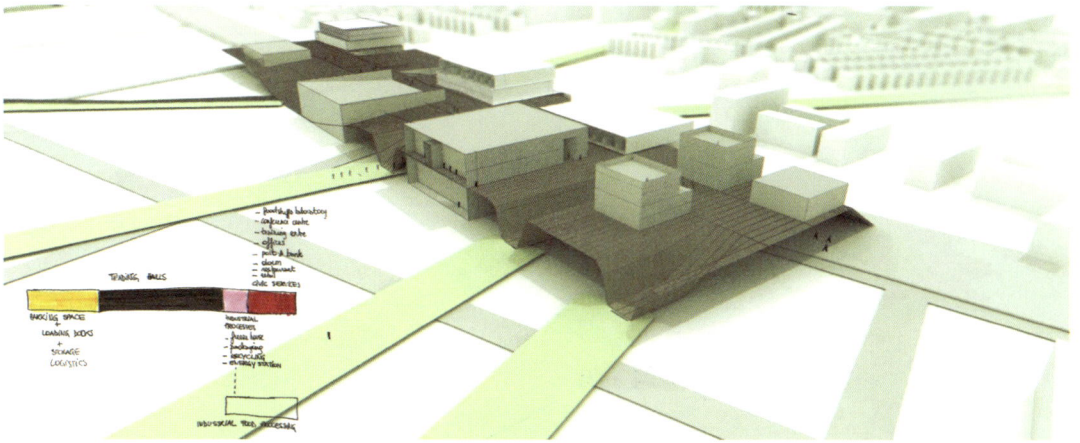

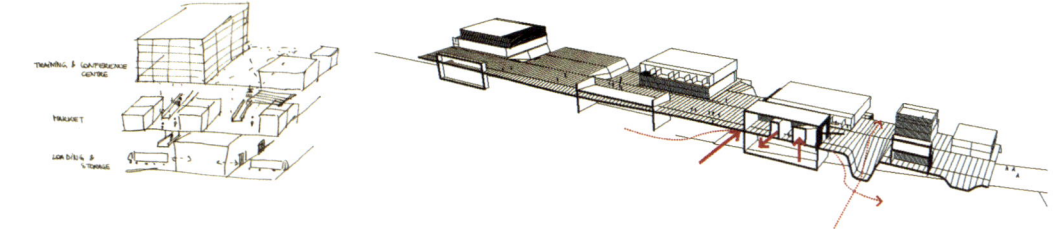

1

2

The London design workshop studied the Lower Lea Valley as a potential location for new knowledge-based economies and a more productive urban condition.

1. Lower Lea Valley: Urbanising the industrial park through mixed uses – introducing a wholesale market.
2. Lower Lea Valley: Recycling as a concept for buildings, landscape and economic change.

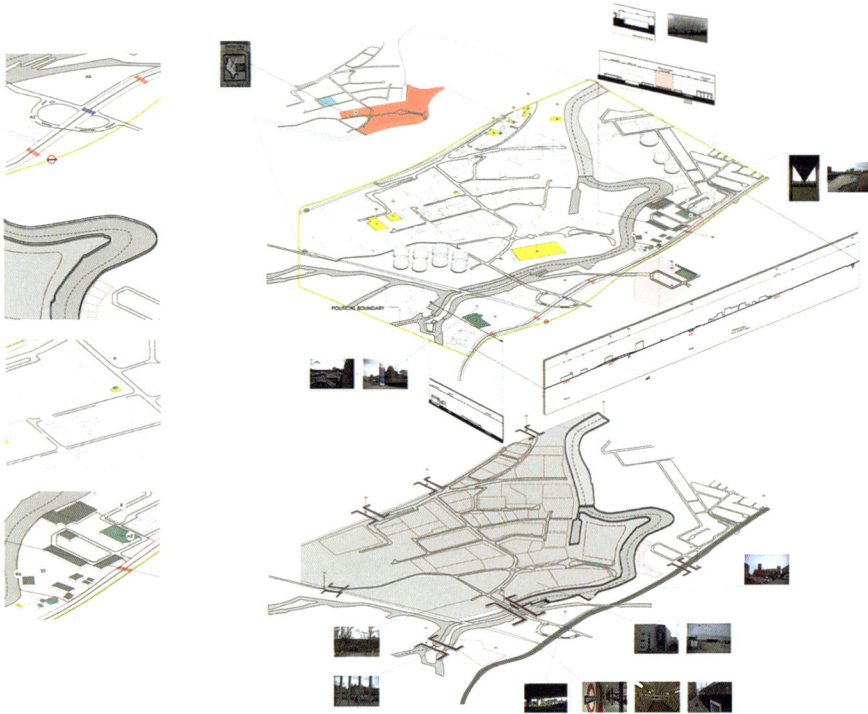

3

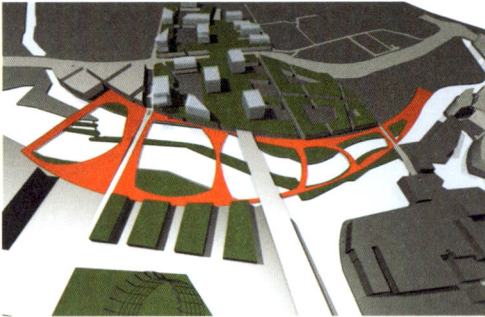

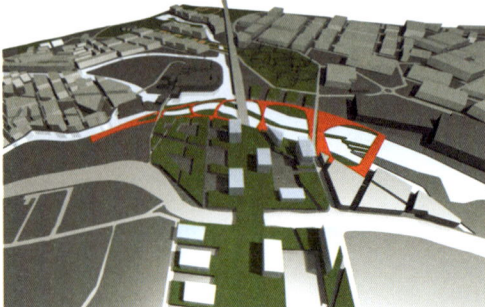

4

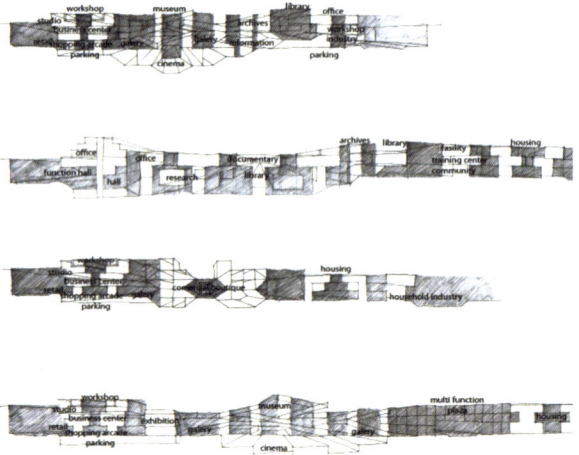

5

3. Lower Lea Valley: Readings of infrastructure
and landscape
4. Lower Lea Valley: Connective void – new bridging
structure activates landscape

5. Lower Lea Valley: Sectional study of void as
connector in creative industries quarter

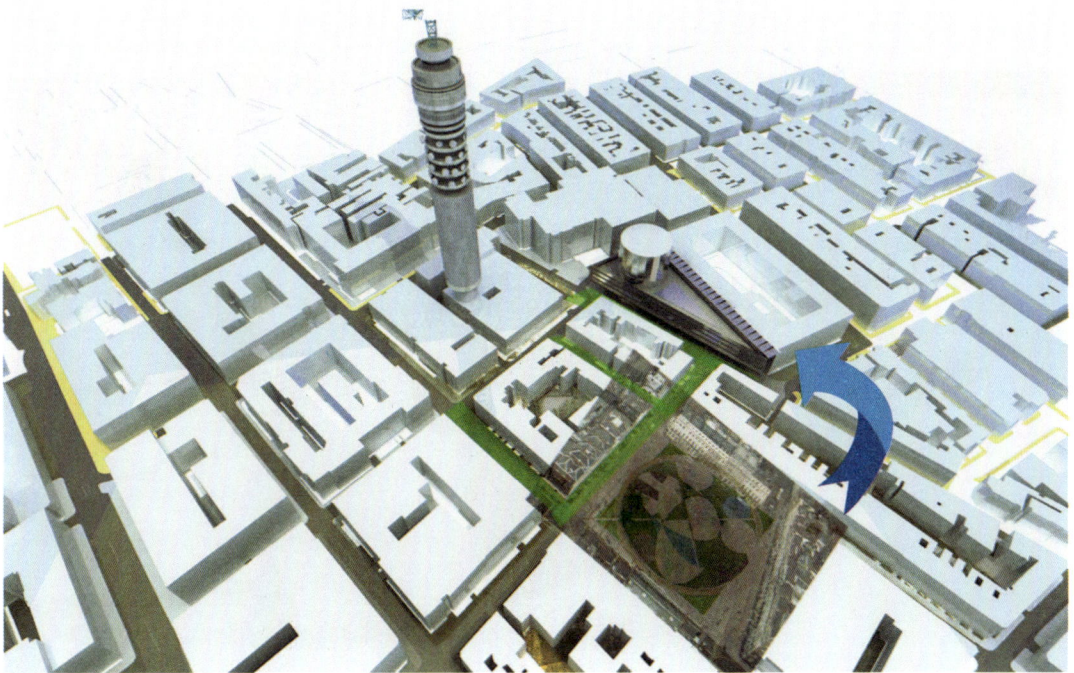

6

SOCIAL DEPRIVATION- 2005

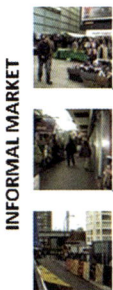

MONEY TRANSFER

REGIONAL CUISINE

FRUIT STALLS

ETHNIC CLOTHES

INFORMAL MARKET

ETHNIC FURNISHINGS

ETHNIC COMMUNITY > 43%

SOUTH AMERICANS
AFRICANS
AFRICAN CARRIBEANS
PAKISTANIS
BANGLADESHIS
INDIAN BENGALIS

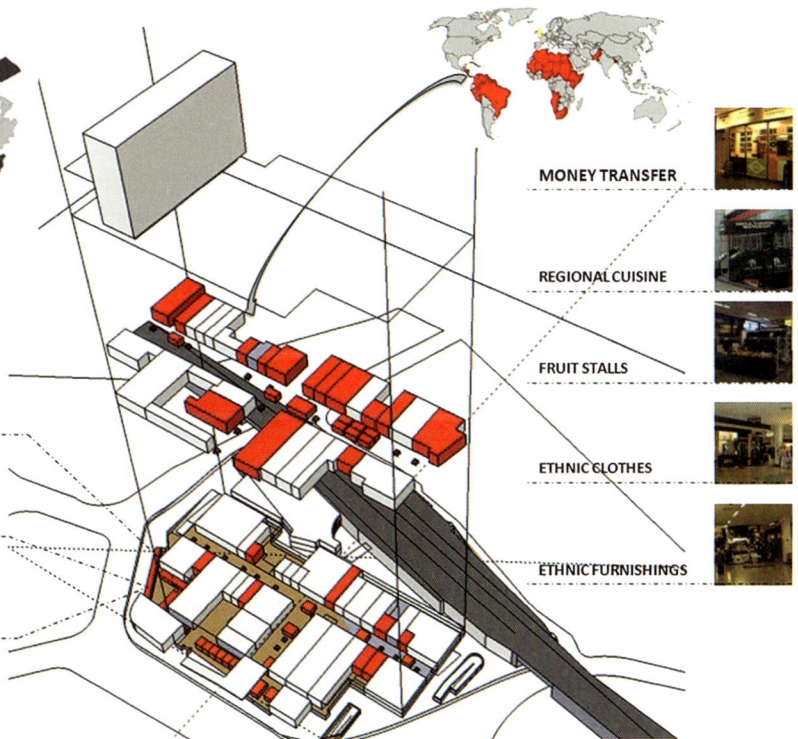

7

6. Urban Study: Fitzrovia – business incubator and
training centre

7. Urban Study: Elephant & Castle shopping centre –
global and local economies

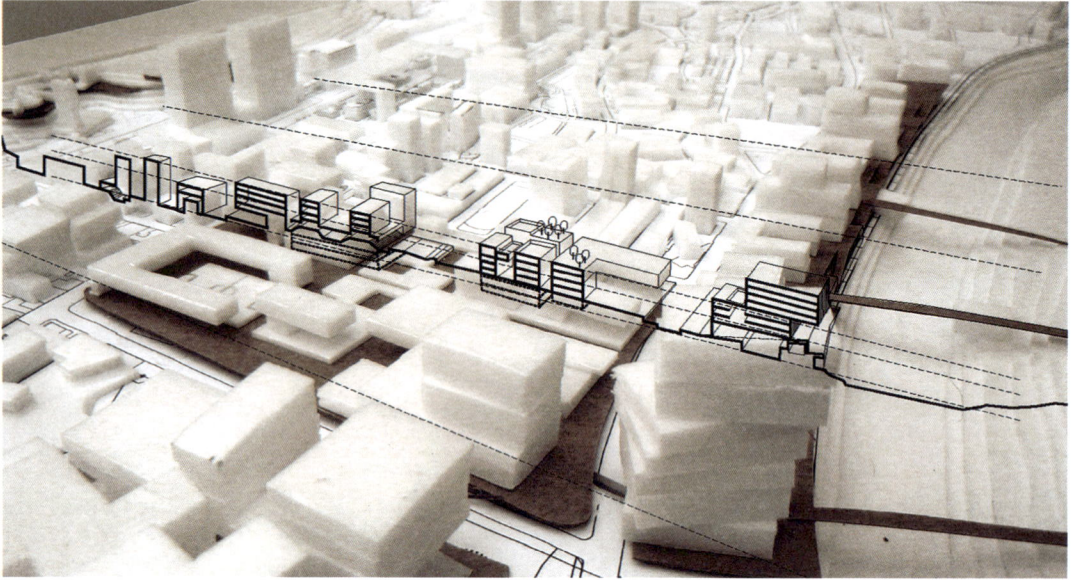

8

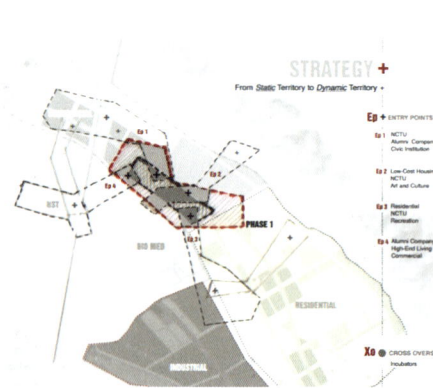

9

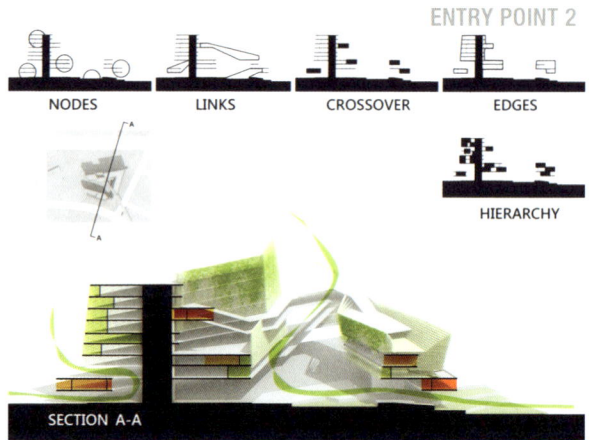

10

Taiwan intensive design workshop: Innovative Regions and Creative Cities
In collaboration with the Graduate Institute of Architecture of NCTU, four teams addressed the urban and regional implications of the evolving knowledge-based economy at two sites. One is an abandoned factory site in Nangang, Taipei, and we have jointly won a grant from Taipei City government to develop this work. The other was the Jubei expansion area of Hsinchu, which aims to combine a new university campus, a bio-medical research park and residential and commercial development.

11

8. Nangang: Sectional and model study of an evolving music ecology and creative sector
9. Jubei: Dynamic Territory
10. Jubei: Study of an entry point

11. Taiwan intensive design workshop: Innovative Regions and Creative Cities work in progress

LANDSCAPE URBANISM

Sprawl, post-industrialisation, rapid urbanisation and 'natural' disasters pose significant challenges to normative design practice, requiring an approach beyond the quick fix. Landscape Urbanism has emerged as a new discipline which responds to the demands of these conditions. Here, 'landscape' is a model of connective, scalar and temporal operations through which the urban is conceived and engages a complex ecology.

Landscape Urbanism integrates techniques from environmental engineering, urban strategy and landscape ecology and employs the science of emergence, the tools of digital design and the thought of political ecology.

Prototypical Urbanities 03: The Yangtze River Delta
China's economic boom, combined with migration from the countryside, produces new cities instantly and transforms the faces of older towns. This directional urbanisation has brought the phenomenon of globalisation, its foreign capital and generic architecture, to the smallest villages.

Expanding on research established over the past two years, LU maintained its focus on China's ambitions to build 400 new cities by the year 2020 – with 12 million people expected to move from rural to urban locations – as the basis for its brief. Far from resisting this development, we engaged opportunistically with 'proto-strategies' for new large-scale agglomerations as a means to critically address mass-produced urban sprawl. Our testbed was the Yangtze River Delta, including Shanghai, Nanjing, Hangzhou, Suzhou, Ningbo. Students explored three issues:

Metabolic rurbanism: Explore modes of urbanisation emergent from the 'desakota' fabric in which urban and rural processes of land use are combined.

Tactical resistance: Locate fault lines in the clash between top-down masterplanning and developed urban cores, where informed and territorially specific urbanism might be produced.

Material identities: Explore infrastructure as a material alternative to prevailing urban settlements with an instant 'identity', based on either vernacular or western styles of building, in the context of 'post-traditional' urbanisation.

STAFF
Eva Castro
Alfredo Ramírez
Eduardo Rico
Tom Smith
Douglas Spencer

VISITING STAFF
Alex Wall
Steve Graham
Erik Swyngedouw
Simon Marvin
Mike Hodson
Chris Reed
Alberto Clementi

STUDENTS
Fiona Kirkwood
Ana Bachina
Carlos Umaña
Karishma Desai
Golara Jalapor
Athanasios Kourniotis
Mak Mun Pheng
Tzu-Hui (Teri) Kao
Jian-Jie Zhou (Tommy)
Diana Helena
  Araya Muñoz
Leonardo Robleto
Swepta Gupta
Manuel Navarro
Chen Chen
Zhuo Li
Nicola Saladino

1. The Easter workshop was framed as a collaboration with Trento University and the municipality of Bolzano, Italy. AALU students worked on an area of southern Bolzano, between the A22 Brenner highway and the Virgolo Hill. Students combined the study of urban typologies incorporating the vineyard terracing systems in south-facing slopes with more infrastructural approaches in dealing with the highway and freight railway crossing the site. The project was shown to the urban authorities in Bolzano and presented in different newspapers and local television.

Ship path
60 min
30 min
Shanghai
Lingang
Touristic boats' paths
2.00 hr
Fishing boats' paths
Touristic ports
1.30 hr
Sheng Shan
Touristic ports
Dahuangiong Shan
1.30 hr
Local boats' paths
2.00 hr
2.30 hr
Dachangjushan
Xia Shan
Zhoushan
Jintang Shan
Puto Shan
Zhu Jia Jian
Taohua Dao

Touristic ports
2 km around the lands (boats barrier)
30 min distance by ferry
Local ports
Touristic boats' paths
Local boats' paths
Fishing boats' paths

Time taken by ferries passing through barriers

Shanghai
Shanghai port
Korea
Yangshan container port
Shanghai
Container ship routes
Lingang
Ningbo
Yangshan port
High pressure
Japan
Yangtze river delta
Hong kong
Ningbo port

Ports
Main cities
Boat station
50 ships from Japan (annually)
50 ships from Korea (annually)
50 ships from Hong kong (annually)

Current - Container ship routes

Zhoushan archipelago, Shengsi Island, Floating fish farms integrated with touristic development
48000000 mm3/month
Runoff accumulation
Adjusted mesh to existing built
17600000 mm3/month
Sijiao mountain
Base Lake beach, Touristic beach
Accesibility mesh (touristic walking path)
- 4.00
- 3.80
- 3.60
- 3.40
Height : 100m
40000000 mm3/month
7200000 mm3/month
- 3.20
- 3.00
Shengsu island
Shizhucun villages
Height : 100m
Adjusted mesh with existing settlements
52000000 mm3/month
8600000 mm3/month
Adjusted mesh to fish pond size requirement
6400000 mm3/month
Xiaoguan Aocun villages

2. Golara Jalalpor

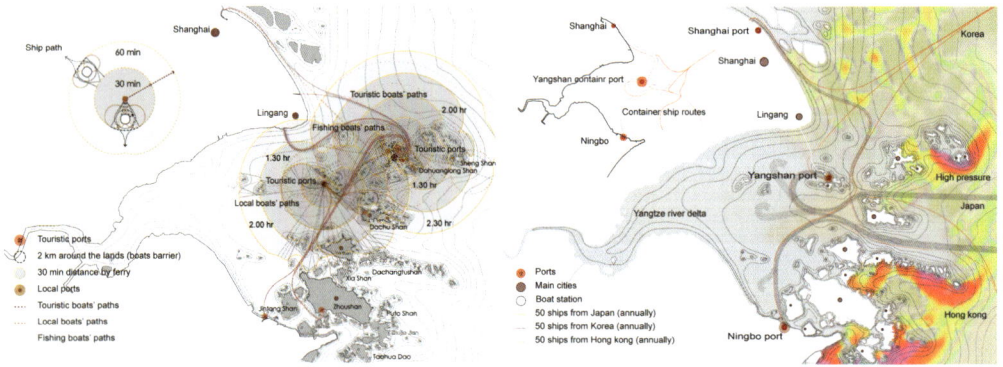

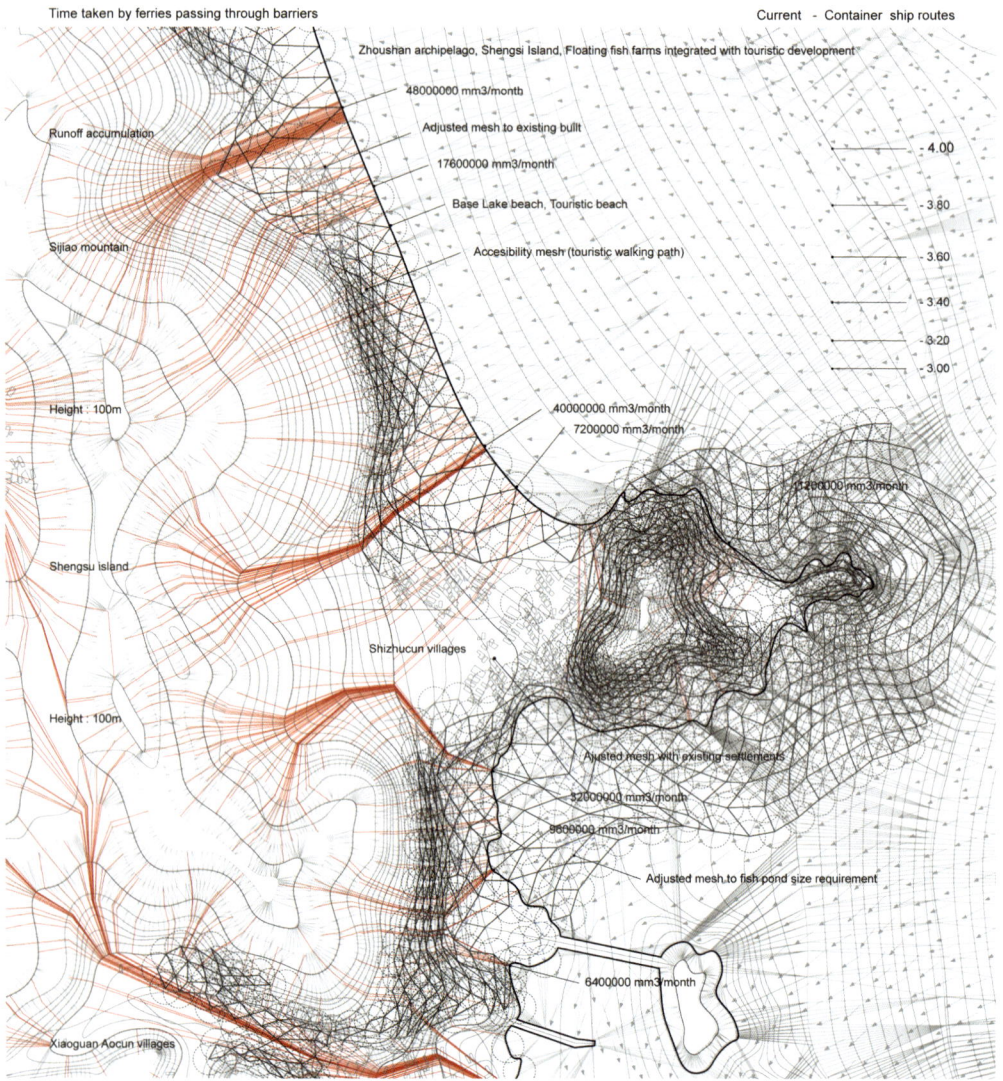

As a result of the construction of Yangshan port [which connects to Shanghai by Dounghai bridge], Gouqi Shan can be reached from the mainland within a few hours. It is the biggest island in the Shengsi archipelago, containing China's largest beach. Its strategic location has made it a tourist destination in recent years, leading to the conversion of agricultural land into new developments. The project strategy is to integrate local agro-based activity with the ecology of the site, by proposing floating fish farms and floating agricultural plots which also act as tourist attractions.

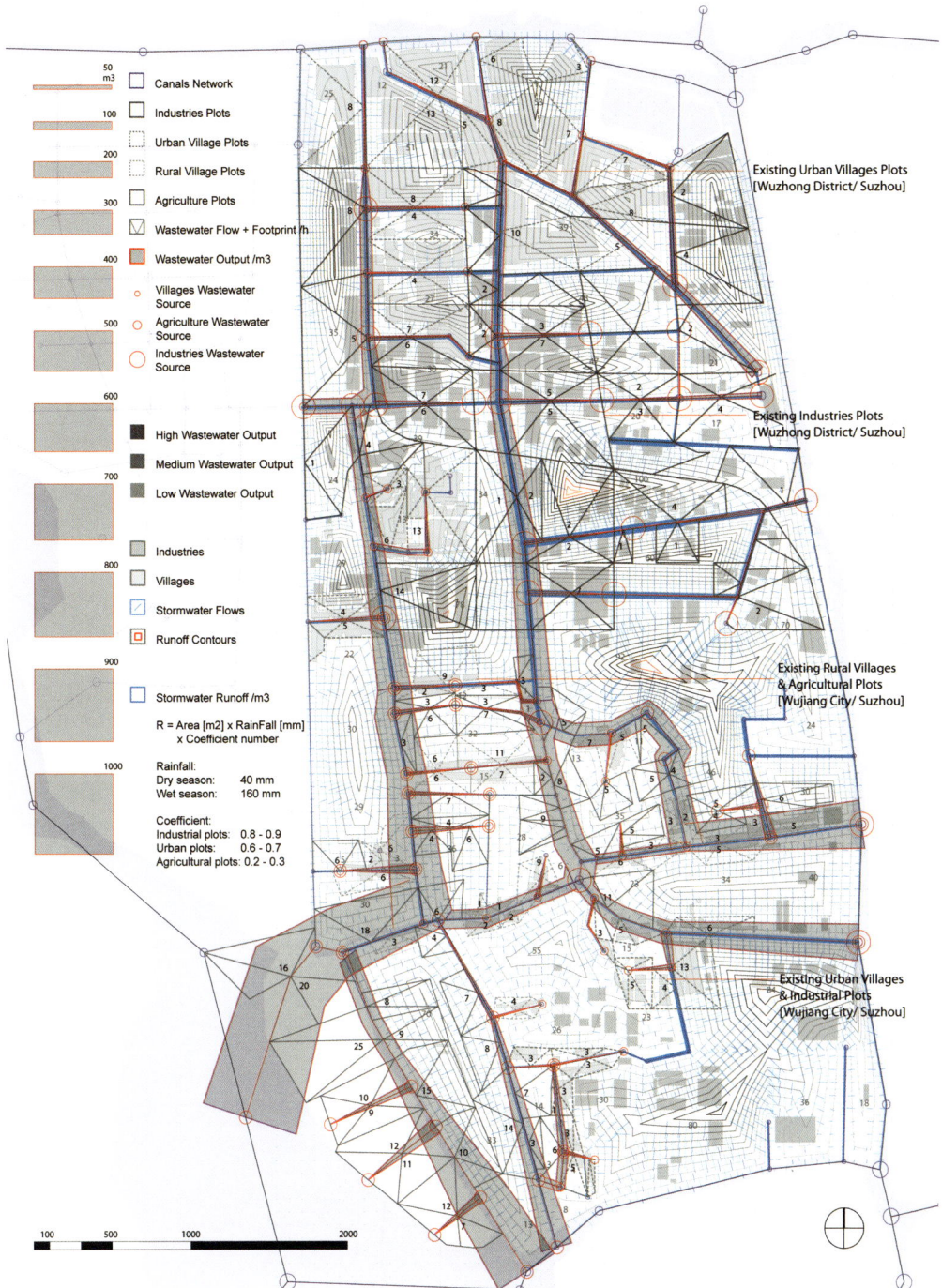

Legend:

Canals Network
Industries Plots
Urban Village Plots
Rural Village Plots
Agriculture Plots
Wastewater Flow + Footprint /h
Wastewater Output /m3

○ Villages Wastewater Source
○ Agriculture Wastewater Source
○ Industries Wastewater Source

High Wastewater Output
Medium Wastewater Output
Low Wastewater Output

Industries
Villages
Stormwater Flows
Runoff Contours

Stormwater Runoff /m3

R = Area [m2] x RainFall [mm] x Coefficient number

Rainfall:
Dry season: 40 mm
Wet season: 160 mm

Coefficient:
Industrial plots: 0.8 - 0.9
Urban plots: 0.6 - 0.7
Agricultural plots: 0.2 - 0.3

Existing Urban Villages Plots [Wuzhong District/ Suzhou]

Existing Industries Plots [Wuzhong District/ Suzhou]

Existing Rural Villages & Agricultural Plots [Wujiang City/ Suzhou]

Existing Urban Villages & Industrial Plots [Wujiang City/ Suzhou]

3. Jian-Jie Zhou, Rurbanscape
The scheme challenges the generic industrial zoning and polluted livelihoods resulting from inadequate wastewater treatment amongst a group of rapidly industrialising rural villages between Wuzhong and Wujiang in Suzhou. It proposes to hybridise mechanical and natural wastewater treatment processes as a responsive infrastructure, generating an alternative morphological framework and self-sufficient urban configuration.

221

Testing the angles of branching with changing proximities of canals

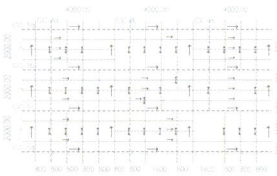

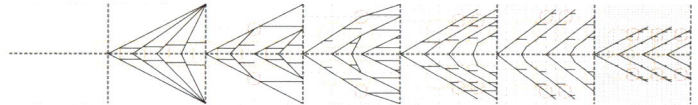

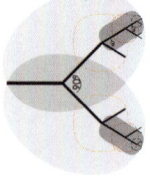

Existing Canal system: discontinuity leading to stagnancy and inefficient water movement

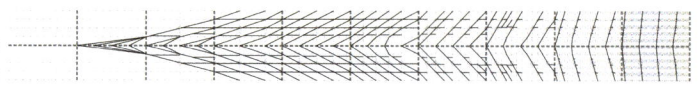

Testing the angles of branching with changing proximities of canals

MELON ON THE VINE SYSTEM:
The system provides efficiency in lending clear hierachy to the canal system (from A to B). The system is used as a method of organizing the territory by varied geometric explorations

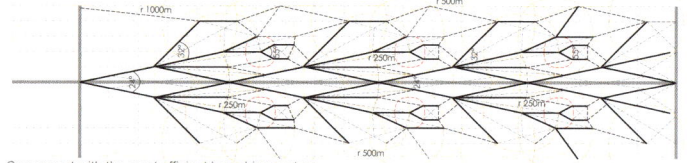

Component Proliferation on Site

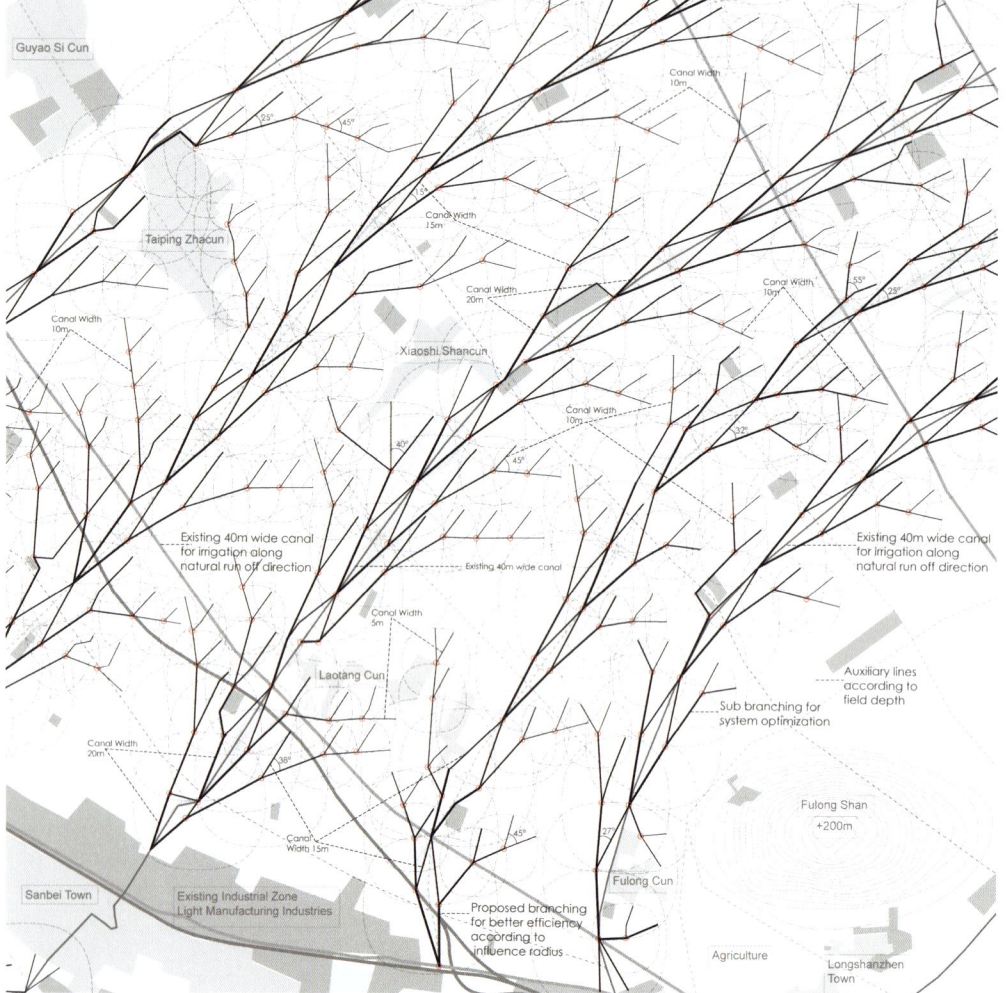

Component with the most efficient branching system

Guyao Si Cun

Canal Width 10m

Taiping Zhacun

Canal Width 15m

Canal Width 20m

Canal Width 10m

Canal Width 10m

Xiaoshi Shancun

Canal Width 10m

Canal Width 10m

Existing 40m wide canal for irrigation along natural run off direction

Existing 40m wide canal

Existing 40m wide canal for irrigation along natural run off direction

Canal Width 5m

Laotang Cun

Auxiliary lines according to field depth

Sub branching for system optimization

Canal Width 20m

Fulong Shan +200m

Canal Width 15m

Fulong Cun

Sanbei Town

Existing Industrial Zone Light Manufacturing Industries

Proposed branching for better efficiency according to influence radius

Agriculture

Fulong Cun

Longshanzhen Town

4. Karishma Desai
The Yangtze River Delta is one of the most intensely developing regions of the world today, experiencing issues of large-scale migration, pollution and loss of arable land as a result of massive urbanisation. The expansion of Port of Ningbo is part of this development trend, affecting the Hangzhou Bay area ecological zone which is home to a mix of agro-based and industrial systems.

Adaptive spatial strategies harness the material conditions of the site by amalgamating 'water infrastructures' to generate new forms of social, infrastructural and industrial programming – bridging otherwise fragmented entities.

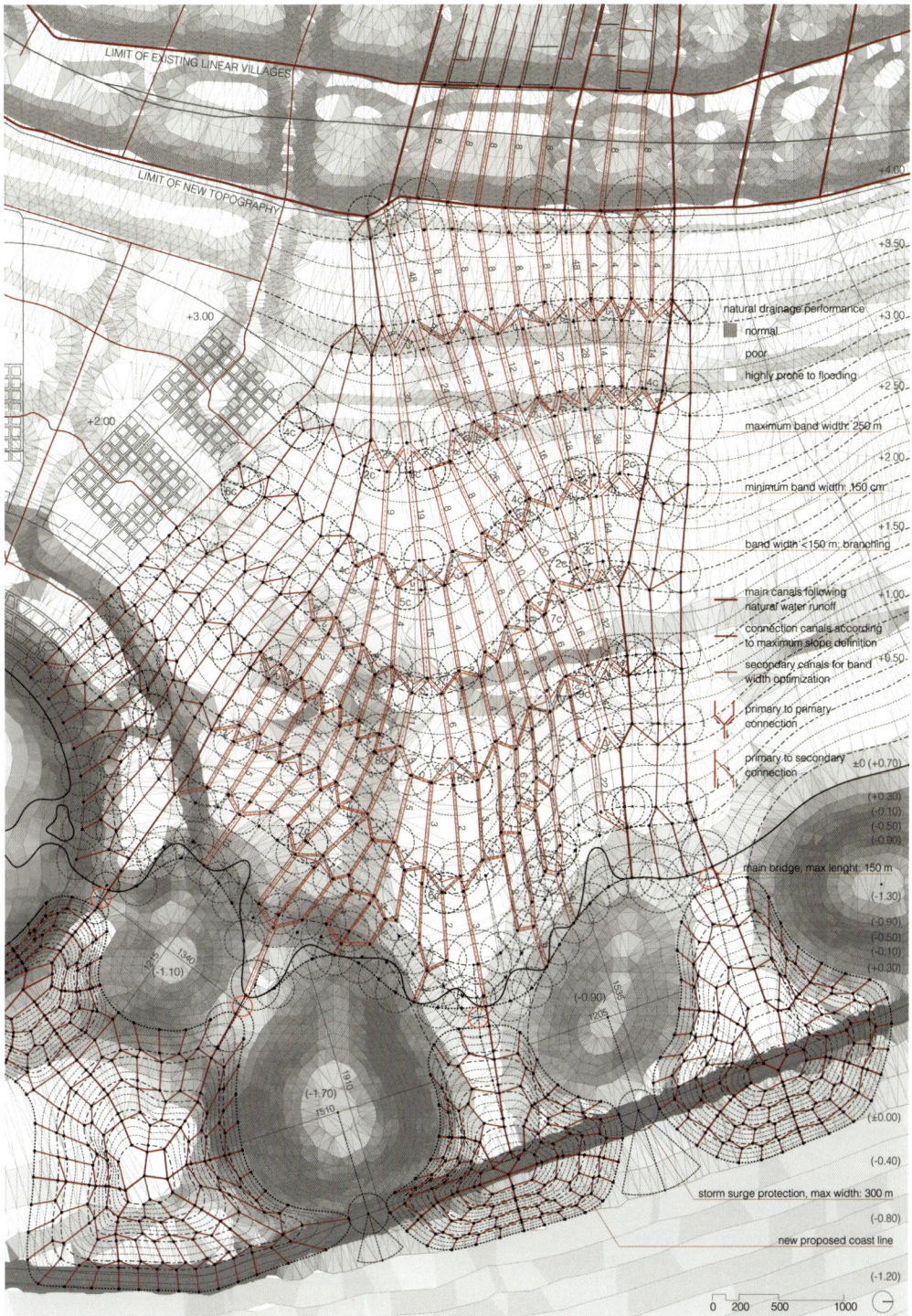

Legend labels (right side of map):

LIMIT OF EXISTING LINEAR VILLAGES

LIMIT OF NEW TOPOGRAPHY

natural drainage performance
normal
poor
highly prone to flooding

maximum band width: 250 m

minimum band width: 150 cm

band width <150 m: branching

main canals following
natural water runoff

connection canals according
to maximum slope definition

secondary canals for band
width optimization

primary to primary
connection

primary to secondary
connection

main bridge, max lenght: 150 m

storm surge protection, max width: 300 m

new proposed coast line

0   200   500   1000

5. Nicola Saladino

The city of Lingang sits on reclaimed land that floods easily during the rainy season. A new network of canals and bodies of water connect with the existing patterns of linear villages, improving drainage and structuring the future growth of the city. The design treats water as a crucial element of public space and, by maximising the coastline, generates higher land values that compensate for the costs of necessary dredging and earthworks.

223

SUSTAINABLE ENVIRONMENTAL DESIGN

The main research objective of the Masters programme in Sustainable Environmental Design is the relationship between architectural form, materiality and environmental performance and how this relation evolves in response to climate change and emerging technical capabilities. Sustainable environmental design is not a fixed ideal, but an evolving concept that must be redefined and reassessed with each new project. The first part of the taught programme is structured around team projects aimed at developing participants' conceptual and analytical skills. Projects are supported by weekly lectures on the theories and practices of sustainable design and by training in the use of computational tools and research techniques. The second part of the programme is devoted to dissertation projects. The focus of this year's studio projects was housing design. In the Autumn Term fieldwork in selected schemes around London encompassed a broad spectrum of dwelling typologies and environmental characteristics. The Spring Term studio focused on low-energy design briefs for new housing and conversions in London and Madrid. The third stage of the year's agenda takes the lessons of these exercises into dissertation projects started in May 2010 by 42 MSc and MArch candidates working under 14 interrelated thematic groupings. MArch projects begun last May on sites in Athens, Bangkok, Belgrade, Bogota, London, Pune and Chile were successfully completed in February this year.

STAFF
Simos Yannas
Klaus Bode
Gustavo Brunelli
Joana Soares Gonçalves
Alberto Moletto
Raul Moura
Barak Pelman
Jorge Rodriguez Alvarez

GUEST SPEAKERS & REVIEWERS
Pierandrea Angius
Nick Baker
Michael Bruse
Paula Cadima
Peter Chlapowski
Mario Cucinella
Asif Din
Bill Gething
Joy-Anne Fleming
Hattie Hartman
Catherine Harrington
Richard Hawkes
Amy Holtz
Ben Humphreys
Gary Hunt
Snighda Jain
Jessica James
Victor Lopez-Roboo Gil
Federico Montella
Farah Naz
Rudrajit Sabhaney
Rosa Schiano-Phan
Ekachai Sophonudomporn

Spyros Stravoravdis
Becci Taylor
Alexandros Tombazis
Kim Waller

STUDENTS
Phase I MSc
Hiroki Abe
Carole Aspeslagh
Evgenia Budanova
Aaron Budd
Francisco Casablanca
Joanna Conceicao
Cristina Crespo
Melpo Danou
Anna Gkouma
Alfonso Hernandez
Kristin Hoogenboom
Shao-Fan Hsu
Shashank Jain
Amygdalia Kyropoulou
Masoudeh Nooraei
Joram Orvieto
Jeewon Paek
Niken Palupi
Silvia Piccione
Sameena Rajendra Singh
Gemala Rinaldi
Liliana Rodriguez
Roshanek Sajadian
Rohin Sher
Gabriela Ferreira Tristao
Kalliroi Tzimika
Marco Vitali
Ruofan Yao

Phase I MArch
Suraksha Bhatla
Miguel Cardona
Xavier Cordero
Ruth Dominguez
Celina Escobar
Pablo Gugel
Constanza Jorquera
Pamela Kravetsky
Amy Leedham
Didar Ozcelik
Rodrigo Rodrigues
Francisco Ramirez
Fanor Serrano
Orapim Tantipat

Phase II MArch
Isha Anand
Chanasit Chalasuek
Olga Conto Sterling
Antonio Espinoza de Tudela
Anuja Pandit
Katerina Pantazi
Gilda Riveros
Konstantina Saranti
Milena Stojkovic
Alexandra Theodorou

For this year's study trips, visits to architectural practices and building projects, thanks to Mecanoo Architekten, TANGRAM, West 8, KCAP, Cie and VMX Architects in the Netherlands; Kate Cheyne, Jake Ireland, Mooarc, Julia Manheim, Ken Taylor, Peter Thomas, Catherine Du Toit and ZEDfactory for building studies in London; and in Madrid, Jose Maria de Lapuerta, Fernando Altozano, Carmen Espegel, Sebastian Severino and their colleagues and students of the Masters Programme in Collective Housing at the Escuela Tecnica Superior de Arquitectura de Madrid. Thanks to Kazuo Iwamura, Ben Nakamura, Miwako Nakamura, Koji Itonaga and Masanori Shukuya for the workshop on environmental research in Japan and the Architectural Institute of Japan's Low Carbon Society 2050 research project.

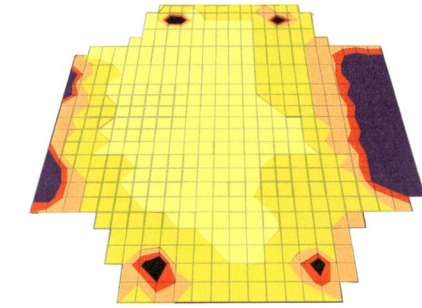

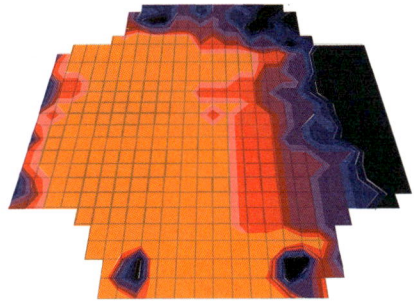

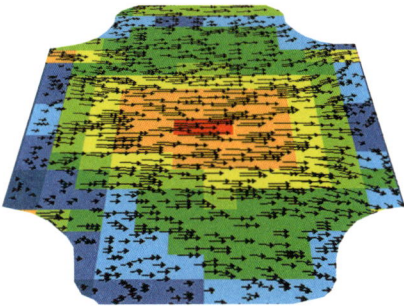

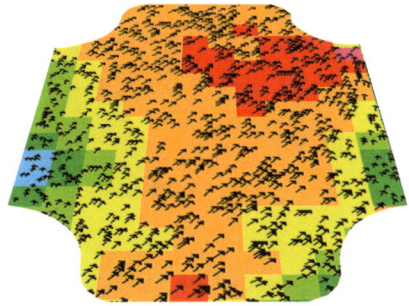

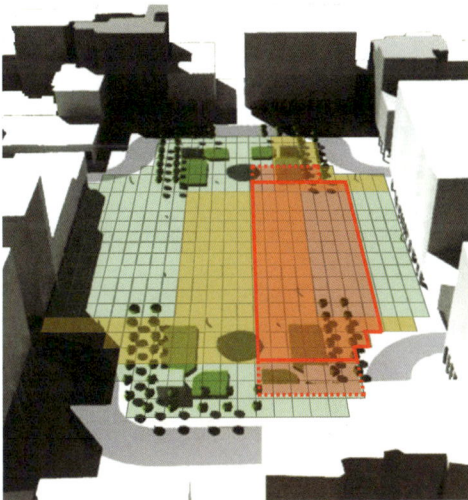

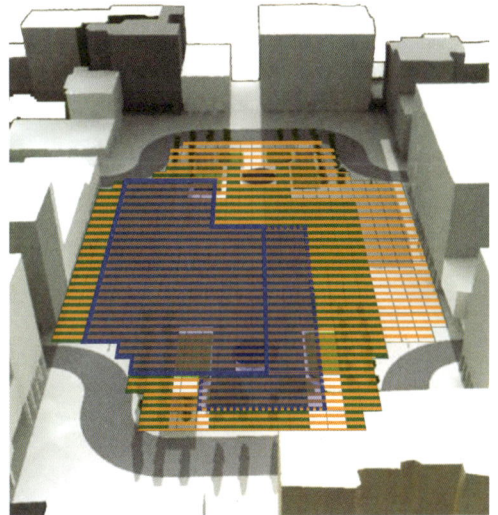

1. Konstantina Saranti, microclimatic interventions on an
urban square in Patras, Greece. MArch dissertation
project

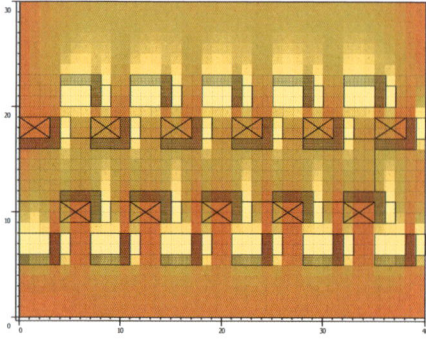

2

3

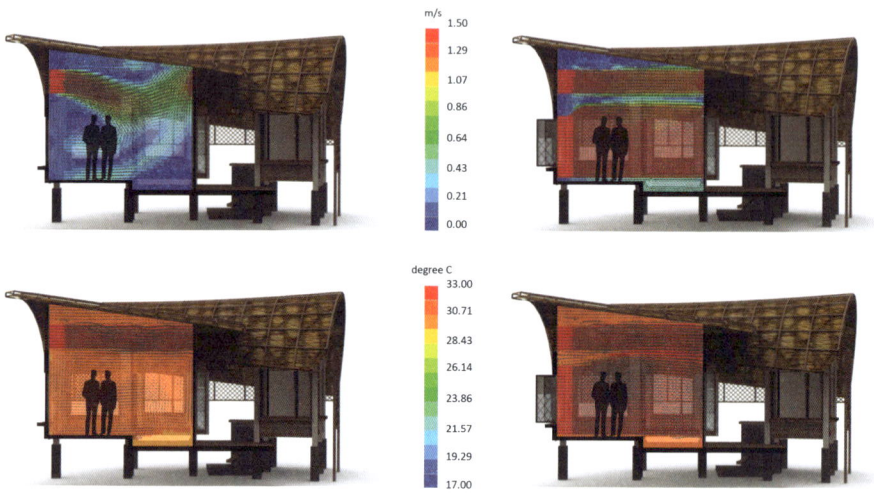

4

5

2–5. Chanasit Chalasuek, sustainable low-income
community in Bangkok. MArch dissertation project

6

7

6 & 7. Antonio Espinoza de Tudela, post-disaster housing
for Chile. MArch dissertation project

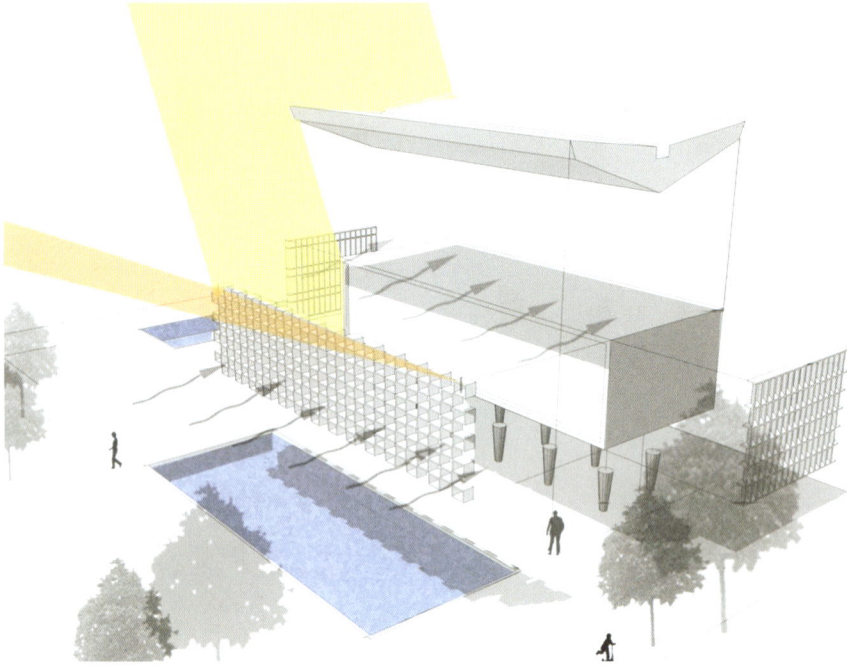

8

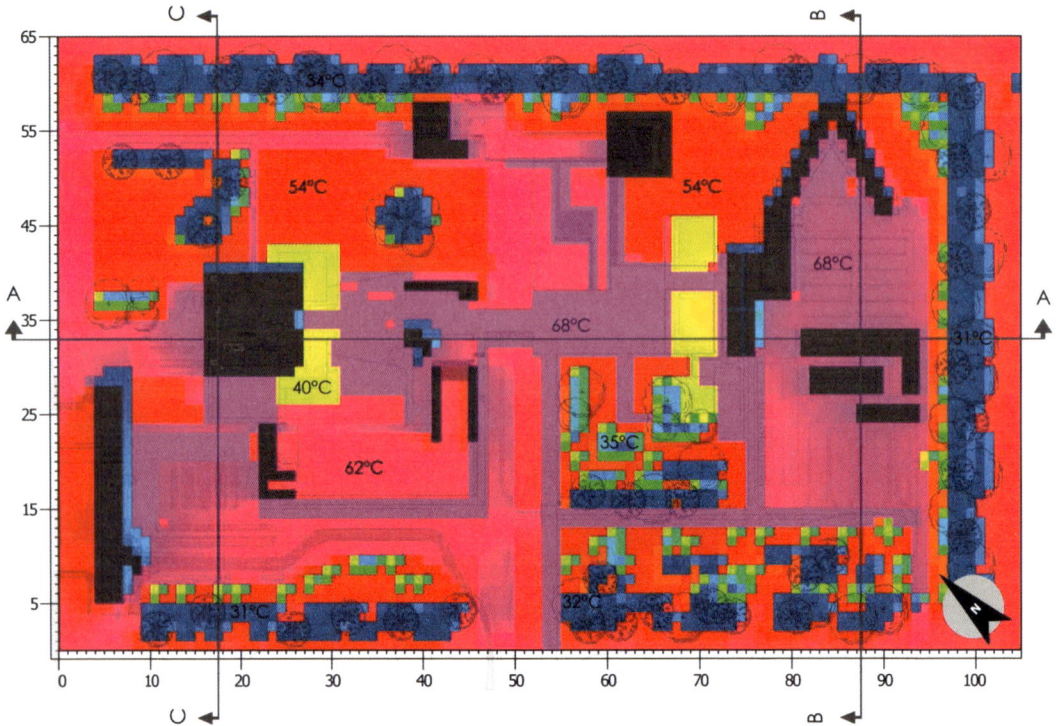

9

8 & 9. Nitin Bansal, 'Corbu' in the tropics: a study of
environmental strategies by Le Corbusier in Chandigarh.
MSc dissertation project

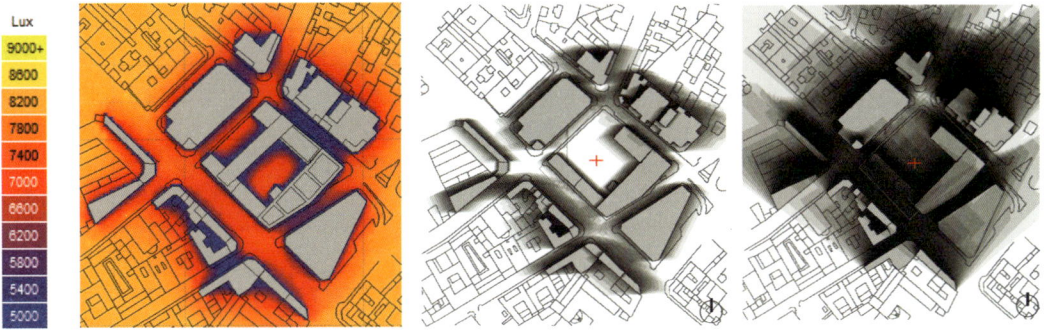

10

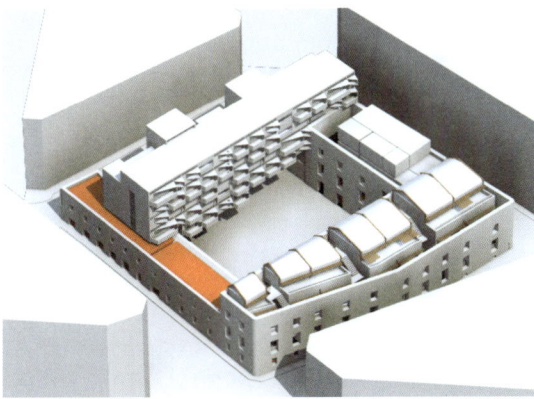

11

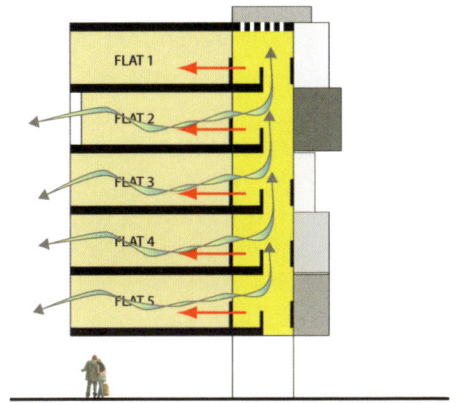

12

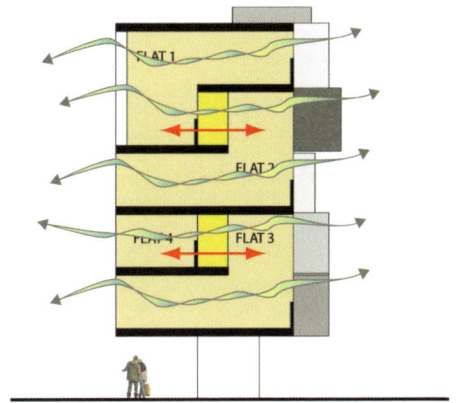

13

10–13. Francisco Casablanca, Ruth Dominguez, Pablo Gugel, Jeewon Paek, Palacio de Ustariz Term 2 urban living environments project

CONSERVATION OF HISTORIC BUILDINGS

The Conservation of Historic Buildings course awards a Graduate Diploma on completion of its two-year, part-time programme of studies. The course aims to develop awareness and skills in the core areas of Historic Knowledge and Cultural Appreciation; Research and Report Writing; Philosophies of Conservation; Traditional Building Materials; Structures of Historic Buildings; Fabric Deterioration and Repair; Building Investigations and Assessments; Regeneration and Conservation; Design in Modern Urban Contexts; and International Projects. In addition to developing a wide range of knowledge concerning historic buildings from all periods, the programme continues to emphasise twentieth-century buildings and environs, along with the current political and social issues of change, regeneration and urban redevelopment. Recent visits to sites exemplifying contemporary urbanisation issues have included King's Cross/St Pancras and the Shoreditch/Hackney/Spitalfields district, which couple conservation with regeneration. This year, our annual tour travelled to Oxford to view the Castle and Ashmolean Museum redevelopments.

The course continued its involvement with the ongoing EU-funded project to develop 'Criteria for Assessment of Heritage at Risk' as part of the Heritage without Borders programme in conjunction with participants from seven countries in southeastern Europe. Director Andrew Shepherd attended workshops in Dubrovnik and Pécs, Hungary in addition to lecturing and leading a building repairs workshop at the Swedish Foundation Cultural Heritage without Borders Training camp in Gjirokastra, Albania. The 'Heritage at Risk' project will be completed in 2011, after which we will participate in a project on recording industrial archaeology together with teams from Hungary, Romania and France.

The course continues to engage with the proposed conservation of Kurt Schwitters' Merz Barn at Elterwater in the Lake District, through consultation and the presentation of a paper at the annual Elterwater Seminar.

STAFF
Andrew Shepherd (Director), Judith Roebuck (Year Master, part of the year), Russell Bateman (Year Tutor, part of the year), David Heath (Thesis tutor), Clement Chung (Supervisor), Jenny Devine (Coordinator)

VISITING LECTURERS
John Bailey, Neil Burton, Ian Bristow, Sharon Cather, Robert Demaus, Andrew Derrick, Michael Drury, Keith Emerick, Helen Ensor, Claire Gapper, Alan Greening, Richard Halsey, Julian Harrap, Harriett Harriss, Richard Harris, Elain Harwood, Paula Henderson, Jacques Heyman, Ian Hume, Shawn Kholuchy, Stephen Levrant, Alyson McDermott, Ian McInnes, Cathy Oakes, David Odgers, Sam Price, Alan Powers, Rosemarie McQueen, John Redmill, Geoff Rich, Clive Richardson, Eric Robinson, Veronica Sekules, Sally Strachey, Robert Thorne, Tony Walker, Andrew Wiles, Roger White

FIRST YEAR STUDENTS
George Allan, Duncan Berntsen, Calvin Bruce, Nick Chapple, Effie Dalrymple, Irene Georgakis, Udo Heinrich, Inga Sievert, Jeananne Wells

SECOND YEAR STUDENTS
Natasha Brown, Alan Dickinson, Nicola James, Chris Kiernan, Monica Knight

THESES SUBMITTED
Lydia Blaszcynska – *Animal Pounds in and around London: An Unexpected Survival*

Natasha Brown – *History and Conservation of Eighteenth/Nineteenth-Century Stage Machinery Today*

Alan Dickinson – *Timber Towers and Spires of Romney March and Hinterland: A Developmental and Conservation Study*

Monica Knight – *A Study of Charles Edward Mallows (1864–1915): Mallows's Garden Houses of Biddenham in comparison to those of Mackay Hugh Baillie Scott: Value and Survival*

Rosemarie Shaw – *Save Brixton Market: Protecting Cultural Values*

Sybil Thomas – *Water Wells and Hand Pumps: Their Working History, Demise and Potential Future: A Study for Conservation in Uttlesford, Essex*

Jade Young – *Inconvenient Survivals: When Form is Without Function*

1

2

1. Spitalfields visit with the Spitalfields Trust

2. Visit to SPAN housing, Twickenham

PhD PROGRAMME

The AA's PhD Programme fosters critical discourse and innovative research in the fields of architecture and urbanism. The thematic and methodological origins of current projects derive from three main areas of research: architectural theory and history (mainly the critical reassessment of twentieth-century architecture and urbanism); architectural urbanism (its role in addressing central issues in contemporary urban conditions and debates); and sustainable environmental design (its critical dimension and innovative applications in architecture and urbanism). The programme combines advanced research with a broader educational agenda preparing graduates for practice in global academic and professional environments. This year sees the completion of over half of the programme's PhD projects and the start of eight new ones.

Winyu Ardrugsa
'Stranger' and 'Home-Land': The Spatial Negotiations of the Muslim Minorities in the Practice of Prayer in Contemporary Bangkok, Thailand
Since the 1970s, Islamic resurgence and urbanisation have altered general conceptions of identity and place for Thai Muslims. This thesis investigates the relationship between subject formation and spatial negotiation through the everyday prayer practices of the Muslims of Bangkok.

Francisca Aroso
Performative Bio-Intelligent Architecture within the Metabolism of Mediterranean Cities
In nature, biological processes show that the capacity for adjustment is fundamental to the success of future generations. Likewise, the design of architectural structures should take change into consideration, to develop responsive structures with adaptable behaviours and functions.

Merate Barakat
Sonic City Networking: The Acoustic Effect of a City on the Human Sensorium
Every city has a unique set of sonic characteristics as a result of regional ecology, cultural influences and current technology. Expanding on past research in Barcelona, this thesis examines Istanbul and its rich acoustic character.

Doreen Bernath
On Architecture of Building the Picture – China and Pictorial Introjection
Projects in contemporary Chinese practices are often visualised and even realised on the basis of highly effective computer renderings – effect drawings – while representations in plans, sections and elevations become a posterior exercise of 'fitting into the picture'. This thesis traces the link between these pictorial strategies and a traditional Chinese aesthetic preference for idealised frontal configurations. New forms of digital software, which have furthered architectural design as an introjective process, are considered significant beyond a specifically Chinese context.

1

2

3

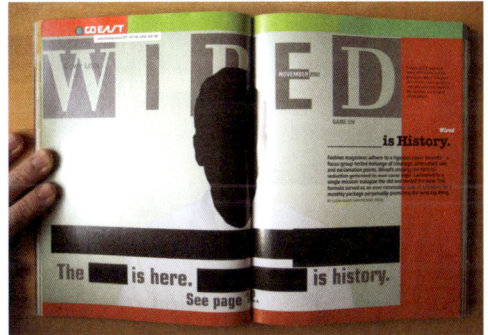

4

1 Chittawadi Chitrabongs presenting her PhD on
The Politics of Dressing, completed this year
2. Emanuel de Sousa, Photomontage: Teatro del Mondo
by Aldo Rossi / Arrival to Dubrovnik (August 1980)

3. Elif Erdine, tower research initial diagram based
on Patrik Schumacher's 'Proto-Tower' brief
4. Kirk Wooller, The Architecture Magazine as a Project

Alejandra Celedon F.
Beyond the Modernist Plan: The Beginning of the End(s) of Planning
This proposed thesis departs from the debates that shaped the postwar
era. By analysing specific systems of urban representation it aims to revise
claims for a reorganisation of architectural knowledge in the post-CIAM city
to be conceived in terms of an expanded field for architectural practice.

Chittawadi Chitrabongs
The Politics of Dressing Up
This thesis documents the hygiene reforms carried out by King Rama V of
Siam (1868–1910). Rama V sought to improve royal authority in Bangkok by
imposing distinctive ideas of order and neatness and was willing to import
objects and practices from the west. The crux of the argument is that his
reforms were not 'westernisation', but a highly developed fantasy.

Nerma Cridge
Drawing the Unbuildable
This thesis is concerned with unbuildable drawings, speculating whether
they can still be considered as a field of architectural investigation that
reveals pertinent facts independently from the construction of buildings.

Elif Erdine
*Mathematics in Nature: Self-Organisation in Parametrically
Generated Morphologies*
The major questions to be examined: how do the principles of geometry
shaping natural formations relate to form, structure, material and
efficiency? How can we integrate nature's self-organisation processes into
design research? What can context-specific architecture learn from nature?

Eva Eylers
*Hygiene and Health in Modern Urban Planning: The Sanatorium
and Its Role within the Modernist Movement*
This thesis centres the programmatic typology of the sanatorium, its
engagement with the city and its instrumental role in the planning debates
of the modern city. Using this building type as an analytical device and
considering the medical and psychological conditions created by the
modern metropolis – of which the sanatorium is a product and a response
– this thesis discusses how the tuberculosis sanatorium provided a cure
not only for TB but for diseases associated with the experience of the city.

Valeria Guzmán-Verri
Graphic Form as a System of Regulation
This thesis explores the rise of a series of printed forms which began
to formally organise ways of thinking across a number of fields in the
nineteenth century. It argues that the systematic use of numerical
data, together with its representation, developed a certain typography
in which modern architects, urban planners, sociologists, economists
and administrators were captured.

Kensuke Hotta
Programmable Architecture
The Metabolists of 1970s Japan have a certain presence in recent architecture and urbanism, but their influence is difficult to trace in the fabric of cities today. Yet the necessity for intelligent buildings and their aggregation into metabolic urban systems has increased. This thesis will explore a model for urban metabolism and the design of intelligent buildings and blocks that can modulate their surfaces and spatial configurations in response to climate and ecology, coupled with economically driven programmatic changes.

Dong Ku Kim
Climate-Interactive Building Design in a Korean Climate
Continuous adaptation to surrounding environmental change is essential to sustain life. Like living beings, buildings can provide a comfortable environment adjusted to outdoor climate variation. This thesis focuses on the potential of climate-interactive building design strategies for the Korean climate and its significant seasonal variations.

Pavlos Philippou
Cultivating Urbanism: The Architecture of Cultural Institutions
Beginning in the late nineteenth century and codified by the early twentieth, cultural buildings acquired a salient role in urban reasoning. This thesis pursues the architectural richness of this reasoning in three case studies which exemplify the themes and strategies linking cultural buildings to the spatial politics of the liberal metropolis. Within a complex urban discourse, they make visible the continuities as well as the dynamism and differentiation architecture brings to the urban field.

Ivonne Santoyo Orozco
The Rise of Housing: Architecture's Relation to Liberalism
This thesis argues that housing, as a category of urbanism, arose from the burgeoning liberalism of nineteenth-century Europe. In this sense, architecture is inseparable from this form of government, its aims and concerns, and thus assists in the so-called formation of the modern subject. The new role of the architect and the aesthetic techniques acquired for housing in the modern city are also examined.

Camila E. Sotomayor
To Survive or To Collapse: Exploring the Urban Critical Threshold
Cities thrive at the peril of their surrounding environment, often depleting natural resources to such an extent that collapse ensues. Diminishing resources affect the city in a variety of ways; pockets of the population migrate, areas of the city are abandoned, climate changes are magnified. The aim of this research is to design a dynamic system model set to unfold over a period of time. The nature of the system will emerge from a reciprocal exchange between city and landscape, in which the impact of one has a positive effect on the other.

Emanuel de Sousa
Heterotopia: Reframing Spatial Practices and Boundaries, 1960–present
This thesis problematises the dissemination of the notion of heterotopia as an alternative way of thinking spatiality that has challenged established modes in architecture and the history of the built environment. From an unusual distribution of elements of corporal space in medical terms – through histological processes in the isolation of a functional, two-dimensional section of tissue in contrast to a paradoxical 'internal surface' – to the reorganisation of space in cultural and architectural terms – perceiving the relativity of difference and its local status in the organism's architecture with effects in three-dimensional space – heterotopia assumes an exaptative role in questioning spatial practices and histories.

Fei Fei Sun
Achieving Suitable Thermal Performance for Residential Buildings in Different Climatic Regions of China
With the Chinese economy soaring, increased energy efficiency is essential to achieve sustainable future development. This thesis identifies new technologies and existing practices that will significantly increase the indoor comfort of residential buildings in China, in five different climatic regions. Its proposals rely heavily on passive and natural techniques.

Aldo Urbinati
Architectural Effects
This thesis is designed as a case study; for each situation or condition a specific architectural effect will be addressed. The operative intersections function as a conceptual nest or matrix in which to discuss the relevant points about each building, landscape or city. This multiple condition of the architectural effect can offer a strategic vantage point for understanding the critical moment in the history of architecture.

Kirk Wooller
Changing the Criteria for Innovation: The Architecture Magazine as a Project, c.1956–2006
This thesis explores the diminishing role of judgement in contemporary architectural writing and its implications for architectural knowledge. Focusing on the historiographical argument that the architecture magazine is a site for innovation, this thesis examines specific publications over the last 50 years, taking those of Reyner Banham and Rem Koolhaas as case studies in the transition from 'architectural criticism' to 'architectural intelligence'. This thesis shows that a decline in judgement hinders the reader from establishing a position either for or against what is registered.

Arthur Aw
The Architecture of Innovation Environments: Hidden Patterns and New Relationships

Pablo León de la Barra Vargas
Art and Architecture: The Creation of Space and Place in Contemporary Art

Katharina Borsi
Urban Domestic: The Diagram of the Berlin Block

Luciano Dutra
Design Process and Environmental Information: Applicability of Design Support Tools

Choul Woong Kwon
Transitional Spaces: The Role of Sheltered Semi-Outdoor Spaces as Microclimatic Modifiers on School Buildings in the UK Climate

Tania Lopez Winkler
Clues in the Detection of London: Evidence of the Construction of Knowledge of the City in Nineteenth-Century London

Frances Mikuriya
Time-Space Pathologies

Carlos Miranda
The House: Energy Efficiency and Architectural Expression

Kristine Mun
Vitalising Technology: On the Mode of Invention

Jose Alberto Tovar-Barrientos
Urban Form and Regional Strategies of Innovation Environments: The Case of Biotechnology Clusters in Cambridge-London

Enrique Walker
The Infra-Ordinary City: George Perec's Lieux Project

Jose Zavala
Towards a Multidimensional Approach in the Design of Housing Policies

SUPERVISORS
Simos Yannas
Lawrence Barth
Geoffrey Bennington
Tim Brittain-Catlin
Mark Cousins
David Dunster

Jorge Fiori
Hugo Hinsley
Marina Lathouri
Ronaldo Ramirez
Modjtaba Sadria
Rosa Schiano-Phan
Patrik Schumacher

Peter Sharratt
Edward W Soja
Teresa Stoppani
Anthony Vidler
Michael Weinstock

PhD degrees are administered by the Architecture & Urbanism Management Group set in partnership with the Open University.

INTERPROFESSIONAL STUDIO

Seed to Scene
This year's project of the Interprofessional Studio 'Seed to Scene' (S2S) is the result of new forms of collaboration within the creative disciplines. Therefore S2S cannot merely be defined as architecture, as a performance space or as a social and political event, but rather as the sum of these components.

With S2S we created a platform for the discussion of experimental collaboration in the creative field. Bringing together various components of design, the events in London's Covent Garden have demonstrated new innovation strategies for creative networks and are the starting point for a series of further events in the UK and Europe.

The studio aimed to explore the scalability of creative processes. Taking inspiration from the structural scale of seeds at a microscopic level, S2S is also literally the seed of the discussion on how to frame creativity today and offers a platform for artistic performances, interactive installations and workshops. S2S develops into large-scale social projects through the negotiation between different participating disciplines, finally expressed in a multi-dimensional film scene documenting the creative network in operation. The overall space of the scene begins to shift the perception of event, daily activity, scale, time, physical and virtual construction, and with this the remit area of activity of the creative disciplines.

AAIS has collaborated with many professionals and individuals including film producer Rosa Bosch; music producers Ben Wolff and Andy Dean (Music Technology Ltd); and organisations such as New Deal of the Mind initiated by Martin Bright, which seeks to create employment opportunities for the creative industries; c/o pop, the organisers of Europe's biggest creative industries convention in Cologne; and the dancers of New Movement, who brought the installations to life.

The entire design of the set from furniture to stage design and installation, fashion and music was produced in close collaboration with this year's participants. We achieved a lot in trying to make the impossible possible – in the environment of the AA such innovation becomes reality.

STUDIO DIRECTOR
Theo Lorenz

STUDIO MASTER
Tanja Siems

STUDIO TUTOR
Jan Hendrik
 Brueggemeier

AAIS PARTICIPANTS:
Emu Masuyama
Eugene Soler
Lori Solondz
Prayrika Mathur
Raluca Grada
Vikrant Tike

WORKSHOP/LECTURERS
Ben Wolff
Jonathan Laventhol
Hugo Hinsley
Rocio Paz
Mohammed Makki
Steve Webb
Wolfgang Stubby
Alexandra Papadakis

Thanks to:
Christina Smith, Will Wright, Ben Wolff, Andy Dean, Rosa Bosch, Hannah Price, Arthur Cauty, Dominic Lutyens, Tal Rosner, Steve Webb, Anita LeRoy, Anna Hodgson, Magnus Finnes, Richard Wentworth, Ilona Sagar, Patricia Okenwa, Clara Barbera, Gemma Nixon, Jonathan Goddard, Renaud Wiser, Joe Walkling, Nick Elias, Miraj Ahmed, Simon Beames, Will Kallaway, Anna Cusden, Claudia Jericho, Martin Bright, Markus Mason, Kit Friend, Barbara Gunnell, Jo Phillips, Stuart Dale, Fereday Pollard Architects, Brett Steele, Esther McLaughlin, Nicola Quinn, Stephen Livett, Joel Newman, Collin Prendergast, Leszek Skrzypiec, Peter Keiff, Mathew Hanrahan, Anita Pfaunstch, James Keiff, Nick Wayne, Charlie Cole, Valerie Bennett, Darko Calina, Pascal Babeau, David McAlmont and Guy Davis

Photos by
Takako Hasegawa

1. The design of the entire installation Seed to Scene, the dress, the hexagon wall and the dark seed, is inspired by the formal and performative qualities of 'seeds'.

2

3

2. Edgewood building tests at Hooke Park   3. David McAlmont in concert at AAIS Seed to Scene

4. Dance performance of New Movement
in the 'soft room'

5

6

7

5. Andy Dean, Richard Wentworth and Simon Freedman
in conversation at Seed to Scene
6. The 'Darker Space' designed by this year's AAIS
participants Emu Masuyama, Eugene Soler, Raluca
Grada, Prayrika Mathur and Vikrant Tike, is made
from edge wood, giving the design a dark rough
outside and a smooth light inside.

7. The smooth Hexgon Dress contrasts with the
rough timber of the Darker Space.

8

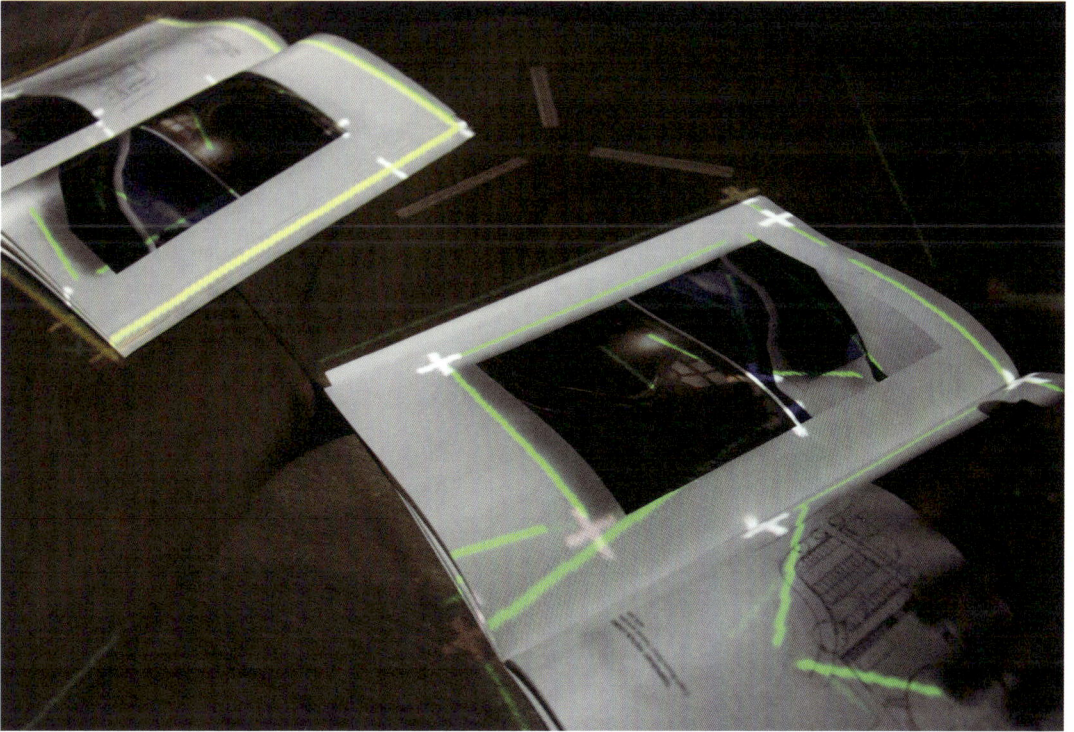

9

8. AAIS in the music studio with Marcus Finnes and
Ben Wolff

9. Interactive table workshop with Daniel Fischer

HISTORY & THEORY STUDIES

First Year: Elements of Architecture

The course focuses on key 'elements' of architecture theory and practice in order to establish a foundation for design thinking. It aims not only to redefine key concepts but also to outline the relationships that have been formed (or severed) between them: technique and process, size and scale, form and programme, decoration and surface. These relationships are investigated through theoretical arguments and practical experiments, establishing their relevance to contemporary architectural conversation. The coursework supports crossovers between written and graphic investigations, as students learn to conceptually advance and visually articulate their emerging methodological positions within the broader disciplinary framework. Ultimately, the course initiates a long-term corre-spondence between research and design.

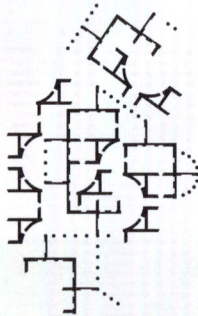

One interesting thing about Villa La Rotonda's transformation from an object to a field, is the fact that the very things that make it a pure example of an object – its two axes – also provided a solution to making it a field. The symmetry of the axes makes the individual parts generic, and that was exploited in its field incarnation. By combining the different parts in new ways – at angles, mirrored etc. – using the fact that they actually fit together in multiple ways, a more field-like condition was created. I wonder what Palladio would have thought?

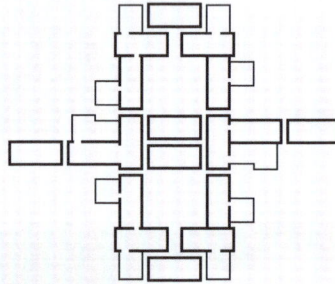

By applying the two axes of Villa La Rotonda on the distribution pattern that makes up Habitat 67, a hybrid was created that has substituted a parts of the field conditions present in the latter by the strict geometry of the former, in the process loosing its dynamic expression. It is much harder to imagine how to add or subtract parts from this hybrid whilst staying true to its initial manifestation than it was when it was configured as a field.

Olle Eriksson, HTS First Year, Object / Field

Second Year

How is, and how should, architectural history and theory be taught? Over several months, Mark Cousins developed a comprehensive argument that culminated in the spring symposium 'Architecture and its Pasts'.

The distinction between past and history was taken as the difference between things that have happened before and the constructed linear narrative of those things. While each of us has a history, we intuitively recognise it to be quite incongruous with our past. In reorganising the events of the past into coherent narrative structures we forcibly alter their meaning – the act of history-making is in essence the *construction* of a past, far more than the re-presentation of a past. The pedagogical rel-evance of this distinction is that by rejecting a history of architecture in favour of architectural pasts, a number of myths and inconsistencies used to construct that accepted history are exposed.

Perhaps the most important example of this is the oft-cited myth that architecture began with the Egyptians, or Vitruvius, or any other arbitrary point in the development of human habitation. In fact, Cousins argues, the notion of architecture is almost completely a nineteenth-century invention. The emerging profession applied the term retroactively to contexts which had no conception of architecture in the modern sense, as a method to authenticate its own existence. In particular, we spent several weeks analysing the validity of terming the Parthenon an architectural design.

While the emerging profession may have convinced society that architecture did indeed exist, and that it always-already was of ancient lineage, it nonetheless failed to establish ownership of what it claimed to be its exclusive field. Whereas law and medicine invoked venerable precedents (habeas corpus and the Hippocratic oath respectively) and subsequently monopolised their fields – only a doctor can practise medicine and only a lawyer can practise law. In this respect any failure of architecture as a profession might be tied to its inability to dominate its own field, by failing to delineate what it intended to do.

The resulting question, What does an architect actually do?, is neither naïve nor simplistic, and Cousins related it to his initial enquiry: What has the architect historically claimed to do, and to what extent is this actually true? Of course no irrefutable solutions were provided. What began instead was an honest enquiry into the role of architectural history in the contemporary education of the architect. *Jack Self*

Third Year
This year we tackled the twentieth-century 'canon'. From the Amsterdam Bourse and 'Ornament and Crime' to CCTV and 'Junkspace', we scrutinised the buildings and texts that define contemporary architecture. '16 Canonical Buildings and Texts' aimed to make the discourse of modern and contemporary architecture more intelligible and ground the idea of an experimental or critical practice, including the relationship between architectural theories and projects. It presented architecture as a form of knowledge and cultural discourse where history and theory are not seen as secondary to the essential work of an architect, which is the invention, promotion and communication of new ideas about architecture. Selected abstracts from student essays are listed below.

Gustav Toftgård
'Continuity and Change'
This essay examines the work of Sigurd Lewerentz (Swedish, 1885-1975), specifically his project for the Chapel of the Resurrection (Stockholm, 1925), by examining Lewerentz's application of architectural elements through the concept of disengagement. Toftgård takes a personal approach to the historical, cleverly mixing both biography and analysis. He addresses the fragmentation and isolation that predominate in modernity and modern architecture, through rigorous archival research of the main case study and several secondary case studies, triggering a connection between Lewerentz and the Neo-Gothic of Karl Friedrich Schinkel.

Lyn Hayek
'Le Corbusier's Beistegui Apartment: A Surrealist's Design'
This essay addresses a lesser known work of Le Corbusier's, the Beistegui
Apartment (Paris, 1930) by connecting it to the Surrealist art movement
as a representation of Le Corbusier's perception of modernity. Hayek's
argument develops through detailed research of several key features within
the case study despite there being limited documentation of the project,
demonstrating a keen understanding of an underplayed project in Le
Corbusier's oeuvre.

Camille Steyaert
'Monumentality: The Expression of Man's Highest Need'
Through challenging several statements made by Sigfried Giedion, José
Luis Sert and Fernand Léger in '9 Points on Monumentality' (1943), this
essay formulates the notion of 'projection' as an apparatus in analysing
monumental architecture. There is a strong and unparalleled use of semiot-
ics in discussions of architecture's monumentality. Steyaert explicitly
confronts several key notions of the course curriculum, including modernity
and memory, attacking them with meticulously articulated language.

Scrap Marshall
'The Eames Case Study House No. 8: A Framework for a Projected
Image of Modern Life'
This essay focuses on the Eames Case Study House No. 8 to formulate
the 'modern' house as a device which enables and controls the image of
domesticity in modernity. Marshall's argument develops organically
through a series of strong historical interpretations of domesticity, house/
home and just how much the 'image' is embedded in modern culture. He
is able to unify the issue of architectural production versus image production via an array of authors and perspectives that support and strengthen
his main argument.

Diploma School
The following titles refer to exemplary essays produced by students this year.

Jan Nauta, 4th Year
'Government of Space: The street, infinity and inclusive design.
The Via Giulia and the Battersea Powerstation development'
Pier Vittorio Aureli, The Project of Architecture

Li Gan, 4th Year
'An Indexical Intervention: Liberating Choreography'
Judith Clark, Curating Fashion

Michael Kloihofer, 5th Year
'Iconographic Ornament: The Lost Medium of the Message'
Oliver Domeisen, Architecture's Battle Royal

Tom Fox, 4th Year
'A Problem of Organisation: Typology in the Brittle City'
Chris Lee/Sam Jacoby, Projective Cities

Oscar Gomes, 4th Year
'All Quiet at the Planning Office: What are the possibilities for architects
to act as meaningfully productive agents in a controlling planning system?'
John Palmesino, Polity and Space

Aram Mooradian, 4th Year
'Why Hitler Saved the Ponte Vecchio: How Political Regimes
Reconstruct Collective Memories and How Individuals Cope With It'
Ines Weizman, Cold War Architecture

Nathaniel Mosley, 4th Year
'What Does It Mean to Live in a Culture That Finds It So Hard to Produce
New Domestic Architecture?
Patrick Wright, Landscape and Mobility

Aditya Aachi, 4th Year
'Case Study: St Mary's Secondary School, Wallasey UK, The "Solar School"'
Simos Yannas, Myths and Theories of Sustainable Architecture

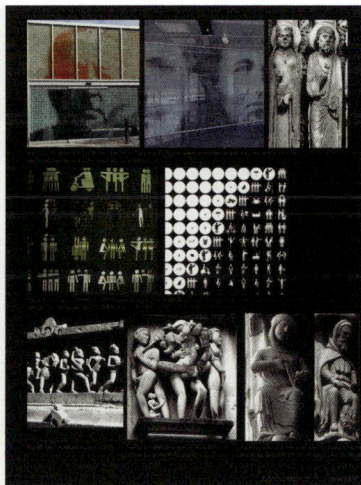

Michael Kloihofer, 5th Year, 'Iconographic Ornament'

TECHNICAL STUDIES

The Technical Studies programme consists of lecture courses, experiments and tests, group and individual research exercises and design projects. Lecture courses form a portion of yearly requirements, particularly in the First, Second and Fourth Years, when students concentrate on critical case studies, analysis and material experiments.

However the pinnacle of Technical Studies is the Detail Technical Design in the Third Year (TS3) and the Technical Design Thesis in the Fifth Year (TS5). For many years it has been the aim of the Technical Studies director and staff to integrate as much as possible the content of the teaching programme into individual unit agendas. This accounts for the great variety of themes and approaches in the TS3 and TS5 samples published here. In the Third Year, students conduct research to explore and resolve the technical issues of the main project of their unit portfolio, whereas Fifth Year students undertake a Technical Design Thesis (TS5), contextualised in a broader critical dialogue, and pursue extensive research through case studies and material experiments. In other words, TS3 and TS5 showcases the work of individual students engaged over the long term. And yet, TS supports a collaborative process; success stories (High Passes) are invariably the result of cooperation between Technical Staff and Unit Masters, as well as consultants hand-picked not only from amongst the leading UK practices but also from abroad. From a pedagogical perspective, TS3 and TS5 represent the application of the Technical Programme to the individual student's project – which amounts to a truly personalised experience.

DIPLOMA MASTER
Javier Castañón

Diploma Tutors
Mike Weinstock
Javier Castañón
Wolf Mangelsdorf
Toni Kotnik
John Noel
Martin Hagemann

INTERMEDIATE MASTER
Wolfgang Frese

Intermediate Tutors
Wolfgang Frese
Manja Van de Worp
Phil Cooper
Dancho Azagra

COURSE LECTURERS
Marissa Kretsch
Phil Cooper
Anderson Inge
Carolina Bartram
Ian Duncombe
Wolfgang Fresse
Martin Hagemann
Emanuele Marfisi
John Noel
Randall Thomas
Simos Yannas
Mohsen Zikri
Toni Kotnik

Special thanks to:
Mike Weinstock, Belinda
Flaherty, Fernando Perez
Fraile and Fridrich
Schneider

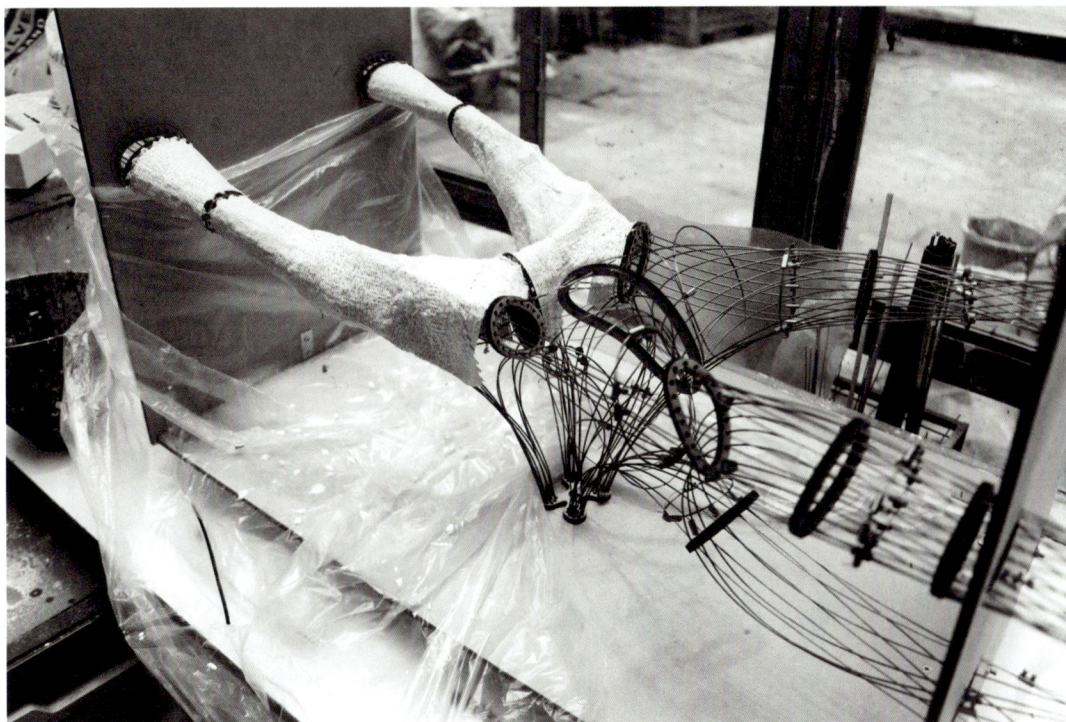

1

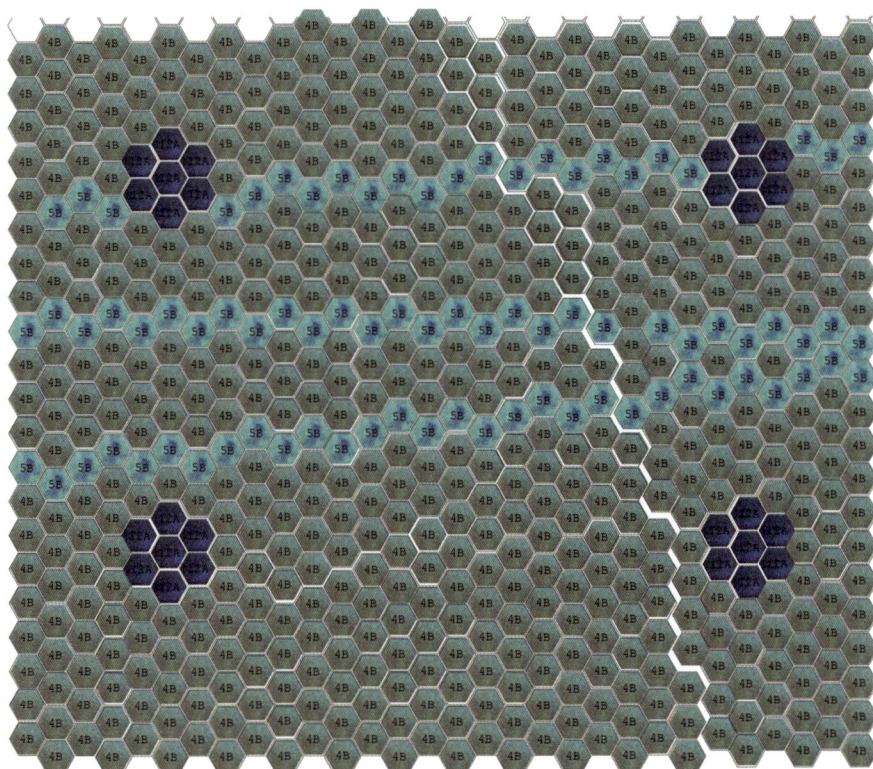

2

1. Arya Safavi, Diploma 2
Test model of the structural supports to test the
critical position of the reinforcement and the method
of construction

2. Rebecca Crabtree, Intermediate 9
Barcelona ceramics, section of external tile patterns

3

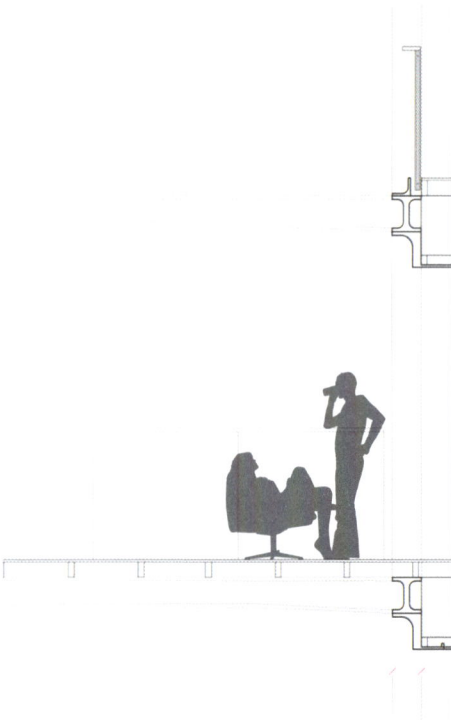
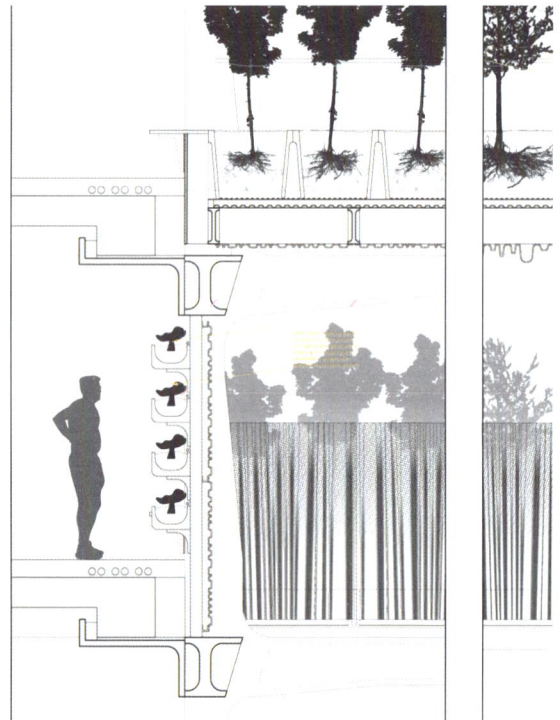

4

3. Jorgen Tandberg, Diploma 14
The reveals of the facade panels have been designed
to maximise the effect of the reflected natural light
coming through the windows.

4. Andrew Tam, Diploma 7
Partial sections showing the layers added to the
existing facades of a derelict hotel in order to create
hydroponic allotment gardens.

5

6

5. Manjeh Verghese, Intermediate 6
Brick, a more versatile building component.
Transformation of the Saatchi advertising agency
based on camouflage techniques

6. Maria Brewster, Intermediate 3
The river water and its purification as a programme
for a spiritual spatial experience at the Ganges in
rural India.

MEDIA STUDIES

Media Studies addresses the many different ways design-based projects are produced. As methods of fabrication, visualisation and information are continually reassessed, the programme includes a comprehensive set of courses that encourages students to use production techniques as a means to both materialise and reinvent their design approach in architecture. This year's courses range from video, photography and drawing to automated machining processes and digital information-based projects. In addition to studio-led courses, the department also administers digital skills-based courses focusing on major applications to help students learn contemporary tools quickly and effectively to develop their architectural ambitions.

While Media Studies are a compulsory part of the curriculum in the First Year and Intermediate School, the programme draws the participation of students from across the entire undergraduate school and other parts of the AA. This widespread integration of students from a highly diverse set of backgrounds allows for an active discussion through production techniques. Beyond the courses provided by Media Studies, the department also participates in exhibitions and workshops that serve to engrain the concept of technique as an integral component of the conceptualisation-to-production pipeline of architectural design. The department is composed of staff with an extremely wide range of interests and expertise, from architecture to the arts and technology. This diversity provides a comprehensive and established collection of courses that equip students with vital skills relevant to contemporary architectural production.

www.aa-mediastudies.net

DEPARTMENT HEAD
Eugene Han

**DEPARTMENT STAFF
(CORE)**
Sue Barr
Shajay Bhooshan
Valentin Bontjes Van Beek
Monia De Marchi
Shin Egashira
Trevor Flynn
Matej Hosek
Alex Kaiser
Tobias Klein
Toni Kotnik
Zak Kyes
Antoni Malinowski
Joel Newman
Anne Save de Beaurecueil
Goswin Schwendinger

**DEPARTMENT STAFF
(LAB)**
Ran Ankori
Shajay Bhooshan
Brian Dale
Christina Doumpioti
Andres Harris
Pavel Hladik
Joel Newman
Edgar Payan Pacheco
Suyeon Song

WORKSHOP TUTORS
Trevor Flynn
Anderson Inge

1. Student: David Chen
Course: Rendering Environments (Matej Hosek)
Studies of isolated render passes to understand the
effect of light and material simulation parameters

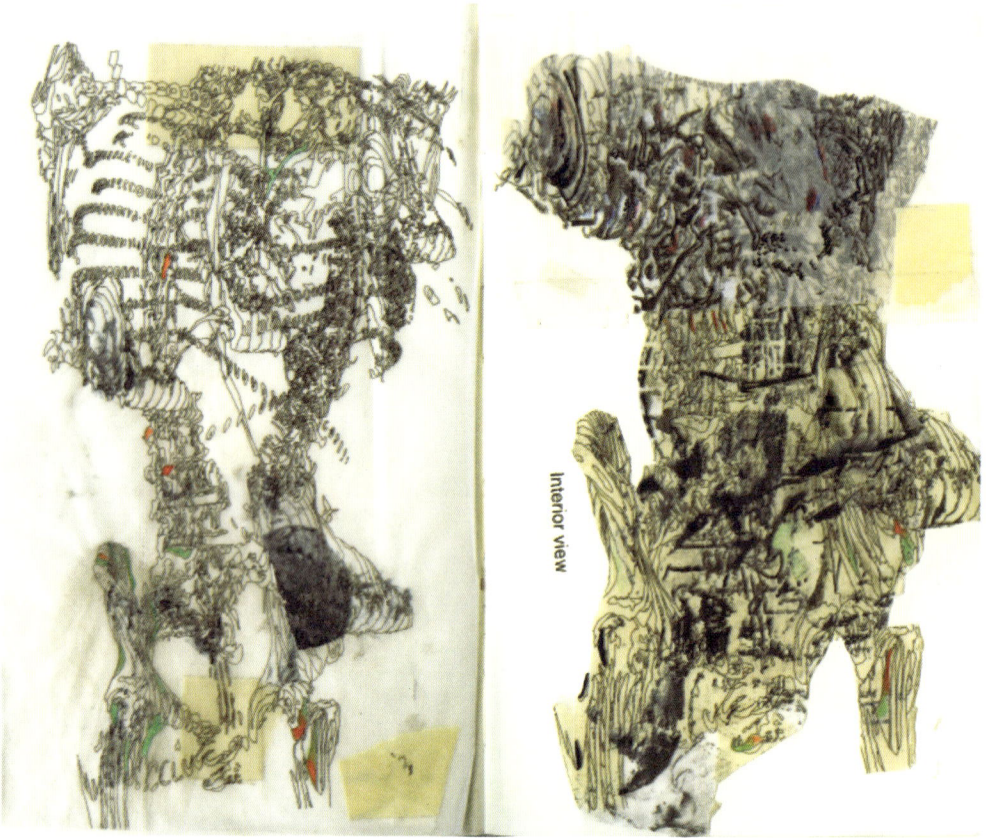

Interior view

2

3

2. Student: Quiddale O'Sullivan
Course: Embodied Landscapes (Tobias Klein)
Investigation of perception via the relationship
between image and reality through a collection
of drawings and documentation

3. Student: Nathalie Matathias
Course: Painting Architecture (Alex Kaiser)
Digital painting using assemblage and texture
through manipulation of layered image information

4

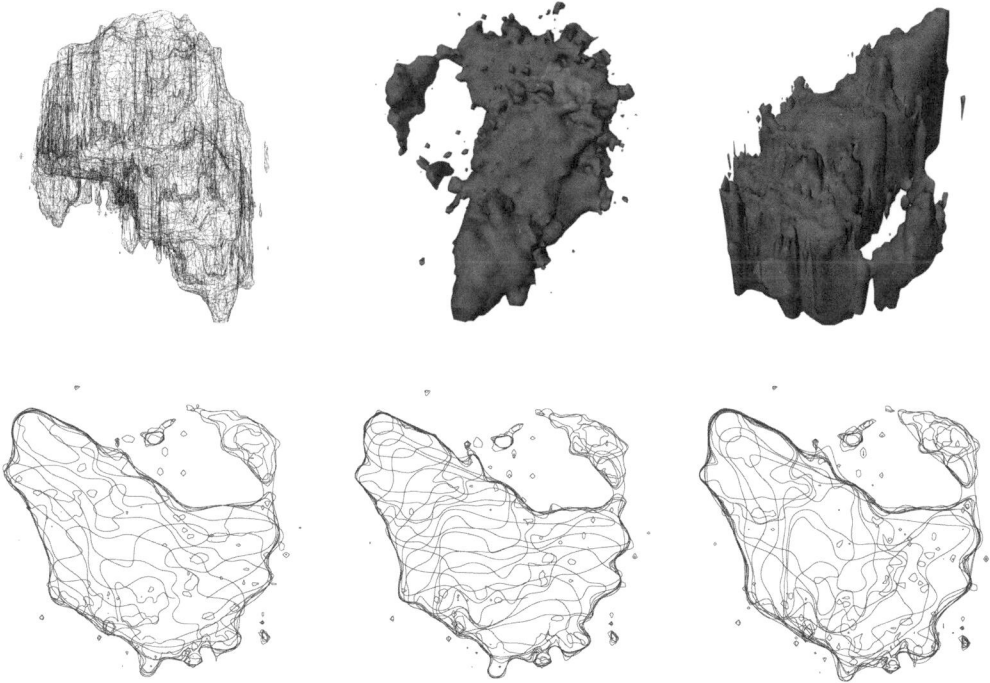

5

4. Student: Song Jie Lim
Course: Painting Architecture (Alex Kaiser)
Digital painting using assemblage and texture
through manipulation of layered image information

5. Student: Nora Nordgard Nilsen
Course: Embodied Landscapes (Tobias Klein)
Conversion of voxel cloud into a surface to define
peripheries, definition of irregular contours for
visualising organisational parameters

255

WORKSHOPS

The AA operates four independent workshops located at its home on Bedford Square and at the Hooke Park facility in Dorset. Students are encouraged to use and combine technologies from the different facilities to experiment with a range of tools and materials and to learn about fabrication aspects of the design process.

The technologies offered in the different workshops are partially overlapping and range from traditional hand tools for wood and metal work to computer numerically controlled prototyping machines.

The Workshop includes machine and hand tools for working in steel and some nonferrous metals, as well as hardwoods, softwoods and panel products, stone, concrete, ferrocement and some plastics and composites.

The Model Workshop provides indoor and outdoor working space for a wide variety of activities, including mould-making and casting, kiln work in ceramics and glass and vacuum-forming. Projects are realised using a wide variety of materials and techniques and range in scale from traditional model-making work to 1:1 concrete castings.

The Digital Prototyping Lab offers a number of digital fabrication technologies including five laser-cutting machines available to individual students, four CNC milling machines and two 3D printers operated by lab staff. The lab offers tutorials on file preparation for digital fabrication to groups and individual students and organises independent workshops open to students across the school.

The Hooke Park facilities offer a unique setting and a spacious workshop featuring various machines for wood and metal work including a large CNC machine. Usually organised through units, Media Studies or graduate programmes, groups of students can use the facility to experiment with the manufacture, assembly and testing of large-scale working prototypes.

WOOD & METAL WORKSHOP
Robert Busher
William Fausset

MODEL WORKSHOP
Trystrem Smith

HOOKE PARK
Charles Corry Wright
Bruce Hunter-Inglis
Chris Sadd

DIGITAL PROTOTYPING LAB
Jeroen van Ameijde
Karleung Wai

STUDENT ASSISTANTS
Francisca Aroso
Frederik Bo Bojesen
Evgenia Budanova
Luis Costa
Michael Dosier
Tyson Hosmer
Sarah Huelin
Tobias Jewson
Conrad Koslowsky
Oliviu Lugojan-Ghenciu
Miguel Miranda
Thiago Mundim
Bryan Oknyansky
Quiddale O'Sullivan

1

2

1. Workshop

2. Digital Prototyping Lab
Photos Valerie Bennett

HOOKE PARK

Hooke Park is the AA's 350-acre woodland site in Dorset, southwest England, which contains a small campus centred on a wood-working workshop. Since becoming part of the AA in 2002, Hooke Park has provided a venue for activities that use the workshop as a site for experimentation and fabrication, and the forest as an alternative to the central London environment of Bedford Square.

The 2009–10 academic year marked the beginning of a new phase of activity at Hooke Park, through which the AA will extend the physical infrastructure of the campus and develop new academic programmes. The plan for development of the site, with increased accommodation, workshop and other teaching spaces, was awarded approval of outline planning permission by West Dorset Council in May 2010. Central to this development is the new MArch Design & Make course, which will commence in Autumn 2010.

Based at Hooke Park, this programme will design and build the components of the enlarged campus on a yearly cycle, with the students fully engaged in the issues of experimental sustainable construction. Through the activities of Design & Make and the ongoing visitor groups from London, the AA will develop Hooke Park as a site for exploring prototypical rural architectures, the crafts and technologies of construction and fabrication, and innovative approaches to timber use in building.

The output of Design & Make will add to the existing buildings at Hooke Park, which were designed by collaborations between Richard Burton of ABK, Frei Otto, Buro Happold and Edward Cullinan. Each building is a remarkable demonstration of an intelligent approach to maximising resources provided by the forest – by using green round-wood poles provided by forest thinning, a silvicultural waste product.

DIRECTOR
Martin Self

WORKSHOP SUPERVISOR
Charlie Corry Wright

ADMINISTRATOR
Bruce Hunter Inglis

FORESTER
Christopher Sadd

1

2

1. Diploma 7 busy in the Hooke Park workshop
Photo Andrew Tam

2. Timber being sawn from Hooke Park's spruce
trees to provide material for the Caretaker's House
Photo Rebecca Spencer

3. Student Forum visit to Hooke Park, October 2009
Photo Zeng Junjie

VISITING SCHOOL

In 2009/10 the Visiting School produced its first comprehensive 48-page prospectus describing the 19 unique academic programmes, workshops and events (six taking place at the AA's home in Bedford Square and 13 global schools at locations worldwide), which together cover four continents and include over 700 students. Its lollipop-coloured B5 cards describe an array of innovative programmes that encourage a global audience of participants to confront the leading issues and technologies shaping architecture, design and urban culture at the outset of the twenty-first century.

Characteristic of the Visiting School is its emphasis on engaging the widest range of prospective and young students, academics, practitioners and other design professionals as well as current AA undergraduate and graduate students, for a period ranging from one week to an entire academic year in an intensive studio culture supported by an influential public programme. It takes advantage of a dimension of the school that fosters and promotes cross-cultural experimentation and innovation.

New global schools in the 2009/10 summer include: 'Hyper | Threads' in Bangalore; 'Biodynamic Structures' in San Francisco; 'Micro-Revolutions' in São Paulo; 'Manufacturing Simplexities' in Tehran and 'The City After-Image' in Tokyo.

DIRECTOR
Christopher Pierce

COORDINATOR
Sandra Sanna

2010 Visiting School cards

TEL AVIV

8–17 July 2009
AA CSI: Connections, Surfaces, Infrastructures

The AA CSI Global School at Tel Aviv University was the first in a series of annual summer workshops focused on developing innovative techniques for synthesising drawing and 3D printing. Working with Objet Geometries' high-resolution, liquid 3D printing technology, workshop participants invented and tested 2D, 'thick 2D' and 3D digital prints and rapid proto-types. The 10-day programme worked with a wide range of media – archi-tectural drawings, cartographic maps, hydrographic blueprints and digital photography – that was synthesised to form intricate 2D and 3D forms experimenting with the parameters and meaning of drawing. The varied material production emphasised the making and craft of contemporary architectural production. Work was purposely scale-less and contextless. Instead, it prioritised issues of aesthetics and design processes while challenging and experimenting with the relevance of digital technologies, especially their precision and processes, in relation to architecture.

The workshop's overarching objective was to deliver an atlas of objects/ prints from each participant that will be incorporated into future theoretical and built projects and publications, giving the programme a wide-ranging material and intellectual influence.

DIRECTORS
Christopher Pierce
Chris Matthews

TUTORS
Ruth Kedar, Eran Neuman
Aaron Sprecher, Jeroen
van Ameijde

TEACHING ASSISTANTS
Chen Jin, Edith Wunsch

LECTURERS
Yossi Abu, Erez Ella,
Yael Gilad, Galit Shif

Special thanks to:
Nataly Matathias
Emmanuelle Siedes
Evan Saarinen
Samantha Lee

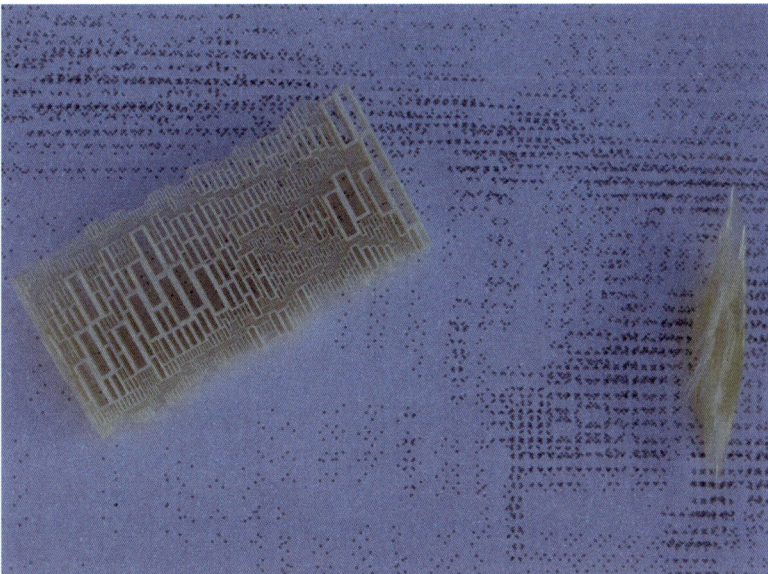

Ruth Ezroni and Evan Saarinen, Connex 500 3D print

AA SUMMER SCHOOL, LONDON

13–31 July 2009
Minicity: Smallness in an era of city-boom slow-down

Is the age of bigness over as the world scales back its architectural and urban ambitions? MINICITY turned its attention to the micro and the modest: diminutive buildings, tiny projects and mini-inserts in small spaces, in an attempt to understand the city as an aggregation of miniature moments instead of the heroic account of iconic projects. The twenty-first century places its great hopes in the 'nano-', whether increasingly powerful microprocessors or relief housing for disaster victims around the world.

The Summer Architecture School examined this 'big' issue from a number of compelling perspectives: social, economic, ecological, cultural and technological. Once again, London served as an experimental laboratory of ideas and actions.

DIRECTORS
Shumon Basar
Natasha Sandmeier

TUTORS
Adam Furman, Marie Isabelle de Monseignat, Steve Bates, Joshua Bonnetta, Douglas Moffat, Julika Gittner, Sarah Entwistle, Geraldine Dening, David Knight, Finn Williams, Ulf Hackauf, Inigo Minns, Onkar Kular, Noam Andrews, Rene Barownick, Yeena Yoon

Minicity Unit 6 models. Photo Valerie Bennett

SINGAPORE

15–24 July 2009
Designed Geographies

For the fourth consecutive year, Singapore provided the focus for broad reflections on prospective tools for dense urban fields. Designed Geographies developed cross-referencing layers of urban conditions and produced complex readings of the city. The workshop investigated experimental ways of observing the city, informed by an introduction to contemporary methods of physical and digital mapping, modelling and advanced design processes and research. Architectural ecology was placed within a larger context of environmental and artificial geographies conceived as part of a systemic approach to urban growth.

DIRECTORS
Nathalie Rozencwajg
Michel da Costa
Goncalves

TUTORS
Jeroen van Ameijde
Naiara Vegara

STUDENT ASSISTANTS
Calvin Chua
John Naylor
Kai Ong

Special thanks to:
School of Design
(Singapore Polytechnic),
Ng Lye Hock Larry (URA
Singapore), Tan Szue
Hann, Peng Beng Khoo

The terrain group: a topographical reading of a nodal traffic way and surrounding programmes in Singapore.

MADRID

16–25 July 2009
Urban Endurance & Hybrid Spaces

The inaugural Madrid Visiting School Workshop focused on the redesign and redevelopment of an iconic site in the core of the city. The AZCA district in Madrid underwent a rapid transformation in the middle decades of the twentieth century. Designated as a special zoning district, the 190-hectare site was envisioned as a great business centre with high-rise buildings for finance, offices, housing, hotel, commercial use and open space. Following models derived from old principles, it was driven by a combination of factors that quickly contributed to its demise and disuse. Like other large-scale developments elsewhere in Europe, it became obsolete as it failed to keep pace with the many ways in which building types, open spaces and public use patterns evolved since the time of its construction.

The workshop explored the ways in which emergent urban ideas, experimental design strategies, process-driven working methods and hybrid public initiatives are brought to bear on such sites in order to fundamentally improve public life in the city. Students investigated ways of working across new design platforms, collaborative media and material systems in order to visualise proposals and to energise larger political, professional and public discussions about the fate of the AZCA district.

DIRECTOR
Ricardo de Ostos

TUTORS
Peter Ferretto, Ricardo de Ostos, Jose Ballesteros

Special thanks to:
Martha Thorne, Javier Quintana de Uña, Juan Lago-Novás Domingo, Cristina Díaz Moreno, Efrén García Grinda,

Gerardo Mingo,
Nannette Jackowski,
Jose Ballesteros

Francisco Borja, narrative exploration of site strategy through bombing device

DAEJON

11–18 August 2009
The Rebirth of the River

To understand Korea's complex history and culture, it is necessary to understand how human habitation has coexisted with the topography, and in particular the river networks that permeate the peninsula. In recent years, however, this interrelation has been neglected, disconnecting the nation from the influence of architectural and urban practice.

In response to the South Korean government's recent decision to 'reconstruct' the course of four important rivers, including the river Han (Seoul), the workshop focused on new experimental strategies for reconnecting the urban environment with the river network and waterfronts. Students investigated alternative architectures and critical ways to galvanise wider political, professional and public discussions about the future of the rivers.

DIRECTOR
Peter Ferretto

TUTORS
Kate Davies, Nannette Jackowski, Shin Egashira, Valentin Bontjes Van Beek, Matthias Moroder

Special thanks to: Professor Byung-yoon Kim of the KIA, the Korea Institute of Architects and Daejeon University for organizing and hosting the AA/SAKIA summer workshop 2009.

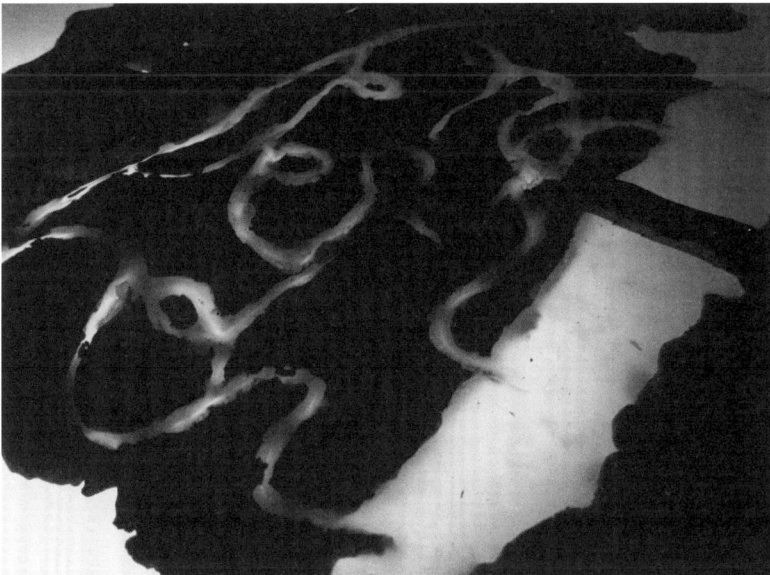

Unit 1 group model proposing to flood the obsolete Daejon Expo site with a series of artificial canals

SUMMER DLAB, LONDON

3–14 August 2009

The two-week Summer dLab considers contemporary computational techniques as a starting point for addressing the transformations brought about by advances in digital workflows. It provides a laboratory for free experimentation and speculation on the possibilities of digital tools in design and architecture, overcoming the discrete specialisations that typically govern their use.

Organised as a series of design workshops, seminars and presentations, the programme offered a unique setting in which professionals and students engaged with alternative forms of computation-driven design. Working intensively with a unit tutor, small student groups developed projects based around a unit brief that was worked through in the digital environment as well as with rapid prototyping machinery. Alongside digital modelling techniques, participants were instructed in CNC-machining, laser-cutting and 3D-printing. In line with the dLab's ambition of reassessing the roles of design and production, computational and prototyping processes were treated as parallel strands rather than as successive stages of a project.

DIRECTOR
Eugene Han

TUTORS
Unit 1
Toni Kotnik
Lorenz Lachauer

Unit 2
Shajay Bhooshan
Chikara Inamura

LECTURERS
Cristiano Ceccato, Fabian
Scheurer

Thanks to:
Mike Weinstock, Chris
Yoo, Jeroen van Ameijde

Elora Brahmachari, Pierluigi D'Acunto, Ed Pearce:
Reverse Dynamism – studies of articulated composite
surface structures
Tutors: Toni Kotnik and Lorenz Lachauer

SHANGHAI

14–22 August 2009
Parametric Prototypes

The Shanghai Summer School, held at the University of Hong Kong Faculty of Architecture Study Centre, investigated new computational design approaches in architecture and urbanism within the context of Shanghai, one of the world's fastest growing cities.

The conventional point-block tower and low-rise sprawl have been the primary (and default) typologies of Shanghai's urban densification and expansion over the last 20 years. Given the complications arising from global economic turmoil, there has never been a more crucial time to challenge and propose alternatives to these dominant models of urban growth, which are tied to China's continuing policy of urbanising an additional 400 million of its citizens over the next 20 years. The workshop developed computational design tools and research concepts able to engage with the development of alternative social, spatial, structural and material systems. It sought to formulate new discourses on contemporary computation and production, including the use of code-based modelling and simulation techniques, in relation to the disciplines of architecture and urbanism.

DIRECTOR
Tom Verebes

TUTORS
Yan Gao, Ercu Gorgul, Lydia Kim, Bittor Sanchez Monasterio,

Eric Schuldenfrei, Andrew Tirta Atmadjaja

Special thanks to:
Brett Steele, Ralph Lerner, Koon Wee, Tracy Cui, Xiangning Li,

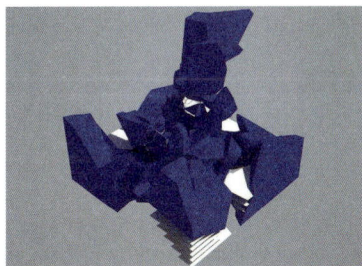

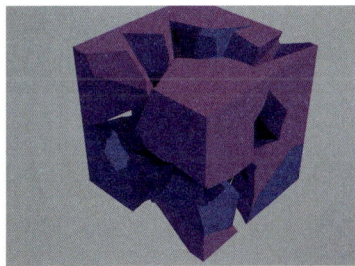

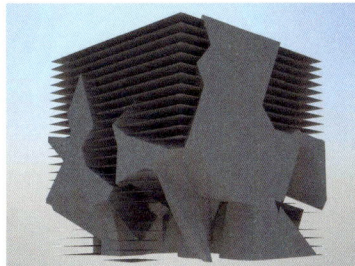

Su Yunsheng, Lin Wan, Vivi He, Yuyang Liu, Defne Ayas, Pascal Berger, Vincent De Graaf, Lutz Dickmann, Judit Klostermann

Chen Yanjing, Stefano Verrocchio, Zhu Jiayi
Series of diagrams indicating zones of aggregate public programmes inserted into the megablock

269

BERLIN

4–12 September 2009
The City as Laboratory

Post-wall Berlin has emerged as the foremost player for contemporary cultural production in Europe, if not the world. Labelled 'poor but sexy', the city has been colonised by a vast creative community making use of the unique economic and spatial conditions and its concentration of skills. Harvesting this exceptional energy, AA Berlin Laboratory explored modes of creative production and their manifestations in the city. Two workshop units used the city as a field for investigation and intervention. The 'Mapping Unit' tracked the dynamic relationship between the art world and the fabric of the city, while the 'Notation Unit' explored and intervened in Berlin's voids in search of a performative paradigm. Visits to artist studios included Larissa Fassler, Jorinde Voigt and Olafur Eliasson as well as a special walk along the Avus racetrack with landscape artist Bertram Weisshaar. The workshop took place at Aedes Network Berlin Campus (ANCB) and was accompanied by a public programme with participants from architecture, science and art focusing on the notions of 'Laboratory' and 'Experimental Systems'.

DIRECTORS
Olaf Kneer
Marianne Mueller

TUTORS
Jens Casper, Christopher Dell, Sven Pfeiffer, Stefano Rabolli Pansera

LECTURERS
Rory McLean, Hans Jörg Rheinberger

Special thanks to:
Olafur Eliasson, Larissa Fassler, Jorinde Voigt, Bertram Weisshaar,

Justus Pysall, Frank Barkow, Carson Chan, Fotini Lazaridou-Hatzigoga, Antje Buchholz, Thomas Arnold, Susanne Hoffmann and Kristine Freiress, Hans-Jürgen Comrell, Micheal Roper

and Julia at Aedes Network Campus Berlin

Mapping Berlin's evolving art scene

SANTIAGO

6–15 January 2010
Game (On) Santiago

In Chile the construction of new sports infrastructure to house the 2014 South American Olympics – ODESUR – is being treated as an unparalleled opportunity to transform a range of environments. Sponsored by the Chilean Olympic Committee and hosted by the School of Architecture of the Catholic University in Santiago de Chile, the workshop proposed design alternatives to plans currently in development, defining strategies applicable at different scales. This research encouraged explorations of material properties, construction processes, parametric design and digital fabrication, while considering also Chile's local culture and landscape. Students experimented with new tools and concepts for mapping, indexing and diagramming different types of urban information (infrastructural, ecological, social) and designed prototypical models of urban scenarios for the site of the National Stadium Complex in central Santiago, which served as the testbed for team design exercises.

DIRECTOR
Pedro Ignacio Alonso

TUTORS
Monia De Marchi, Eva Castro, Holger Kehne, Rodrigo Pérez de Arce, Arturo Lyon, Alejandra Bosch

LECTURERS
J. Parrish, Diego Damm, Jose Luis Lopez

Special thanks to:
Jose Rosas, Juan Ignacio Baixas, Luis Valenzuela, Alex Moreno, Ian Bertie, Victoria Saud, Lia Aliaga,

Nicolas Riveros, Nicole Rochette and Pamela Prado at the Catholic University in Santiago

Sponsors:
Masisa, Atika, Knauf, Hunter Douglas, Plataforma Arquitectura

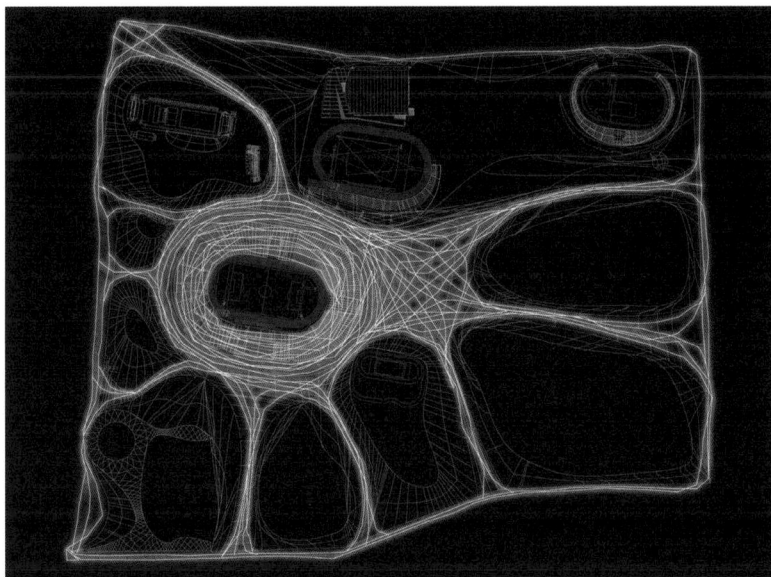

Daniel Mahony, Daniel Portilla, Gonzalo Carrasco and Robert Krumhansl: Mapping intensity of circulation towards the definition of new inner and outer boundaries to the National Stadium Complex

BEIJING

30 January – 7 February 2010
Super-Blend

This winter the AA held its first annual Beijing Global School at the Digital College of CrystalCG in collaboration with the Parametric Studio of Tsinghua Architectural Design & Research Institute. The course focused on emerging computational approaches in the context of Beijing, one of the world's most architecturally eclectic cities. As the capital of the world's fastest growing country, Beijing has become an experimental platform for many architects, making grand statements encouraged by the obsession for so-called iconic buildings. But does Beijing need more of these structures? Do these projects respond to the city's history and culture or instead create an entirely new context?

The workshop's objective was to evolve a coherent architectural prototype by 'Super-Blending' conflicting elements co-existing in Beijing (e.g. Hutong and boulevard, courtyard and skyscraper, culture and technology, old and new, nature and artefact, order and chaos). Students toured parts of the city prior to working in a team-based design studio, which familiarised them with essential parametric design techniques.

DIRECTOR
Yan Gao

TUTORS
Bittor Sanchez-Monasterio, Elif Erdine, Ercument Gorgul,

Ling Fan, Raymond Lau, Lydia Kim, Diego Perez-Espitia

GUEST LECTURERS
Brett Steele
Christopher Pierce

Minsuk Cho
Patrik Schumacher
Roberto Bannura
Tom Verebes
Ted Kane
Wei Guo Xu

VISITING JURORS
Jonathan Solomon
Debra T M Cheung

3D PRINT COORDINATOR
Qiang Chang

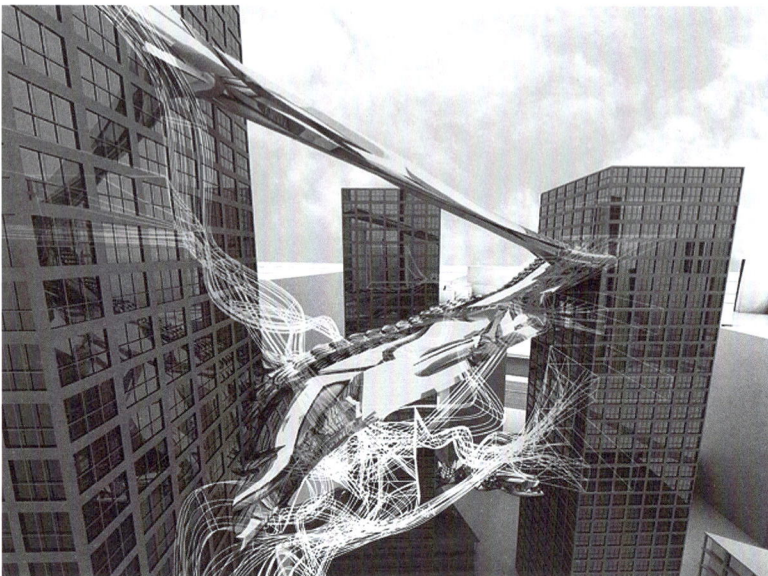

Project Name: Anti-Icon Net
Team: Liang Cao, Shuai Guo, Tomas Labanc, Xin Ying
Tutors: Ercument Gorgul, Yan Gao

SPRING SEMESTER PROGRAMME

18 January – 14 May 2010
London Calling

As in previous years, the Spring Semester Programme investigated the development of urban projects that engage with the rapidly changing conditions found in London, a world city that is undergoing radical transformations in its built environment, public spaces and urban infrastructures. Students explored two alternative briefs, the first one focused on the formulation of urban retreats and the second exploring the problem of a compact city.

In *Urban Retreats For London* students used architectural forms and narrations to construct ways of retreating within the city. Projects varied from a retreat for workaholics to a monastic enclosed retreat, and from the retreat / rehab for space abusers to a retreat for architectures.

London Plan of Tomorrow v2 explored the idea of the compact city through performative urban structures and prototypical urban habitation, attempting to visualise, redefine and propose high-density.

DIRECTORS
Urban Retreats for London: Monia De Marchi
London Plan of Tomorrow: Sam Jacoby with Ridzwa Fathan

Thanks to Meneesha Kellay, Ruth Lie, Sandra Sanna, Christopher Pierce, Brett Steele, Alex Kaiser, Andres Harris, all the jurors, and the maintenance departments

Final Jury at the AA: Erin Ota presenting her project, The Reprocessing Centre for Loss: A retreat for space abusers

RESEARCH CLUSTERS

Research Clusters are independent research groups initiated by tutors from across the school. The Research Cluster programme was launched in 2005 as a platform to trigger discussion and exchange across the AA through a body of focused research. At present, each Cluster runs on an 18-month cycle and is managed by Charles Tashima, AA Academic Head, in consultation with cluster researchers.

An important ambition of the Research Clusters is to consolidate expertise within the school, not only enhancing territories of research and knowledge, but also exploring innovative ways in which work can be produced and discussed. This has taken the form of symposia, workshops, performances, competitions, publications, off- and on-site exhibitions, fabrication as well as interdisciplinary collaborative research with specialists from outside the AA.

Currently there are five Research Clusters, four of which are continuing into the next academic year.

AAIFAB: A Platform for Material and Manufacturing Innovation AAIFAB has been led by Alan Dempsey and Kristine Mun, with initial assistance from Yusuke Obuchi. With support from leading companies in the UK and Europe, AAIFAB established two awards providing funding and resources for innovative research projects in the emerging application of digital design and fabrication technologies in architecture.

The 2008 Prototyping Design awards were open to all full-time AA students and staff. They offered an opportunity to pursue a project to an advanced stage of development, establishing direct collaboration with a wider network of industry specialists. Four projects were selected and two eventually given full research awards: Urban Toys by Shin Egashira, Rubens Avezedo and their team, and Inflatable Pneus by Mehran Gharleghi and Amin Sadeghi. This work formed the centrepiece of the exhibition with full-scale prototypes as well as smaller models and mock-ups. The 2009 Designing Fabrication awards asked designers around the world to submit recently built projects that exemplify the innovative integration of design and fabrication processes through digitally driven design systems and protocols. Six selected projects were presented through large-format prints and rapid prototype models. All of the aforementioned work was displayed alongside innovative projects submitted by 18 other designers in a large public exhibition and symposium during the London Design Festival.
www.aa-fab.net

Beyond Energy: When Energy Becomes Form was launched at the 2009 Venice Art Biennale to explore the relationship of art, architecture and energy. Coordinated by Intermediate Unit Master Stefano Rabolli Pansera, the work is being conducted by a series of research teams comprising architects, artists and scientists from across Europe. Different forms of energy are explored, including nuclear, mechanical, potential, mass, electric, thermal, chemical and gravitational energy. The methods of working, areas of interest and applications are as diverse as each participant's background. The prototypes, which include a time-machine, a self-balancing mechanism and a platform to exhibit the invisible network of energy supply, will be presented at the Venice Architecture Biennale from 27 August 2010.

beyondentropy.aaschool.ac.uk

Concrete Geometries
Directed by Marianne Mueller and Olaf Kneer, Concrete Geometries investigates the intimate relationship between spatial form and human processes, whether social or aesthetic, and the variety of new material entities this relationship might provoke. Concrete Geometries is a work-in-progress term derived from the notion of 'concrete' as existing in reality or actual experience and 'geometries' as shorthand for spatial form. In Januray 2010, the cluster launched an international call for submissions with two thematic fields: 'Geometry and Perception' and 'Geometry and Social Processes', attracting 415 entries from the fields of art, architecture, design and the humanities. Some questions posed by the work include: How does spatial form choreograph human processes? Can it stimulate emotional or behavioural responses or create particular aesthetic experiences? Can social cultures be patterned through formal configurations of space?

Following PREVIEW, an exhibition at the AA Back Members' Room of selected competition submissions, a symposium will be held in October 2010 with invited participants drawn from the call. A final shortlist of works will be selected for an exhibition and book launch in January 2011.

www.concrete-geometries.net

City Cultures
Launched in October 2008 by Marina Lathouri, City Cultures seeks to develop new conceptual frameworks to redefine what has historically been constructed and institutionalised as the 'city'.

In recent years, architects have become more involved than ever in the design and building of new cities. Although continuing urban growth has prompted elaborate arguments on economic policies, new organisational models, environmental strategies and sustainable development patterns, there seems to be a lack of reflection on the fundamental question of the city as a composite environment and political space.

A central objective is to approach this question through a diversity of design practices and organisational forms, seeking to interrogate typical representations of the 'living in community' and experiment with laws and procedures of urban formation which are distinct from the regulations of urbanism. Constructing the object of study in this type of effort often means operating at the intersection of multiple disciplinary forms of knowledge and techniques for research. However, the ways in which architecture and design research can formulate a judgement about these theoretical and methodological challenges is most relevant.

The cluster launched a call for Contemporary Positions on the City and held one open seminar and a symposium that brought together AA tutors and outside visitors to identify a range of approaches and forms of

research. The positions, formalised in the AA/CC website and a print document to be distributed in June 2010, as well as the ideas generated in these events, will build up to a 2010 workshop, conference and publication seeking to establish a network of emerging issues and venues of research.
aacitycultures.blogspot.com

Urbanism and the Informal City

Launched in October 2009 by Jorge Fiori, Elena Pascolo and Alex Warnock-Smith, the cluster's aim is to explore the concept of the 'informal' as a parallel modality that shapes the urban condition. Previously associated with cities in developing or emerging economies, the informal is now a pervasive phenomenon spanning a spectrum of economies and cities. Is a threat to formal processes of city formation and the institutions which govern them, or does it define an alternative response to producing and planning cities? Can these contrasting ways of producing and appropriating cities, with their different logics and rules co-exist? With particular emphasis on spatiality, the cluster seeks to discover ways in which 'informal' processes contribute to a radical re-thinking of the city and its institutions.

The team is identifying unexplored themes and contradictions for designers, thinkers and practitioners to consider at a series of unit 'open-mike' sessions, talk-shops and a symposium at the AA. The results of these findings will initiate an international design workshop in 2011, followed by an exhibition and publication.

1. 'Still Live' (2003–04), selected project submission
by British artist Fran Cottell for 'Concrete Geometries
– Spatial Form in Social and Aesthetic Processes'

2

3

5

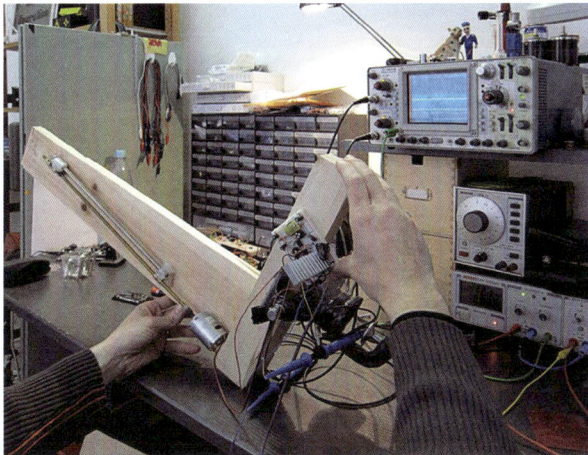

4

2. Informing the city: a Shanghai neighbourhood in the shadow of redevelopment; sleeping rough in New York (with widescreen TV); weekly gathering of Philippino domestic workers in Hong Kong
3. Mechanical Energy: prototype of a Time Machine by Shin Egashira and Andrew Jaffe

4. Energy as Mass: prototype of a self-balancing machine by Rubens Azevedo, Ariel Schlesinger and Vid Stojevic
5. Adaptive Pneus prototype by Amin Sadeghi and Mehran Garleghi at the AAIFAB exhibition during the London Design Festival 2009

DIGITAL PLATFORMS

www.aaschool.ac.uk is the AA's window to the world with over half a million unique visitors from 160 different countries since our new site launched in July 2009; representing a 300 per cent increase in traffic. The most popular pages for our targeted audience of public, students, members and potential students are Projects Review, the video archive and application pages.

Our strategy for presenting the AA seeks to mirror the diversity and independence of groups within the school. We encourage programmes, units, research clusters and visiting schools to build micro-sites with their own distinct content and aesthetic, which AADP then supports under the umbrella of the main site. Our portfolio pages link to over 50 micro-sites showcasing the breadth of activity within the AA.

Online video from the AA Public Programme is fully integrated – lectures can be streamed within 24 hours of their delivery at Bedford Square. Since July 2009 the 200+ lectures archived online have been viewed more than 34,000 times.

During the past year, Digital Platforms overhauled our back-end systems using a stripped-down content management scheme to allow for rapid and more flexible updating. Internally, we are building systems to ease administrative workloads and improve interdepartmental communication. With new staff in the department and this groundwork nearly complete, we are embarking on a series of projects aimed at greater membership and student participation, such as a membership projects map and mobile phone application. AADP's long-term goal is to maintain the AA website's primacy as an online resource for architectural study.

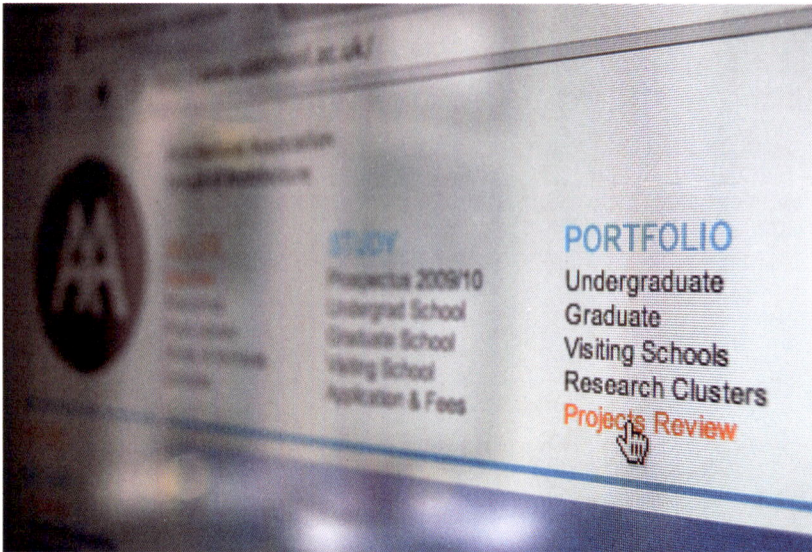

AADP TEAM
Head: Frank Owen
Editor: Rosa Ainley
Designer/Developer:
Zeynep Görgülü

Editorial Assistant
Emanuel Sousa
Microsite Developers:
Jack Self
Susanna Wong

eyond Entropy int
Martin Creed
7 December

TSCH

MEGAI

FRONT

FIREW

FIRST V

SEPTEMBER

24 September
AA FAB: DESIGNING FABRICATION
The AA FAB cluster opens an exhibition of its work at Village Underground in Shoreditch, London.

OCTOBER

2 October
ENZO MARI
Autoprogettazione Revisited
Nine artists and designers respond to Mari's instruction-based furniture plans with their own set of instructions.

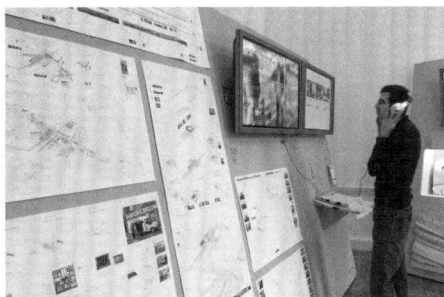

2 October
DIPLOMA HONOURS 2008/09
Exhibition of the three winners of the 2008/09 AA Diploma Honours: Edmund Fowles, Adam Johnston and Tarek Shamma.

8 October
JESSE REISER
Continuous Variation
'Today we can consider modernism from the point of view of persistence and of novelty. This necessarily involves inverting certain assumptions inherent to modernism.'

13 October
SIR KEN ADAM: In Conversation
Originally trained in architecture and interior design, Sir Ken Adam's infamous war room in *Dr Strangelove* (1962) became an icon of Cold War paranoia. In conversation with AACP director Shumon Basar, Adam discusses highlights from an extraordinary career stretching back over 60 years: the transition from architecture to film, the origins of his iconic James Bond sets and the unique relationship he developed with legendary director Stanley Kubrick.

23 October, 5 February, 12 February, 19 February, 5 March, 12 March
MARK COUSINS: The Neighbour
Since the invention of agriculture and rise of the city, human proximity has been a central issue for culture. Judeo-Christian and Islamic thought grants the neighbour supreme value – Love Thy Neighbour – whereas in philosophy the neighbour is seen more in terms of the *polis* than a community. Relations with neighbours have always been tense, even to the point of hostility. Architecture and urbanism have yet to provide an alternative.

27 October
ALICE RAWSTHORN
Design critic Alice Rawsthorne speaks with AACP director Shumon Basar about today's challenges to design, the role of the critic and the future of content in a journalism landscape under threat.

29 October
JOSE PEREZ DE LAMA
Hacking in Public!
hackitectura.net explores new territories demarcated by electronic networks and flows, focusing on the production of digital infrastructures and temporary public spaces.

NOVEMBER

3 November
WILFREDO PRIETO AND ROBERTO TROTTA
Cuban artist Prieto and physicist Trotta discuss subatomic particles with Stefano Raboli Ponsera and other dark matters.

5 November
The Sin Centre and the Beginning of the Archigram Syndrome
Mike 'Spider' Webb re-presents his AA thesis project, the Sin Centre for Entertainments in Leicester Square (1961–62) – a project repeatedly rejected by Diploma examiners.

5 November
ZBIGNIEW OKSIUTA
Biological Habitat
What is the bare minimum required for physiological existence? Oksiuta and students use biological polymers as building materials.

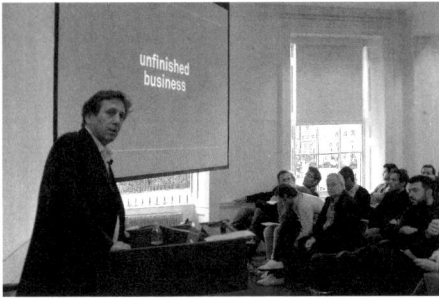

6 November
BRETT STEELE: STATE OF THE ASSOCIATION
Lecture by AA director Brett Steele in advance of the vote by the school community on his directorship.

7 November
PROJECTED LANDSCAPES
Curated by Harry Hardie of Foto8, the exhibition brings together the work of four UK-based photographers: Aaron Schuman, Caroline Molloy, Kate Peters and Corinne Silva.

13 November
ZBIGNIEW OKSIUTA WORKSHOP
Visiting artist Zbigniew Oksiuta creates his inflatable Biological Habitat with David Greene and students from the First Year.

16 November
MASSIMO BARTOLINI
The Vision of What is There
Beyond the visible, conditions arise for the development of mathematical intuition, poetic logic and theoretical sophistication. Bartolini's work is experiential and highly unstable.

19 November
MARK WIGLEY AND BRETT STEELE MODERATED BY MARK COUSINS
Elastic Pedagogies
Heads of schools at Columbia and the AA, Wigley and Steele discuss how contemporary urban culture influences the teaching of architecture today.

24 November
MANUELLE GAUTRAND
Re-enchant the City
Gautrand works with emotion and surprise; without preconceptions.

6 November
FIRST WORKS: Emerging Architectural Experimentation of the 1960s and 1970s
Curated by Brett Steele and Francisco González de Canales, the exhibition examined projects undertaken internationally during the period of profound social change in the 1960s and 1970s, when new conditions for architecture and the city arose. First Works is an exercise in tracing the origins of contemporary architecture through the formative projects of its most celebrated figures.

9 November
TOYO ITO: My First & Latest Work
Since the Aluminium House (1971), Ito has worked to redefine the relationship of nature to architecture beyond modernism. Notable projects from his almost 40-year career include the Sendai Mediatheque (2001), Serpentine Gallery Pavilion (2002), TOD'S Omotesando Building (2004) and the Tama Art University Library (2007). Ito has won the Golden Lion in Venice and the RIBA Royal Gold Medal. He continues to give sustainable architecture a good name in Japan and abroad.

20 November
STORYTELLING – *VOLUME* MAGAZINE AT
TWENTY: Jeffrey Inaba, Tom McCarthy,
Dave Mckean, Brett Steele, Mark Wigley
Recently, various unfolding dramas have
competed for attention within the architecture community: housing crisis,
pandemic, recession. But the effort in
following events leaves little time to
contemplate causes. *Volume* 20 revealed
that although truth is important, in the
task of elevating fact, so too is fiction.
Fantasy is needed to build a precise story
for architecture's future.

23 November
MONICA PIDGEON Memorial Symposium
In 1946 Pidgeon became editor of
Architectural Design, the same year she
divorced her husband. With Theo Crosby
she transformed the journal, then outlast-
ed a string of his replacements. Insistent
that history not be included in *AD*,
Pidgeon committed to creating it.
She died in September at the age
of 95. Former technical editors Kenneth
Frampton, Peter Murray and writers
Sam Webb and Michael Manser spoke
of their memories of her.

25 November
BJARKE INGELS
Yes Is More
BIG's 'programmatic alchemy' mixes conventional ingredients such as living, leisure, working, parking and shopping into new forms of symbiotic architecture.

26 November
FRÉDÉRIC MIGAYROU
Architectural Mathesis
A generation of architects working with new analytical processes has anchored architecture directly to Mathesis. What are the aesthetic and socio-political consequences?

DECEMBER

1 December
ERIC PARRY
Architecture Visible Image of Invisible Thoughts
Eric Parry mostly builds in London. His Westminster projects are embedded in a situational narrative.

4 December
PETER COOK
Ten Themes – Ten Sounds
In the first of his series of lunchtime AA lectures, Cook speaks about music and image.

5 December
21st CENTURY BAMBOO
John Andrews + Johan Granberg, Greg Votolato, Ivana Wingham, Cambell Drake, Lee Dalby
Bamboo is an underappreciated, emotive material: versatile, malleable and strong.

7 December
MARTIN CREED
The nonplussed Turner Prize winner
talks about the Duveen galleries,
commissioned runners at Tate Britain
and some other things.

8 December
THOM MAYNE
Morphosis and maintaining coherency,
emphasising differentiation, articulat-
ing hybridity.

9 December
MAGNUS ERICSON, SARA TELEMAN,
MARTIN FROSTNER, ZAK KYES
Iaspis and the AA launch *The Reader*,
featuring conversations between
graphic designers from the exhibition
'Forms of Inquiry: The Architecture of
Critical Graphic Design'.

10 December
ABRAHAM THOMAS
Owen Jones and The Language of
Design Reform
Some thoughts on the late impact
of the Victorian design reformer's
sourcebook *The Grammar of Ornament*.

JANUARY

6 January
RADIM PEŠKO: INFORMAL MEETINGS
The exhibition includes a selection of
photographs by Radim Peško made
between 1999 and 2009, with an
accompanying publication, *Informal
Meetings,* published by Bedford Press.

290

27 November
RAFAEL MONEO
The First And Latest Projects
Moneo spoke on the relevance of the Diestre Transformers Factory (Zaragoza, 1964–67) in his corpus and the recently completed Columbia University Northwest Science Building (2009). His significant projects include the National Museum of Roman Art (1985), the Moderna Museet in Stockholm (1998), Our Lady of the Angels Cathedral in Los Angeles (2002) and the Prado Museum extension in Madrid (2007). Moneo won the Pritzker Prize in 1996.

5 February
PETER EISENMAN
Lateness and the Crisis of Modernity
In 1959 Eisenman already thought Gropius was a fraud. His State of the Union (of Architecture) address at the AA isn't much more optimistic: architecture today struggles between space and surface; image squelches the grammar and the rhetoric of the meta-critical project while Parametric Process Disease runs rampant. Who shops in the Brooks Brothers store at Newark Airport anyway?

13 January
BECOMING FICTION
Exhibition of images taken by
Foundation students who were asked
to construct an image that depicts a
personally resonant moment.

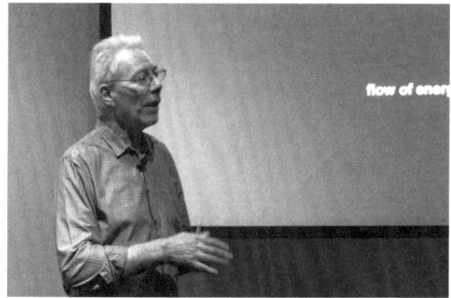

19 January
MICHAEL WEINSTOCK
The Metabolism of Cities
The dynamics of individual and
collective metabolisms from which
social and spatial orders and
intelligence emerge are related to
the proliferation of cities.

20 January
ALEXANDROS TOMBAZIS
**Concerning Architecture: Thoughts
and Visions**
Since 1963 Tombazis has specialised
in low-energy and bioclimatic design,
with projects in the Middle East and
across Europe.

21 January
PAUL NAKAZAWA
Next and Again
Architectural and landscape practice
in the post-recessionary period,
considering the computer industry's
boom as allegory.

22 January
TOM WISCOMBE
Extreme Integration
'For example: the hammerhead shark's
head was not always shaped as a
hammer.'

25 January
DAVID CLAERBOUT
Untitled
'How does photography's past witness
relate to how we look at it today?... I
feel myself like a diplomat between
conflicting situations within one single
picture.'

28 January, 4 & 25 February
PETER COOK
Stuff
In the second of his lunchtime AA lectures Cook talks about stuff.

28 January
OLYMPIC SITE VISIT
AA Members enjoy a rare opportunity to step into the Olympic stadium building site, thanks to AA alumni William Chen and Tina Gröne of stadium architects Populous.

29 January
ANDREA BRANZI
Weak Modernity
In the 1960s and 70s Archizoom demonstrated how extreme radicalism ultimately achieves the opposite of what it sets out to do – while at the same time they opposed 'good design'.

FEBRUARY

1 February
GIOVANNI ANCESCHI
The Vertigo of the List
A founder of Kinetic Art and Gruppo T in the 1960s, Anceschi is interested in how specific technologies allow an audience to take a particular position on issues.

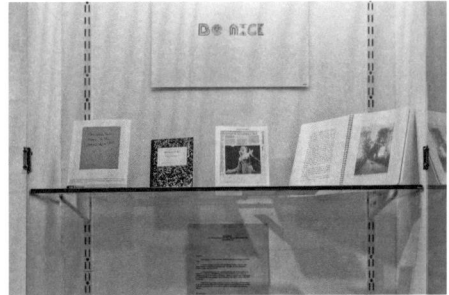

2 February
EXHIBITION PROSTHETICS
BOOK LAUNCH
Exhibition Prosthetics by Joseph Grigely explores the artist's use of language and images as a means of representation that further the reach of the real.

2 February
INTERMEDIATE UNIT 6 CAMOUFLAGE:
A CATALOGUE OF EFFECTS
Exhibition explores how the process of becoming changes our perception and how this can be used to develop surfaces and spaces through the manipulation of pattern.

4 February
MATHIAS MULLER AND
DANIEL NIGGLI
Both And
After Venturi: 'we do not recognise a single great truth, but find in the fractures of reality a ground in which to anchor architecture'.

5 February
JÖRG STOLLMANN
urbaninform – Tools and Prototypes
for the Informal City
An internet platform that supports knowledge-sharing in the informal city, specifically in São Paulo and Addis Ababa.

8 February
AA ARCHIVES REVEALED:
Highlights from the Collections
Exhibition of a small selection of items from the 1000-plus architectural drawings and 14m³ of documents and objects held within the AA Archives.

12 February
OPENING UP THE AA ARCHIVE
Organised in association with Archives for London, the event examined the material of the archive, its academic value, accessibility and current cataloguing priorities.

12 February
ALFREDO JAAR
On the problem of representing genocides, epidemics and famines in art and public desensitisation to these types of images.

16 February
CHRISTOPHER DELL/dra
Thinking Space Musically
'Improvisations on Urbanity' and
'Tacit Urbanism' use music to
conceptualise space.

22 February
ARIEL SCHLESINGER
Train Hopping and Reverse
Engineering
Temporary Autonomous Zone: 'when
you secretly catch a ride on a railroad
freight car'.

27 February
LONDON +10
The London +10 exhibition
concentrates on London over the
last 20 years and speculates on the
relationship between the live realm
of the city and its urban fabric.

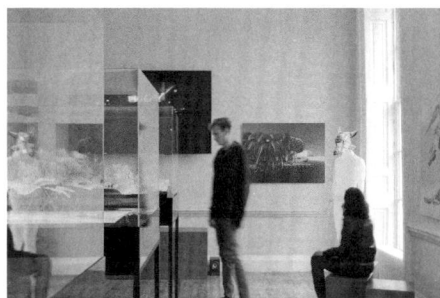

27 February
ENABLING: THE WORK OF
MINIMAFORMS
Exploring ideas of social and material
interaction, this exhibition shows
recent work including a pavilion
developed with Stelarc and a redesign
of David Greene's Living Pod project.

27 February
LIQUID THRESHOLD: 20 YEARS OF
ATELIER ONE
Exhibition of photo essay by Magnum
photographer Peter Marlow in the AA's
Back Members' Room in tandem with
the publication of a book on the firm.

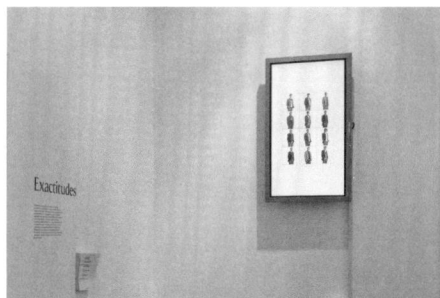

27 February
ARI VERSLUIS & ELLIE UYTTENBROEK
EXACTITUDES
Versluis and Uyttenbroek document
the dress codes of different social and
cultural groups, inviting strangers off
the streets to be photographed in their
studio.

23 February
IAIN SINCLAIR
Ghost Milk
(Calling Time on the Age of the Grand Project): 'Expeditions in the Lower Lea Valley, Freedom Pass bus rides down Will Alsop's SuperCity highway, the M62 from Liverpool to Hull. How National Socialism in Berlin in 1936 provides the working model for New Labour's culture of surveillance and media control. Post-architectural infill among the Olympic wastelands of Athens.'

12 March
TOM McCARTHY
'Greenwich is the seat of time; the novelist's obsession.' McCarthy's conceptual installation *Greenwich Degree Zero* describes one man's attempt to rewrite time: 'What really sparked Rod's and my imagination about this [1894] episode was this sense that Martial Boudin's real target in his doomed act was not really the Observatory building; it was time itself. He was trying to blow up time – an artist of the impossible. Of course, he just blew himself up.'

MARCH

1 March
STEPHEN AND THEODORE SPYROPOULOS: Enabling
The minima as moment, form as an evolving act. See also: '(War Veteran) Vehicle' with Krzysztof Wodiczko; a pavilion with Stelarc; David Greene's Living Pod Project revisted.

2 March
LARS MÜLLER
Communicating Architecture
Müller speaks of the potential of the book as a medium for the communication of architecture and the differences between digital and analogue media.

3 March
NEIL THOMAS AND ARAN CHADWICK / ATELIER 1: Why Not
Structural engineers Atelier One take complex propositions and translate them through a language of first principles, resulting in some extraordinary conclusions.

4 March
WORK YOUR TALK
Theory to engagement: Expeditio (Montenegro), re:ACT (Singapore), Espacio Expresion and (Y)NCLUYE (Peru) and Posibilidades del Paisaje (Colombia) apply discourse directly to their communities.

5 March
MARK GARCIA AND GUESTS
Diagrams Symposium
Since the 1980s the diagram has been the preferred method for researching, communicating, theorising and making architectural designs.

5 March
EYAL SIVAN
Sivan investigates the way in which memory is used for political purposes, working from an archive common to victims and perpetrators – in this case Palestinians and Israelis.

8 March
MARCEL ODENBACH
'In Still Waters Crocodiles Lurk' (2004) ponders the Rwandan genocide of 1994. 'Turning Circles' (2009) considers the Majdanek Mausoleum, built on the site of the Lublin concentration camp in 1969.

9 March
PUBLIC OCCASION AGENCY
ICA talk
The AA's student-led POA invited Stefano Rabolli Pansera to the ICA to talk about his Beyond Entropy research cluster.

9 March
JOHN GRAY / AA FILES: Science and Magic – What Technology Can and Can't Fix
'A high-tech Green utopia in which a few humans live happily in balance with the rest of life is scientifically feasible but humanly unimaginable.'

9 March
TATIANA BILBAO
Two Public Art / Architecture Projects in Mexico
New social urban approaches at the Botanical Garden in Culiacan; Sinaloa and Pilgrimage Route in Jalisco.

10 March
ARI VERSLUIS
Exactitudes
Street anthropology: the Exactitudes oeuvre from Rotterdam's Hardcore Gabberscene in 1994 to Evry, a Paris suburb, in 2009.

11 March
JEAN LOUIS COHEN
Architecture Drafted: Designing for World War II
'Guernica and Hiroshima have been fundamental to the process of modernisation and, arguably, the dominance of modernism in architecture.'

18 March
AA MEMBERS IN LITTLEHAMPTON
AA members travel to Littlehampton's West Beach to review the first built project by recent AA graduate Asif Khan.

APRIL

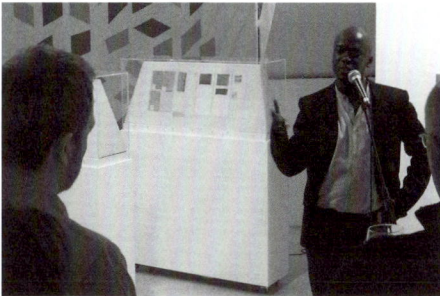

30 March
DAVID ADJAYE AT THE DESIGN MUSEUM
A glamorous crowd gathers for an exclusive AA preview of David Adjaye's photographic journey, 'Urban Africa', at the Design Museum.

23 April
BOOKABLE SPACE
Books produced by AA students in the last five years through which they learn to communicate the architectural project. Organised by Natasha Sandmeier.

26 April
LARS LERUP
How Blue The Sky Was
The positivity underlying the suburban city has a fascinating history, rooted in the myth of America as utopia. Enthusiasm ensues in the face of toxic ecology and fading consumer society.

29 April
CHARLES JENCKS
The Architecture of Hope
Maggie's Centres take a fresh
approach to both architecture and
health. The hybrid genre cancer care
centre offers a new mixed building
type for healing.

29 April
FRANÇOIS ROCHE: Ecosophical
Apparatus & Skizoïd Machines
Machines always pretend to do more
than they are programmed to do.
The anthropomorphic psychology we
project onto them creates both inter-
pretative and productive potentiality.

30 April
FRAUKE STENZ FOR
MASSIMILIANO FUKSAS
'The speed of change today is indi-
cated by the images that are projected
so quickly they seem to come from a
fast-moving car. Days and months are
lived in just a few moments.'

MAY

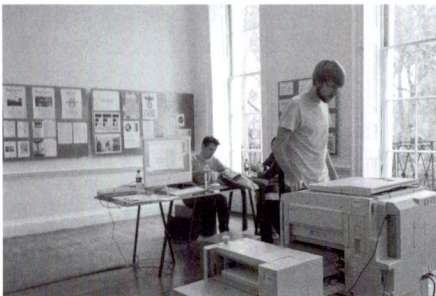

7 May
ON-SITE
An editorial intervention by the
AA's new imprint Bedford Press.
Printed ephemera and publications
are produced on site in the Front
Members' Room.

12 May
DAVID RUTTEN
Computing Architectural Concepts
'Can innovative software like
Grasshopper be the ideal platform
to marry computation, creativity and
ecologic thinking?'

7 May
RENDERING SPECULATIONS
SYMPOSIUM: Marjan Colletti,
Ziah Fogel, Zaha Hadid, Andrew Jones,
Lebbeus Woods
Specialists speculate on speculative visualisation and virtual design. Can architecture be a lens through which digital visions are imagined? Now that actual and virtual environments coalesce more and more, the symposium stimulates debate on how emerging media might best articulate architecture's conjectures for tomorrow.

21–22 May
ARCHITECTURE AND ITS PASTS
Mark Cousins, Adrian Forty, Tony Grafton,
Brian Hatton, Jeff Kipnis, Reinhold
Martin, Brett Steele
The symposium looked at the teaching of architectural history within architectural training and addressed the question of why so many students do not find their history programmes useful or interesting. In doing so it considered how problems within architectural history might be productively changed by a different approach to the architectural past.

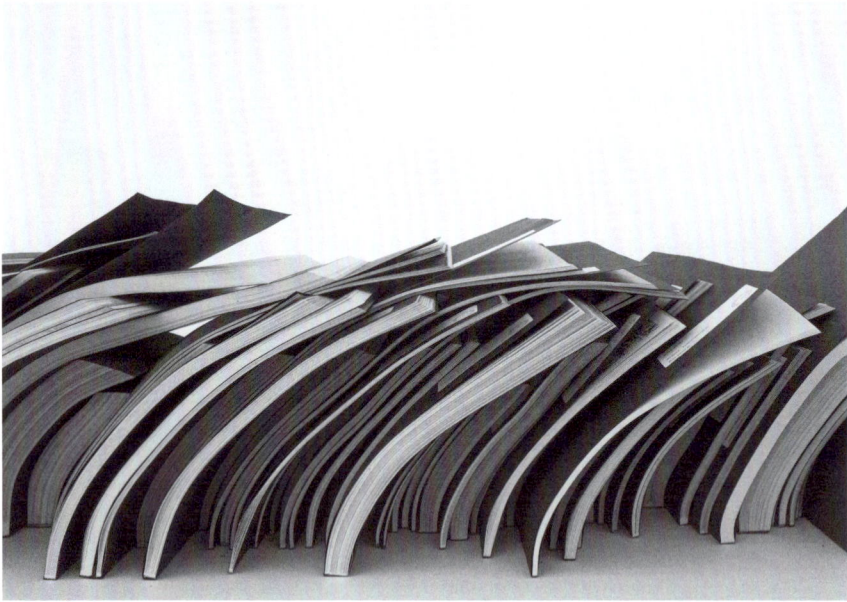

7 May
OMA BOOK MACHINE
'The book is a block of information'
The first retrospective of the books
produced by OMA and its many
collaborators, including graphic designers
(Bruce Mau), clients (Prada) and cultural
institutions (Hans Ulrich Obrist). 'OMA
Book Machine' offers a previously
invisible portrait of a defining architectural
office of our time and of an architectural
culture promoted, developed and
polemicised through the circulation of
books and the printed page.

27 May
PUBLIC OCCASION AGENCY
Invisible University
As part of the Bedford Press ON-SITE
exhibition, Public Occasion Agency invited
the Invisible University to address the role
of publishing in architectural production.
David Greene, Samantha Hardingham
and artist John Walter conducted a test
in re-printing, re-thinking and over-
printing the missing pages of L.A.W.u.N
Project #19. Using material brought in by
the speakers as well as the audience, ten
pages were produced in one hour.

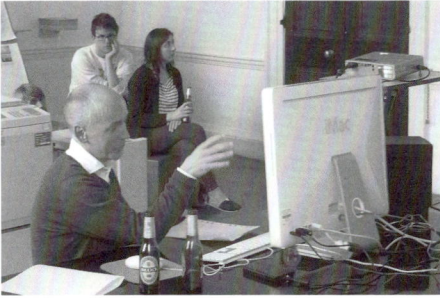

13 May
TOM BENSON
Subject to Change
Bedford Press launches Benson's
In Black & White. 'A pleasant,
accomplished neutrality quick
to browse and to close again'.
– Jens Peter Koerver

14 May
**SARA MACKILLOP: Some Things I
Like About Making Books**
How does the reader pass through a
book? The artist rearranges, annotates
and miniaturises the object and the
narrative.

14 May
MARIANNE MUELLER & OLAF KNEER
**Concrete Geometries: Spatial Form in
Social and Aesthetic Processes**
Concrete Geometries Research Cluster
PREVIEW exhibition opens, exploring
the role of spatial form in social and
aesthetic processes.

14 May
AA CITY CULTURES
**Marina Lathouri with Douglas
Spencer, Peter Carl, David
Cunningham and Sam Jacoby**
In need of re-evaluation: contemporary
positions on the city.

JUNE

2 June
**HAVANA... THE DEAD BODY OF
PARADISE**
Exhibition showing glimpses of
research work carried out by Inter 8
students on the unit trip to Havana
in January.

21 May
MAX BILL: FORM, FUNCTION, BEAUTY = GESTALT
Max Bill (1904–1994) was a virtuoso designer whose work overlapped disciplinary boundaries, encompassing architecture, painting, sculpture, industrial and graphic design as well as education. This exhibition of a selection of his work was held to accompany the launch of the latest book in the AA's Architecture Words series: Max Bill, *Form, Function, Beauty = Gestalt.*

3 June
AL MANAKH: GULF CONTINUED
A conversation with Rem Koolhaas
Rem Koolhaas and editor Todd Reisz discuss the implications of OMA's continuing work in the Gulf region and the book *Al Manakh: Gulf Continued*. A follow-up to the first instalment of *Al Manakh*, this 536-page book of interviews, travelogues, analyses, propositions, infographics and photography explores the growing interconnectedness of the region and the complex impact of the financial crisis.

Public Programme photos: Valerie Bennett, Sue Barr, Wayne Daly, Camille Steyaert

Open

Work-in-progress fro

on Studio ound Floor		First Sec
SESSION 2 **2.30PM**		**SESSION 3** **10AM**
Highways Diploma Unit 12 *Nip and Tuck*		**Digital design,** **technique and** **material science**

TENDER IS
THE NIGHT

The full-time, three-week Summer School offers an exciting approach to architectural design for anyone interested in exploring architecture as a profession or as an extended field of research.

www.aaschool.ac.uk/summerschool

'The lonely loner seems to free his mind at night (at, at, at night)

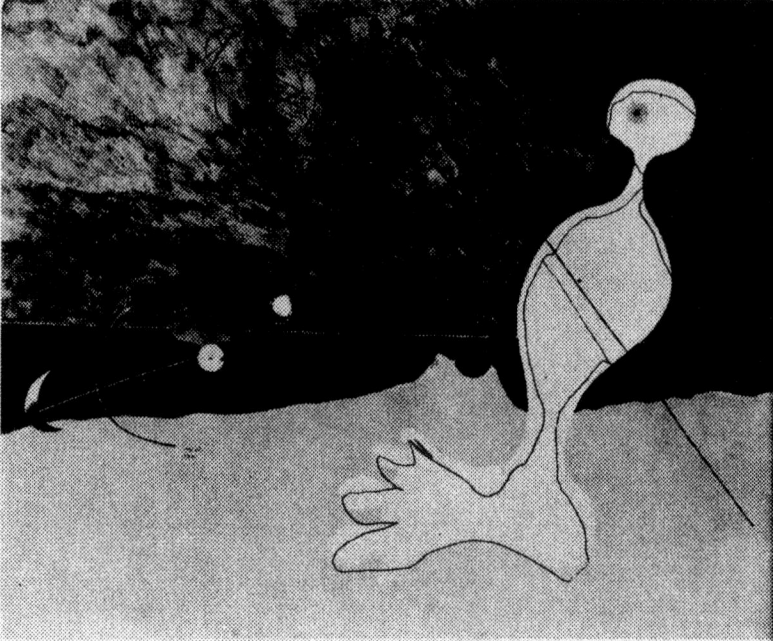

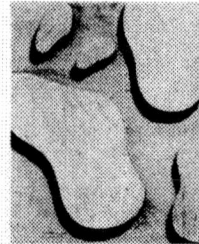

JOAN MIRO. *Person Throwing a Stone at a Bird.* Oil, 1926
The Museum of Modern Art, New York

One of today's psychological commonplaces is that the human mind is like an iceberg, most of it is sunk beneath the surface, moving at levels that lie below its conscious functioning and with meanings that are not, in the ordinary sense, rational or logical. In modern painting, the surrealists have made the most use of this new knowledge. Throughout their works runs the principle of an apparent incongruity, the line of consistent inconsistency. Employing an imagery that (like dreams) has a logic of its own, they create unexpected juxtapositions and strange situations, so to surprise the observer into a sudden new awareness.

16

Sara MacKillop, *Modern Art in Everyday Li*

ara MacKillop's talk *Some Things
Like About Making Books* will focus
n the artist's various uses of books
s object, found material and narrative

Sara MacKillop is an artist l
and working in London. She st
at the Royal College of Art ar
University. Recently she has l

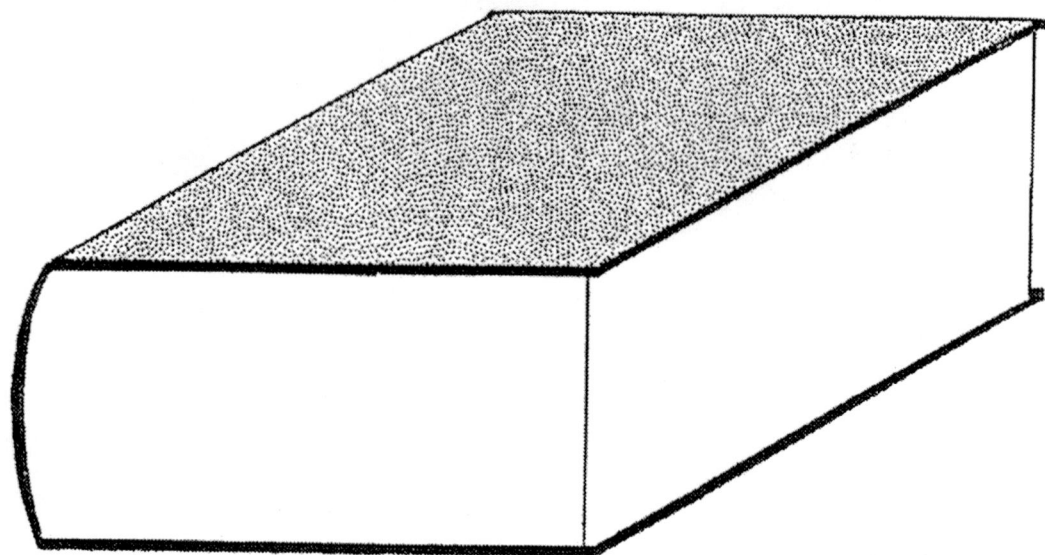

The book is conceived as a block of information.

OMA sketch for the preliminary design of *S,M,L,XL*
From *OMA by OMA*, unpublished booklet, 1989

Technical Studies spaghetti structure testing. Photo Valerie Bennett

Biological Habitat workshop with Zbigniew Oksiuta. Photo VB

BUILDING

New restaurant furniture by Valentin Bontjes van Beek. Photo VB

Hapkido class, tutor Philip Hartstein. Photo VB

Sustainable Environmental Design study trip to Madrid.
Photo Alberto Moletto

CERN visit, Geneva, Beyond Entropy Research Cluster. Photo VB

WORKING

Digital Prototyping Lab. Photo VB

First Year Studio. Photo VB

WORKING

LISTENING

Technical Studies spaghetti structure testing. Photo VB

Brett Steele, AA Director, presents to school community. Photo VB

LISTENING

Launch, *The Architecture of Emergence* by Mike Weinstock. Photo VB

A&U DRL Phase II Jury. Photo VB

PRESENTING

Intermediate 6 meeting. Photo VB

Diploma 16 Jury. Photo VB

PRESENTING

MAKING

AA Student Forum carve Hallowe'en pumpkins. Photo VB

In the workshop. Photo VB

MAKING

First Year Studio. Photo VB

Technical Studies second year bridge-building. Photo VB

INSTALLING

Cinema Lalibela opening at the Truman Brewery. Photo VB

Kiteweb, Diploma 7 trip to Beirut. Photo Toby James

INSTALLING

Algorithmic Structures workshop. Photo Jeroen van Ameijde

AA Interdisciplinary Studio (AAIS) at Hooke Park. Photo Takako Hasegawa

MODELLING

AA School model by Scrap Marshall. Photo VB

Model workshop. Photo VB

MODELLING

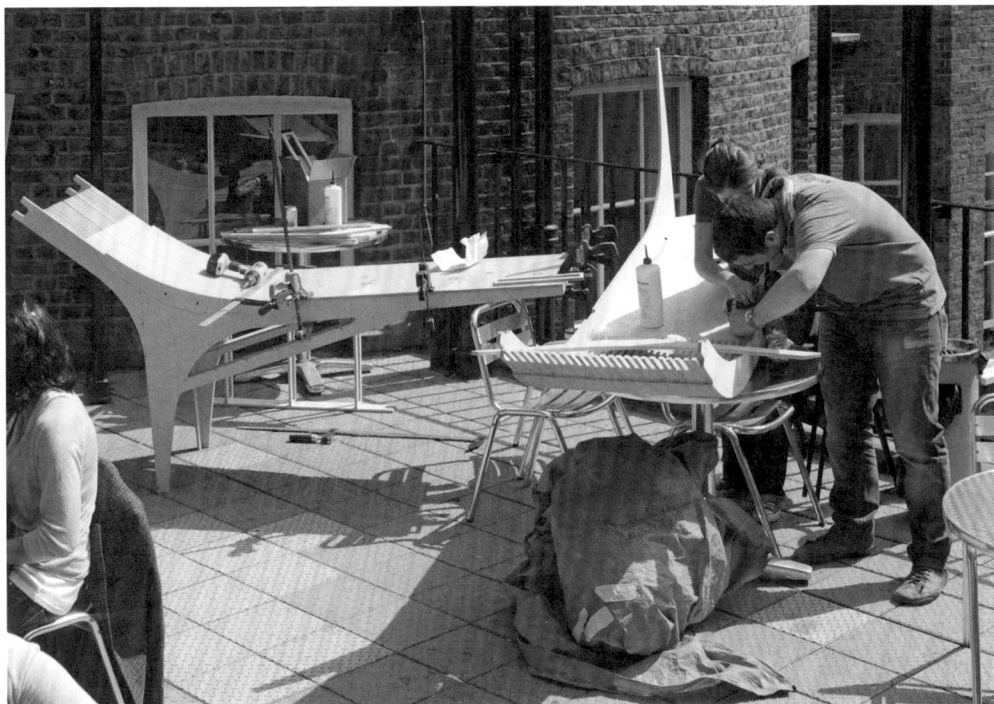

Emergency Slide, Intermediate Media Studies, tutor Valentin Bontjes van Beek. Photo VB

Diploma 11 models. Photo VB

OPENING

Pascal Schöning opens AA Cinema. Photo VB

AA Bookshop anniversary. Photo Timothy Iveson

AA Publications was founded as a means of opening up the interests of the AA to wider debate. All of its titles are derived in some way from the activities of the school. Some are directly connected to public events – to exhibitions, conferences and lectures. Others reflect more general concerns with developments in architecture and urbanism and the fields that touch upon them – engineering, landscape and art.

In addition to the annual *Projects Review*, *Prospectus* and twice-yearly *AA Files*, we publish around eight titles a year. All titles are generally produced in-house with our editorial and production teams who include Thomas Weaver (Editor of *AA Files* and Managing Editor), Pamela Johnston (Publications Editor), Zak Kyes (Art Director), Wayne Daly (Graphic Designer), Claire McManus (Assistant Graphic Designer), Clare Barrett (Editorial Assistant) and Phill Clatworthy (Bedford Press). Marketing, distribution and promotion are handled by Marilyn Sparrow and Kirsten Morphet. Promotional activities include attendance at two major international book fairs each year (Frankfurt Book Fair and London Book Fair) and book launches – often coinciding with exhibition openings at the AA. We also hold book sales twice a year to give students the opportunity to purchase our titles at reduced prices.

Since 2008 the AA has also operated its own bookshop. Stocking a wide range of books on architecture, including all titles published by the AA, the bookshop is able to supply recommended course books and any title that is in print.

AA Agendas

AA Agendas is an ongoing series of books launched in 2006. The series is designed to capture work generated through any number of the school's design units, courses and other AA events and initiatives. Through the range of projects illustrated, the series reveals the breadth of the AA's teaching practices and the vitality of the resulting student and staff work.

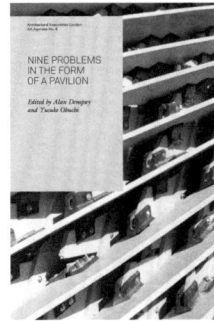

AA Agendas 8
Nine Problems in the Form of a Pavilion
Forthcoming
Created as part of the 2008 tenth anniversary celebrations of the Design Research Laboratory, the AA DRL TEN Pavilion was one of those built projects that pushed convention in architecture, engineering and manufacturing. This book recounts the story of the creation of the pavilion, illustrating its design, development and assembly as well as the structure's place within the evolving teaching methodologies of the DRL as a whole.

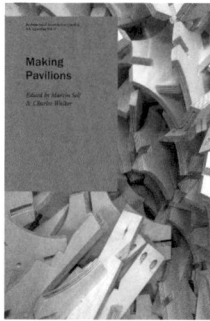

AA Agendas 9
Making Pavilions
Forthcoming
Over the past four years students of the
AA's Intermediate Unit 2 have designed
and built a series of experimental
pavilions. Structured to follow a year
in the life of the unit, this book presents
the processes of the pavilions' design
and production, from concept ideas to
workshop fabrication. Essays by the
unit's tutors, Charles Walker and
Martin Self, explain the ambitions and
pedagogic basis of the programme,
rooted in the idea of experiential
learning. The educational validity of
this innovative design-build programme and its architectural output is
explored through the voices of students, tutors and critics.

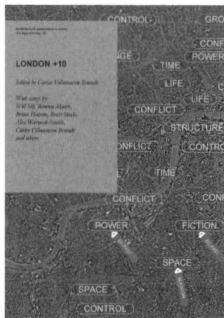

AA Agendas 10
London +10
February 2010
London +10 focuses on London over
the last 20 years and features projects

carried out by the AA's Diploma Unit 10
that have attempted to integrate the
live realm of the city into the design of
alternative urban strategies. In addition, a series of essays by contributors
including the writer Will Self and the
journalist Rowan Moore provide an
overview of London, questioning and
celebrating the city and generating
possible scenarios for its future.

Architecture Words
Architecture Words is a series of texts
and important essays on architecture
written by architects, critics and
scholars. The words are edited and
the pages designed in a way that
acknowledges the ability of graphic
and printed forms to communicate
architectural ideas; not only the ideas
contained within each volume, but
also the enduring power of written
ideas to challenge and change the
way all architects think.

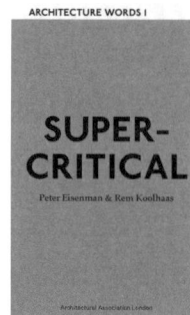

Architecture Words 1
Supercritical:
Peter Eisenman & Rem Koolhaas
December 2009
In January 2006 Peter Eisenman and
Rem Koolhaas came to the AA for an
evening of conversation. Their dia-
logue is the centrepiece of the first
Words book, a series that emphasises
the written word as the basis for debate

by contemporary architects and theorists. Each architect states his own views about the terms of architecture, including its theories and relationship to the city. A number of responses from the audience follow these statements and the book is introduced with an essay from AA director Brett Steele.

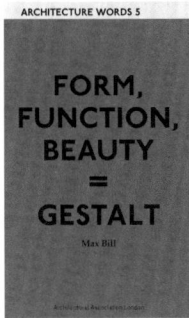

Exhibition Catalogues
Continuing a long AA tradition and in recognition of the vitality of the AA's exhibition programme, each year also sees the publication of a number of catalogues, produced to coincide with the opening of various shows and exhibitions.

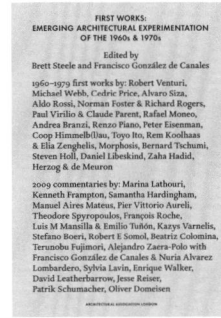

ARCHITECTURE WORDS 5

FORM,
FUNCTION,
BEAUTY
=
GESTALT

Max Bill

FIRST WORKS:
EMERGING ARCHITECTURAL EXPERIMENTATION
OF THE 1960s & 1970s

Edited by
Brett Steele and Francisco González de Canales

1960–1979 first works by: Robert Venturi,
Michael Webb, Cedric Price, Alvaro Siza,
Aldo Rossi, Norman Foster & Richard Rogers,
Paul Virilio & Claude Parent, Rafael Moneo,
Andrea Branzi, Renzo Piano, Peter Eisenman,
Coop Himmelb(l)au, Toyo Ito, Rem Koolhaas
& Elia Zenghelis, Morphosis, Bernard Tschumi,
Steven Holl, Daniel Libeskind, Zaha Hadid,
Herzog & de Meuron

2009 commentaries by: Marina Lathouri,
Kenneth Frampton, Samantha Hardingham,
Manuel Aires Mateus, Pier Vittorio Aureli,
Theodore Spyropoulos, François Roche,
Luis M Mansilla & Emilio Tuñón, Kazys Varnelis,
Stefano Boeri, Robert E Somol, Beatriz Colomina,
Terunobu Fujimori, Alejandro Zaera-Polo with
Francisco González de Canales & Nuria Alvarez
Lombardero, Sylvia Lavin, Enrique Walker,
David Leatherbarrow, Jesse Reiser,
Patrik Schumacher, Oliver Domeisen

ARCHITECTURAL ASSOCIATION LONDON

Architecture Words 5
Form, Function, Beauty = Gestalt
Max Bill
May 2010
Max Bill (1904–1994) – a product of the Bauhaus at Dessau, pupil of Walter Gropius, Vasily Kandinsky and Paul Klee – was a virtuoso designer whose work overlapped disciplinary boundaries, encompassing architecture, painting, sculpture, industrial and graphic design, as well as education. What unites all the work is a clarity and precision of expression. Through both his designs and his writings Max Bill has long been a major figure of reference in the German-speaking world. This collection makes many of his key texts available in English for the first time.

First Works:
Emerging Architectural
Experimentation of the 1960s
& 1970s
November 2009
During a tumultuous period in the 1960s and 70s, a new generation of architects began their careers amidst a period of profound social change. *First Works* tells the story of this period through a selection of 20 projects, including works by Cedric Price, Zaha Hadid, Rafael Moneo and Toyo Ito. Alongside these first works, 20 invited critics, including Kenneth Frampton, Sylvia Lavin and Pier Vittorio Aureli, offer contemporary commentaries on these projects and their place within the architects' subsequent careers.

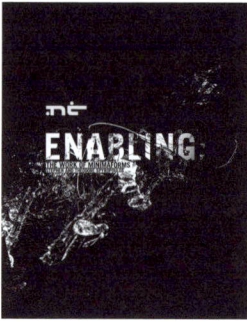

Enabling:
The Work of Minimaforms
February 2010
This book highlights the work of the design and architecture practice Minimaforms. Founded in 2002 by brothers Stephen and Theodore Spyropoulos, the practice has developed a diverse body of work that explores new forms of communication through correlated systems of interaction. Using installations as a primary mode of research, the studio creates public performance-based interventions that engage material and social interaction. The book features recent work developed in collaboration with Krzysztof Wodiczko, a pavilion produced with the performance artist Stelarc, a video piece with artist Mira Calix and Minimaforms' light installation in Trafalgar Square, Memory Cloud. Accompanying the projects are texts by David Greene, Stelarc and Krzysztof Wodiczko

AA Files
AA Files is the AA's journal of record. Launched in 1981 by the school's then chairman Alvin Boyarsky, the journal, edited by Thomas Weaver, appears twice a year and looks to promote original and engaging writing on architecture. It does this by drawing both on the AA's own research, lectures, exhibitions and events, as well as by a rich and eclectic mix of architectural scholarship from all over the world.

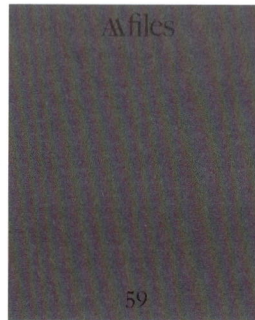

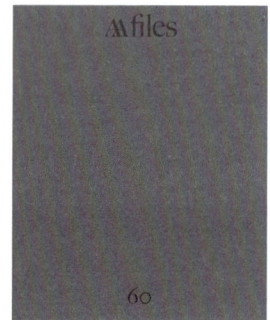

AA Files 59
October 2009
Features essays by the writer William Firebrace on Marseille, the psychotherapist Adam Phillips on getting lost, the architect Adam Caruso on analogue architecture, the critic Irénée Scalbert on parklife, the historian Pier Vittorio Aureli on Palladio and a conversation between architect Tom Emerson and artist Richard Wentworth.

AA Files 60
March 2010
Features essays by the architect Bernard Cache on Barack Obama, the geographer Matthew Gandy on cyborg urbanism, the critic Igor Marjanovic on Alvin Boyarsky, the design historian James Mosley on the English Vernacular, the Oxford professor of French Michael Sheringham on the project,

the photographer Toby Glanville on
jelly and a conversation with architect
Léon Krier.

Bedford Press
Established as an imprint of AA Publications Ltd, Bedford Press aims to
create a more responsive model of
small-scale publishing, nimble enough
to encompass the entire chain of
production in one fluid activity, from
initial commission to the final printing.
The products of the press include
publications as well as ephemera such
as pamphlets, posters and limited
edition prints.

Exhibition Prosthetics
Joseph Grigely
January 2010
Exhibition Prosthetics by Joseph
Grigely explores the artist's use of
language and images as a means of
representation that further the
reach of the real. Grigely uses the
term 'exhibition prosthetics' to
describe an array of these conventions, particularly (but not exclusively)
in relation to exhibition practices.

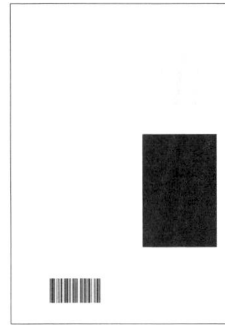

In Black & White
Tom Benson
April 2010
Published on the occasion of 'Tom
Benson, Registers and Greyscales' at
Stiftung für konkrete Kunst, Reutlingen
in 2006, *In Black & White* is the fourth in
a series of publications by Benson
which consider the separation of
exhibition and book, employing the
publication as a site for reinterpreta-
tion rather than replication.

Informal Meetings
Radim Peško
February 2010
Informal Meetings is a collection of
photographs by Amsterdam-based
graphic designer Radim Peško, made
during travels to different cities between 2001 and 2009. The photographs
show poetic glimpses of seemingly
unremarkable encounters between
space and architecture that suggest
their own stories.

Since its founding in 1847, the AA has remained independent and self-supporting. A pioneering higher educational UK educational charity, the AA School receives no statutory funding for either its internationally renowned teaching activities or its acclaimed public programme, which operates one of the world's largest calendars of lectures, exhibitions and other public events dedicated to contemporary architectural culture. Each year the AA attracts the world's foremost architects, engineers, designers, critics, theorists, artists and other leaders as part of its academic and cultural programmes.

Supporting The
Architectural Association
The AA actively pursues its role as an independent setting for the teaching, learning, discussion and debate of contemporary architecture, including the vital role architecture can play in bridging between public, professional and political interests in the future of the world's cities and built environment. Like the world city of London that is its home, the AA School today is distinguished by its international and multicultural make-up. Maintaining the AA's independence is the key to the school's ability to remain at the forefront of architectural education. The AA School's leading position is greatly enhanced each year through the generous support, both financial and in-kind, provided by many individuals and organisations throughout the world. The AA's Development Office cultivates mutually beneficial relationships between the school and individuals, organisations, institutions,corporate companies and neighbours.

The AA Foundation
In 1989 the AA Council established the Architectural Association Foundation as an independent charitable trust designed to particularly benefit the students of the Architectural Association. The Foundation's trustees are Keith Priest (Chairman), Harry N Cobb, Robert F Emmerson, Baroness Howe of Idlicote, Alan Leibowitz (Hon Treasurer), Lawrence Malcic, John Winter. During 2009/10 the AA Foundation has made available more than £200,000 towards scholarships and bursaries for AA students, which were distributed through the AA Bursary and Scholarship Committees. Named awards managed by the AA Foundation include the Baylight scholarships, Stephen Lawrence scholarship, Mercers' Bursary, Fletcher Priest and Mike Davies awards and other awards in memory of Eileen Gray, Elizabeth Chesterton, David Allford, Alvin Boyarsky, Martin Caroe and the Nicholas Pozner Prize.
For further information contact Alex Lorente, AA Foundation administrator, on +44 (0)20 7887 4074.

Support for Students and
Special Projects
2009/10 has been another successful year in the AA School's development of outside partnerships in support of units and programmes across the entire school. The school extends its thanks to the dozens of sponsors and partners from the UK and abroad for backing projects, study visits and special events. In particular, the AA School is very excited to announce a new award by Foster + Partners to students who have demonstrated outstanding advancements in the field of sustainable infrastructure. The award will be made for the first time this year at Projects Review.

Furthermore, the AA is delighted to announce the major sponsorship of the Research Cluster Beyond Entropy/When Energy becomes Form which has been graciously sponsored by Olivetti/Digital Technology Solutions, RePower and *Abitare* and is part of the Mostra Internazionale de Architettura, La Biennale of Venice 2010.

Funds are channelled directly to our students' and staff's academic activities. Individual thanks for this support can be found in the introductions to the units and programmes in this book.

Thanks to
Christina Smith, The Mercers Company, Rosa Bosch – B & W Film, Webb Yates Engineers, Honeysuckle Bottom Sawmill and Fereday Pollard Ltd for their support of the AAIS.

Maeda for their support of the Maeda Workshop and exhibition by Shin Egashira and his students.

Hewlett-Packard for their continued support of the AA School.

Mike Davies for continuing support of new student scholarships.

The Baylight Foundation for its continuing programme of Baylight scholarships for UK-resident students of outstanding merit and need.

The Fletcher Priest Trust for their continued support of new student scholarships.

Doris Lockhart Saatchi, the Partners at Martin Caroe and Zeev Aram for supporting various student scholarships and bursaries.

Robert and Elizabeth Boas for the continuation of the Nicholas Boas Student Travel Award.

Friends and family of Nick Pozner for their support towards an annual prize for The Single Best Drawing in the Undergraduate School.

Venice Architecture Biennale 2008; Venice Art Biennale 2009.

Norah Garlick and her family for their generosity in honouring the AA with the Horace and Ellen Hannah Wakeford Bequest.

AA Exhibitions would like to warmly thank the following institutions for their ongoing support: Aram, The Czech Centre, The Romanian Embassy and The Swiss Embassy.

Enquiries for 20010/11
Planning and organisation for the numerous activities, special projects and worldwide trips and special events associated with the upcoming AA academic year is already underway. As always, the AA welcomes enquiries and expressions of interest for support by AA members as well as other individuals and organisations whose generous assistance helps make possible our students' future learning.

If you are interested in becoming a supporting partner in 2010/11, please contact Esther McLaughlin, Head of Development at: esther.mclaughlin@aaschool.ac.uk or on +44 (0)20 7887 4090. She will be pleased to meet with you to discuss how your support can be added to the growing UK and international network of AA partners and sponsors.

STAFF LIST

Director's Office
Director
Brett Steele
Personal Assistant
Roberta Jenkins
Academic Head
Charles Tashima

AACP
Shumon Basar
Staff
Francisco González
de Canales
Oliver Domeisen

Registrar's Office
Registrar
Marilyn Dyer
Assistant Registrar
Belinda Flaherty
Registrar's Office/
External Students
Administrative
Coordinator
Sabrina Blakstad
Admissions
(Undergraduate)
Coordinators
Ruth Lie/Meneesha
Kellay
Admissions
(Graduate)
Coordinators
Claire Perry
Imogen Evans
Undergraduate
School
Administrative
Coordinator
Victoria Bahia
Visiting School
Director
Christopher Pierce
Visiting School/
Visiting Teachers'
Programme
Coordinator
Sandra Sanna

Foundation
Studio Masters
Saskia Lewis
William Martyr
Takako Hasegawa
Matthew Butcher

First Year
Studio Masters
Valentin Bontjes
van Beek
David Greene
Samantha
Hardingham
Tobias Klein

Martina Schäfer
Robert Stuart-
Smith

Intermediate
School
Unit 1
Deane Simpson
Mark Campbell
Unit 2
Martin Self
Charles Walker
Unit 3
Nanette Jackowski
Ricardo de Ostos
Unit 4
Nathalie
Rozencwajg
Michel da Costa
Gonçalves
Unit 5
Stefano Rabolli
Pansera
Goswin
Schewendinger
Unit 6
Jonathan Dawes
Fumiko Kato
Dagobert Bergmans
Unit 7
Liam Young
Kate Davies
Unit 8
Francisco González
de Canales
Nuria Alvarez
Lombardero
Unit 9
Christopher Pierce
Christopher
Matthews
Unit 10
Claudia Pasquero
Marco Poletto
Unit 11
Theodore
Sarantoglou Lalis
Dora Sweijd
Unit 12
Sam Jacob
Tomas Klassnik
Unit 13
Miraj Ahmed
Martin Jameson

Diploma School
Unit 1
Marianne Mueller
Olaf Kneer
Unit 2
Anne Save
de Beaurecueil
Franklin Lee

Unit 3
Alison Brooks
Max Kahlen
Unit 4
John Palmesino
Ann-Sofi
Rönnskog
Unit 5
Cristina Díaz
Moreno
Efrén García
Grinda
Tyen Masten
Unit 6
On Sabbatical
Unit 7
Simon Beames
Kenneth Fraser
Unit 8
Eugene Han
Chris Yoo
Unit 9
Natasha
Sandmeier
Monia De Marchi
Unit 10
Carlos Villanueva
Brandt
Unit 11
Shin Egashira
Unit 12
Holger Kehne
Jeffrey Turko
Unit 13
Oliver Domeisen
Tristan Simmonds
Unit 14
Pier Vittorio Aureli
Barbara Campbell-
Lange
Fenella Collingridge
Unit 15
Francesca Hughes
Noam Andrews
Unit 16
Jonas Lundberg
Andrew Yau

Graduate School
Administrative
Coordinators
Clement Chung
Jenny Devine

DRL
Directors
Yusuke Obuchi
Theodore
Spyropoulos
Founding Director
Patrik Schumacher
Course Master
Alisa Andrasek
Marta
Malé-Alemany

Programme
Assistant
Yota Adilenidou
Course Tutors
Jeroen van
Ameijde
Shajay Bhooshan
Christos Passas
Robert
Stuart-Smith
Technical Tutors
Lawrence Friesen
Hanif Kara
Riccardo Merello

Emtech
Directors
Michael Weinstock
George Jeronimidis
Studio Masters
Christina Doumpioti
Toni Kotnik
Studio Tutors
Evan Greenberg
George
Jeronimides
Kostis Karatzas

Landscape
Urbanism
Director
Eva Castro
Programme Staff
Eduardo Rico
Alfredo Ramirez
Douglas Spencer
Tom Smith
Workshop Tutors
Enriqueta Llabres
Bridget Mackean
Jorge Ayala
Teruyuki Nomura
Clara Oloriz

Histories &
Theories
Director
Marina Lathouri
Programme Staff
Francisco González
de Canales
Pedro Ignacio
Alonso
Mark Cousins
Braden Engel

Housing &
Urbanism
Directors
Jorge Fiori
Hugo Hinsley
Programme Staff
Lawrence Barth
Hugo Hinsley
Nicholas Bullock

Kathryn Firth
Dominic Papa
Elena Pascolo
Alex Warnock-Smith

Sustainable
Environmental
Design
Director
Simos Yannas
Programme Staff
Klaus Bode
Joana Soares
Gonçalves
Raul Moura
Jorge Rodriguez
Alvarez
Gustavo Brunelli
Alberto Moletto
Barak Pelman

Conservation of
Historic Buildings
Director
Andrew Shepherd
Programme Staff
Judith Roebuck
David Heath
Russell Bateman

PhD Programme
Academic
Coordinator
Simos Yannas
Programme Staff
Lawrence Barth
Mark Cousins
Jorge Fiori
Hugo Hinsley
Marina Lathouri

Professional
Practice
Professional
Studies Advisor
Alastair Robertson
Professional
Studies
Coordinator
Rob Sparrow
Part 1
Javier Castañón
Future Practice/
Part 2
Hugo Hinsley

Interprofessional
Studio
Studio Director
Theo Lorenz
Studio Master
Tanja Siems
Studio Tutor
Jan Brüggemeier

STAFF LIST

History & Theory Studies
Administrative Coordinator
Belinda Flaherty
Director
Mark Cousins
Course Lecturers
Mark Cousins
Maria Fedorchenko
Christopher Pierce
Brett Steele
Consultants
Pier Vittorio Aureli
Mark Campbell
Judith Clark
Mark Cousins
Paul Davies
Oliver Domeisen
Brian Hatton
Sam Jacoby
Christopher M Lee
John Palmesino
Martin Self
Brett Steele
Ines Weizman
Patrick Wright
Simos Yannas
Programme Staff
William Firebrace
Teaching Assistants
Mollie Claypool
Emanuel de Sousa
Ishraq Khan
Marlie Mul

Media Studies
Director
Eugene Han
Programme Staff
Sue Barr
Shajay Bhooshan
Valentin Bontjes van Beek
Monia De Marchi
Shin Egashira
Trevor Flynn
Matej Hosek
Alex Kaiser
Toni Kotnik
Zak Kyes
Antoni Malinowski
Joel Newman
Anne Save de Beaurecueil
Goswin Schwendinger
Tobias Klein

Technical Studies
Director of Research & Dev
Michael Weinstock

Administrative Coordinator
Belinda Flaherty
Intermediate Master
Wolfgang Frese
Diploma Master
Javier Castañón
Programme Staff
Phil Cooper
Martin Hagemann
Anderson Inge
Kostis Karatzas
Toni Kotnik
Wolf Mangelsdorf
John Noel
Manja Van de Worp
Simos Yannas
Consultants
Carolina Bartram
Ian Duncombe
Marissa Kretsch
Emmanuele Marfisi
Randall Thomas
Mohsen Zikri

Research Clusters
Alan Dempsey
Olaf Kneer
Theo Sarantoglou Lalis
Marina Lathouri
Marianne Mueller
Stefano Rabolli Pansera

Media Services
Audiovisual Manager
Joel Newman
Audiovisual Assistant
Nick Wayne
Head of Computing
Julia Frazer
Assistant Head of Computing
Mathew Bielecki
Computer Engineers
Amos Deane
Andrew Ennis
David Hopkins
Syed Qadri
Kevin Seddon
Computing Course Coordinator
Eugene Han
Digital Photo Studio
Sue Barr

Digital Platforms
Head of Digital Platorms/ Web Designer
Frank Owen
Web Designer/ Developer
Zeynep Görgülü
Content Editor
Rosa Ainley
Images & Videos
Joel Newman

Workshops
Model Making
Trystrem Smith
Wood and Metal Workshop Technicians
Robert Busher
Will Fausset
Head of Digital Prototyping
Jeroen van Ameijde
Prototyping Lab Technician
Kar Leung Wai
Hooke Park
Bruce Hunter-Inglis
Charles Corry Wright
Chris Sadd

Association Secretary
Kathleen Formosa
Secretary's Office Personal Assistant
Cristian Sanchez Gonzalez
Head of Membership
Alex Lorente
Membership Coordinator
Jenny Keiff
Membership Events Coordinator
Luisa Miller

Development Office
Head of Development
Esther McLaughlin
Special Projects Officer
Jan Brüggemeier
Research and Proposal Development Manager
Nicola Quinn

AA Foundation
Secretary
Marilyn Dyer
Administrator
Alex Lorente

Exhibitions
Head of Exhibitions
Vanessa Norwood
Exhibitions Project Manager
Lee Regan
Exhibitions Coordinator
Luke Currall

Library
Librarian
Hinda Sklar
Deputy Librarian
Aileen Smith
Archivist
Edward Bottoms
Cataloguer
Beatriz Flora
Serials/Library
Web Developer
Simine Marine

Print Studio
Print Studio Manager/Editor
AA Files
Thomas Weaver
Publications Editor
Pamela Johnston
Editor, Events List
Rosa Ainley
Editorial Assistant
Clare Barrett
Art Director
Zak Kyes
Graphic Designers
Wayne Daly
Claire McManus

AA Publications
Marketing & Distribution
Kirsten Morphet
Marilyn Sparrow

Bedford Press
Directors
Zak Kyes
Wayne Daly
Print Technician
Phill Clatworthy

Photo Library
Librarian
Valerie Bennett

Accounts Office
Manager
Steve Livett
Assistants
Lauren Harcourt
Linda Keifff
Eve Livett
Fozia Munshi

Drawing Materials Shop
Manager
Maria Cox

Facilities
Manager
Anita Pfauntsch
Assistant Manager
Peter Keiff
Maintenance & Security
Matthew Hanrahan
Lea Ketsawang
James McColgan
Adam Okuniewski
Colin Prendergast
Leszak Skrzypiec
Mariusz Stawiarski
Bogdan Swidzinski
Sebastian Wyatt

Front of House
Reception & Switchboard
Mary Lee
Hiroe Shin Shigemitsu
Public Programme/ Graduation Administrator/ Outside Events
Philip Hartstein

Catering/Bar
Manager/Chef
Pascal Babeau
Deputy Manager/ Barman
Darko Calina
Catering Assistants
Brigitte Ayoro
Daniel Swidzinski
Miodrag Ristic

Human Resources
Head of Human Resources
Tehmina Mahmood

AA Bookshop
Bookshop Manager
Charlotte Newman
Bookshop Assistant
Luz Hincapie

COLOPHON

AA Book
Projects Review 2010

Editor:
Kari Rittenbach

Contributing Editors:
Rosa Ainley
Valerie Bennett

Art Director: Zak Kyes
Design: Wayne Daly
Design assistance:
Claire McManus
Phill Clatworthy

Titles and headers set
in Correspondance,
designed by Radim Peško

Printed in England
by Beacon Press

ISBN 978-1-902902-93-7
ISSN 0265 4644

© 2010 Architectural Association
and the Authors. No part of this
book may be reproduced in
any manner whatsoever without
written permission from the
publisher, except in the context
of reviews.

AA Publications are initiated by
the Director of the AA School,
Brett Steele, and produced
through the AA Print Studio.

AA Book: Projects Review 2010
and back issues are available from:

AA Publications
36 Bedford Square
London WC1B 3ES

T + 44 (0)20 7887 4021
F + 44 (0)20 7414 0783
publications@aaschool.ac.uk

www.aaschool.ac.uk/publications